CW00552963

Black Knight
RITCHIE BLACKMORE

Black Knight
RITCHIE BLACKMORE

JERRY BLOOM

OMNIBUS PRESS

LONDON / NEW YORK / PARIS / SYDNEY / COPENHAGEN / BERLIN / MADRID / TOKYO

Exclusive Distributors
Music Sales Limited,
14/15 Berners Street,
London, W1T 3LJ.

Music Sales Corporation,
257 Park Avenue South,
New York, NY 10010, USA.

Macmillan Distribution Services,
53 Park West Drive,
Derrimut, Vic 3030,
Australia.

To the Music Trade only:
Music Sales Limited,
14/15 Berners Street,
London, W1T 3LJ.

Every effort has been made to trace the copyright holders of the photographs in this book but one or
two were unreachable. We would be grateful if the photographers concerned would contact us.

Typeset by Phoenix Photosetting, Chatham, Kent
Printed by Creative Print & Design (Ebbw Vale) Wales

A catalogue record for this book is available from the British Library.

Visit Omnibus Press on the web at www.omnibuspress.com

Contents

"Sixteenth Century Greensleeves is [Rainbow's] idea of a castle where the **black knight** lives. The **black knight** of course being Ritchie and the **black knight** periodically comes out of his castle and captures a young peasant maiden from the village."

Ronnie James Dio

Introduction

Rock musicians by their very nature are generally mercurial, larger than life characters. However, few have been as influential as Richard Hugh Blackmore has been to generations of aspiring guitarists. Revered for his immense talent, he has also been castigated more times than anyone would care to recall for his belligerant attitude towards anyone and everyone. No doubt about it: he's one of rock's moodiest, most difficult yet enigmatic characters.

When editor Chris Charlesworth first approached me to write what would be the first full biography on the 'Man In Black's' career, he stressed the importance of "digging deep" and getting new information. Many of the new stories in this book that have come to light are due to the interviews I conducted with the many friends, associates and musicians who have been involved in Blackmore's career from his schooldays and first professional band the Jaywalkers to his current group Blackmore's Night. All who were gracious in giving their time are acknowledged in the appropriate section of this book.

In truth, had I tried to compile the book primarily with the use of the many interviews that Blackmore himself has given throughout his career the end result would undoubtedly have been puzzling. Anyone who is familiar with the man's character will know only too well that he loves to wind people up, and in the same way that Bob Dylan played mind games with journalists in the mid-Sixties, so Blackmore did likewise in the Seventies, Eighties and beyond, leading interviewers up the proverbial garden path at every given opportunity.

As a perfect example of this, many fans will be aware of Blackmore's interest in all things spiritual. Chatting to *Melody Maker*'s Steve Gett in 1981 he candidly explained that he was first introduced to the mysterious world of séances by Nick Simper when Deep Purple formed in 1968. As you will discover, this was completely untrue and is just one of many fabricated stories he has enjoyed spouting over the years. Being able to decipher when Blackmore is being straight and when he is clearly leading a journalist on a merry dance is something of a skill in itself.

Fortunately one of the most expansive and interesting interviews that Blackmore has conducted in the past 10 years was a lengthy four hour chat arranged and conducted by Alan Whitman for *Record Collector* magazine in 1998. Having never met the man prior to the interview, Whitman was somewhat apprehensive considering Blackmore's reputation, and at the time, as a subscriber to my own magazine, *More Black Than Purple* he contacted me for a few words of advice and encouragement which resulted in me being added to the entourage that flew to New York. I was also delighted to be able to sit in on the interview conducted at the Normandie Inn, Long Island. Fortunately Blackmore was particularly gracious that evening and by and large he was also straight and honest when talking about his career, particularly in relation to his schooldays and formative years as a session and backing musician in the early Sixties.

It remains one of the most detailed accounts of those times and several quotes are to be found throughout this tome. I must also thank noted journalist Neil Jeffries for another excellent Blackmore interview that he conducted in 1995, which was published exclusively in *More Black Than Purple*, extracts from which are also scattered throughout the book. Elsewhere various quotes from press interviews through the decades have been used as I felt it was beneficial to combine current views with those done at the time specific events occurred.

Blackmore's career has always appeared to be shrouded in mystery but this is largely due to a desire to maintain his privacy as much as possible. As a direct result of the spontaneous way he works, he has very little interest in analysing his own music. Although it was never my intention to delve deeply into his personal life, in order to give the reader a better understanding as to why some of the things that happened in his career occurred as they did, I felt it necessary to put them into context with what was going on behind the scenes.

The character behind any person who makes music will naturally intrigue the listener but Blackmore has never been one to show any real desire to explain himself. Certainly I can't imagine he would ever consider writing an autobiography, yet, like everyone else, he is just as intrigued with the personality behind the music. Although he has read biographies on some of his favourite musicians, such as Bob Dylan, and even though he has no interest in retelling his own story, I hope he will at least understand why others would want to know more about him. Conversely, for a man who loves portraying a dark image and to be seen dressed in black, he has certainly lived a colourful life. Despite having a darker side to his persona, Blackmore is also intensely funny and hopefully this book will bring a touch of levity along the way with some amusing stories.

Much has been said about Blackmore's reputation for being 'difficult' though as with many other individuals who have lived on the edge or possess a unique skill this is often a result of obstinate or single-minded behaviour. Although it can never be fully explained or justified I hope that this book goes someway into providing a greater insight into the reasons behind his actions.

Although I approached this book from the standpoint of a long-standing fan of 30 years, I was conscious of not wanting it to be an exercise in hero worship but to portray Blackmore for what he is; a man of intelligence, intolerance, of generosity and yes … of obstinacy. Having been fortunate enough to have experienced his company on numerous occasions throughout the past 20 years I have seen both sides. The people that I interviewed for the book have also experienced Blackmore's moods and while this is reflected in the story, a general feeling of respect shines through even from those left behind.

As a life-long football fan Blackmore would be well aware of the chant, "there's only one …" in honour of a favourite player. In contrast there isn't only one Ritchie Blackmore: in fact there are at least two others I am aware of who have become public figures, one an author, the other a rugby league player. However I'm certain there is only one whose life has been as diverse as the one known as the 'Man In Black.' I hope the reader also reaches that conclusion.

Jerry Bloom,
Bedford 2006

CHAPTER 1

From Weston to Heston
(1945–59)

During the 19th century, Weston-super-Mare, situated 25 miles south-west from the city of Bristol, grew from a tiny village of about 100 inhabitants to a thriving Victorian West Coast seaside resort of nearly 20,000 people and 100 years on its population rose to almost 70,000. The advent of the Second World War brought new industries to Weston; chief among these was aircraft production. Although receiving many evacuees from London and other large cities during the early days of the war, the decision to evacuate people to Weston was ill-advised given its involvement in producing aircraft. By June 1940 the first bombs fell on the town with the worst blitzes taking place in January 1941 and June 1942. Large areas were destroyed, especially in the Boulevard, High Street and Grove Park areas of the town.

On April 14, 1945 WWII was finally drawing to a close with the news that the British Army had reached the outskirts of Bremen, the US Army had captured Gera and Bayreuth, and the Canadians had assumed military control of the Netherlands. Meanwhile, in humble Weston-super-Mare, Lewis and Violet Blackmore of 33 Addicott Road were celebrating the birth of their second son, Richard Hugh, at Allandale Nursing Home.

Ritchie Blackmore wasn't the only famous figure to be born in Weston; the small Somerset coastal town was also the birthplace of former Conservative party chairman, Jeffrey Archer, Monty Python comedian John Cleese and the slain journalist and broadcaster Jill Dando. When speaking to Michael Parkinson in 2001, Cleese said, "You have to be subversive if you're

1

from Weston-super-Mare." While Weston wasn't exactly the most striking of English towns, it would be stretching things to suggest, as Cleese did, that everyone who hails from there tends to be argumentative and contrary. Yet that element in Cleese's psychological make-up is also apparent in Blackmore's.

Although the name Blackmore is thought to be of English origin, Lewis John Blackmore was born in Cardiff, Wales. When talking to Welsh television in 2001 Ritchie spoke about his Welsh heritage: "I think my grandfather was from Swansea. I'm well aware of the Welsh contingent. My father was from Cardiff. I have my father's stubbornness. I don't know if that's Welsh!"

Little is known of the Blackmore family history other than Lewis, who worked within Weston's aviation industry, married Violet Short from Bristol and their eldest son was named Paul. Whether it was the cost of one shilling and six pence for the first 12 words, and nine pence for every six additional words that deterred Lewis from placing a notice of Richard's birth in the *Weston Mercury & Somersetshire Herald* is unclear. It may well have been that Lewis was generally unmoved by such natural events – something he passed on to his second son. The same day Ritchie was born, five shillings bought entry to the Saturday Night Palais De Danse at the Winter Gardens Pavilion for Weston residents wanting a night out. Tickets cost just three shillings for forces members, and no doubt primarily directed towards servicemen, the paper carried a Ministry of Health advertisement, warning "the most important thing about VD is to avoid the loose behaviour which spreads disease."

The paper also reported that "the town clerk reported a circular from the Ministry of Health regarding 30,000 temporary houses from America for erection in areas which had suffered from enemy bombing." Although the Blackmore home in Addicott Road was not directly affected by the bombings, as with most families, the immediate post-war years were tough. Many wartime factories were no longer required for the same work and the Borough Council heavily promoted the area as an ideal base for light industry. For those within the aviation industry, it was a case of moving to another trade or to another town. In 1947, with Richard just two years old, Lewis took the opportunity of working at London's airport, resulting in the family departing from the West Country to set up home in Middlesex, just west of the capital.

The Blackmore's set up residence close to Heathrow airport at 13 Ash Grove, Heston, in a modest three-bedroom semi-detached. Family holidays were spent back in Weston where Lewis made Richard aware of his Welsh heritage. "Going to Weston-super-Mare for every holiday I had up to about

15, we often came across to Cardiff and Swansea and did the whole thing," he told HTV in 2001.

While Richard grew up in a stable middle-class environment, he also came of age during one of the century's most transitional decades: the ten years from the end of WWII saw astonishing change in an era where the general attitude was 'out with the old and in with the new.' Some of these, such as the acceptance of modern architectural developments, are now generally viewed as an error of judgement, but the one area that proved to be far more durable was the change that occurred in popular music.

For the youth seeking an alternative to classical or jazz, there was little on offer apart from big band swing such as the Glenn Miller or Ted Heath Orchestras or 'crooners' like Bing Crosby and Frankie Laine. By the mid Fifties a new style of music emerged on the scene with Bill Haley & the Comets' 'Rock Around The Clock', the first hit record of the genre given the name 'rock 'n' roll' by American DJ Alan Freed. The fact that this new music was seen by the pre-war generation as a bad and disruptive influence only helped increase its appeal to rebellious children such as Richard Blackmore. In fact Haley's 'Rock Around The Clock' along with Elvis Presley's 'Hound Dog' were amongst the first records he acquired.

Unfortunately there was very little media outlet in the late Fifties for youngsters attracted to rock 'n' roll. In Britain, the conservative BBC Light Programme was virtually all that was on offer as an alternative to classical music. Fortunately Radio Luxembourg, broadcasting on 208 metres, proved to be a guiding light for rock 'n' roll fans. "It was a big highlight of my life back then," said Blackmore. "I'd listen to it from eight to 10 at night, but after 10 o'clock I had to listen to it very quietly, because my dad thought I was sleeping! Radio Luxembourg was a big thrill to listen to at the time; they played Buddy Holly and Duane Eddy, who were my heroes. The bands I played in as a teenager did a lot of Buddy Holly and Duane Eddy songs."

By the time he was 11 Richard had got his first guitar. "I pestered my dad to get me a guitar; I'd been listening to performers like Elvis Presley on the radio, so that would have been Scotty Moore I heard playing guitar. He bought me a Framus acoustic at the local guitar shop; it cost about seven guineas, and that was a lot of money in those days. I remember him telling me, 'If you don't learn how to play this thing, I'm going to put it across your head.'" Lewis Blackmore was all too aware of his son's easily bored tendencies and having invested the equivalent of a week's wages he insisted Richard took lessons and mastered the instrument properly. "I was lucky, because I went to lessons at the very beginning," Blackmore told Steve Gett in *Melody Maker*, "so I got off on the right footing. I had to ride my bicycle to lessons; I had to hold my guitar and try to steer the bicycle, and such trips were interesting, because I had to travel six miles."

Richard had classical tuition for a year, which not only installed a good degree of discipline into his playing but also taught him correct techniques that later held him in good stead. Lewis initially helped his son's musical aspirations as best he could. "I don't really have a musical background from my parents," Blackmore told *Guitar Player* in 1978, "but my father was a kind of mathematician and he helped me with the notes in a purely mathematical way. I would show him some music and ask, 'Why is this like this?' and he would work it out without knowing why, which I couldn't do at that age. And that's what I've been doing since I was 11."

Although initially inspired by Buddy Holly and Duane Eddy it was seeing Tommy Steele, one of the very first English rock 'n' rollers, on television, that became the spark that ignited Blackmore's passion for wanting to play this new music. "I wanted to play like him; I'd watch him on *6.5 Special.** I used to watch and strum along with my guitar; although I couldn't play any chords, it looked good."

Little is known of Blackmore's earliest years at school but having failed his eleven-plus examination, instead of attending the local grammar school that his parents had wished for, Ritchie spent his remaining academic years at Heston Senior School. "I didn't go to grammar school, so I'm going to be excommunicated. I was like, 'I don't want to die yet! Help! Give me a guitar. I can do this. I can do a bit of this …' and I thought, 'I'm gonna show people, I'm gonna play the guitar really well.' So they would say, 'He was a terrible pupil, but he could really play the guitar.' That's exactly what they said later on. This was great – the cause – because then I went, 'I've got to apply myself to something to show these people I can do it.' That's the motivation, to show people that you're worthy of something, you're not just an idiot. It would be, 'Oh, Blackmore, he's an idiot. I'll show them. I'll …take up guitar!' I'll need a guitar to do it.

"Small point, but … I failed my 11-plus, so I was automatically a reject after that. You know, that hit me hard, 'cause my father and mother said, 'Well, now you've failed that, that's terrible.' I was 11 years old. But I couldn't follow anything they taught me at school. It's the way they would teach. We had very puritanical teachers; my school was like a Victorian school – it was like, disgusting! If you missed something: 'Please sir, I didn't

---

* An influential TV programme, broadcast on the BBC channel at 6.05 pm, *6.5 Special* was one of the first British attempts at a pop music-based television show. Director Jack Good went on to helm such other rock related TV shows as *Oh Boy!* and, in the US, *Shindig!*

understand' … 'You didn't understand Blackmore? Go and stand in the corner.' 'Sorry sir!' It was just like *Tom Brown's Schooldays*; very similar."

As a child Blackmore had all the usual interests that most young boys indulged in, and from an early age, he showed a natural aptitude for sport. He excelled at athletics, and javelin throwing was one pursuit he became particularly adept at, representing his school at county level and becoming the best in his age group as Middlesex county champion. Aside from the usual sports the P.E teacher, Mr Pegram also gave the class lessons in morris dancing. "We were the only school to have the morris dancers, we were a very sporty little group of kids," recalls Valerie Morris. "When I used to ride to school on my bike I used to catch up with him down Cranford Lane or join him and we used to ride along together and he had his guitar slung over his back. He used to play it during playtime – he was very much into it. He was always playing, and when it was school concerts he was always up there along with everyone else. I can still see his little face from school."

The success he achieved through his sporting achievements was offset by his general attitude to other subjects, telling Gett, "I used to do athletic events like javelin throwing and swimming and they kept presenting me with all these awards. After hymns at assembly the headmaster would say, 'Blackmore's done it once more – he's put Heston up there' and I'd be given some medal for some sport. By the afternoon I'd be in his office getting the cane and being threatened with expulsion. I was always talking in class. I couldn't stand classes; I was always being caught out. I remember my physics teacher saying, 'Blackmore, never become a criminal' and when I asked him why, he told me 'Because you look so bloody guilty all the time – don't bother.' Meanwhile Bunsen burners would be going strong and we'd have blown something else up. I'll never forget his words though. 'Blackmore, never become a criminal, because you look so bloody guilty.' I was terrible at school and I think I was threatened with being expelled every week."

Whether Blackmore's stories of being both a bully and mischievous at school actually occurred or have been imbued with the type of image he wanted to portray, they certainly don't ring true with Valerie Morris who remembers him as the reserved type. "He was very, very shy and quiet. I don't remember him around the bike sheds when we used to go there. Who would have thought then that he would have gone on to be so famous?"

Even though he wasn't the most academic child, what skills Blackmore did possess were often undermined by the inflexibility of his teachers which damaged his confidence. When interviewed in 1998 Blackmore was still bitter about his schooldays: "You're very impressionable between the ages of 11 and 15. My father used to teach maths, and he taught me a certain way of doing maths, which I would take to school, and they would turn round and go, 'How did you come to this conclusion?' And I would go, 'Well, I did this,' and the guy would say, 'Yes, I know what you did, but I didn't teach you that.' I would go, 'No, you didn't, my dad taught me that. It's a much simpler way of doing it.' I remember him going through the whole book. They were all correct answers, and he would cross out all the answers. 'No, that's not the way I taught you, so it's wrong!' Something hit me that day, like 'This world is really messed up.' That teacher – his ego's been hurt because I figured out a way of doing something – I didn't figure it out, I was taught another way, which was much simpler. But he didn't teach me that way. So, that didn't help. But it did, in a way. It gave me that … 'I'll show them …'"

This "I'll show them" attitude was to become the major catalyst through-out Blackmore's professional career. Not only did his school experiences shape a dislike for authority, something that still holds with him today, but his self-determination would also lead to numerous run-ins and altercations with many future colleagues and associates. "When I was about 13, I got the impression – and I think a lot of people may have got this impression when they were at school – that you're kind of picked on, although I was a school bully. But in school I kind of felt a little bit … I didn't really study, so I felt a little bit distanced from being accepted in school. You were either in or out, you know. In those days you were either brilliant at history, geography or maths, English – and if you didn't do that you were just a reject."

The skiffle craze of the mid Fifties, as exemplified by the likes of Lonnie Donegan and Wally Whyton, appealed to many youngsters including Blackmore. While still at school he joined his first group but as they already had several guitarists in Glen Stoner, David Cox (nicknamed 'Oxo'), David Rodham and Victor 'Bugsy' Hare, he wasn't initially considered good enough to replace any of them. "The very first band I was in was called the 2 I's Junior Skiffle Group. Because there was a 2 I's Coffee Bar Skiffle Group with Wally Whyton and people like that, and we were the junior band. That was my first band, and I played washboard in that! Then I went on to better things – I played the dog box. There were about 20 guitarists involved and none of them could play. We were playing Lonnie Donegan stuff – 'Rock Island Line' and things like that. But first I started playing what you call a dog box; it's a piece of string attached to a broomhandle, which goes through a tea chest and gives you certain notes. And any one of the notes will do, as long as it goes boom. Then I progressed to the washboard with thimbles and things."

Like so many musically motivated kids his age, Blackmore's first live per-formance was at a school show: "It was quite funny – we did 'Rebel Rouser' by Duane Eddy. The audience started clapping, and it just drowned us out!

You couldn't even hear what we were playing. It was great at the beginning then (*mimics clapping*) – 'Where are we?' Then the teacher comes on stage and says, 'OK, that's enough – next!' And it was a ballet act or something. But that was my first. It was interesting that when we were rehearsing for that school thing, I couldn't get the amplifier to work – which was a little radio, two watt radio – and I kept plugging it in, taking it out, fiddling with it, couldn't get it to work. And in the end, by mistake, I had the guitar lead and I plugged it straight into the mains – imagine coming out of a pick-up straight into the mains – and I blew the whole mains in the school. All the lights went out in the whole school."

There were other short-lived bands at school including one with Barry Lovegrove. "We went through school together playing in local bands and stuff like that. All we did at school was talk guitars and bands. We used to meet in the bike sheds and talk bands. [Blackmore] was just a natural though; he was brilliant actually. We were always in each other's houses. He would come over to my house. I had a music room, which was just a little room in this house in 1 Eldon Avenue. We would jam together playing over the top of Ricky Nelson LP's and such, thinking we were the greatest. On the ceiling in that small room I had all my guitar buddies sign their name with a thick black marker that I brought home from BOAC. Ritchie's autograph is probably still there under the paint. It was a novelty for us at the time so we just closed the door, put the amplifiers on and just played and pretend we were in a band. We used to rehearse in his room until the neighbours complained. We used to blast the room out and we had these French windows. We closed them once because the neighbour said her husband was working night shift, so we closed them up and put the volume up louder." Ritchie and Barry got a little group together as Lovegrove vaguely remembers, "In this group there was a guy called Clive on the drums, I don't remember his surname, Allan was on the bass and I was on rhythm."

Long before he became better known as 'Ritchie' most people referred to him as 'Blackie' or 'Ricky'. Despite being a shy kid, even at such an early age Ricky had an eye for the ladies, and not long after he started at Heston Senior School he started dating his first girlfriend Pauline Walton, as she recalls in a letter to the author: "It was about 1958. We were inseparable for at least two years. I think we were quite grown up for our respective ages. We walked home from Heston School together, until he turned off, I think at Springwell Road. Even if we didn't walk home together from school I could be 100 per cent sure that he would be at my house every single evening by 5.30. During summer evenings we would walk to Cranford Park. During the winter when it was too cold to walk over the park, we

7

would stop at the local off licence to buy a packet of Smiths Crisps and then walk back to my house.

"My mother bought a Dansette record player for me but Blackie and I loved sitting together in my parent's dining room. We would have a smooch on the sofa while we listened to Eddie Cochran on Radio Luxembourg. Blackie was thrilled when, in about 1959 his father bought him his first [electric] guitar. It was his pride and joy and he couldn't wait to bring it round to my house in Brabazon Road. He wanted me to have a guitar also, so my mother purchased one for me. Blackie would spend lots of time trying to teach me but all I could play was a little of 'Tom Dooley.'

"Sometimes he walked all the way to the house carrying his guitar and amplifier. He would happily play away and the house shook as my parent's small lounge became his stage. They were very tolerant. My mother frequently called us out into the back garden to take photos of us. Blackie was always very shy, even sullen. He had a beautiful smile but was always quiet. He always told me he would be a professional musician at some stage and I knew he would. Even though he couldn't read music, when I asked him to play something he would play it after simply hearing it once.

"His taste in clothes never really changed. He loved black clothes and nearly always wore a black jacket with a very tiny check. Often black jeans, a black shirt with open collar and black suede shoes. His most particular asset was his lovely dark hair. He combed it at least every hour, the sides combed back flat and the front dropped over his forehead, similar to a quiff as we then called it. It was that front piece that he was so particular about. Each time we were out, he would always be combing his hair in the reflection of a shop window. I often had to stop and wait a couple of minutes while he checked his coiffure. He wouldn't let anyone touch his hair, sometimes if I raised my hand to touch it he would duck his head, nothing or nobody dared spoil his hair. He couldn't get it wet in the rain!

"Sometimes we would go Sunday afternoons to Hounslow to the cinema, the Regal or the Granada. We always waited for the 111 bus at Kingsley Road to take us home up Cranford Lane. He never got off the bus at his stop but always escorted me all the way home first. The only times we were apart were when my parents took me to St. Austell in Cornwall and his parents took him to his grandparents at Weston-super-Mare. During these separations we wrote letters to one another nearly every day. He always put S.W.A.L.K on my envelopes. It was ages before I discovered that SWALK meant 'sealed with a loving kiss.' His favourite guitarist at the time was Duane Eddy and he signed his letters to me 'Richard Duane' or 'Duane Eddy Blackmore.' One time he came home from Weston with a cream handbag for me. He was always sweet, thoughtful and kind. I think in those days we both considered our love was the real thing and it would last forever. We thought we were so grown up. Sadly, after we both left school about 1960, we saw less of each other and eventually went our own ways."

Whether or not it was due to Blackmore's shyness is unclear but in all the time he dated Pauline he kept it a secret from his family, something that to this day she still finds a little odd, as Walton never met Blackie's parents or brother.

Aside from an interest in girls, sport and his personal appearance, music was undoubtedly Blackmore's main passion and he paid attention to the top guitarists of the day such as country players Jimmy Bryant and Speedy West and top rock 'n' rollers Scotty Moore and James Burton. Despite his classical tuition, rock 'n' roll players employed different approaches and techniques to anything that his tutor had taught him and while appreciating the value of the classical lessons, he desired to play like his rock heroes.

Among the top players in Britain at the time was 'Big' Jim Sullivan, guitarist with the Wildcats, Marty Wilde's backing band. Although he was only four years older than Ritchie, Sullivan had already built one hell of a reputation and in January 1960, Marty Wilde and the Wildcats were included on the bill for a tour of top US acts Gene Vincent and Eddie Cochran. Cochran's first visit to Britain was a huge event and Sullivan was fortunate to pick up many new licks from listening to Cochran play. In fact Cochran would often travel on the train to gigs with the support groups, throwing a few guitar lessons in along the way. The fact that Sullivan toured with the great Cochran was made all the more poignant when Cochran was tragically killed in a car crash in Wiltshire at the end of the tour on April 17.

Fortunately for Ritchie, Sullivan lived nearby in Hounslow. "My brother's girlfriend knew him and he would come over to the house," Blackmore told Steve Gett, "of course after I heard him play I idolised him. I would always be around his house trying to learn different things – I used to sit on his doorstep because he wouldn't answer the door, so I'd sit there. Then he'd answer the door: 'What do you want?' 'Jim, can you teach me that riff?' He was phenomenal at the time. It was amazing to see somebody that good. He was good because I could see how far I had to go to try and keep up. At first I thought, 'Oh, no, I'll never make it if this is just the guy around the corner,' but luckily not everybody was like him. It just so happened he lived around the corner and it was like having a genius around, and you think everyone else is the same way. He was teaching me classical Bach, and things like that – and he was teaching me to read better than I was. He said to me once, 'Whatever type of music you're going to play, you must stick to it; don't be a jack-of-all-trades.' So I decided rock and roll was the thing."

Nearly half a century on Jim Sullivan recalls those lessons. "I could only teach him what I knew, which at that time was quite limited stuff. He did all the things he was supposed to do but it wasn't like a teacher-student thing. It wasn't like that, I didn't charge him; he just wanted to know how to do certain things." Ironically, despite Blackmore's desire to learn rock 'n' roll, the first thing that Sullivan taught him to play was Bach's 'Gavotte', a melody that Blackmore has subsequently employed throughout the years. There were many other significant things that Blackmore learnt from Sullivan, most notably, how to bend notes, and to use all fingers including his thumb. "I said, 'Look, how many fingers have you got? You've got to use all of your fingers and that includes the thumb over the top.' He said, 'Oh my classical teacher said you can't use your thumb' and I said 'Well it's another digit' and I showed him a couple of chords you could play using your thumb that you couldn't possibly play without. Blues players and jazz players use the thumb a lot because with some chords you want some bass notes and you can't play them without using your thumb."

The other significant policy that was installed into the 14-year-old was to be original and not copy others. In truth Blackmore found it difficult to copy others regardless. "He took my advice, and nobody plays like him," says Sullivan. "He doesn't copy anybody. He doesn't have the need to copy anybody – his own personality came through. You would say to him just do what you want to in there and he'd do exactly the right thing, but if you said I want a little bit of soul guitar he'd clam up. Whether he knew and said, 'Well sod you, I'm gonna play what I want to play, I'm not going to play what you want.' Which I think he's right in, to be honest."

Even at this early age Sullivan could also see the young player had lots of ability. "He had talent even then. You can tell somebody with talent. I couldn't see what he was going to become but I knew he was going to be a good guitarist that went without saying really. One of the things I think he learnt from me, it's all very well copying other people but by doing that you lose your individuality. So you have to play what you are as a human being rather than what you think people are. That was one of these things … I had this kind of philosophy when I was young. And I helped quite a lot of people by doing that."

Sullivan also recalls how shy and introverted the young Blackmore was. "The confidence thing in those days wasn't there and I think that's what makes him walk around with this black cloud over him today. I think that shyness still pervades in certain ways but it's kind of overcome by bravado. He's not exactly outward going: his view of an intellectual conversation is hello and goodbye. He's a very hard man to talk to."

As for his own perception of his abilities, Blackmore has always insisted that playing didn't come naturally and he had to fight in order to master the instrument, an indication of the dedication and determination he had in those early days by practicing for hours and hours. "I found it very hard at first," he told *Guitar Player* in 1978. "It was very difficult. The first six months were difficult and then it became very easy; then after about three years it became very difficult again."

With his son's dedication to the instrument now apparent, as Pauline Walton recalls, Lewis took Ritchie to Albert's in Twickenham to buy him his first ever electric guitar, after Ritchie made attempts to electrify his Framus model. "I put three pick-ups on it myself and I used to have to plug it into the radio because I didn't have an amp. My first electric was the Hofner Club 50 – it was a great guitar. I remember playing my first date with it at Feltham Town Hall. It was much easier than my Framus, which would always break down. I had this amplifier called a Watkins Dominator amp – and I was in the Dominators at the age of 15-and-a-half – and it would always break down every time we'd do a show. It would blow up. So I'd go and take it back to Selmer's in Charing Cross Road. To get there I'd have to go on the train from Hounslow West, with this amplifier. I'd take it back. 'Oh, we'll give you another one,' 'Alright, great.' So I took the other one back, and then the next weekend I'd be playing, and as soon as we opened up, sure enough ... bong bang ... the usual.

"So the following Monday I'd be taking it back to Selmer's. This happened five times! Every week I took it back, and they said, 'What the hell are you doing, why do you keep blowing this amp up?' They said, 'Next time you come in here, bring your guitar in, so we can see what you're doing.' So I took the amplifier back. They said, 'Right, got your guitar?' 'Got it with me.' The guy was really nice. He said, 'Just plug your guitar in – what are you doing?' I said, 'Well, I turn the amp up like this,' and they had a brand new one, and I started playing until it blows up. It blew up, right in the shop. They couldn't believe it. They couldn't believe I blew it up in the shop. I said: 'There you go, look.' 'Cause it was getting like a Monty Python sketch – I was getting used to it by then. They said, 'Take this amp.' 'Can I try that amp?' 'No, don't try that out. Get it out of here!' And that amp never let me down. Sixth amplifier."

Blackmore's own recollections of his early career are patchy to say the least and most biographies mention his involvement with a band called the Satellites but the group's drummer Mick Underwood is adamant that

11

Blackmore was never a member.* What is certain is that the group in question included another guitarist, Rodger Mingaye who was a couple of years Blackmore's senior. "I was playing rhythm guitar in the band," Blackmore recalled. "Rodger Mingaye – brilliant guitarist – was the lead guitar player. We used to play places like Vicky Burke's in Twickenham, a dance place – we used to play down there. That was my first introduction to playing live in front of people. And Rodger was the main guitar player; I just played rhythm 'cause he was just brilliant."

Mingaye, like Blackmore, cannot remember the group's name but he does recall what they played. "We were doing all Lonnie Donegan's stuff. I don't think we even had a name to be honest. It was those kind of days where you just played anywhere that would let you play. I remember we had a tea-chest bass, and I think we had a guy called Bill Piper, who I went to school with, who wasn't really a musician. None of us were bloody musicians anyway. I can't remember who was singing or if we even had a singer. It certainly wasn't Ritchie. I don't think he ever opened his mouth. I remember I really hated him because he had a Hofner Club 50 and I had some really crappy old guitar. It only lasted two or three months."

In later years Blackmore claimed that the family's move to West London had no affect on his direction in music and his future would have been the same wherever he lived. However, being so close to London's burgeoning music scene fuelled his ambitions and it's doubtful whether the excitement of the early Sixties would have had the same effect in sleepy Weston-super-Mare. Apart from Jim Sullivan, the West London area from Shepherd's Bush to Hayes in Middlesex was a hotbed of young musical talent. Jimmy Page, Pete Townshend, Dave Wendels, Mick Underwood, Nick Simper, and Ian Gillan were just some of the other lads in the locality who were all making their first tentative steps into the music business.

According to local musician, Frank Allen, who knew of Blackmore during his schooldays and also became bassist with Cliff Bennett & the Rebel Rousers and later, the Searchers, Blackmore's reputation as a terrific guitarist was already established at this early stage. Word soon spread around the locality, reaching the ears of Dave Wendels, who was three years Blackmore's senior. "I was playing in one of the local bands at that time in the Hounslow area and the singer in that band said, 'Hey you've got to hear this guy Ritchie he's unbelievable' so this friend of mine took me over to this house in Heston. And there was this gangly kid playing Duane Eddy things at 9,000 miles an hour and that was just amazing. Certainly no one

---

* In fairness, Blackmore has said that he can't remember for certain the group's name.

12

played that fast at that time. The rest of us were trying to struggle our way through 'Peggy Sue' and 'Apache' and here was this kid just ripping through this stuff. I also remember he was into the classical guitar and could play Segovia type things even at that age which was remarkable.

"That's a very distinct memory because you don't forget stuff like that. A lot of us guitar players had to work at it, but Ritchie and Albert Lee were the two guys that were better than the average person. Ritchie was amazingly and obviously gifted from a very early age for anyone who saw that. We all practised and there's a certain amount of learning to get where we need to be with our craft but it comes easier to other people so he had a natural fluidity that the rest of us didn't have. We had to practice playing fast whereas it just rolled off his fingers."

Apart from Bert Weedon's influential but basic *Play In A Day* instruction manual, the only way to really learn guitar was by listening to records and trading licks and pointers with another guitarist. Blackmore and Wendels often sat together doing just that, but Blackmore was hell bent on playing everything as fast as possible. "One of the earliest times we sat down in his living room in Heston, we sat and played together," Wendels recalled. "I tried to show him the solo to 'Bluejean Bop' by Gene Vincent, which is basically not 9,000 miles an hour. It's fairly intricate but not ridiculously fast. He couldn't grasp it. He could get it, he could play the notes but he did it in this enormous flurry of speed and I'm saying, 'It's a bit slower than that.' He was prone to do that, play everything ridiculously fast. Something that was slow and in a groove was a concept he hadn't quite discovered at that time."

Having learnt all that he could from sharing tips with other guitar-playing friends, listening to radio and watching TV, in 1960, at Southall Community Centre, Ritchie saw his first gig. "I got to see a band called Nero & the Gladiators when I was 15 – that was my favourite band – and they were big heroes for me. I will always remember – they were unbelievable. Just a three-piece band with a pianist, and they did 'In The Hall Of The Mountain King' and things like that. It was all classical stuff, but to rock 'n' roll, and that to me was … well, this is it! They dressed up as Romans."

The Gladiators were one of the top bands on the circuit and hugely admired by hordes of aspiring young musicians that attended their concerts.* Guitarist Colin Green, one of Britain's top players of the day, was held in high esteem by Blackmore but before long Ritchie would be gaining equal amounts of admiration from his contemporaries.

---

* Their 'rocked up' rendition of Grieg's 'In The Hall Of The Mountain King' was banned by the BBC for fear of offending classical music lovers.

CHAPTER 2

Sutch An Apprenticeship
(1960–62)

In early Sixties Britain it was still possible to leave school before the age of 16 and Blackmore jumped at the opportunity. "I left school when I was 15 and I couldn't wait to get out. I was like a drop out." Initially he took a factory job, which, to the best of Pauline Walton's recollections, was for EMI Records in Hayes – coincidental considering so many of his future recordings would be done for that company. It appears he only lasted there a few weeks. With both his father and elder brother Paul working at London Airport, Ritchie followed in the family tradition when Cunard Eagle employed him as an apprentice radio mechanic.

The tradition of ridiculing young apprentices by sending them off for a 'long weight (wait)', or to get some 'rubber nails' was something the young Blackmore fell victim to as he recalled to *Melody Maker's* Steve Gett in 1981: "I used to work at Heathrow Airport for a company called Cunard Eagle who have since merged with the shipping company and no longer fly. I used to work in the hangers and one day, about two weeks after I'd started, I was in the main office when the telephone rang. At the time I was only 16 and it was my job to observe what was happening and take note of everything that was going on. Anyway, the guy in the office answered the phone and after a short while said, 'Sure, I've got someone here, I'll send him over.'

"I was standing there like a dummy and the guy told me to take a huge piece of equipment over to central area, which was by the control tower. This meant going across all the runways, dodging planes en route. There was

14

a plane over there and they wanted to check the aerials. So I had to take this big unit over and it weighed a ton. Eventually I reached the aircraft and although I had 'radio mechanic' written across my overalls I didn't know the slightest thing about it. Three guys were standing there and no one was in the plane and they all turned round and said 'Ah thank goodness the radio man has arrived. We're saved.' So they told me to give them a reading and I didn't know what to do. All the time they were praising me saying. 'I do admire you radio men, it's so involved I don't know how you lads do it. You're the salt of the earth.' These guys were qualified pilots and I was just an apprentice. I didn't know how to work this unit and they couldn't figure out why the man in the cockpit wasn't getting a reading. I had about 16 aerials out and absolutely nothing was happening. I should have sent out a frequency and they should have picked up a reading. This whole procedure went on for about 15 minutes until one of these pilots asked me if I knew what I was doing. I replied that I didn't and they went crazy. I felt so small it was such an embarrassment. The whole thing had been a complete practical joke and when I went back to the office they were in hysterics."

Being on the receiving end of practical jokes had an affect on the young Blackmore as he would go on to be one of rock's greatest exponents of the art. While suffering at the hands of others during his days at Heathrow, he was also capable of causing chaos: "One of the jobs was to clean out the air filters with a huge long hose. But you were supposed to curl the thing up so that not too much air came out. I didn't know how to work this filter and when I turned it on it blew absolutely everything down the hanger. There was a guy spraying a plane with paint and he went shooting down the end of the hanger. That didn't go down too well. Again. I felt such a fool."

Working at the airport at least gave Blackmore the opportunity to put his practical skills to use for his own benefit. "When all the planes were out it was great fun. Everybody was doing something for the home, making chairs and tables. I made a guitar. I built parts – I got the parts of the amplifier and put it all together." Ritchie also got the chance to join his first proper group, the Dominators, which included Barry Lovegrove on rhythm guitar, bassist Alan Dunklin and a drummer called Clive. Although the Dominators only lasted a matter of months there were personnel changes and at one point they included Mick Underwood on drums and Bob Danks on vocals and rhythm guitar. The Dominators were the first band in which Blackmore would get the chance to earn some money, playing live to supplement his meagre wage.

"We played in the pubs on a Thursday night," recalls Lovegrove. "We had these amplifiers that we took apart and tried to make them more powerful.

We were quite thick when we were young because we both had cheap guitars and Vox amplifiers and we even repaired our own echo chamber back in those days with a single piece of tape that went round. That was Rick's job to make sure we had enough spare tape when we went on stage so we could change it if one broke. I remember once he put banjo strings on his guitar instead of regular strings and got this weird sound and he arranged our own version of the Grieg classic 'Hall Of The Mountain King'."

Mick Underwood: "We used to rehearse up at a school in Harlington. We played Johnny B. Goode, some Shadows. We did some Presley stuff, 'Baby I Don't Care', Cliff Richard stuff. We did a BBC audition with some Shadows stuff and failed miserably. At that time you could write in and get an audition. We were looking at TV. In those days you could contact them and they'd grant you an audition. It was the days before people had tapes. I think they thought we were a bunch of scruffy little kids, which we were! We played one or two tunes, I know one of them was 'Apache' but I don't think the BBC was overly impressed."

During his time with the Dominators, having recently split from his school sweetheart Pauline Walton, Blackmore found a new partner who was, by all accounts, a very pretty girl by the name of Jacqueline Shirley. Mick Underwood: "I remember being somewhere and she came up on the train where we were. He met her after school; I know when he met her because I'd got a singer who started playing with the Dominators called Tony Parsons. She came from that area where Frankie Allen lived, that was in the same area that Tony Parsons lived." With the Dominators only in existence for a matter of months, Lovegrove recalls that Blackmore also played in his next band, Dave Dean & the Cruisers Combo, though probably not on a regular basis.

By 1960 a new music store had opened in Hanwell at 76 Uxbridge Road, run by former big band drummer Jim Marshall. It was a highly significant focal point for young musicians in the West London area and the amplifiers and speakers Marshall started producing defined the generations of rock musicians that followed. Dave Wendels: "Marshall's was the hang out, the place we all used to go for the legendary Saturday jam sessions. Jim Marshall's was the place."*

Around the same time that Marshall's shop opened; a new band emerged on the local scene led by a colourful eccentric from South Harrow called David Sutch. It's fair to say that Sutch wasn't particularly talented; his

---

* Proprietor Jim Marshall, doesn't recall jam sessions taking place.

singing was poor, but he was without doubt a visionary and a pioneer in British rock 'n' roll. In the late Fifties and early Sixties, British popular music was still extremely conservative. American artists like Elvis Presley, Eddie Cochran, Jerry Lee Lewis and Little Richard were far more animated in their recordings and stage presence than anything Britain had to offer. Sutch saw that there was a place for an artist with an extremely visual and theatrical show. Taking his cues from the uninhibited approach of Screamin' Jay Hawkins, Sutch took stagecraft to another level with numerous props including a coffin and a totally over the top performance that left an indelible impression on anyone who witnessed it. Giving himself the grandiose name of Screaming Lord Sutch, with his long hair (unheard of in those days) and helmet with buffalo horns, he looked like the "wild man of Borneo" and suitably named his backing band the Savages.

It didn't take long before a reputation built around London and beyond, for despite his lack of talent, Sutch managed to attract some of the area's best players, and along with Nero & the Gladiators, Screaming Lord Sutch & the Savages became the band that aspirant musicians looked up to. By May 1961, the Savages were auditioning for new personnel including a guitarist. Blackmore saw it as an ideal opportunity to establish himself with a name band that had already turned professional by the time he went along to the audition. Unfortunately for Blackmore his former bandmate Rodger Mingaye was among the other guitarists who applied for the post. Carlo Little, then drummer with the Savages, recalled that it wasn't an easy choice. "The audition for a guitarist proved more of an ordeal. Ritchie Blackmore, who could have only been 15 at the time, came along with his girlfriend and his dad. We heard about seven or eight blokes, but it was a toss up between Ritchie and Rodger Mingaye. Rodger just had the edge, because he was older and more experienced."

Disappointed at failing the audition, Blackmore continued working at the airport, staying there a total nine months before joining an outfit called Mike Dee & the Jaywalkers. Lead singer Mike Wheeler who used the stage name of Dee, bassist David Tippler, drummer Terry Maybey and rhythm guitarist Brian Mansell were seeking a replacement for guitarist Brian Cell. "They wanted to go on the road professionally," says Blackmore. "That's when I was 16. So I went on the road with them. And that was when I started being professional, travelling up and down the M1 with the door half open on a Bedford van. It gets really cold!"

Such details seem to be forever etched in musicians' memories of struggling to make a living and Wheeler echoes Blackmore's recollections. "We all lived pretty local, Terry and me lived in Twickenham, Brian lived in

Whitton, Dave lived in Feltham and Ritchie by the airport there. We had a Bedford Dormobile. Our manager Phil Jay had hit a wall or something and the van had sliding doors and once he'd hit the wall the door wouldn't slide back properly so he wedged an old raincoat in it and it used to be freezing in the back. He never got it repaired and there were no heaters in it."

The Jaywalkers were nothing more than boys, all just 16, except Wheeler who was a year older than the rest. Mike Wheeler: "We had only just left school and at that time there were only a handful of professional bands in the country. Very few and far between, we were unique really in that way and of course we were local heroes around where we lived." Although professional, by all accounts the Jaywalkers were nothing exceptional; an all-round pop band that played the chart hits and standards of the day such as 'What'd I Say' and 'Money', Bobby Darin and Shadows songs.

They had been together for a year or so when Ritchie joined. Mike Wheeler: "We had turned professional and the guitarist who was with us before was a lad called Brian Cell, who actually formed the band but our manager Phil Jay wanted to get us in with the Cooper Agency. Phil Jay compered a lot of the Larry Parnes tours called 'Star Spangled Nights' so he was obviously employed by Parnes – he was from that stable as it were. Because he wanted to get a backing band for Vince Eager and all these Larry Parnes boys – they were all booked through the Cooper Agency. We went to do an audition for the Cooper Agency, which Phil took us to, and they liked the band but unfortunately they didn't like the guitarist so they said they would sign us up but not with that guitarist. So of course we knew Ritchie because he was a local lad and we knew he was a really good player so when we asked him he said 'Yeah' because he was working at London Airport at that time. He jacked it in to join up. He was called Blackie, that's what he was called round our way; everyone called him Blackie, long before he was Ritchie. And he had a band called Blackie and the somebody's – I can't remember who they were. I only remember seeing him once. At that time in Twickenham we used to have what they called a rhythm band competition and all the local bands used to go and play and Phil Jay somehow got to compere it. That's how he found the Jaywalkers but Ritchie was on one of them as well at the same time."

Having been approached by the band as opposed to the other way around, 'Blackie' didn't have an arduous audition to contend with. According to Wheeler, "He just came along and it was almost like a practice, the job was filled really – we knew that he'd be the man for the job if he wanted to join. My dad had a big band, played piano and he said 'He's [Blackmore] definitely a bit special' and that was then. I can remember Jim

Sullivan saying, 'He'll make it one day, he's definitely got something.' He could play classical guitar even when he was with us. He had a Spanish guitar and he could read and play things like 'Greensleeves' all finger style, he played all that finger style stuff then because he was quite into Chet Atkins."

Although Blackmore was still not a domineering figure, he nevertheless expressed his opinions as soon as he joined the group. Mike Wheeler: "Like all musicians when they join a band, they influence you in different ways and at that time the instrumentals in the band were more the Shadows. Ritchie didn't like the Shadows; he was really mad keen on Nero & the Gladiators. We were like, 'We normally do the Shadows' but he was like 'I don't really want to do the Shadows, I don't like the Shadows very much.' 'Anyway what do you want to do?' 'Hall Of The Mountain King' and 'Entry Of The Gladiators' were his main two instrumentals. So that was his influence on the instrumental side. He was very much into that. He liked Colin Green who was the guitarist in Nero & the Gladiators, that's where that influence came in so he changed the band around a little bit in that respect. But at that time, when he first joined we were doing a lot of Cliff Richard stuff and Billy Fury and that kind of stuff. But then we changed to more Bobby Darin stuff, and threw in 'Mack The Knife' and 'Bill Bailey' and 'Black Magic' and different things like that. We used to do 'The Bells Are Ringing', 'Summertime' and 'My Blue Heaven' which we put our own arrangements to. 'Nature Boy' was another Bobby Darin one we used to do and 'What'd I Say' by Ray Charles. We'd come out of the rock 'n' roll thing and looking back now, more into swing stuff really."

Even at a young age Blackmore's character showed through in his playing. Mike Wheeler: "When he first joined us he had a Watkins Dominator Amp and a Hofner Club 50 guitar and he could get an amazing sound out of it. I don't know how he did it." Blackmore was also fortunate in that his parents continued to encourage and support him. Within a short while of joining, Wheeler remembers Blackmore surprising them with some new acquisitions. "He was only with us a few weeks and his dad said, 'Come and see what we've bought him' and he had a Vox twin, a Vox Echo and a Gibson 335. All in one day, we couldn't believe it because to us that was a fortune in those days. I'd never ever seen a Gibson 335. He couldn't wait to tell us. The gear and the standards of the bands at that time were really poor. The bands that we had as support bands with us were very poor and they were absolutely amazed by Ritchie, he was certainly a bit special."

Although the cherry red Gibson ES 335 was second-hand, it was still quite special for such a young player to own, and was the same model and colour as the one used by Chuck Berry. Blackmore soon became dissatisfied with the Vox Echo, but came up with a novel idea that would give him much amusement as Wheeler relates: "He took the Vox Echo badge and put it on his Twin and all these other bands used to come up to us and say 'How do you get that fantastic sound?' He used to tell them he'd got a Vox Echo built into his Vox Twin just to wind them up but he just had a unique style."

By now, apart from the obvious rock 'n' roll influences, Blackmore was also educating himself in other musical styles, showing a particular interest in jazz players, most notably Les Paul, Django Reinhardt and Wes Montgomery. Although the group had signed with one of the top agencies, the George Cooper Organisation, many bigger named acts such as Joe Brown, Danny Rivers, Nero & the Gladiators, and Johnny Kidd & the Pirates, were also on Cooper's books so Phil Jay & the Jaywalkers were lucky to get two or three gigs a week. They took whatever work they could, mainly backing the likes of Vince Eager, Johnny Gentle, Tommy Bruce – all acts from the Larry Parnes stable. The common setup of the time was for the support group to play its own set for half an hour followed by a stint backing the headline act. Sometimes there would be two other acts on the bill so they would end up doing three spots: a half hour with Mike Dee and a half hour each with the other two.

Mike Wheeler: "A lot of them were those backing type gigs. We ended up as a backing band really. We weren't alone. I think there were other lads around the country that backed these lads because they didn't have a band, they just used to turn up at the gig. You'd rehearse with them and that was it and if they wanted to put a new song in they normally did it in the dress-ing room or on a soundcheck."

Looking back, Wheeler is amused by the primitive and minimal amount of equipment at the group's disposal. "I laugh about it now – these cinemas where the tours played and they'd have a Reslo mic and a 30 watt linear Concorde amplifier and some 12 inch speakers each side of the stage and we thought we were loud! But we didn't know any different. But we had three Vox Twins and not many bands had them at the time, it was only the Shadows that would have those sorts of amps so we were quite privileged. And when we started the only PA you could buy was the one I bought that was Italian or something like that and that was long before Jim Marshall started building PA stuff. So you just got a couple of boxes with 12″ speakers in and a linear Concorde amp but they were only about 30 watts in a big metal case with two carrier handles. There was no echo or effects. There were a lot of village halls we did. Some of them had never seen a band."

ship (1960–62)*

Despite the primitive equipment the band certainly managed to get some prestigious gigs such as Southall Community Centre, the very place where Ritchie had seen the Gladiators only a year or so earlier. Mike Wheeler: "We played there a few times. That was a Sunday night gig but it was a big gig to have. Jerry Lee, Gene Vincent, Little Richard all played there. I think we backed Tommy Bruce there."

Nick Simper, then with The Renegades, remembers seeing the Jaywalkers at Southall Community Centre: "Once he appeared at Southall with the Jaywalkers a lot of people started to talk about him. I think musicians like him and Mickey Green [of the Pirates] and other good guitarists probably didn't realise at the time how important they were. I remember Johnny Kidd saying he couldn't believe that so many people had gone to see Mickey Green and I think the same thing happened with Ritchie because he made such an impression. What made Ritchie stand out was that he was 10 times faster than anybody else. People used to try and do fast little licks like Duane Eddy's '3.30 Blues' and there's a break in it where it stops and goes into a fast run and nobody could, you would just bluff and it sounded like a fart! But Ritchie could do it note for note and we thought this guy's a bit sharp he can do it just like the record. The Jaywalkers stood out because of him, they were just an ordinary run of the mill band, pretty good and polished but nothing spectacular but he was the one guy. Everybody looked at the guitarist. Didn't matter how good the singer or drummer were, with guys like Hank Marvin to the fore it was the most important thing as far as blokes were concerned. And he did stand out. Everybody used to mention it and talk about him. When you saw somebody like Ritchie Blackmore you knew you had seen something a little bit special."

Blackmore also got to make his first ever recording while with the Jaywalkers, thanks to Phil Jay who arranged a recording session with Decca Records. The band went to Decca's studios in West Hampstead to lay down two tracks. Jay was working in conjunction with one of the agencies the band was signed to and the whole enterprise was highly coordinated as one of the partners from the agency wrote a song called 'Stolen Hours' and was obviously pushing it to get the publishing monies. The other track was 'My Blue Heaven.' Mike Wheeler: "That was actually going to be the B-side, because 'Stolen Hours' had been written for us and that was going to be the A-side and 'My Blue Heaven' the B-side. But we went to Decca and did them but for some reason someone didn't like them and they never released them. I did actually have a demo of them but they got lost over the years."

Because both numbers were in the group's live set there wasn't much rehearsing required and the whole recording was completed in a day. When Blackmore recalled the session decades later, he wasn't particularly enamoured by what had been achieved. "'My Blue Heaven' they wanted it rocked up. That was the very first thing I ever did – we did it with Decca Records. It got turned down, but that was what we recorded. It was dreadful, awful." Even though the record was rejected the group started to get cocky and decided they no longer needed Jay, something that Wheeler now accepts was a mistake. "We got a bit big headed towards the end and we sacked Phil and said we can do it on our own. Dave Tippler got a driving licence and his dad bought him a van so we thought we can do without Phil's fifteen per cent or whatever he was taking but it was our downfall really. The gigs used to come through the agency and every month Phil would just give us a date sheet with them all on so we knew roughly where we were. There would be a few last minute ones. There was at least one a week but on average two a week, maybe three."

"We had gigs up in Newark, Grantham a hundred miles away which I could never understand why," Blackmore told John Tobler in 1982. "It would be places like Hammersmith Palais then Grantham the next day."

The Jaywalkers got their first big break in November '61 when they joined a package tour headlined by one of Britain's top performers of the day Billy Fury, with a bill that consisted of Eden Kane, Karl Denver, the Allisons, Chas McDevitt, Dave Sampson, Gordon Peters, and Shirley Douglas. It was only because Shirley Douglas took ill that the group got such a prodigious gig, albeit briefly as Wheeler explains, "We got a phone call in the morning – could we come on, at Dartford I think, and replace her. That's how we got on that Billy Fury tour. We thought this is it, in the back door here on one of these big stage tours. I think we were all pretty excited. We only did three or so gigs. Funnily enough the other Jaywalkers were on that tour because they were backing Eden Kane."

Because they were last minute stand-ins the presence of Peter Jay & the Jaywalkers caused some confusion for Wheeler and his boys. "There was a dressing room with Jaywalkers on the door and the dressing room was full up because it was us and them; the Jaywalkers and the Jaywalkers!"

Unfortunately for the West London Jaywalkers, after the gig at the Dartford Granada on the 20th and Portsmouth Guildhall the following evening, their brief flirtation with the big time was over when Douglas was well enough to regain her place on the tour. The Jaywalkers had already been dropped by the George Cooper Organisation so instead they signed with the Rudy Stanton Agency and wasted no time in trying to get maximum mileage out of the Fury tour by placing an advert in the December 2 issue of *Melody Maker*.

"ALL ENQUIRIES FOR MIKE DEE and the JAY WALKERS (recently having appeared in the Billy Fury/ Eden Kane Tour) Phone or write to: RUDY STANTON AGENCY 41 GT. WINDMILL STREET, W1, 2nd Floor WHI 5973 BOW 4711."

Neither the advert nor the reflected glory of the Fury tour could guarantee them further work. The band struggled to get more gigs although five days after the Portsmouth show they were back at Southall Community Centre this time supporting Gene Vincent. It was the second occasion the group supported the crazed American rocker having originally done so at the Carlton Ballroom in Slough three months earlier. Although supporting Vincent was certainly another boost for the group's kudos, Blackmore could not have foreseen how much of an effect Vincent would have on his career several years later.

Personality wise Ritchie and his girlfriend Jacqueline appeared ideally suited but she seemed to show little interest in his guitar skills according to Wheeler, "She was very quiet, she hardly ever came to any of the gigs." By April 1962, because of the confusion with Peter Jay's lot, the group decided to change their name to the Condors but unbeknownst to them they had once again ended up with a name that was already being used by another combo. The 'other Condors' were also Johnny Milton's regular backing group and things weren't made any easier when adverts appeared claiming Milton's band was soon to appear on tour with Gary 'US' Bonds. On April 1 Johnny Milton's Condors got a gig in Stoke backing Gene Vincent but it was no April Fools' joke when the mix-up over the shared name actually worked in their favour. They were mistakenly booked on to the Gary 'US' Bonds/ Johnny Burnette/Gene McDaniel package tour which also included all-vocal group the Kestrels, Danny Rivers and Mark Wynter – all of whom the Condors were employed to back, meaning that Dee wasn't required. This was academic as the group folded straight after completing the dates.

Prior to the tour, Blackmore was fortunate that David Sutch was once again seeking a guitarist. Sutch had dropped in on a Jaywalkers gig to check on the guitarist. Mike Wheeler: "I knew something was up because it was at Southall Community Centre where we were playing. Sutchy came down and Ritchie was chatting with him and I knew he hadn't come to see us. Then Ritchie said, 'I've had a really good offer from Sutch.' The reason

23

Ritchie left really was because we were averaging £10–£15 a week and Sutch offered him £20, plus he was one of the best payers on the road. He worked more than everybody else; he was a really big pull. That's why all the big guitarists played with him because he paid so much."

In view of this it was ironic that the Condors last tour was the busiest period of their brief tenure, playing 21 dates in as many days:* three weeks of solid gigs kicking off in Glasgow exactly one week after Blackmore's 17th birthday and finishing in Walthamstow on May 13. The Condors received little recognition for their performances but a reviewer at one of the last shows at the Bedford Granada described the overall line-up as "the swingiest, rockiest candy-box to be opened at Bedford this year."

The Kestrels who opened the show, with backing from the Condors, "took the tempo way up high." Their arrangement of 'Michael Row The Boat Ashore' was by all accounts a "real toe-tapper." Danny Rivers also proved popular and his rendition of 'One Night With You' "really set the fans screaming." However the headlining American names were not quite the attraction the promoters thought they were and audiences at both houses at this Wednesday night concert were among the smallest on the tour. It's doubtful that anyone in attendance at this provincial show paid the young guitarist from Heston any attention but this was soon to change.

The chance to play with Screaming Lord Sutch was too good to turn down for Blackmore even though it would be on a temporary basis as a result of previous guitarist Bernie Watson, along with pianist Nicky Hopkins having left the Savages to take up a residency with Cliff Bennett and the Rebel Rousers in Hamburg. With Blackmore fulfilling obligations to the Condors he asked his mate Dave Wendels to fill the vacant spot for a few weeks until his commitments with the Condors were completed. "I did it for him until he could join," Wendels says. "He was always the guy Sutch wanted because the word was out by then that Ritchie was the hot guy and Sutch wanted him in the band. Whatever else Sutch was he was very perceptive when it came to musicians. He always had the best guys."

The period in which Blackmore joined the Savages in late May 1962 until his stint ended in October, would prove to be the guitarist's first big break. Playing alongside drummer Carlo Little, bassist Ricky Brown and pianist Andy Wren he was left in no doubt as to the status of the band he'd joined. "I was thrown in the deep end really because they were touring everywhere. Very professional band, very good musicians and I had to learn

*The fact that they were doing two shows a night actually made it 42 shows in 21 days!

quick. I used to play through an echo chamber and things like this and the first thing they said to me was, 'You're going to have to get rid of that echo chamber for a start, and you have to move.' "

Because Sutch had a reputation for the quality of his players various local musicians took note of the Savages. Drummer Carlo Little, who was already established as one of the best around, drew the attention of a budding young drummer by the name of Keith Moon. Moon was a huge Savages fan and attended many shows, primarily to watch and learn from Carlo. In anecdotes posted on his website,* Little recalled that Moon was a little disappointed when he discovered that Nicky Hopkins and Bernie Watson had left the band to team up with Cliff Bennett and the Rebel Rousers but in Little's words, "Keith couldn't blame them: he would have jumped at the chance himself to get out of London and play in a foreign country. No, what really got his back up was that the new guitarist was even younger than Watson, a Middlesex boy by the name of Ritchie Blackmore whose devastating runs up and down the guitar were leaving people gasping for breath."

Indeed these few months playing the length and breadth of Britain with the Savages was a pivotal time for Blackmore. Many eyewitnesses, such as Nick Simper, recall being left aghast at the speed and dexterity of the 17-year old's playing. "When [Ritchie] got into the Savages I was really pleased because the Savages were always one of my favourite bands; Ricky Brown was the best bass player around without a doubt. Carlo was definitely the top drummer; they were probably the best band on the London scene. Ritchie's individuality hadn't developed by then, he didn't have a particularly great sound or style in those days. What set Ritchie apart was pure speed; nobody could keep up with him. When he joined Sutch he started doing the fast instrumentals it was bloody great."

Rodger Mingaye hadn't seen Blackmore play since the brief foray with their skiffle outfit and was highly impressed with his mate's progress. "It was New Brighton we were there with the Outlaws and we went over after the gig to see them. I hadn't seen him for about two and a half years, then I heard him in the Savages and I thought, 'Fuckin' hell, is that the same guy?' "

During Blackmore's first stint with the band, Freddie 'Fingers' Lee, who had been Sutch's original pianist returned to the fold, replacing Andy Wren. Lee was in no doubt as to Blackmore's talent as a guitarist but as far as his personality went, Lee was forthright. "He was as thick as fuck. That's what I remember of Ritchie. He was so thick. He was a good-looking lad, all the birds used to really fancy him. He'd get their addresses to write them letters

---

* Carlo Little passed away on August 5, 2005.

and we'd be sitting in the van telling him what to write as he had no idea. We'd tell him what to write and he'd post the letter off. He wasn't very intelligent put it that way but give him a guitar and he was unbelievable."

Although the Savages were top musicians, a popular trick they employed was to play each other's instruments during soundchecks, so that anyone listening, such as the other acts on the bill or club managers, was given the impression that the Savages were hopeless musicians. By the time they took to the stage everyone was blown away by their talent. It wasn't just musical dexterity where Blackmore had to develop quickly; during those few months with Sutch the guitarist started to really learn about showmanship.

Working with the most visual British band at that time was an important turning point in Blackmore's life as it started to bring the shy and retiring teenager out of his shell. In truth, he had no option as Lee explains, "The whole band were showman, and you had to be to keep in the band. You weren't allowed to sit still in anyway. He made you get involved. The other band's stood still like wooden planks. But with Sutch you never stood still."

In the days when guitarists used a single small amp set-up, according to Big Jim Sullivan: "We were all pretty well animated on stage in those days, it was part of being young and being energetic. I can't think of any specifics but for instance, and I know Ritchie used to do the same thing. We used to have our amplifiers in front of us instead of behind and what would happen, we'd be playing away and come to the solo and leap over the amplifier and land on our knees and things like that."

Initially Blackmore was so lacking in confidence that he hated the idea of his family showing up to see him play. Reports of Sutch having to literally drag him on stage were confirmed by Blackmore to Alan Whitman. "Oh yes! Hiding behind the guitar amps and in the wings. They used to grab me, 'Come on!' and pull me out. It's very true. I learned a lot of showmanship from him. He taught me that you can go out there and act like an imbecile and people would think it's wonderful. But – it's very interesting, like a whole psychology kind of thing – if you get out on stage and you look self-conscious, people will watch you. But if you go out there, throw yourself around and act like a fool, they'll go, 'Oh, yeah.' It's like a show, a whole masquerade. But the moment you start taking yourself seriously and go into your shell, people see it immediately. But [Sutch] taught me that. Just get out there and run around. I'd go, 'Well, I feel an idiot. In the end I'm running around with a Tarzan outfit on, and I'm going, 'These people are going for this; I can't believe it.'"

David Sutch was evidently proud of the way he developed the visual aspect of the Savages and in particular the way he managed to turn

Blackmore into an extrovert. "We taught the Savages to be visual and move around a lot. I'd run around a lot on the stage, so we taught the band to move as well. That's one of the main factors. There was a marching routine with the baton and bass player; they would march forward, left right, left right and go towards the crowd. The drummer and the pianist would move side to side. Then jumping across the stage and leaping up in the air, all this sort of stuff was taught to the likes of Ritchie Blackmore, who used to just stand in the corner when we first got him. We had to drag him round the stage and put a bit of life into him."

Neil Newsome, then drummer with Jamie Lee & the Atlantics remembers being a support act to the Savages on a few occasions. "When they came on stage they all wore leopard skin suits. With the Savages you didn't hear the sound you felt it! With Carlo Little's drumming and the noise, the bass and drum riff and the infill of Ritchie it used to crash at you. Then Sutch used to come screaming on stage with these horns on, wielding a big axe. Ritchie used to move about a little bit with the band but he was more of a reserved guy. I think he was dedicated to his playing more than antics."

However Newsome was in no doubt as to just how good Blackmore's playing was. "I remember standing in awe in front of Ritchie. Even without our band we would go and see them. I've always revered him. You can't take it away from the other guitarists but he's always been my firm favourite. At Morecambe Floral Hall he sat down on his amp with his guitar and Billy Clarke (Atlantics guitarist) sat down and he was showing Billy harmonics. He played a number called 'Czardas', like a Russian type speeding up thing and the speed on the guitar was phenomenal. He just sat there and played it ad-lib with Billy. We just stood with our mouths open. Bear in mind he was only 17 years old then."

Blackmore freely acknowledges that Sutch taught him about showmanship but he was initially shell-shocked when joining the Savages: "The very first night with Screaming Lord Sutch, the guy enters – I didn't know, but by the time he enters the stage he's in a coffin: I was not amused by that. I thought, 'This guy is nuts!' And I'm playing in his band. I didn't know what was going to happen. I just rehearsed with him, and we played 'Jack The Ripper.' And we'd open with that, and I didn't know what the stage set-up was until I did it. We'd rehearse then on stage he'd come out of the coffin. I'm like, 'What's going on?' Of course he's got hair down to here and I thought, 'I've got to go home with this guy tonight – he's driving the van!' I wasn't too amused at that!"

If Blackmore's comments appear a little overdramatic bear in mind a gig the group played at the Conservative Club in Bedford on August 16 was billed as 'In person – direct from the nuthouse – the one and only – Screaming Lord Sutch and his Savages.' If that wasn't enough to make the 17 year-old feel uneasy, Sutch gave his band members seemingly unexplainable nicknames. Apart from getting used to being on stage with one of Britain's most eccentric performers, leaping out of coffins and running through the audience scaring the females, Blackmore also had to live with the name 'Bluebell' over the ensuing months.

The Savages live repertoire was built around a few of Sutch's own tunes and several Chuck Berry numbers that remained Sutch mainstays for decades. Dave Wendels: "If you were in the Savages you had to have a certain degree of ability. Sutch didn't have anybody that was bad in his bands. It was a high quality band, it was high energy. One of the first sort of heavy bands, when that word didn't even exist. They were loud! Carlo was one of the loudest drummers around. As we know Sutch couldn't sing to save his life but he was a great showman and very knowledgeable about the music. When it came to music and musicians he knew the difference. The fact that his own talent was marginal was neither here nor there. It was a great training ground." Wendels got to see Ritchie live a few times with the Savages and was impressed with his stage movements. "Ritchie did it very well. That was the genesis of his very live stage presence. If it was an act and at that time not a part of his personality then he was a great actor. He was very lyrical, very accomplished, very technical."

David Sutch spoke about these times three years before his tragic suicide in 1999: "I always had a high standard of musicianship, good musicians, plus a good visual show. I come from the musical area, so I see a lot of musical alliance. So I literally put that musical vaudeville to rock 'n' roll, and that's how we presented a show." Although he adopted the moniker of Lord, Dave Sutch, as his friends referred to him, didn't have an ounce of aristocracy in him. Although it has already been stated that Sutch paid more than other bands, in reality this wasn't the case. Most musicians who were in the Savages talk of the man now immortalised as one of the tightest bandleaders when it came to money. Playing in the Savages was a lucrative gig purely because the band had such a full diary.

Whereas most bands were lucky if they got three gigs a week, the Savages were playing non-stop. Freddie Lee: "It was only because we were working every night, £3 and £21 a week was a good wage then. Then it went to £4. You had the choice of a wage for £20 a week or nightly. The band was on for 45 minutes and Sutch was on for about 15–20 minutes. We did all the work and he got all the money. Sometimes two sets. But he knew he had that much work on, he knew he could get anyone he wanted. That's why everyone went with Sutch. It was the biggest band in England at the time. I'm proud to have been a part of it. It made me so confident. That's where I learnt it."

Compared to America or indeed other parts of Europe, Britain was relatively underdeveloped in the early Sixties, and in the days before motorways, fast food joints, credit cards and numerous other luxuries now taken for granted, life on the road for travelling groups was a lot more demanding as Freddie Lee explains: "There was only one motorway and it stopped at Watford Gap. We used to leave at seven in the morning sometimes – now it's unheard of – to get to Prestatyn in North Wales for the gig that night. If you had to get digs [Sutch] wouldn't pay for them. If you couldn't afford to stay in digs you slept in the van."

It was commonplace in the early Sixties for various groups to frequently bump into each other and Frank Allen remembers encountering Ritchie during this time. "When he joined Lord Sutch's Savages our paths crossed often as I was in Cliff Bennett's Rebel Rousers. But when the groups stopped at the great gathering place, the Blue Boar [café] at Watford Gap, on the way home from shows he would rarely get out and join everyone, preferring to stay in the van. He had a reputation for being extremely moody, something I can't confirm or deny as I never spent enough time in his company to witness it."

Newsome who frequently crossed paths with Blackmore in those days reinforces Allen's observations: "We used to meet up with the bands in local pubs in Doncaster or wherever and have a beer. He liked a game of darts did Ritchie. He was such a quite person. Not a gregarious person. Now and again he would have a bit of a laugh and a joke."

Although his time with Sutch was short-lived, after his last show with the Savages at Putney on October 12, Blackmore had no need to sign on at the Welfare Exchange because he once again found himself in another top band.

CHAPTER 3

The Meek Shall Inherit The Outlaws (1962–64)

The recognition that Blackmore had gained from his six-month stint with the Savages was sufficient for him to get an invitation to join the Outlaws, another highly regarded group of the day. The Outlaws had started in 1960, having already produced one album and numerous singles, and were seeking a replacement drummer and guitarist for the recently departed Don Groom and Rodger Mingaye. Mick Underwood had just taken over Groom's drum stool and told the group's producer, Joe Meek about his former band mate from the Dominators. "Joe Meek heard about this and said, 'How about joining my band the Outlaws?'" recalled Blackmore. "So I said 'OK, it sounds good to me.' The Outlaws were more well-known than the Savages so I was quite pleased."

However it wasn't a simple case of transferring from one group straight into another. Blackmore had some tough competition to contend with as the Outlaws rhythm guitarist Ken Lundgren recalls. "Nicky Hopkins and Bernie Watson auditioned. We actually thought about changing the line-up to make it a piano-guitar thing but Chas [Hodges] wanted to play the piano as well so we didn't go for that. We held auditions at the 2 I's coffee bar in Soho. A number of people including Jimmy Page auditioned for the band, because we'd had some records in the charts and we backed John Leyton on a couple of things which were number one hits so the Outlaws had a pretty big name. All of these young guitarists, that were like the second wave, up and comers and really good players all auditioned for the band. Jimmy Page wouldn't join. He said our stage set was too physical and he had to jump around a bit and he wasn't interested in that, he just wanted to stand still and let his art shine for its own sake. But Ritchie had been playing with Lord Sutch and he was into it. He said, 'I'm a member of the Savages and stage antics are part of my professional make-up' and we tried him out and he was great.

"As far as his guitar skills were concerned he and Jimmy Page were at least on an equal footing at that stage. If you came out of Sutch's band we were really interested because we knew what kind of a show he put on and it tied in with us because we wanted to be the antithesis of Cliff & the Shadows. They were very regimented and wore neat little outfits and did dance steps. The Outlaws were the opposite and fully trying to appeal to the male audience as opposed to girlies and did it by being outlaws basically: trying to look as macho as possible in a Sixties context and playing really rough music; music that wasn't pretty; rock 'n' roll and rhythm and blues, we were really into that.

"Ritchie wasn't a team player ... He was definitely a Ritchie player, which was great for us at the time because he was so good that it gave us an edge and we would get all these tours largely because we had a really good musician's musician in Chas and a spectacular player in Ritchie. When he joined the band and we were driving along he would always have this imaginary horse called 'Dobbin.' None of the rest of us ever did that kind of role play but Ritchie who was the kind of loner in the band anyway would keep referring to his phantom horse 'Dobbin' wherever we went."

The Outlaws had already established themselves as the resident session band for Joe Meek. Having originally been an engineer at IBC, in the days of white-coated engineers and stuffy in-house producers, Meek broke the mould by becoming an independent – a highly radical move at the time – and started producing numerous recordings from his home. Though referred to as Joe, his full name was Robert George Meek, hence the name of his company RGM Productions. By 1960 Meek had relocated to 304 Holloway Road, renting the floors above Shenton's Leather Shop. He converted the second floor flat into a studio, and against all the odds, produced hundreds of recordings on a meagre budget, many of them becoming hits. Meek was without doubt a true pioneer, employing sound effects, multi-tracking and numerous editing and production skills that were often beyond the comprehension of his contemporaries.

Operating from a flat wasn't the easiest of environments as Patrick Pink, who was employed as Meek's assistant, explains: "It was chaos all the time. For the first hour of every session it was chaos but it did calm down. But if

Joe had a bunch of musicians in there he knew there wouldn't be a lot of chaos with people that worked with him all the time. The chaos would die within 10 minutes but if it was a fresh band there could be chaos right the way through."

Not only was Meek a homosexual at a time when this was still a criminal offence in Britain, but he also had a strange interest in the spiritual world. In later years it emerged that Meek had a protection racket placed on him by the notorious Kray Twins gangsters. By late 1962, Meek had already enjoyed huge success with records such as 'Angela Jones' by Michael Cox and even bigger hits like his superb production of 'Johnny Remember Me' by John Leyton, backed by the original Outlaws line-up, that made it to number one the previous year. What would turn out to be Meek's biggest ever hit reached the top of the charts just before Blackmore joined the Outlaws. The instrumental 'Telstar' by the Tornados, arguably the finest moment in Meek's career was the first British song to top the charts on both sides of the Atlantic.[*]

Derek Lawrence, whose career path became inextricably linked with Blackmore's during the early days of Deep Purple, was looking after a group called Laurie Black & the Men Of Mystery who had won a talent competition in Harrow. Among the judges was Meek with first prize being a session at Holloway Road. Lawrence went with them in to the session which quickly started going wrong when Meek stormed down the stairs, unhappy with the group's progress. Lawrence made some suggestions and in his words, "Meek heard it then he came up and said, 'Well you're useless but you've got some idea. So why don't you come and work for me for a while.'"

Lawrence recalls how Meek's records would often come together. "What he would do when he was writing a thing, like a hit record at the time was sing a song over it and it usually had nothing to do with the record that he was doing. So he would give it to Chas or Ritchie or Big Jim [Sullivan] or whoever and they would work it out."

Although Blackmore was aware of Meek's track record, he also learnt of Meek's others interests but as Lawrence points out, "We all knew. We basically all said, 'We don't care what you are but if you come near us we'll break your legs!'" Blackmore's heterosexuality was never in doubt as he appeared to have little problem in pulling women. "Ritchie wasn't afraid to put it about," says Lawrence, seeing Blackmore's shyness as part of the attrac-

---

[*] 'Telstar' went on to sell millions and stayed in the UK charts for an astonishing 25 weeks.

tion. "The women love all that, everyone wanted to mother him. And he just wanted to climb back where he'd come from." While Meek's sexuality was of no concern to Blackmore, the producer's interest in spiritualism, along with RGM's chief composer Geoff Goddard, would prove to have a lasting effect.

"Joe was very secretive about the things he did," Blackmore recalled. "I used to come into a session sometimes and he would say, 'I've been speaking to Buddy last night.' 'Buddy?' 'Yes Buddy Holly and he told me that we must do this record.' He actually thought he could communicate with Buddy Holly and people like that."

From the moment that he joined the Outlaws in October '62, Blackmore was kept incredibly busy by Meek's relentless workload. The group spent countless hours recording the backings for the artistes who filed through Holloway Road: Heinz Burt, Jennifer Moss, Burr Bailey, Glenda Collins, Mike Berry, Davy Kaye, Freddie Starr, Gunilla Thorne, the Sharades, Valerie Masters and Jess Conrad to name but several. Unfortunately Meek's session documentation was non-existent and for this reason it's impossible to be definitive about all the records Blackmore played on. Moreover, Meek's production techniques often resulted in numerous overdubs adding orchestration, additional vocals and numerous sound effects that sometimes made the original backing tracks difficult to hear.

One of the very first Meek records that Blackmore is thought to have worked on was 'In The Night' by Jamie & the Atlantics, released by Decca in January 1963. Neil Newsome confirms that there were overdubs on the record. "Our guitarist Billy Clarke definitely played on it but it was augmented by others. I know Joe overdubbed some drumming on top of my drumming and I know there was some guitar work done but we weren't in the studio when it happened." Some tracks that Blackmore almost certainly featured on contain so little audible guitar that it's extremely difficult to ascertain what involvement (if any) he had. The Outlaws incessant recording schedule was important in helping Blackmore hone his craft. Apart from one brief foray into the studio with the Jaywalkers, Blackmore had developed his style from live work up to this point. Working in a studio environment was, he later admitted, more restrictive than what he had been used to. "It's rigid. I was pretty good, until they'd say to me, 'Play this melody.' And as I didn't read music – we'd just read chord sheets – that threw me. I could not remember melodies to save my life, except certain melodies. Chas, our bass player, used to play the guitar – I would leave it to him."

Meek had unusual ways of working. Patrick Pink: "Joe would advance plan things. If he knew he had a band in the next day that was doing 'x' record, after Ritchie or whoever had finished the session they were on he would get them to lay down something else and that would probably get used in two days time unbeknown to them on someone else's record. Another band would come in and add to it. That's where Ritchie would find himself playing on something he never even knew he played on. That happened a hell of a lot. That's why there's a mangle today with people saying they played on this and that. They didn't intentionally play on it, it was the way Joe planned things. There were hundreds of tapes with various things on them that Joe would pull out a year later. The tape would be put in a box and flung on a pile with the rest. Around '65 it took me a month of Sundays to mark up most of the tape boxes. Until I was allowed to touch stuff upstairs there was tape everywhere. He had a memory of where tapes were. He could go to a pile and pull a tape and know exactly what was on it."

Pink describes a typical day's session: "They'd come in about 11 o'clock and they'd be out by three. They'd nail it very fast: a couple of sides. Quite often it would be a finished product on the day." The musicians had a great ear as sometimes, "down in the living room in the morning the acetate would go on, they'd listen to it two or three times then up they'd go and tell Joe they'd learnt it. Joe would listen to the first playback and alter what he wanted then they would go ahead and record it. Sometimes the record was made on the Monday and it was released on the Friday!"

Because recordings were done at such an alarming speed in the early Sixties it was commonplace for producers and managers to use one band for studio work and a different band for live performances. Bands of the Outlaws calibre were so quick in learning tunes that it made common sense. A good case in point was Freddie Starr[*] & the Midnighters, from Liverpool. "When I was working with Joe I went up to Liverpool and I brought down Freddie Starr & the Midnighters," Lawrence recalls.[†] "There was a great story about Freddie Starr & the Midnighters supporting Little Richard in Germany and Freddie went on and did Little Richard's act! Great singer, really good pop singer. They were a great band. They got involved in all that Liverpool scene, the Beatles weren't the best band up

---

[*] Starr later become known as the clown of UK comedy and something of a national institution with such antics like dressing up as Hitler at FA Cup finals and eating a hamster thanks to a notorious tabloid headline.

[†] While Lawrence claims he brought Freddie Starr & the Midnighters to London, others including Midnighters bassist Brian Woods recall that Dave Adams was the man responsible for setting up their recordings with RGM.

there." By '62, Freddie Starr & the Midnighters were one of the top acts on the emerging Merseybeat scene, something that Blackmore cited when talking to the author in 1998: "Apparently when they played with the Beatles they blew them off stage. The Beatles could not follow them, in Liverpool, in '62!"

Starr released three Meek-produced singles and although the first two were credited as being with the Midnighters, the Outlaws backed Starr on several of his Holloway Road recordings. According to Meek archivist Tom Casey, "Ritchie with the Outlaws played on all of Freddie Starr's tracks except 'Peter Gunn Locomotion'; that is the Midnighters. There are also two unreleased tracks by Freddie from Joe Meek's time that feature Ritchie, 'I'm Not A Juvenile Delinquent', the old Frankie Lymon song and 'The Lips Are Redder On You', which was covered by Gene Pitney on the B-side of his record 'I'm Gonna Find Myself A Girl'."*

Even in those days Starr's clowning was legendary and being a constant joker, many a session was livened up by his outrageousness. Blackmore vividly recalled one particular session when Starr started acting the fool: "It takes a lot to make me laugh – Freddie Starr had me crying. 'Cause I was backing the guy … I first met him in Joe Meek's studio. At the time he was just in a rock 'n' roll band. Chas is sitting there half asleep – still got his pyjamas on. He actually had his pyjamas on underneath his trousers. You could see his pyjamas sticking out at the bottom. I'd go, 'What's that?' 'Oh! It's nothing.' 'It's pyjamas!' And he was always late because he would get on the bus to come down to the studio and he would fall asleep. And then the bus would go back again to where he'd started! So he kept going back and forth to get to the studio and when he got there, Joe Meek used to go, 'Where've you been?' 'Joe, you'll never believe this' – I remember this story once – 'I was walking along, and this little bird was on the ground. It had fallen out of its nest, so I had to take it to the vet's …' And Joe starts laughing. That was it, because he had a soft spot for Chas. Of course, Joe was very gay.

"Anyway, Freddie Starr would come into the studio … we'd start playing … In those days … sometimes you'd have to put the solo down as you're playing. Not like today, when you'd stop, do the rhythm 400 times then do the solo. In those days it was – right, now we're coming to the solo, and I'd start playing the solo. Freddie Starr dropped his trousers in the studio while I'm playing, and he's now got his thing and he's trying to put it in my ear!

---

* Casey believes there were possibly further tracks recorded but if so, they are now sadly lost.

I'm like, 'What's going on? Get off! Get off!' And I'm trying to play the solo. Of course, Joe Meek heard the mistake – I made a mistake. In those days you didn't have a see-through thing (*control room window*), he'd have to come around the room to see what we were doing. He came storming round. 'What the bloody hell's going on here … oooh!' I'm going, 'This is getting to me. I'm 17 years old and people are sticking things in my ear.' That was my first introduction to Freddie Starr– he was completely nuts!"

This was just one of the bizarre situations with Starr the young, naïve guitarist found himself in. "I remember going to a party once somewhere – a debutante's party. It was a very high society kind of place … 'This is the Screaming Lord Sutch …' and we all walked in. Freddie would walk in, go straight up the stairs, and start washing his hair, dyeing his hair – in somebody else's house! So he comes down – we're all having tea – he pops his head in: 'Have you got any more of that dye?' Who is this? It's Freddie Starr – he's just helped himself to the hair dye. Very odd! Another time when I went somewhere on a train with Freddie, he sat on one side of the aisle facing a young girl and I sat on the other side of the aisle facing a man in a suit, reading a newspaper. Suddenly Freddie, who said he had a dose of some anti-social disease, was talking very loudly to me in an upper class accent: 'Richard, what am I to do? I've got all this white stuff coming out of the end of my thing! What is it Richard? What should I do?' While the horrified girl tries not to look, the guy hides behind his paper, and I'm trying desperately to pretend I have never met him before in my life."

Meek also used Blackmore to enhance some RGM recordings done in a single day's session by Tommy Scott & the Senators, a Welsh beat group fronted by Thomas Jones Woodward, who used the stage name Scott. At the time none of the record companies showed any interest in the recordings but by 1965 Tommy Scott had changed his name to Tom Jones, signed a deal with Decca and had a number one with 'It's Not Unusual.' Meek cashed in on Jones' sudden popularity by issuing two of the tracks, 'Little Lonely One'/ 'That's What We'll All Do', in May of that year, much to the singer's annoyance. When speaking to *New Musical Express* Jones said, "We really pinned our hopes on the recording session. 'Little Lonely One' was one of seven we did that day. Joe said he was going to get it released, but we didn't hear anymore. It was two years before a chance came again and now they bring out this relic from the past. I'd like to disassociate myself from it." Meek responded by saying, "I honestly maintain this is a good record" and followed it up with another single 'Lonely Joe'/ 'I Was A Fool' in October. The other recordings remain unreleased including an alternative version of Jones' first Decca release 'Chills And Fever' that includes Blackmore's guitar work.

The quick-fire way Meek operated partly explains why he wasn't renowned as an easy person to work for; he wasn't renowned for his patience, didn't suffer fools gladly and certainly had a short fuse. Patrick Pink: "There were times when just banging the drums on the stairs on the way up would be enough for Joe to say 'Fuck off, I don't want you here.' I used to warn people out on the streets, these are the rules, and if you don't believe me you won't be there very long." Pink recalls Blackmore as being generally compliant. "He'd always ask Joe, 'Is that okay, is that what you want?' or whatever. I can't recall Joe and Ritchie ever having a shouting session at each other over anything."

Despite Meek and Blackmore's efficient working relationship, on one occasion, Meek's paranoia and short fuse resulted in Blackmore and Lundgren getting their marching orders, as the latter recollected, "One day Ritchie and I were in the office, just a little tiny hole with a telephone in it, and I was phoning Don Arden's office, checking on a gig and for some strange reason Joe thought we were laughing at Heinz [Burt, bassist with the Tornados]. He grabbed the phone and threw it on the floor and told us to get out. I phoned Chas and said 'We've just been fired by Joe' so he said, 'I'll sort it out' and he called Joe a little while later after he'd cooled down and Joe admitted that he just lost it and reconsidered and we were allowed back in."

In a 1982 interview with John Tobler, Blackmore, who often claims his memory of the Sixties is clearer than that of the Seventies, mentioned also backing Danny Rivers and Mike Berry. However Rivers recorded three singles for Meek between 1960 and 1962, *before* Blackmore was in the Outlaws. As for Berry, the Outlaws certainly were his studio backing band for a spell, but again prior to Blackmore joining.* "Joe Meek liked my playing so he used to have me on sessions," Blackmore told Tobler. "The Outlaws was the standard band that did all the session work for Joe Meek. There would be a point – unlike now – where I would listen to the radio and go 'I know that song, I played on it!' I'd hear so many songs on the radio, and I'd played on nearly all the records!" Although Blackmore's recorded involvement with Berry remains unclear, the Outlaws continued

---

* In that same interview Blackmore mentions a Buddy Holly tribute record that Berry recorded. 'Tribute To Buddy Holly' was released in 1961, and although an EP of the same name was released in 1963, again it was recorded by an earlier Outlaws line-up. However there is thought to be a whole album's worth of unreleased Mike Berry tracks – mostly Buddy Holly songs – so it could be these that Blackmore is referring to, though Meek archivist Tom Casey has concluded Blackmore never recorded with Berry.

as Berry's live backing band when he initially joined the group. One of his earliest Outlaws' gigs was on October 26 at Preston Public Hall, billed as a 'rock 'n' roll spectacular', with support from the Syd Munson Orchestra and a then little-known beat combo from Liverpool called the Beatles.

Apart from the numerous sessions backing other artistes the Outlaws also got to cut four of their own singles during the year and a half Ritchie was in the line-up. The first single featuring Blackmore and Underwood, the suitably titled 'The Return Of The Outlaws,' was released in February '63. Despite the band posing on a railway track in the midst of the coldest British winter for 16 years, sales froze and the record failed to chart. The follow-up, 'That Set The Wild West Free' fared no better when released six months later.

Although the Outlaws invariably performed as a group, Meek also used Blackmore independently on sessions, something that gave him a reputation of being pampered by Meek. As far as Lundgren was concerned this was not surprising. "Joe spoilt Ritchie because he was totally in awe of his incredible playing. He was so fast that I don't think Joe Meek had seen anyone play like that before." Because of Blackmore's desire to play as fast as possible, often the end results were not in context with what the record should have sounded like. Ken Lundgren: "Quite often Chas had to overdub the melody because you couldn't tell where Ritchie was coming from as part of a record." Although Blackmore sometimes struggled to play in the manner that was required, he was undoubtedly a devoted student of his instrument as far as Lundgren is concerned. "He used to practice six to seven hours a day. Even before he was doing it for a living, he incessantly practised. Not like kids today when they get an amplifier and make horrible noises and disturb the neighbours he would literally sit there and practise without the guitar turned on."

Blackmore seems unconcerned with taking any credit for helping to put Meek's recordings together, explaining, "We'd go in, in the morning, and the producer would say, 'This is the song that I want you to do today.' And he would either play us a demo or he would sing it to us. And he couldn't really sing, so that became embarrassing. Chas was brilliant. Chas would make up his own melodies. Chas would go, 'What do you want on this, Joe?' And Joe would go (*sings out of tune melody*). 'Do you want?' (*plays in-tune melody*) 'Yeah, that's what I want.' And of course you could see what was going down. Chas was writing it for him."

Although the musicians that worked for RGM took a set fee for each session, normally a cash payment of around £7, there was always the option of a royalty payment instead. However despite some of the records being hits, the vast majority of RGM's productions were not huge sellers, in fact numerous sessions involving Blackmore were never released and the Outlaws always took the cash option.

"The sessions were for everybody, even for Tom Jones at times," Blackmore commented to *Guitar Player* in 1978. "But half the time they were backing tracks, so we didn't know who they were for. Occasionally we'd see the artists, but the people were really not well-known." Heinz Burt and Glenda Collins were some of the artists that the Outlaws would actually play alongside in the studio. The attractive young Collins, "used to turn up for sessions with her dad," recalls Underwood. "He kept an eye on her all the time."

One evocative first hand account of the RGM recording process was documented in *Record Collector* in 1998 by writer Kingsley Abbott, then a budding young drummer who had written to Meek enquiring about his studio and was invited to witness a session first hand. It happened to be one involving the Outlaws backing Glenda Collins on 'In The First Place' and 'If You Gotta Pick A Baby', released as a single that November (1963). "Some degree of confusion reigned as the Outlaws arrived, apparently late, for the session, but once they were all set up, we all moved upstairs to the second floor, where the studio was, in what once would have been the front bedroom. He [Meek] directed me to stand just outside on the landing, but a bit back towards the stairwell so that I wouldn't interfere with his frequent trips in and out of the studio. It proved to be a most advantageous location as the only person I couldn't see directly was the drummer, Mick Underwood, who was over by the window. The three guitarists, Ritchie Blackmore, Chas Hodges, and Ken Lundgren, sat in a low line just outside the door, which was wedged open. Glenda Collins stood by an open mike a little more into the room. Everything was done live at each take: there were no attempts that day at overdubbing. I would guess the song ('In The First Place') was done 16 or 17 times before Joe was satisfied. Occasionally he would stop a take early on, but more often than not he would let it run right through before he would give instructions.

"My untrained ears could not differentiate exactly what was right and wrong about each take, but it was evident that Joe knew exactly what he was trying to achieve. He would get very loud and agitated as he rushed back and forth between the studio and the control panels, but never resorted to swearing or any abuse that went beyond heavy cajoling. The band just kept on delivering what he requested, and I found myself watching Ritchie Blackmore's furiously fast fingers and wondering how someone could play that well so consistently. When they finally nailed the song to Joe's satisfaction, there was a short break before work began on 'If You Gotta Pick A Baby'. This took a few less takes, and was obviously the stronger number. Joe said that he still had a good deal of work to do on the tracks, but without Glenda and the Outlaws. The session must have ended in mid-afternoon, at which point Joe was visibly quite tired."

Meek's tiredness manifested itself in his unpredictable behaviour. Derek Lawrence: "The band was always upstairs and Joe would just storm down and the boys would just carry on getting it together. The thing with Joe was, he'd come steaming down the stairs, slamming and banging and saying 'Get them all to fuck off' and you would say 'Alright Joe' and about 20 minutes later he'd come out with his sheepish little boy's grin on his face and then carry on." As an example of Meek's volatility, he threatened his perceived miscreants with a shotgun. Lawrence remembers an incident when Meek actually fired the weapon at the television set, blowing it to smithereens in the process.

Given such behaviour it was perhaps fortunate for Blackmore that he didn't spend all his time at Holloway Road. The Outlaws were an in-demand live act and the first few months after Blackmore joined were spent as Mike Berry's backing band. But by early February '63 Berry was telling journalists he had ceased using the Outlaws. "In the next week or so I'll be getting a new group to replace the Outlaws, from whom I've parted."

Life on the road with the Outlaws was just as tough for Blackmore as it had been with the Savages. The band would frequently sleep in the back of their van after gigs and during the 'big freeze' winter of '62/'63, Neil Newsome recalls meeting the group when they were gigging up north. "We knew they were in the area. They'd played at the Empire Theatre, York the night before then they came across to Dewsbury to play this little club and they said 'We are setting off back to London tonight.' It was perishing but they said they were going to stop off and just kip in the van. I said, 'No way; we've only got a little house but you're welcome to kip down.' They stayed in our house on the big bed settee with the gas fire on. Ken actually used our little kiddie's plastic potty to have a wee and we had an outside toilet down the yard. Obviously it was frozen solid so we couldn't use it. We said the best thing you can do is use the potty discreetly and then go out and tip it down an outside drain somewhere. He set off out in his cowboy boots and he left the top step and did an amazing back flip somersault and threw this potty full of urine in the air. He rolled over and it landed to one side of him and within a minute it had frozen solid!"

Newsome also recalls another spontaneous on the road incident with the

40

Outlaws: "Once we [the Atlantics] were playing noon and night they came piling into this bar. I think it was Bentley Pavilion at Doncaster and they were appearing at night somewhere else in Doncaster. Ritchie and the lads came in and sat down with us and said, 'Any chance we can get up and have a knock?' We said, 'We're not bothered' so I had a word with the concert secretary and said, 'These lads are from London, any chance they can get up and give us a couple of tunes?' I said, 'There's no money involved they're just doing it for a laugh" and he said, 'Yeah, the more the merrier.' So they got up to give us a bit of a gig and Ritchie and Chas were saying there was this singer who's just cutting his first record, we want to give him a bit of an airing and the guy who got up on stage and sung was Long John Baldry."

Already by this stage in his career, with the confidence gained from his time in the Savages, Blackmore wanted to show off his talent and upstage other musicians at every opportunity. However, as musical director, Chas Hodges would invariably decide the songs the Outlaws would perform and it was Blackmore's job to work within that framework. Ken Lundgren: "When he joined the Outlaws Ritchie wasn't the centre, Chas was, but he put up with that because he was hired to be a guitarist. If he would play an inappropriate solo just because he could that was just him being good as a backing musician in his mind, but he was not in a position to dictate how that music should fit in. On several occasions Chas would say, 'Don't do that,' he would say 'You're playing way too much in that, you don't need that' and Ritchie would agree and as soon as no one was looking he would stick something else in. In the same way, he wasn't in the position to tell the Outlaws what their songs were going to be every night."

However Blackmore had his own agenda and whether it was during the show or even before it he was determined to upstage the competition. Ken Lundgren: "One time we were on a package show, and it included Bert Weedon. Bert and Ritchie were on the stage when we were doing our sound-check and of course Bert was showing off doing a finger style version of something, 'Etude in E' that most guitarists play to show they know what they are doing. Ritchie watched him for a couple of seconds and launched into 'Flight Of The Bumble Bee' just to bowl over Bert Weedon who'd had a number one hit at the time, and was a good player. But Ritchie was of that nature, 'Here comes Bert Weedon who is really famous and I'm going to knock him over' and he did it almost maliciously in a sort of Ritchie Blackmore good-natured way. The rest of us were standing there going 'Come on Ritchie, leave it out' because there was no need for that. Everybody knew how fast Ritchie was but he wanted to put it in people's faces."

★ ★ ★

Joe Meek was already planning his next move in launching Heinz Burt as a solo performer. Because of his blind infatuation, Meek couldn't see what others around him could: that Burt was not and never would be an Elvis Presley or an Eddie Cochran. However Meek was convinced he could turn Heinz into a star and had already recorded his first single 'Dreams Do Come True' with the Outlaws providing the instrumentation. Because of the success the Tornados had gained from 'Telstar' it wasn't that difficult in promoting Heinz as a solo artist. With the Outlaws about to hit the road backing Mike Berry, second on the bill to Brenda Lee on a 21-date tour of the British Isles, it was announced that the Outlaws would be backing Heinz on forthcoming live performances. When asked to comment on the new line-up, Meek told *Record Mirror* that it was, "a settled group now and one I think can finally make the breakthrough. Ritchie Blackmore models his style more on Les Paul than anyone else but can turn out a big gutty sound when necessary. Maybe this will establish them finally as real personalities."

The Brenda Lee–Mike Berry tour kicked off at the Capitol Theatre, Cardiff on the March 11 and concluded at the Tooting Granada on the 31st. Berry had just come out of a convalescent home and had little time to rehearse so on the tour's opening night he stuck to performing Buddy Holly numbers, being songs the Outlaws were most familiar with. For Blackmore, playing on a bill with top US singer Brenda Lee was of little consequence and his general attitude to the headlining act was irreverent. Much of this could be attributed to his short attention span. Derek Lawrence: "The thing about Ritchie, you'd get in the car at Holloway Road and you were doing a gig at Birmingham Town Hall, by the time you got to the railway arch it would be 'Are we nearly there yet I'm bored?'"

When not performing, Blackmore relieved his boredom by indulging in a variety of pranks. According to Lundgren, "he had a penchant for shit" and laid a series of turds around Brenda Lee's dressing room toilet. "Henri Henroid the tour manager was berating us because he figured it was one of us that did it but we didn't even know that Ritchie did it until he was smirking in the corner when everyone else was being told off."

Lundgren also remembers the tour as the first time he encountered groupies. Up to this point the concept of girls who made themselves sexually available to musicians on a regular basis wasn't really heard of. "There were a lot of episodes that happened on that tour, like the Phantom Gobbler, a girl from the Midlands somewhere who was actually the first groupie. She would go into a dressing room and give blow jobs to everyone on the tour and she would do it in the dark. Ritchie even had his turn and she was renowned throughout that part of the world as the Phantom Gobbler. No one really knew her. However she had a friend who would let the guys in the band know that she was in there and ready to do business and she just did it for free. It was one of those strange phenomenons. She was a well-educated person and this was her hobby. You'd get a band like Sounds Incorporated and there were seven guys in that band and they'd all get really excited because they were into that, 'Hey the Phantom Gobbler is in there!' and they would all be lined up outside the dressing room. Ritchie actually lined up and told us afterwards what it was like and he wasn't that impressed. He probably had far better action from people he knew."

In May the Outlaws landed a prestigous slot as part of a package tour with top American performers Jerry Lee Lewis and Gene Vincent, thanks to Meek managing to get Heinz on the bill. The group got to open the show with their own set before providing the backing for both Heinz and Jerry Lee. For Hodges and Lundgren, working with Jerry Lee was a dream come true but playing alongside 'The Killer' didn't draw the same level of excitement from Blackmore. Ken Lundgren: "Ritchie probably thought it was impressive but he wasn't a fan of Jerry Lee Lewis, he was more a fan of Ritchie! He was a guitarist's guitarist; he was more into Les Paul. If we had been backing Les Paul he would have been really knocked out. Playing with Vincent and Lewis wasn't a big thing for Ritchie. I mean for Chas they were his idols, but to Ritchie it was like 'Yeah, you know, good isn't it?'"

The tour, promoted by top impresario Don Arden, was a major coup for the Outlaws.* Vincent, who was being managed by Arden, had been touring the UK regularly for the past few years but Lewis was returning for the first time since his disastrous and controversial tour in 1958 ended abruptly when British authorities discovered that Lewis' 13 year-old cousin Myra, who had travelled to Britain as part of the tour entourage, was actually his wife. After considerable effort on Arden's part, in 1962, Home Office officials granted Jerry Lee a UK work permit for the tour.

Lewis had a reputation for being difficult to work with and despite the chance to back one of the truly great rock 'n' roll pioneers, Blackmore was considerably apprehensive: "Jerry Lee Lewis was interesting, because we were supposed to have a week's rehearsal with him. Don Arden said we were supposed to rehearse for a week. Then it was five days, then three days, and then it was, 'When are rehearsals going to start – we don't know what

---

* Future record producer Mickie Most, then still a solo performer/guitarist, was also on the bill.

we're doing?' The tour was coming up, and I hadn't played one note with him. The day of the show we get to play with him – in the afternoon, he strolls in. And we're there, like, petrified, because I'd been told by Sounds Incorporated that 'If Jerry doesn't like you he'll give you a whack in the face!' So I'm there, petrified, playing. Luckily he liked me! He wanted to bring me back to Memphis, where he lived. He'd come over to me and go, 'Play, boy.' I'd play, and I'd be looking up waiting for that whack. I'm like … [*imitates scared look*] This was before the show. Then when we'd finished he'd go [*extending hand*] 'Put it there'."

Lundgren recalls that Jerry Lee's idea of rehearsing was minimal to say the least. "We were there and ready to go when Jerry Lee Lewis walked in. He had his own way of rehearsing. He had his own drummer so Mick didn't get to play on the Jerry Lee segment of the show so he and his drummer would sit down and play maybe four bars of each thing and that was his idea of a rehearsal. Because Chas and the rest of us knew all these songs anyway that was fine, that was all that we needed because they were all 12-bar straight ahead rock 'n' roll tunes. Ritchie's solo work was Ritchie, he wouldn't try and copy whatever the guy on the record did he would just take centre stage and play like crazy whenever Jerry Lee signalled for him to do that. Jerry loved it, he was a strong enough performer in himself that nobody could steal his show and just having a really great guitar player in it was just more in his favour. He didn't feel threatened by that at all and that was good for us because it just made the Outlaws look like a stronger backing group. We were really into what Jerry Lee Lewis represented as a rock 'n' roll performer and Ritchie's playing in that context was totally appropriate."

Blackmore learnt a lot about stagecraft from Jerry Lee. Ken Lundgren: "If you got an hour with somebody before the show you were lucky. It was very simple really. All that would happen, if you knew the intros and outros of the guy's songs and you could follow all his signals; he would tell you when to lay down and when to come back up again. He would tell you when to take a solo: You were guided by the guy and once you had done the show once you knew pretty much what was going to happen. It was pretty impromptu anyway because he changed his set as he went along depending on how he read the crowd."

The day of the tour's opening show the Outlaws had been up since early morning filming at Pinewood Studios. Meek had arranged for them to appear in a B-movie flick *Live It Up!* designed to showcase Heinz and also featuring Gene Vincent (backed by the Outlaws) and young actors Steve Marriott (pre the Small Faces) and Jennifer Moss (who played Lucille

Hewitt in *Coronation Street*). As well as providing the backings for Moss' numbers, (that had been pre-recorded at Holloway Road) the Outlaws also had their own two minutes on screen, performing a Meek-composed instrumental 'Law And Order,' dressed in white workmen's overalls atop some scaffolding. Once filming was completed the group didn't even have time to remove their make-up and with faces still powdered, they headed off to Birmingham Town Hall for the tour's first 'house'.

In a *Melody Maker* interview published days before the tour commenced, Heinz was extremely upbeat about his future as a solo performer, "I see myself as a beat singer, and I'd like to do Eddie Cochran stuff. I've worked out material with my group the Outlaws that will keep things moving all the time. The audiences won't know what's going to happen next."

Although the Outlaws stage performances were nowhere near as theatrical as the Savages, they certainly made efforts to present a full audiovisual show. When doing their own spot before Heinz appeared they would use the sound effects from the intro to 'Ambush,' an earlier single from the original Outlaws line-up. With the sound of Wild West-type gunfire reverberating through the theatre's sound system, as the curtains opened Blackmore, Hodges and Lundgren would move towards the front of the stage in crouching positions, their guitars pointed forward like weapons. The group then launched into 'Ambush,' invariably followed by a rock 'n' roll tune. Ken Lundgren: "I think one of the favourite starters was 'You Got The Right String Baby But The Wrong Yo-Yo'. We didn't do a heck of a lot of our own records because we were trying to do a rock 'n' roll thing that was suitable to back Jerry Lee Lewis or Gene Vincent.

"Ritchie would use the guitar very menacingly. He looked as if he was going to stab somebody with it. That was because of his guitar style too. He played it very aggressively. Because he was playing lead guitar it would show up more on his part than the others who were playing rhythm and bass." While the objective was to produce a more rugged sound, Blackmore also had his own agenda as Lundgren relates: "He would take front and centre when the guitar solo came up. He would make his move; he wouldn't look over to us and smile or something, he would step forward and be dramatic about it. He was definitely doing it for the girls. He was definitely interested in women. In his case he wasn't going to look like a pop star for women but he personally was playing for the girls. A lot of what we did was certainly male orientated it wasn't aimed at girls but when he did his little bits on stage he would be eyeing some girl in the audience. The band was playing for the whole thing but he was playing for the girls."

Meek went along with Lawrence to Birmingham to see how Heinz fared. Despite Meek's good intention of using the tour to launch Heinz's solo career, putting him on the same bill as established hard hitting (and hard living) rockers like Lewis and Vincent proved tough going for Meek's young protégé who was seen as a wimp by the predominantly male audiences compared to their American idols.

As soon as the Outlaws returned to the stage with Jerry Lee on the opening night of the tour there was pandemonium as his army of loyal fans were treated to a 35 minute performance that frequently had the kids on their feet and jiving in the aisles. Jerry Lee whipped it up with the likes of 'Hound Dog', 'Don't Be Cruel', 'Good Golly Miss Molly', 'Whole Lotta Shakin' Goin' On' and 'Great Balls Of Fire'. The fact that the Outlaws hadn't had time for anything but the most basic of rehearsals just before going on stage spoke volumes for their professionalism. When reviewing Lewis's performance in *New Musical Express* Eric Woodward mentioned that, "His only slip was when paying tribute to the group backing him – he called them the Saints but a hasty whisper told him it was the Outlaws!"

Roger Drew, then playing drums in a group based in Barnet, north London, saw the tour's fourth show at Fairfield Halls, Croydon, on May 9 and confirmed the audience reaction to Heinz: "He struggled through his first song amid a torrent of abuse and catcalls. Halfway through the second number he was running for his life under a hail of coins and anything that could be thrown. He did not return."

Meek, not wishing to admit his unwise move, tried to put some of the blame on the Outlaws but as Lundgren defends, the combination just wasn't right. "On stage we almost felt kind of embarrassed. [Heinz] came out in his little black and white outfit and his guitar that didn't actually work. The bridge wasn't fixed on it. He would look like he was going to do the Eddie Cochran bits but it would be Ritchie who was playing them. From that point of view we had no respect for him as a musician even though we knew he was only putting on an act and it wasn't his fault, Joe put him up to it. We liked him as a person but we just thought he was a victim of circumstance." Derek Lawrence distinctly remembers that Blackmore seemed unmoved by the audience reaction. "As they were throwing things at the stage, he just ducked and played on."

It was around this time that the Outlaws started to build their reputation for outrageous behaviour, born out of the boredom of travelling up and down the country. Ken Lundgren: "Ritchie has to take credit for that. He was the one who started throwing things out of the van." Hodges elaborated to Pete Frame, "One day we were driving along and one of us happened to throw a stale cheese roll out of the open door and it bonked this old geezer.

Obviously we found this very funny so we began to explore the possibility of other missiles."

Lundgren recalls a trip to Jersey, in the Channel Islands during a tour: "Ritchie threw a piece of soap out of a window and hit a traffic guy who was doing point duty, on the head and the guy was knocked out. The police came into the hotel looking for whoever had thrown this and they came in and woke up Chas, Mick and I and Ritchie was hiding in a different room. Then everyone got into it. In some places we would load up the van with eggs and flour bags for the drive up to the next gig. Largely we would pelt Heinz's car, then we got into pelting everybody with it. One time in Wales Ritchie threw a flour bag and hit some guy bent over the engine of his car. The guy was really incensed so he hopped into his car and chased us all over Swansea. We finally got to the hall after taking a devious route because this guy was following us. We parked up and the guy drove up and wanted to know who threw the bag at him. Of course Ritchie had disappeared and ran into the hall and hid somewhere. It went on for some months then other bands started doing it too but I think it was initiated by Ritchie."

Chas Hodges: "We found out that the little half pound flour bags were best. If you made a two inch slit in the bag and threw it out, it burst all over the recipient! Ritchie was a dead shot – never missed his target! So whereas we used to regard long hauls – say from Scarborough to Cornwall with gloom, we began to look forward to them."

Blackmore's enthusiastic missile throwing ensured that anyone in any-place was a potential target. Ken Lundgren: "We were in the Blue Boar one night, and Frank Ifield had a hit at the time with 'I Remember You.' He was seated in the same room but not near us. When we were getting ready to leave Ritchie threw a bun at Frank Ifield and it landed on his head. Frank didn't know where it came from. He got up and was with his road manager and at the time he was quite a star. He was really shocked and surprised. We got out of there quickly because Ritchie was laughing so much. He would have given the game away in a second but that was typical Ritchie. He didn't really have any respect for anyone. It wasn't that he felt he was so important it's just that he didn't feel any reverence to any other people."

The Jerry Lee Lewis–Outlaws combination was successful enough for the UK tour to be followed by a six-night stint in Hamburg along with gigs at various American air bases in Germany, which according to Underwood were, "pretty grim – one place they didn't even have a piano. Jerry just played a few songs on the guitar and the band didn't play."

It was Blackmore's first visit to Germany and it had a lasting effect on him: "I saw a different country and I immediately took to it. They seemed to work harder and enjoy life more than the English. In those days, back in '60 to '63, they were a bit class conscious in England – I don't know if it's still there, I think it's gone the other way now – but there was this class system thing which used to get on my nerves. You'd go into a shop and ask for a bar of chocolate or something and it's like – it'd give me the creeps – there'd be the upper class accent. And people judged you on your accent ... It drove me nuts, whereas in Germany I couldn't understand anybody, they couldn't understand me, and that was perfect: a great arrangement. To me, the English language never meant much. I thought talking was people trying to cover up what they were up to. So going to Germany and hearing people speak a language that I couldn't understand what they were saying, it didn't matter what I was saying – let's just play music."

Even before the war Germany was a far more liberal country than England and by the early Sixties the St Pauli district of Hamburg had built a reputation that made Soho in London's West End seem monastic. As with all major ports, prostitution was a popular industry but unlike Britain's attitude towards the world's oldest profession, it was out in the open and legal in Germany, especially on the Reeperbahn, Europe's most notorious red light street. With prostitution came the inevitably associated crimes and Hamburg had more than it's fair share of gangsters. For a fresh-faced Mick Underwood, not yet 18, Hamburg was a whole different world. "We got briefed when we first went out there, 'If you get hassled to go into a club, because they will try and drag you in, get money out of you, think you are sailors or whatever, just say "Capella Star Club" and they'll walk backwards two steps and won't mess with you.' It was a very dynamic live scene. You had to be careful but the thing with the Star Club ... let's say the gangsters were frightened of the Star Club. That says it all."

At the end of the Fifties, Manfred Weissleder had worked in the city's St. Pauli red light district as an in-house electrician but had worked his way up the club hierarchy, opening the Star Club at 39 Grosse Freiheit on April 13, 1962. The club's name became the guiding principle of the new venue and up to eight groups would appear per night, being booked mostly as house or resident acts. Initially the bulk of these were Americans such as Gene Vincent, Little Richard, the Everly Brothers, Bo Diddley and Ray Charles. Up and coming British groups had also gone to Hamburg prior to the Star Club's opening and found work in other venues within the district, most notably the Beatles who had already gained a reputation at the Top Ten Club among other venues.

As far as Underwood was concerned the tour with Jerry Lee was a relatively easy time for the Outlaws: "We had it cushy out there. The Beatles and the other bands were doing numerous sets a night working their butts off. All we did was two sets a night. An early one and a later one and we were off the hook." Each set consisted of a warm-up slot of about 15 minutes with the Outlaws playing their own songs and then a set backing the star attraction, Jerry Lee Lewis.

Returning to Britain Jerry Lee and the group played a handful of ball-room dates in the last week of May including a show at Wallington Public Hall on the 28th where Jerry posed alongside Blackmore, Lundgren, Hodges and Underwood for *NME* photographer Harry Hammond. On June 1 they embarked on one of the most bizarre gigs of their career. A couple of years earlier Don Arden had come up with a novel promotion of a ferry day trip to France with main attraction the Shadows. As it proved so popular the exercise was repeated on an annual basis. Billed as 'Rock-Twist-Jive Across The Channel' headliner Jerry Lee (backed by the Outlaws) joined several top acts including Nero & the Gladiators, the Flee-Rekkers and Ricky Valance aboard 'MV Royal Daffodil' for the day trip from Southend to Boulogne.

Some 800 punters splashed out on £57/6s tickets for this highly novel event and were greeted on board with a written statement: "Hello, Rockers. Twisters and Jivers: Welcome aboard the MV Royal Daffodil. We intend to make this the most enjoyable and exciting trip yet. We have organised for you a day packed with many things to help you to enjoy yourself. There will be plenty of opportunity to dance all your favourite dances and to the non-stop music provided by all the top line artists aboard the ship, and when you arrive in Boulogne you will be greeted by the Mayor and other prominent members of the community.

When you disembark in Boulogne, you are free to go where you please, but there will be a terrific Teen-beat show in the Casino, with French, American, and English stars specially selected for your entertainment."

During the journey across the Channel, the Outlaws performed their own set and on arrival in Boulogne headed off for the Casino where they performed with Jerry Lee. Meanwhile some of the English fans, no doubt fuelled by the alcohol consumed on the boat trip, appeared hell bent on trying to re-enact the battle of Agincourt. Ken Lundgren: "When we got to the other side all the English kids started rioting on the beach. Jerry Lee and us went to do our concert at the Casino and then we came back to the boat. But while we were doing that the riot happened on the beach and people were being chased back to the boat but we didn't know what was happening." When the time came to depart the groups were nearly left stranded on the French shoreline as Underwood recalls, "We got hassle getting back on the boat. We had palled up with Nero & the Gladiators and the captain of the boat wanted to leave before we got our gear on and Tommy Brown, the Gladiators drummer and me stood on the gangplank so we could get our gear on. It was quite mental."

With all finally on board, from the deck of the ship, around half a dozen English youths hurled bottles at the French kids on the quayside, sufficient to attract some Sunday tabloids who ran exaggerated accounts of drunken youths fighting with French police. The following day's front-page headline in the *News Of The World* – "Jazz Boat Kids Riot" – showed how schooled their reporter was in beat music. Homeward bound fans were treated to a terrific Jerry Lee Lewis and the Outlaws performance lasting nearly an hour which *Record Mirror* described as "probably one of the best sessions Jerry has had here, so atmospheric and tremendous was it."

As an indication of the tough touring schedules groups were expected to adhere to in the early Sixties, the Jerry Lee – Outlaws tour concluded the following evening at the Liverpool Empire. By mid '63 Liverpool was fast becoming the centre of popular music attention with the advent of the Merseybeat sound spearheaded by the Beatles, Gerry & the Pacemakers, the Searchers and many others. Although Jerry Lee Lewis, largely due to his explosive stage performances and past reputation, could still sell out concert halls, many Fifties rock 'n' rollers and instrumental outfits were now having to play second fiddle to this new wave of beat and vocal harmony groups. "62–63 we were into a very heavy kind of rock; Johnny Kidd & the Pirates, Screaming Lord Sutch, very basic rock with a rhythm and blues base," Blackmore described. "Then the Beatles came along and it was all harmonies, along with the Hollies and one had to sing. I didn't sing; I could hardly talk at the time. I was just into playing the guitar, very hard rock 'n' roll, distorted solos, which were out of vogue at the time. It was all pleasant vocal harmonies."

Although the debacle of the Lewis–Vincent tour resulted in Heinz gaining a new backing band, the Saints, the Outlaws continued to provide the backing on the majority of his Decca releases, including 'Just Like Eddie' a tribute to Eddie Cochran that featured the first Blackmore guitar work to be heard by the masses. 'Just Like Eddie' was a huge hit in August 1963, reaching number five on the hit parade and even made number one in Sweden. Irrespective of the large sales, because the band had chosen the session fee option, there were no extra financial rewards to be gained for them.

Having played the home of Merseybeat with Jerry Lee, the Outlaws returned three weeks later, this time backing Gene Vincent, whose hard drinking and unpredictable behaviour was very much the Virginian rocker's trademark. By the time the Outlaws started backing Vincent, Arden had hired Peter Grant to act as tour manager. Grant would go on to achieve massive success as the force behind Led Zeppelin and became established among a pantheon of well-known rock 'n' roll managers that included Colonel Tom Parker, Brian Epstein, and Albert Grossman.

Vincent had been left permanently disabled with a damaged leg as a result of a motorcycle accident eight years earlier and to counteract the constant discomfort he suffered, he used alcohol as a painkiller. The consequent effect was a catalogue of wild and erratic behaviour that many US promoters saw as a liability. In the early Sixties Vincent's career was still on track in Europe, despite his drink-fuelled antics, something that even 23-stone Grant was at times unable to control. Others, such as Vincent's former road manager Hal Carter, who quit because of his behaviour, told stories of the troubled star threatening people with knives and of general drunken obnoxiousness.

Blackmore's experiences working with Vincent turned out to be far worse than anything he'd imagined with Jerry Lee. If Vincent got a certain thought into his head and he was adamant he was right, there was no convincing him otherwise. Ken Lundgren: "He would drink himself sick and sometimes he would be delusional." Vincent took an instant dislike to Blackmore and treated him with utter contempt. Mick Underwood: "He was unpleasant to him face to face but Ritchie never reacted to it, which was very surprising. He was fine with me, fine with Chas and fine with Ken but there was something about Ritchie he didn't like. And I can't think what it could be. He liked the antics of Ritchie. He was in the van once or twice when the flour bags went out, he loved it, he was well up for that. There was something of a clash between him and Ritchie of some sorts, but it wasn't of Ritchie's doing."

Lundgren feels part of the friction between the two may well have been as a result of Blackmore's uncompromising approach, both to his playing and towards other people. "When we were backing Gene, if he was supposed to do a Cliff Gallup (Vincent's original guitarist) kind of solo he wouldn't, he would do a Ritchie Blackmore type solo and that was disconcerting to Gene Vincent who expected the band to sound like the record he'd put out, which we would do except that as soon as Ritchie was unleashed he would go mad, he would overplay. Ritchie didn't become one of the lads easily. He wasn't disliked but it was kind of like three people and Ritchie, and Gene Vincent wanted to be one of the guys. In fact he stopped going to his own private room and stayed where we stayed in bed and breakfast places. That's how much he wanted to be one of the guys. So he found that Ritchie and he were not the same as Gene and me or Chas or Mick. He thought of Ritchie as being this mysterious person who was there, who was part of the whole thing but a step removed."

Most of the time, it was Vincent's alcohol problem that would trigger the friction and as much as Grant tried to keep him away from the bottle, Vincent would regularly manage to get drunk before going on stage. On such occasions Vincent's dislike of Blackmore often resulted in torment or embarrassment, something the latter openly commented about to *Guitarist* magazine in 1990. "I think he taught me how not to behave on the road, how to get into trouble, how to be really obnoxious. He was either really polite and call everybody 'Sir' or 'Mam', but if he'd had a bottle of whisky he'd turn around to us and tell us we were purposely playing wrong notes! He was really paranoid he used to go to the agent and tell him we were playing wrong notes. Of course we weren't."

While working with Vincent, the Outlaws made several radio appearances, and the first of these broadcasts on July 20 '63 was for the BBC Light Programme's *Saturday Club*. Apart from backing Vincent on five tracks they also got the chance to do a song on their own, 'As Long As I Live.' Mick Underwood: "We did that at the Playhouse Theatre, Charing Cross and we sat in the auditorium part and watched Billy J. Kramer also do his bit." As previously mentioned, the decision as to what songs the Outlaws played in their own sets was predominantly down to Hodges. Ken Lundgren: "Chas would say what they were and I would write them out. There was no question about it except on two or three very notable occasions when Ritchie wanted to do a particular thing. One of them wasn't even musical. He wanted to do a number where we took the little hand brake out of the van and use it as a percussion device with a scraping sound and do a sort of a cappella number. We actually did but it didn't work because the crowd expected us to do what they expected and for us to do this funny little noisemaking thing didn't work."

During the summer season on August 18, Vincent and the Outlaws played at the ABC Theatre in Blackpool. Marty Wilde, who was spending the summer in Blackpool and was also providing a weekly column report for *Record Mirror*, reviewed the gig and commented: "My only criticism of the Outlaws is that the lead guitar was too deafeningly loud and tended to drown everything. Volume apart, the Outlaws played with a great driving sound and Gene was on top form." What friction existed between Vincent and Blackmore went unnoticed by Wilde because Blackmore's own recollections to *Guitarist* magazine about that particular gig were far more candid. "I remember one night we were at Blackpool when Marty Wilde was there with Cliff Richard. They're in the wings watching and I'd said to Gene, 'Which act are you going to do tonight?' – because we used to put the act together in the dressing room – and he said, 'Hey man, we'll just play, but it's going to be fast! 'Be-Bop-A-Lula', whatever you like.' And he's drinking. So we get on stage and the place is packed, and I'm really nervous because there are all these famous faces and Marty Wilde was doing the write up.

"Gene said to the audience, 'The next number is a song I wrote quite a while ago, and it goes like this. . .' He's got the mic and he looks at me and it's got to be 'Be-Bop-A-Lula,' which is in E. So I strum the chord to give him the key and he's looking at me, and I'm strumming E again and there's nothing; he's just looking at me. I'm still playing E and he's still looking at me – this time like he could kill me – and I'm thinking, 'Oh no!' There was absolute silence – in those days the audience just sat there – and at that point you could hear a pin drop. I went through A, B, C, D, nothing! And he was still looking at me … Then he said, 'It seems like our guitar player has forgotten the song.' In fact he'd forgotten what the hell he was supposed to be singing! I mean, 'Be-Bop-A-Lula', but it was my fault! And sure enough, we found out afterwards that he'd forgotten what he was singing. That was embarrassing. He went to Don Arden and Don had us all together and said, 'Gene says you're not playing the right notes. You're trying to mess him up.' I mean we were one of the best bands around, almost note perfect."

For most of the people attending, the backing bands were of little consequence, however, Vincent archivist Derek Henderson recalls a gig where it was impossible to ignore the onstage discord: "I've one clear memory although I can't put an exact date to it. At the instrumental break in a song Gene was really goading Ritchie to 'Go!', whacking the mic stand down near him and moving closer in an obviously aggressive manner, with Ritchie looking decidedly overwhelmed and disconsolate, not looking Gene in the face but watching his fingers … And I have to say, not playing in a very fluid manner."

Vincent's treatment of Blackmore undoubtedly had a negative affect and as a hired hand, Blackmore was in no position to criticise or argue against Vincent's actions. One act of retribution was Blackmore offering to fetch Vincent's booze for which he would mark up the price, charging him an extra ten shillings each time. When Blackmore wasn't suffering at the hands of Vincent, he indulged in the usual pranks with the rest of the band. At one show they were approached by a starstruck stagehand who was hellbent on becoming a performer and asked how to go about becoming a singing star. A mischievous Hodges gave him a fictitious story of how Gene Vincent made his name by running on stage and singing during an Elvis Presley performance. As the band took the stage for their own opening spot, Hodges' wind-up resulted in the stagehand running onto the stage shouting at the guys to play 'Johnny B. Goode.' They duly obliged with Vincent watching in the wings, unable to contain his laughter. The stagehand was later seen outside the stage door after the show signing autographs as 'Leon Outlaw.'

Having already had his first brush with the occult, thanks to Joe Meek and Geoff Goddard, an experience at York's Rialto Theatre would trigger Blackmore's lifetime interest in the spiritual realm. Mick Underwood: "We had a Sunday gig, we were playing somewhere on the Friday, we didn't have a gig on the Saturday night but we had this Sunday afternoon type thing at this theatre. We had driven a fair way and thought there's no point in going back to London and driving back up again so we pitched up at York early Saturday evening and they said we could sleep in the theatre so we just went to one of the dressing rooms. During the evening there was a dance going on downstairs and I walked across the circle which was curtained off and I didn't like it up there, it was really strange. I'd never experienced anything like that before. In the morning Ritchie reckoned someone was whispering names in his ears. Aubrey was one he reckoned he'd been visited by. We were all in the same room but no one woke me up. He was really into that and when we spoke to the people who worked there they said it was a very strange place. They'd had doors opening, lights going on and off and all sorts of things. Ritchie was adamant, he wasn't stringing us along, and he wasn't doing a wind-up. It didn't wind us up but he was definite about it."

Even though Underwood didn't experience any ghostly visitations, Lundgren independently verified the strange happenings. "I felt a sudden chill in the room. It was quite warm when we went in there but around midnight the room got very, very cold and I was going to pull my coat over the top of my shoulders to keep warm but I couldn't because I felt a presence right in front of my face that was so frightening I didn't dare look at it. The same time this was happening Ritchie was hearing somebody say to him the name Aubrey. When we told the theatre manager the following morning that we didn't sleep too well because we had ghosts in the room he said, 'That's pretty likely, we have ghosts in this building' and the name Aubrey was apparently the name of the ghost who was an ex-performer or janitor or something."

By the summer of '63, in Underwood's view, the Outlaws started to go downhill. Things were fine musically but the group was imploding largely due to their destructive and some would say anti-social behaviour as Blackmore recounted: "We used to buy these flour bags and split them open along with eggs and tomatoes and just throw them at people we'd see on the way. Preferably old women in wheelchairs but it got out of hand and we became very cocky and started throwing them at policemen and all sorts of people. It was great fun but it got us in a lot of trouble. Until nearly every week we'd be doing a session at Joe's and he would say, 'There's a policeman downstairs, who is it this time?' And it would always be me. I was in trouble so much that I think Chas had to cover for me. I said, 'Chas if you don't cover for me they're going to put me away for three months' so he said it was him who did it. One of the things was, when we would be throwing these flour bags and doing all this nonsense we had our telephone number in big bold type above the van saying please call the Outlaws, and of course the police did that. That's why we were caught out so many times."

"We chucked a flour bag at this teddy boy at this bus stop and a policeman took our number and they traced us," Hodges told Meek biographer John Repsch. "The police soon discovered that irrespective of any missile throwing, the van wasn't insured." As Joe Meek Associates owned the van, it was ultimately Meek's responsibility but despite his business partner Major Wilfred Banks being unaware that Meek had even bought the van, Banks, Meek and the group were all summoned to a court appearance in Shrewsbury. As the Outlaws had to travel to court overnight after a gig, as Chas recalled, "We looked like a load of gypsies." A charge of mischief was brought upon the group with a hefty fine of £100 and Lundgren, behind the wheel at the time of the incident, was banned from driving for a year.

"After the court case it got serious," Hodges recalled to Repsch, "and they said, 'You've got to stop it.' We went on to the gooseberries then. Ritchie was the best shot. There was a traffic jam in Charing Cross Road and we had the old sliding doors and there's this bird looking in one of the shop windows. Ritchie's gone 'wallop', and hit her right up the arse with this gooseberry. She screamed, looked up in the air, but she didn't think to look into the traffic. We must've been stuck there for 15 minutes. We waited for her to calm down and Ritchie's gone 'wallop', hit her again. She turned around and said something to this geezer and they're both looking, up to the windows. As he's looking, Ritchie's gone 'wallop' and hit him right in the back of the neck, 'whack.' He must have hit him five or six times and not once did they look into the traffic."

Lundgren remembers it as another nail in the bands coffin: "That was one of the things that really ended our relationship with Joe Meek. He wanted his van back at that point, which he had bought for us, so after that we had to start renting vans again."

Directly after the Blackpool show, Vincent and the Outlaws moved on to Wolverhampton where they spent a week performing on a 'Tops Of The Pops' variety show at the Grand Theatre, topping a bill that included Billy Fontayne, Nat Gonella and compere Kenny Cantor. Given the lads' reputation a variety show was hardly conducive to respectable behaviour. Mick Underwood: "There were these acts on there, a very famous trumpet player called Nat Gonella and various other people including two tap dancers, absolutely bizarre and after five minutes we were all very bored with it. We had to do matinee and evening gigs at this theatre. They gave Gene the star's dressing room and we had a room as well, which was alright but the rot set in after about a day and Ritchie got very bored, we all did to be honest but when he gets bored he has to do things. It was just a totally bizarre, surreal situation.

"We used to sit in the audience and there was a comedian on. There was nobody in the audience. We would probably make up three quarters of the audience on a matinee and laugh at the wrong time and when it came to the punch line – nothing. And there was a singer, and the pit orchestra was some bloke playing the piano, another on the trumpet, bass player and drummer and it was dreadful. At a matinee show there would be a couple of OAP's in the audience and that was about it and this guy was singing 'Granada' and there was a big build up at the beginning, it was hilarious, I fell off a chair! He's going right the way through and he got right to the pinnacle of the build up at the beginning of the song and the bass player dropped his bow. There was an almighty clatter from the orchestra pit and the guy stops singing and there's a little voice from the orchestra pit 'Sorry.' There was a riser mic that came up for one of the singers so Ritchie got this hamburger, it looked like a turd actually, and he fixed it to the riser so as the riser came up there was this non-specific thing sitting at the top of it. Gene almost set fire to his dressing room. They wound up taking him out and putting him backstage with two orange boxes and a plank across it with a mirror. Anyway with all the rest of the things that went on we got into quite a lot of shit about that. Big arguments with Don Arden, he was going to have us all ... and all the rest of it. The top and bottom of it, we fell out with Joe and with Joe Meek Associates and everything really."

Having so much time on his hands in Wolverhampton, Blackmore indulged in the full gamut of practical jokes. Stories of him sneaking into the orchestra pit and adding notes to the score, or locking doors and trapping the orchestra members backstage are legendary. Lundgren also recalls that Ritchie had his heart on wrecking the dancing girls' performances: "He threw these peppermints on the stage so the tap dancing girls would trip up, at least that was his hope." Despite Blackmore's love of practical jokes, while he could dish it out he wasn't one for taking it back. During one van journey he put chewing gum in Lundgren's hair: "That was a bad thing to do. I got angry and he got angry because I put the chewing gum back in his hair and of course he had his hair nicely quaffed and he was pretty pissed off about that."

Vincent and the Outlaws wound down the disastrous week in Wolverhampton on August 24 and the following afternoon made a personal appearance at Wolverhampton's local electrical store, Cliff and Halifax. Ken Lundgren: "That was one of the few times I got angry at Ritchie. We were all in this store signing autographs and Ritchie was just getting on my nerves and I stormed out. I think he was complaining about something but since I was doing all the driving and most of the organisation, he just got up my nose. He could get on your nerves because he was self-centred and that was the one thing that would bother Chas and I. It's not easy being on the road, everyone has got to be polite and give a bit. If anyone is selfish that is the one thing that really irks the other members of the band."

Following on from their earlier ghostly experience in York, the group started to delve into psychic phenomena and after a show at the ABC in Great Yarmouth the following evening, they decided on a detour. Ken Lundgren: "Chas and I got into reading a bit about haunted houses and we ended up going to Borley Rectory, which was this really haunted place.[*] So we went out of our way from Yarmouth to go to Borley, find the rectory and walk in the garden at midnight to see if we could encounter the spirits but just before we did the place had been exorcised so we didn't encounter anything. But Ritchie was really, really frightened because the thing in York had affected him more. The rest of us just let it roll off our backs but I think it bothered Ritchie. When we said we were going to see Borley Rectory on the way Ritchie was up for it, but when we got out of the van to walk to the churchyard he wouldn't come. He was really quite upset about that. It wasn't because he was chicken, he really felt we would encounter something."

★ ★ ★

---

[*] Borley Rectory was actually demolished in 1944 but supernatural happenings are still reported from the site of the rectory and the nearby churchyard.

In September the Outlaws returned to Hamburg's Star Club for a week's residency with Vincent. During this trip, Blackmore met and fell in love with a blonde girl called Margrit. In the words of Underwood "he was besotted with her." On the previous trip with Jerry Lee, the group had little time for socialising as most of it was spent travelling from air base to air base. Ken Lundgren: "On the Gene Vincent tour we were in Hamburg for a couple of weeks, and people could build up a relationship with others. The rest of us didn't bother, we spent most of our time drinking beer but he wasn't really into drinking and talking so he found Margrit. He was really into being with girls. When he first joined the band he took his girlfriend on tour with him all the time. He'd be snogging in the back with her but taking up two seats and the rest of us had to make do. In a way he wasn't the best travel mate. Even when we were playing a gig, when we were all hustling the gear up the back stage of some Corn Exchange he's found a bird and having a little bit of a snog somewhere, while we were doing the work. It would get under your skin after a while."

It was something of a whirlwind romance and after the Star Club residency was completed Margrit flew to England with Blackmore and the others. Her life in England started in a less than auspicious manner as Underwood recalls: "She flew back with us and she got real hang-ups at Heathrow when we got back. She couldn't just walk through, like we could and she got banged up and interrogated." Once Margrit was given the all-clear to enter the country, she stayed with Ritchie at the Blackmore family home in Heston.

Shortly after returning from Germany, Vincent and the Outlaws were booked for a three-gig trip to Northern Ireland in October. While on most tours Peter Grant was normally employed with looking after the errant singer, on this occasion Grant foolishly entrusted Underwood to act as Vincent's chaperone. "Almost immediately after the Star Club we had to go to Belfast to do a ballroom out there and we flew out and played there the first night and Gene was really weird. We'd done the gig and he came up to me and said, 'I want my ticket. I want to go home.' 'You can't we've got another night to do.' But I was 18 and he was 28, and I couldn't refuse him and he just disappeared."

Vincent's behaviour was just as erratic during a second *Saturday Club* session with the Outlaws. Mick Underwood: "On that [Star Club] stint I was rooming with Gene and I didn't see him all week. Something had gone on but he had the hump about something with his wife. The entire Star Club trip had been weird, he'd not been very good on it, he was very pre-occupied. He'd gone after his wife with a gun and got banged up. Then a day or two after that we've got this session to do at the BBC. I think it was at Charing Cross [again] and he walked in there very shamefaced, quiet and sang his songs, holding her arm and being all lovey dovey."

The 'live' recordings done for *Saturday Club* are among the few examples available that document Blackmore's live performances from this era of his career. Although done at the BBC's studios they were done in one take, just as they would be in front of an audience. Following Vincent's brush with the law he was on his best behaviour during the performances, while Blackmore's playing is relatively subdued throughout the seven songs performed, undoubtedly as a result of the singer's domination over him. Even on the faster numbers such as the Little Richard songs 'Rip It Up' and 'Long Tall Sally,' Ritchie is playing well within the speed capabilities that were his trademark.

'Law And Order', the instrumental the Outlaws performed in *Live It Up!*, was finally released in December to coincide with the film premiere the same month. When reviewing the single for the *NME*, Radio Luxembourg DJ Barry Alldis said, "I feel sure this group will hit the charts hard one day. This new waxing could register in a small way." Alas, it was yet another Outlaws single that failed to make a big impression on the British record buyer.

By early '64 the gigs with Vincent had dried up and an unusual musical pairing occurred as a result of Meek's idea to put the Outlaws together with country singer Houston Wells, who had previously worked with the Marksmen. Houston Wells: "The Marksmen and myself had finished. It was a struggle, we weren't making much money at the time. So they sort of drifted away. I happened to be going to Joe because we were going to do some more recording. We were going to record 'Galway Bay,' so he actually got the Outlaws to do it. I think Joe, from what I've since heard, had in mind for me to stay with the Outlaws but it was never put on the table. But I certainly got a chance to see what kind of guitar player Ritchie was. When we cut 'Galway Bay' Chas is doing a 12-string solo beautifully but Ritchie in the background was doing fast finger work and I couldn't believe how fast his fingers were going … Every time I listen to that record now I never listen to the part Chas is playing though I wouldn't fault that, it was just that I was more interested in what Ritchie was playing. I had a lot of good guitarists on my records, like Big Jim Sullivan but Ritchie was out on his own. If my memory serves me well, I cut seven tracks with the Outlaws. However as far as I know only four of the tracks were ever released, 'Galway Bay', 'Ramona', 'The Wild Side Of Life', and 'Living Alone.' I was in the studio with the Outlaws the whole time.

Unfortunately I wasn't present when the songs were being mixed. Had I been there when 'Galway Bay' was mixed, I would have pushed Joe to bring Ritchie's guitar more to the fore."

All seven tracks were recorded in one session, a common practice for those times and an indication of how talented the group was. Houston Wells: "We knocked them out in one day. That's as I remember it. We may have gone back the next day but I remember meeting the boys and we got stuck into these songs. I thought we were just going to do a couple of songs but once Joe got us in there he said we'll continue and put some stuff in the can because there was nothing arranged to do anymore than 'Galway Bay' and a song called 'Living Alone' and I thought we were just going to do the two. That's what amazed me, how quickly they got on to a song. They heard it and at that particular time I didn't have a lot of bottle in arranging things so I more or less left it in their hands. They more or less did the arranging. What actually happened I'd start singing the song and they would jump in behind and a few suggestions would be made and that's more or less how it was worked out."

With the recordings done Meek arranged for the Outlaws to back Wells on a three-week Irish tour. Although born Andrew Smith in the north of England, the country singer had developed a following in Ireland.[*] For the Outlaws and in particular Blackmore and Underwood, touring the Emerald Isle was a real comedown compared to their experiences in Germany with Lewis and Vincent. Mick Underwood: "It was horrible. It was the total antithesis of the Reeperbahn. Not a lot of fun. We got invited to have a cup of tea with the priest at most gigs because they were in parish halls! We were very well behaved on that tour. There was nothing to do it was just so boring."

For Wells it was a thoroughly memorable time: "On our tour of Ireland we had some great laughs. The [guys in the Outlaws] nearly got us hung in Dublin. We were in the hotel in the main street, about two or three storeys up and they were chucking cups of water out on people walking past. The cops were called and I had to go and sort it out. I had to put the block on that. I got it straightened out. I had a few words with them about that at the time and they possibly realised they'd better watch what they were doing or

[*] 'Only The Heartaches', a track recorded with his previous backing band the Marksmen which made number 22 in the UK charts on August 31, 1963, reached number one in Ireland and stayed in the Irish Top Ten for six weeks. It's thought that Meek also used Blackmore to dub some additional guitar work on the track.

they would get locked up. It was harmless fun really but someone got a bit shitty about it and reported it."

Throwing water about was only half of it as Lundgren describes: "We piled all this furniture behind someone's door so they couldn't get out. We filled the hallway up with these bits of furniture we found in other rooms and completely made it impossible to get out of the room into the hall. We literally blocked the hallway up with divans and Chesterfields and everything we could find. The police came in and the manager kicked us out of the hotel."

Despite Wells' attempts in trying to contain his backing group's behaviour, there were times when he would be more than happy to join in on a spot of mischief. At one point, Wells and the Outlaws played just outside Dublin in an old hotel that was reputed to be haunted. Houston Wells: "Ken and I actually hid behind the curtains in the room and when Ritchie came in we frightened the shit out of him. We'd just had the whole story told to us and Ken and I were upstairs and when Ricky came up we got in the room behind these big drapes. It didn't look like there was anybody in the room and he started to unpack his bag. We made one hell of a racket and came out from behind the curtain and the poor bastard nearly died. I also remember we were playing in Port Stewart just over the Northern border and Chas lined himself up a lady and of course he shot back to the hotel while we were signing autographs and doing all the bits and we didn't miss him and hadn't realised. Of course when we got back to the hotel he'd had the lady in Ritchie's bed and made a bloody mess, I'm not kidding you. It was hilarious.

"Another time we were coming back from a gig at about two in the morning and smack in the middle of the road there is this guy lying on a bicycle. I thought he'd been knocked off his bike by a car. We pulled up, shined the headlights on him and went round to see what had actually happened. The guy was so tanked up, he'd stopped for a piss and he hadn't taken his leg off the bike. He'd just pulled his cock out and started to piss and flaked out and when we got there he still had his cock in his hand. This is fact. I went back to the van where I had a roll of black adhesive tape and I taped his hand to his cock, taped the whole thing there and we dragged him off to the side of the road and left him there. He didn't even know what was happening – he was so gone. I would have given anything to have seen the guy when he woke up in the morning. We had some wild bloody times."

In the days when half hour sets were standard the Irish trek saw Wells and the Outlaws playing on stage for much longer than they had been used to. Houston Wells: "We were on for over an hour, sometimes an hour-and-a-half, sometimes longer, depending on where we played because some of them didn't have another band to fall back on so we had to battle it through. Each show was over an hour anyway. We did stuff that was in the charts and the Irish were mad keen on stuff like 'Blackboard Of My Heart', Slim Whitman and stuff like that. The sound and everything was great and the [Outlaws] certainly went down well with the fans and the women were chasing them like mad. One thing I did notice with Ricky he seemed to disappear pretty quickly right after we finished. I don't know if he was going off with women or what but somehow he kept out of the way because any photograph sessions we had, he never seemed to get involved. I've got photographs of the boys but he's not in them."

Blackmore's inconsiderate attitude didn't always endear him to the Irish as was the case at one of the gigs. Ken Lundgren: "Ritchie didn't stand up for the Irish National Anthem because we didn't know what it was. We realised we were supposed to but Ritchie didn't. He was sort of giggling and making out with some girl while the National Anthem was being played and they went after him and we had to hustle him out of the back window."

Partly due to their image of dressing up in cowboy outfits, the Outlaws were portrayed by some reviewers as a country and western band and touring with Wells merely enhanced that image. With beat groups now taking centre stage, instrumental bands, with the possible exception of the Shadows, were fast falling out of vogue. The Outlaws had already unsuccessfully tried their hands at a vocal number with 'That Set The Wild West Free' and by the early months of 1964, it was sessions and live work that was keeping them going.

Having only known his German girlfriend a few months Margrit fell pregnant and it's quite probable that given the attitudes of the day Ritchie was pressured into marrying Margrit. "Given the Blackmore family I'm sure his father would have said 'Ritchie do the right thing'," says Lundgren. "That's my own opinion of knowing his parents, having met them several times. I don't think Ritchie would have married at that time if that wasn't the case. Ritchie was too self-centred to want a family." On Wednesday, March 18, with Margrit approximately two months pregnant, the couple tied the knot in a low-key ceremony at the local registry office, followed by a reception at his parents' house. Ken Lundgren: "We bought him a clock, which we lost! We clubbed together and bought this nice mantle clock, which we had engraved 'To Margrit and Ritchie from Ken, Chas and Mick' and we took it to an engraver in Chiswick but for some reason we didn't get it back. We went on tour and the clock was left there. We went back months later but the guy couldn't find it!"

For the newly married couple there was no chance of spending a night in the bridal suite of a local hotel because the Outlaws were booked for a gig that evening. Mick Underwood: "A very memorable gig, fancy having a gig on your wedding night! We pitched up in Salisbury at this massive ballroom and there's loads of kids out there jumping about outside and we thought 'Blimey we've got a following here!' but no one had told us we were supporting the Rolling Stones. This is what it was like back then, we didn't even know we were supporting the Stones! People would be cutting their parts off to do it now. We're up their doing our bit in our light blue suits and of course all these teenage girls aren't interested in us – they want the Stones on. There was no security there at all at the front of the stage, and they've got drinks in their hands – Coca Cola. They thought what a cool idea to suck a bit of coke up the straw and then straight out at Ritchie. We all thought it was quite funny actually but Margi didn't and she was a very fit women; quite big, knocked around in the St Pauli part of Hamburg and you don't fuck about there.

"All these kids are doing this, and she's out there. I think she had a leather skirt on if I remember rightly and she's decided no one is going to mess about with her Ritchie any longer so she appears at the front of the stage, kneels down and sets about one of these girls! Then they started on her, Margi stood up and they got hold of her skirt and they were pulling it down! Now remember, we're playing, and Ritchie, he's playing – he ain't done nothing, hasn't stopped! And of course she had no real option, either her skirt was going to come off in front of all these people or she'd jump off the stage so she jumped off and storms into them before the bouncers steamed in and managed to get her out. And guess what? Ritchie never dropped a note! They picked on the wrong one with Margi for a start anyway. She could handle herself. And that was his wedding night! It was hilariously funny."

Ken Lundgren remembers events differently: "When Ritchie saw Margrit go flying in he jumped in after her and we just had to play something fast and keep going. You can't let the crowd get out of control so we just kept on playing and eventually they threw him and her back up."

After falling out with Joe Meek Associates as a result of their wild behaviour, things became tougher for the lads. Mick Underwood: "We were persona non-gratis I suppose, just about everywhere! I think that's when Ritchie decided we weren't going to be doing too much so when Joe said to him … which makes me laugh really because he was the biggest instigator of the shit, he went off and joined Heinz."

Ironically, just before Blackmore decided to take up Meek's offer of joining a newly-created backing group for Heinz Burt, the Outlaws produced their most dynamic single. Abandoning the instrumentals that formed the majority of their previous output both sides featured Hodges and Lundgren on vocals. The A-side was a powerful reworking of Little Richard's 'Keep A Knockin' but it was the B-side, 'Shake With Me' composed by Meek under the pseudonym of Peter Jacobs that featured Blackmore's most explosive guitar playing committed to vinyl up to that point.* 'Shake With Me' was a track that had already been recorded by another of Meek's bands, the Puppets but because the Outlaws had done the backing on that recording, they were already familiar with the track when laying down their own version. When talking to John Tobler for BBC's *Guitar Greats* series in 1982, Blackmore explained how it came about: "Joe had said to me go crazy, play a very weird solo, bend the notes and play with lots of distortion and it came off. I was quite proud of that solo." Despite the quality of the single, as with the group's previous releases, it failed to chart.

---

* The single has since gone on to greater recognition and John Peel later cited it as the first ever heavy metal record.

CHAPTER 4

Wild Ones, Musketeers, Crusaders & The Roman Empire (1964–67)

Joe Meek's offer to Blackmore of taking on the role as Heinz's bandleader wasn't particularly appealing but for the newlywed father-to-be at least it guaranteed a steady wage. Furthermore because Blackmore was highly revered by Meek, by sticking with RGM, he was assured plenty of additional session fees to supplement his Heinz income. Conversely, when the Outlaws continued with replacement guitarist Harvey Hinsley, their session work dried up. As with the transition from Jaywalker to Savage, and from Savage to Outlaw, each move appeared to come just at the right time as far as the individual young guitarist was concerned.

Although none of Heinz's follow-ups to 'Just Like Eddie' were as successful, by early 1964, the peroxide blond singer was firmly established as a popular singer in Britain. Apart from the Outlaws providing the backing on most of his records and their stint on the ill-fated Jerry Lee – Gene Vincent tour, the Saints had up until this point provided accompaniment for the majority of Heinz's live shows. Meek felt that Heinz was capable of achieving greater success if backed by the right group of competent musicians at his disposal. Despite being well aware of Blackmore's mercurial nature, the producer was won over by the guitarist's dedication to his craft and hoped that with Blackmore at the helm the other musicians would provide their best possible performances. At least that was the plan.

In late April '64, the new group was put together. Organist Dave Adams was an obvious choice as not only was he a highly accomplished player but he'd been working at RGM for some time and was hugely instrumental in the writing and arranging of many of Meek's productions. Adams originally recorded for RGM with his sister as Joy and Dave and also recorded for the company under pseudonyms including Burr Bailey.* Completing the line-up was ex-Midnighters drummer Ian Broad and a newcomer John Anderson on bass. Given the name the Wild Ones, no doubt in a bid to toughen up Heinz's image, Heinz and the Wild Ones made their live debut on May 10 at the inaugural night of the Beat City Club, London's answer to Liverpool's Cavern Club, situated on the corner of Oxford Street and Dean Street, followed by TV appearances plugging their single 'Please Little Girl' on Rediffusion's *Ready, Steady, Go!*, ATV's *For Teenagers Only*, and ABC's *Thank Your Lucky Stars*.

It wasn't long before bassist Anderson left and more out of luck than judgement another ex-Midnighter joined the group. Brian Woods recalls the fortuitous circumstances: "After six months off I rang Ian Broad and spoke to his sister. She said he was in London working for Heinz and they needed a bass player so I went straight down to London. I met up with Ian in North London, where he was stopping with some friends then I went for an audition at Joe's flat in Holloway Road. I had already met Joe the previous year when recording with Freddie Starr. It was quiet a nerve-wracking experience, as I had never met Ritchie or Heinz before. I found Ritchie to be quite a subdued sort of person. Quiet in a sort of way but a very good listener. My audition consisted of a few chords from Ritchie and a few bass notes from myself. Not long after that I learnt that I had been playing alongside one of the finest guitarists in the country. From thereon we would rehearse above a pub in Finsbury. Ritchie was a workhorse: our stage workout had to be spot on which is understandable as we would be playing in front of some very large audiences."

Woods was immediately aware that Blackmore was the bandleader, "and he deserved to be as well with his experience. I did admire him as a player because he was superb. He got on well with us. He was very dedicated. I do remember the times when we used to rehearse at his home. He would have

---

* The B-side to his 1963 Decca 45 'San Francisco Bay,' entitled 'Like A Bird Without Feathers,' featured Blackmore, who slots in three excellent but brief solos. The track was credited to Burr Bailey with the Six Shooters. Meek and Adams also worked on a whole album's worth of material under the name Silas Dooley Jr, for which Blackmore did all the guitar work, which was not released at the time.

tape machines all over his bedroom, wires everywhere just like it was at Joe's. He was a very inventive guitarist and a Les Paul fanatic. He would bring out a sound just like that of the great Les Paul himself and nearly as good as Les's fingering. He used to get all the echo sounds as well, at his home and on stage. Ritchie was a true perfectionist but a little moody at times if things were not going his way."

Patrick Pink, who saw the Wild Ones live on many occasions, is adamant that Blackmore's marshalling of the other musicians was simply done as a platform to allow him to shine. "Ritchie would be trying to get the best out of the band so he'd be in the spotlight. They used to do two or three spots without Heinz, warm-up the audience in the middle when Heinz went off and changed and Ritchie would be the star." Heinz resented Ritchie, but not just for his obviously superior talent as Pink explains, "Ritchie was a good looking bloke and had all the girls flocking at his feet. I'm surprised Heinz had him for so long but it was obviously because of the musicianship. If he had been crummy [Heinz] would have dropped him straight away."

Although Meek managed the band, various agencies arranged the gigs; some tours were booked through Robert Stigwood, others with Tito Burns. One of the Wild Ones' earliest gigs backing Heinz was an outdoor show held at Longleat House, the home of Lord Bath, to an audience of around 8,000 on a bill that included the Hollies, the Searchers and headliners Billy J Kramer & the Dakotas. The Wild Ones got special treatment when Lord Bath took them for rides around the park in his open topped car. Brian Woods: "We did all Heinz's stuff, Heinz did Elvis' stuff, a couple of songs and we had our own little act, I sang a few myself. I sang one on my own, a Carl Perkins song called 'Gone, Gone, Gone.'"

By this stage in his career Blackmore had evidently grown in confidence and Woods remembers the novel way that he would show off to audiences. "Ritchie had a little showpiece that used to go down well with the audience. In the middle of playing a solo he would pull out a massive bright yellow comb about a foot long and start combing his hair while playing the guitar with his other hand. This proves he was a master of his own game."

As well as the live performances and sessions, when the opportunity arose, Blackmore took on other work outside the RGM stable. One such session was for Polydor, the German label that was keen to move into the UK market and sign both established and new artistes. One of the latter was Tanya Day, a singer from Walsall who was fairly well known in the West Midlands area. Day had originally been with the Mark Dean Combo and also in the Tremors for a spell and had trod the boards in Hamburg's clubs. Blackmore laid down guitar on 'I Get So Lonely,' the B-side of her debut solo single 'His Lips Get In The Way.' While there was nothing wrong with the backing Day's vocals were dreadfully flat and tuneless and both the single and singer quickly faded from the scene.*

Although Ritchie and Margrit were still living at the Blackmore family home, Joe Meek sublet another flat a few yards down Holloway Road, which by all accounts, was a real dive but it was a place Meek's musicians could stay overnight after a gig. Patrick Pink: "I remember bringing the band back to the flat one night at two in the morning and Ritchie said, 'Fuck that I'm not sleeping here' because the others were all sleeping there, so I took him all the way home to Heston." Within less than a month since the Wild Ones had started, it must have felt like déjà vu for Blackmore when the music press announced that they were going to have to change their name. Another group with the same name recording for Fontana had just released a single 'Bowie Man' so *Record Mirror* ran a competition for fans to select a new name for Heinz's group.

Meanwhile Heinz and the Wild Ones endured a 10 week residency at the Pavilion Theatre, Rhyl, Wales, on a 'Summer Startime' bill with Arthur Askey, Jerry Desmonde and Sheila Southern. Starting on June 27 and finishing on September 5, there were two shows a night; a matinee starting at 6, followed by an evening show at 8.25, six nights a week with Sunday a day off. Just prior to the first performances Meek announced that he would be recording a live EP approximately nine weeks into the season. The plan was to invite fans to attend a special session outside of the group's ordinary performances but sadly nothing ever came of the idea.

Brian Woods: "At times it was bloody boring. On some occasions we would sit up in the balcony of the theatre before the beginning of the second half of the show, knowing that we were not due on stage until later on, waiting for the first act to come on. As I remember it there were two artists performing acrobatics or something, so we knew when to clap and when not to. The audience didn't know, so what we used to do was clap before the end of their performance and all the audience would follow suit. To this day I'm sure the performers still wonder why the audience clapped before the act ended. I fully enjoyed that it was funny. Ritchie was involved with that because he always had a laugh with us."

---

* 'I Get So Lonely' gained some notoriety years later when on May 15, 1977, it ranked at number 10 in Kenny Everett's Capital Radio 'Bottom 30' Records of All-Time). Tanya Day was last heard of working in Hamburg as well as Israel.

Despite the boredom, the pay was good, around £30 a week, delivered in registered letters to the theatre on a weekly basis. By the start of the season Margrit was already about six months pregnant. Being based in one place for the entire summer meant the recently married couple could spend plenty of time together in a bungalow just a few miles from Rhyl. Despite the fact that a steady income was guaranteed, Blackmore wasn't at all happy playing in a variety show for 10 weeks. At Meek's request Pink paid a visit to Rhyl to check on Heinz's progress. "They were staying in a place in Colwyn Bay and Ritchie was pissed off. Grotty little theatre, two shows a day – one in the afternoon, one in the evening and nobody came to see it. I spent four or five days there and went to see the show twice. They were all pissed off. It was an old people's show."

During the middle of the season in July, the band got a call from Meek summoning them back to London during down time. Brian Woods: "We were actually at Rhyl when Joe rang us up and he wanted us to all get back down that weekend and record 'Questions I Can't Answer,' and there was a panic to get there. He'd just got this new sound and he was dying for us to record it. I thought it was one of Heinz's best." Woods also remembers Ritchie developing a unique sound for the recording: "He had his own little amp, and he put small speakers in it to get this sound like distortion. That was the first I had heard of a distorted sound like a fuzz sound. He got it through those little speakers. He didn't have any fuzz machine or foot pedal it was done straight by a speaker. Just overdriving the volume."

At the same time, *Record Mirror* announced that 22-year-old Norma Adnitt had won the competition to pick the group's new name, resulting in a trip to Rhyl and dinner with Heinz! The name change to the Wild Boys wasn't particularly radical and for Blackmore the role of backing musician having to play second fiddle to an infinitely less talented front man was grating. Nor was he enjoying the type of work they were getting. However Woods looks back on the experience fondly: "We all had a great time over the 10 weeks the show lasted and on the final night of the show Ritchie came up with some fun things to do. As I can remember, Ritchie said to us 'Have you noticed quite a few gaps on the stage floor? Why don't we make use of them?' It was decided to fill some empty balloons up with flour and push them through the gaps before you blow them up in the middle of the last performance of the night until they all burst, and they did! You should have seen the face on Arthur Askey and a few others. Arthur was not impressed. The rest of the stage acts, crew and dancing girls had a great laugh along with the audience."

Meek's professional relationship with Heinz had greatly deteriorated after the singer got himself a girlfriend, so Meek tried to arrange as many gigs as possible to keep Heinz out of his sight, including an Australasian tour booked for October. However, no doubt because of costs, Heinz travelled there solo. Brian Woods: "We were booked to play in Australia but it fell through. We never went abroad. Furthest we got was the Isle of Wight, the Isle of Man and Scotland! We flew to the Isle of Man from Liverpool on a little prop."

While Heinz was away in Australia, Blackmore kept busy with more RGM sessions, as well as becoming a father when Margrit gave birth to their only child, Jürgen Richard, on October 7. Blackmore's relationship with Jürgen hasn't exactly been close, but in those early years he had no option but to take what work was on offer while Margrit stayed at home to look after their young son. In later years, having moved to Germany, Jürgen commented about the father and son relationship, "I'd see him when he played in Germany, but there were always other people around. I don't feel comfortable calling him, because I don't know him very well."

Heinz spent three weeks in Australia but a planned American trip to follow was subsequently cancelled. Instead Heinz and the Wild Boys commenced another British tour at the Essoldo, Tunbridge Wells, on October 23, promoted by Larry Parnes in association with the George Cooper Organisation. The 'Your Lucky Stars' package saw the group second on the bill to the Hollies, supported by Jess Conrad, American girl act the Dixie Cups, as well as Heinz's former band the Tornados, with the 14-date tour concluding on November 8 at Coventry Theatre.

With the tour in mind Heinz sold his Chevrolet and bought a new Ford Zephyr Estate, complete with back seats that folded into beds, so the group could travel in reasonable comfort. Life on the road for any touring band in the mid Sixties was a series of tiresome journeys and with the amount of miles travelled the law of averages ensured that accidents would occur, as was the case on the journey to Leicester's De Montfort Hall. Brian Woods: "We were nearly there, the fog was so dense, we were going slowly and suddenly there was an almighty crash into the back of us. The van that hit us ended up in the ditch upside down, and the back of the car was all smashed in but driveable. I'd knocked my face on the seat and knocked my front teeth out but no one was injured apart from that. But the police came and we stood by the side of the road and the policeman said, 'Look at these idiots on the other side' and they were tailgating and banging into each other. We played at De Montfort Hall in the end, an hour or so after leaving the scene."

It wasn't their only lucky escape as Woods remembers averting another potential accident that the rest of the group weren't even aware of. "Although I say it myself I think I saved the band's life on the M1. Coming back down south the lads were sleeping in the back on the floor in between the amps and I couldn't sleep, I'm one of those nervous passengers and I sat in the passenger seat. Our roadie John who was quite new to us was dropping off at the wheel and I had to nudge him. Anyhow I'm looking out the window and the next minute he's dropping off again. And we had to pull onto the hard shoulder. It was a good job I hadn't fallen asleep or we would have all been piled up. It was frightening. It was fate I didn't fall asleep. I thought all of us could have been killed. They were all oblivious in the back fast asleep."

Normally after the shows, the band would relax back at their hotel with a few drinks. However there was a less conventional end to one night. Brian Woods: "I experienced a dark side of Ritchie's life, like Joe, Ritchie was into spirituals and maybe other strange rituals. One evening after one of our many gigs Ritchie asked whether or not we would be interested in contacting any of our families. This was all done in one of our hotel bedrooms under lock and key. Ritchie set up a Ouija board and cut up some paper and cardboard, and got us all to do this with paper slips with the alphabet written on them. We sat around this table with a bit of apprehension. I had never experienced this sort of going on but was willing to partake like the rest of the lads. Ritchie then told us all to be dead quiet. That was difficult at first because I thought it was a bit of a laugh but Ritchie did not. In the end we all realised the serious side of this. The tumbler was in the centre of the table with one of our fingers on it. He asked me would I be happy to contact the spirits. I was a bit concerned at first but said OK. The question I put forward was 'How are things back home?' and it spelt out a health problem with one of my parents, it spelt out – 'There's a health problem.' With this feedback I rang back home that evening to find out that my mother had been taken ill and rushed in to hospital that same evening and unfortunately my mum passed away two months later. It just goes to show Ritchie's belief in the spirits is worth thinking about."

When released in November 'Questions I Can't Answer' was yet another in a string of hit singles that made the Top 50 for Heinz and as a result, more TV appearances were undertaken. While some of these were mimed others were done live such as BBC2's *The Beat Room* on November 12 where, according to Woods, Blackmore came face to face with a fellow guitar rival. "On the *Beat Room* show there was another group on and Jimmy Page was playing with them. Ritchie said, 'He's here! I've got to be playing my best!'

It frightened Ritchie – not frightened of Jimmy personally but frightened of making a mistake. I think he admired Jimmy Page as a rival."

Although the summer season with Arthur Askey had been anything but a rock 'n' roll experience, worse was to come when Heinz and the Wild Boys were booked on a Christmas pantomime season. *Once Upon A Fairytale* billed as a "pop pantomime" was the first of its kind, aimed directly at the young army of British pop fans, with the principal roles being handled by top stars. The bill starred Marty Wilde and his wife Joyce Baker plus Scottish singer Lulu, and her backing band The Luvvers, who were riding high after the success of their single 'Shout.' The concept was devised by Harry Dawson, of the Cooper Organisation, who commented, "We felt that pantomime could do with a little modernisation." A consultant anaesthetist, Jimmy Wilson who was involved with pop music as a hobby, wrote the story.

Irrespective of the weak concept of putting pop stars into pantomime, the lavish production involved £5,000 worth of scenery, not to mention a lot of hard graft from the cast. "We did a lot of rehearsing for weeks on end in a big hall," recalls Woods, who to this day remains upbeat about the whole enterprise. "We had a script and everything. Lulu was the witch! Heinz was the captain of the guards and we were the courtiers. We were all in it; we did the acting as well, it was fantastic."

The full season was planned to run from December 26 through January 23, starting with seven shows at the Doncaster Gaumont. Reviews varied with *Melody Maker* responding reasonably positively: "Heinz and his Wild Ones (*sic*) are always lively and when they found their own little niche in their solo spot they were good. But during the rest of the show they gave little indication of being at all at home." The *NME* claimed the Wild Boys were much too loud and as a result Heinz "didn't come over well."

Despite Blackmore's disinterest and reluctance to be involved in the whole affair, Woods recalls that eventful week in Doncaster: "Ritchie did it as well, he was all right, it went down well. That's part of showbiz – he was in it so he had to do it. The Luvvers were guards and we were courtiers, so we were kind of in the background. We didn't do much. I think we said something but not much but we had to follow the scripts. It was a well-rehearsed show but we did our own spot like Lulu and the Luvvers did. It was an unusual show and we had uniforms to put on. It was quite normal in those days; Lulu was a rocker as well and Marty Wilde. I think Joe [Meek] came in to see how we were getting on towards the end of the Doncaster run, and he was quite worried with things, he got us all together but he looked like a worried man. Things were going wrong about then. We saw the change in him – sad."

Although the shows failed to sell out, the tour continued with six nights at Norwich Gaumont, where they were less well-received. One opening night reviewer said: "Thank heavens it is only *Once Upon A Fairy Tale*. Twice would be too much." Another commented that the pantomime fell between two stools "and some of the acting was amateurish." Midway through their week in Norwich some of the cast indulged in the most un-rock 'n' roll behaviour of a ten pin bowling tournament against the *Cinderella* cast, who were performing at the Theatre Royal. Much to Blackmore's relief, after the last show at Norwich on January 9, the rest of the performances scheduled for Barking Odeon and Worcester Gaumont were cancelled due to poor ticket sales.*

For Blackmore the panto was the final straw and to avoid such further debacles, he quit the Wild Boys in February. Brian Woods: "My mind is very foggy over this, I can't remember what happened. Nothing serious occurred – it was like a drifting. I don't know whether he had an argument with Joe, for all we know he might have had. I know things weren't going too well towards the end, things were going wrong." Even if Blackmore had argued with Meek he continued to fit in RGM sessions, although he was in effect a free agent. For a brief spell he teamed up with bassist Arvid Andersen and drummer Jimmy Evans in Neil Christian & the Crusaders.

Christian & the Crusaders had been a popular live act since 1962, and like the Savages, were a breeding ground for many great young musicians including Albert Lee, Nicky Hopkins and Jimmy Page who had all been in previous incarnations of the Crusaders. Christian was already aware of Blackmore, having seen him play a couple of years earlier. "First time I saw him he was playing with the Outlaws and I thought, 'Very good.' I was introduced to him by a piano player called Tony Marsh who used to work in the Savages. Ritchie wasn't working for anybody and [he was] a great piss taker – sends people up, whatever way you want to take it. He'd only work for people if he thought they stood a chance [of success]. So I was introduced to him and I said, 'If you can't make your mind up come on the gig with us have a blow, see what you think. If you don't rate it forget it, don't worry about it." So anyway we came off the stage and I said, 'What do you reckon?' He said, 'I know a big star in the making when I see one' and we all started laughing. After that I got on great with the man and he joined the

---

* With the Cooper Organisation operating the panto simultaneously around the country with two casts, after a fortnight of performances Harry Dawson put the losses at around £20,000.

band. He was all right, I liked Ritchie he was very dry but I like that sort of sense of humour so we got on well."

According to Arvid Andersen, Christian had tried out just about every available guitarist but none had clicked. "I'd heard of but never seen The Outlaws. [Christian] came round one afternoon in the bandwagon [an old ambulance] for that night's gig. 'We've got Blackmore,' he said, 'he's doing tonight's show.' We drove over to Neil's flat above the tobacconists his dad ran on Paul Street, in Shoreditch. Someone rang the buzzer and Christian said, 'That'll be Ritchie. He's in the Ford Consul parked across the way, why don't you go down and say hello?' I tapped on the car window and let myself in. We looked at each other straight in the eye, shook hands, which was rather quaint and introduced ourselves. Ritchie had his hair combed back in a quiff, which was unfortunate but it didn't look retro, it suited him. He was obviously very direct – a strong guy who didn't look as if he would accept or put up with any bullshit. I liked what I saw. He was sure of himself but not cocky. He spoke really well – you might say urban. He looked good, dressed in dark, well-fitting clothes.

"It was typical – in the way you suss out chords, you suss out people. We got down to business, Ritchie not only knew our repertoire but also all the instrumentals so this was a bonus. It was like talking to a kindred spirit, a brother. Ritchie even asked what side of the stage I used. 'Right – facing out.' 'Great,' he said, 'I only feel good on the left.' This may be a small detail but it was an important factor in our presentation because I moved a lot on stage. Ritchie complimented me on my manoeuvres, told me he was all for that and was enthusiastic about the band, especially Jimmy Evans. Jimmy was knocked out, saying, 'We must keep him, he's shit hot.' We went on stage that night without a rehearsal – it was a church hall in the East End – it was really good and on such occasions Christian would just let us get on with it. [Christian] would slide on stage for a few numbers [mainly Chuck Berry] and then let me carry on with a Little Richard song list plus a few stand-bys like 'Skinny Minnie'. We didn't have time for a drink as the pubs had closed by the time we'd finished so we chatted about all the old bands that had impressed us while we packed up."

When Blackmore joined the Crusaders, work was thin on the ground. In view of Blackmore's familial responsibilities Christian reportedly guaranteed him a retainer. Arvid Andersen: "I can't remember if Ritchie got a weekly bung or not. Jimmy Evans was married as well with a child but he was a watchmaker by trade and worked near home. I occupied a room in the family house in Tolmers Square so my credit was good on that score.

Christian's little side deals kept the band afloat but we did spend a good six months together as the Crusaders."*

Even though he enthusiastically stepped into the Crusaders, the first inklings that Blackmore wanted to form his own band were manifesting, as it was around this time that he discussed forming a band with Jackie Lynton. "We were going to get a band together, when I was about 19," states Blackmore. "When I used to go to work in the workers' playtime they used to play Jackie Lynton & the Teenbeats. This was about 1960 and he was great. I got to meet him in '61 or '62 – very nice guy. Then we tried to get a band together, I think. We met [American scenester/producer] Kim Fowley, who was doing P.J. Proby's stuff, who gave us some demos to learn and to come back. Of course, Jack had the records and lost them and left them on the train! So we never did it. Typical!"

It was also around this time that Blackmore claims to have done a session involving both Jeff Beck and Jimmy Page which, if correct, has never come to light.† "I did a record with Jeff Beck once that Jimmy Page was producing, back in '64 or '65. I can't remember who for. But that was interesting. It was the first time I met Jeff Beck. I always remember him playing a solo – it was a great solo – and I asked him, 'What's your name?' 'Jeff Beck.' 'Who do you play for?' 'The Tridents.' And I made a kind of backhanded compliment like. 'I've never heard of you.' But what I meant to say was, 'I've never heard of you, but you're so good and you should be a name.' It kind of stuck in his head, because when I saw him again in '67 I said, 'Hi! I'm Ritchie.' And he went, 'Ritchie? Ritchie? Sorry, I've never heard of you.' But I didn't mean it that way, and he knew I didn't – bastard! But in '64 he was a great guitar player."

Blackmore's stint with the Crusaders only lasted a month or so and around March time, along with Andersen and Evans, he was back with the Savages for two months. Andersen explains how the switch occurred: "Ritchie didn't join the Crusaders with the express intention of walking off with the band – that would have been tantamount to poaching. We were up for most things against the common enemy: managers/club owners/bookers but poaching was frowned upon within the gigging fraternity.

---

* The period could not have been as long as Andersen describes because Blackmore was still with the Wild Boys in January '65 and was definitely back with Sutch by May.

† In recalling the session work he did with Blackmore, Arvid Andersen says: "We did quite a few together, Ritchie was in demand. I also did a fair bit for [Jimmy] Page. In fact I was signed as a solo artiste by Tony Calder (the business partner of Andrew Loog Oldham) Page was my producer. Ritchie played on those sessions but the tapes were never released."

"If you told the singer he would usually agree to loan [his backing band] out to deputise which carried a certain amount of kudos for all parties. Sutch came up with a tour covering the whole of the UK mainland with some double dates included, which sounded interesting. My guess is Ritchie hustled the gig. At least he told me about it and said, 'But if you're interested, you have to phone Sutch.' I did call and Dave said, 'I'll be really happy to have you guys but I can't walk away with the whole of Christian's band, can I?' I replied that would be our decision. Sutch said, 'OK, great! But you have to tell Christian.' I thought of my usual line on these occasions as I always did the dirty work. I told him I felt mean about it but it was not a question of preference just cold [financial] reality. We had no backers in the Crusaders. Christian looked a bit off colour for a moment but that might have been due to the condition of the road. We were all in the back of a Commer van. He said, 'Yeah, OK,' and that he was thinking of knocking it on the head for a bit anyway. Sutch sacked his existing band as soon as Ritchie told him he was available with a shit hot trio.

"We did one rehearsal at the 'White House.' As a trio nothing much changed we added more songs and kept moving and improving as we played so much more together. We used to talk over arrangements as we travelled Germany by road. We did one show as an opener and then backed the singer. It was like two bands really.* Sutch spent more time on stage than Christian and his act was rather more involved with costumes and transvestite roadies dressed as Ripper victims and occasionally as policemen. Whereas Christian shocked and got us banned by climbing up the stage curtains and dismantling pianos, Sutch's criminal acts were confined to dismembering and causing fires – it was hilarious when it went wrong, usually due to Ritchie tampering with the props. Ritchie never smiled but was always laughing. Jimmy Evans was very calm and did exactly as he liked. Ritchie and I were rogues, always provoking [people]. Not in the band but anybody outside was fair game."

Roger Drew, who had seen Blackmore backing Jerry Lee Lewis in the Outlaws a couple of years earlier, also caught him with Sutch at the California Ballroom, Dunstable around this time: "As a drummer I didn't usually take a lot of interest in guitarists. But on this occasion I realised that my companions [Steve Lovelock and Dave Smith, bass player and rhythm guitarist respectively in Drew's group, the Starliners] were held spellbound

* This Savages line-up also featured four saxophone players, simply referred to as the Four Saxes.

by the playing of this guy who looked no older than us. Eventually Dave regained his voice, turned to me and said, 'That man is an education.' I have never forgotten those words. Even to me, who knew precious little about guitar playing, he seemed pretty special, and so cool too. There was a low overhanging ledge above the stage, and during one breathtaking solo he swung the guitar up and accidentally smashed the end of the neck into the ledge, he did not even flinch or bat an eyelid!"

During his brief second stint in the Savages, Blackmore made his first and only studio recordings with the group on the Joe Meek produced single, 'The Train Kept A Rollin'' b/w 'Honey Hush', released by CBS in June (and credited to Lord Sutch). Sutch and the Savages even managed to do a spot of TV promotion on *Thank Your Lucky Stars*, broadcast May 22.[*] Arvid Andersen: "Dick Errington played the sax solo on that record, he was top notch. He would probably have been happier playing with the Graham Bond Organisation or some real jazz outfit. We did the TV show up [in Birmingham]. The only problem was they only had room for a singer and six musicians – we were seven so one of the sax players had to stay behind. Sutch wanted Errington up front of the camera. Sutch wanted him to leap forward so it would be like he was in the lounge of the people watching TV … Dick was not pleased. I told him how good his solo was and when he saw I was serious and how good Jimmy and Ritchie were, he agreed to Sutch's direction."

Despite being a punchy rock 'n' roller, and devoid of the controversy of earlier Savages recordings such as 'Jack The Ripper', as with all Sutch's previous recordings, it failed to make any impact on the charts, but it did show a degree of maturity in Blackmore's playing.

Having now branched out on his own, former RGM employee Derek Lawrence also called upon Blackmore for several sessions. Lawrence had secured a deal to do several recordings exclusively for the US market and for one of the first Lawrence reassembled the Outlaws to record a B-side.[†] Another session, credited to the aptly named Sessions, featured Chas Hodges, Nicky Hopkins, drummer Jim Evans, and vocalist Miki Dallon. These helped pay the rent as Lawrence explains, "I'd give them a tenner or whatever but they'd probably do four or five a week, it supported them."

---

[*] Unfortunately this and all of Blackmore's other Sixties UK television appearances appear not to have been archived.

[†] Blackmore's replacement, Harvey Hinsley, who went on to play with Hot Chocolate in the Seventies, did the guitar work on the already recorded A-side.

A session at Olympic Studios (then in Marble Arch) backing all-girl trio the Murmaids was completed far quicker than anticipated. Derek Lawrence: "We were doing a thing for Kim Fowley with these three girls called the Murmaids, who were actually an English group whose name was something else, but [Fowley] had been associated with this kind of hit in America with this band the Murmaids* so I think we did a version of 'To Know Him Is To Love Him'. The band was there and the session had finished and there was still time booked in and Kim was like he always was, on the phone hustling and we just laid down two tracks. We'd done the session and there was time left."

Blackmore had always admired Nero & the Gladiators take on Edvard Grieg's 'In The Hall Of The Mountain King' so the studio outfit knocked out their own version, albeit with a different title, 'Satan's Holiday'. Given Blackmore's reputation as a speed merchant the arrangement is relatively pedestrian and doesn't showcase his fast finger work to anywhere near the extent of his capabilities. The 'made up in the studio' B-side, 'Earthshaker,' bagged Blackmore his first co-writing credit. The recordings were released under the name of the Lancasters but Underwood who was the drummer on the session[†] was surprised they ever got out at all. "They're unfinished those tracks, they're not rehearsed just a quick blow through the tune and record it, they were pretty grim. Horrible: one take of not knowing what you're doing." The Lancasters' US-only single is now a highly rare collectors' item.

More notably Lawrence also organised a session for a UK single release on Oriole Records to be credited under Blackmore's own name. Once again familiar faces were brought in for the sessions including the ever-dependable Hopkins, Hodges, and Underwood but to this day it's still unclear who is playing sax on the record.[‡] Derek Lawrence: "Ritchie always loved 'Little Brown Jug' [made famous by Glenn Miller] and 'Getaway' was 'Hall Of The Mountain King' in drag! So it was easy." Underwood also recalls that unlike the Lancaster's single some pre-planning went into the recordings that were done at London's IBC studios. "We spent a little bit of time buggering about at IBC prior to that. When we went in to do Ritchie's record that was a definite session because we went over to Chas

---

* 'Popsicles And Icicles' reached number three on the *Billboard* Hot 100 in 1963.
† The bass player was Ritchie's former Savages band mate, Ricky Brown.
‡ Some claim it to be one Reg Price but Underwood recalls the players from the Savages were drafted in for the session.

Hodges' the day before to routine it, just get an idea of what the tracks were going to be all about so there was a very brief rehearsal if you like. Ritchie was also very taken with a solo on a Jim [P.J.] Proby track.* I think it was Jim Sullivan on it with a fuzz box and they were virtually unknown of over here at that time. Ritchie discovered if he used cheap little speakers and trashed them and then played the guitar through them, they didn't last very long but they fuzzed and he could get the sustain. So it was all pretty well set up before we did that."

From the outset there was never any intention of Blackmore launching a solo career and despite being well-known within musician circles, he was hardly a household name. When the single was released press reports referred to it under the name of the Ritchie Blackmore Orchestra but as with the Lancasters single, it only sold a handful of copies and original pressings now fetch a king's ransom.

When Lewis and Violet Blackmore moved to Camberley in Surrey, Ritchie, Margrit and Jürgen sought new accommodation. Joe Meek offered Ritchie and Margrit his other flat on the first floor at 224 Holloway Road, which he sublet to them for £4 a week. Rob Huxley, better known at the time as Robbie Gale from the Saxons who was by then working with the new line-up of the Tornados, had been living there. "Joe asked us to leave the flat that he had provided for us on Holloway Road just a few doors down from the studio so that Ritchie and his wife could move in there. Joe said that Ritchie needed it more than us as he was married and needed a place." "It was a real dirty doss hole," recalls Patrick Pink, "but when Ritchie moved in, I don't know who decorated it all but they did it up quite nicely."

Meek might have told others that Blackmore needed the flat because of his marital needs but the opinion held by some of the musicians working for RGM was that Meek had Blackmore there for his own agenda. But as Pink explains there was a logical reason for this. "Ritchie worked [at Meek's studio] every day at one point. He's got the best guitar player in the world living on his doorstep, he's going to accommodate him and pull the stops out. He might have been spoilt but he was spoilt for a reason."

With Blackmore now living just a few yards away, whenever he wasn't gigging he would be at the studio. Around this time Meek brought him in

---

* In all probability, either 'Hold Me' or 'Zing! Went The Strings Of My Heart' both of which Proby recorded in 1964.

to assist the Tornados on a few sessions. Although it's uncertain exactly what recordings he features on, Tornados' drummer Clem Cattini's recollections suggest Blackmore at least played guitar on 'Early Bird,'* which when released by Columbia, was billed as 'Tornados '65.'

What *is* certain was that Meek wanted to involve Blackmore in a new version of the original group, being anxious to repeat the same level of success 'Telstar' had achieved. Unfortunately Meek's Midas touch had dried up. Keyboard player Dave Watts remembers some of those sessions for what would have been the New Tornados featuring both Blackmore and future Jimi Hendrix Experience drummer Mitch Mitchell. "We did some absolutely blinding sessions. Joe came in grinning all over his face." Although one of the best drummers that Meek had at his disposal, Mitchell was a very flamboyant player with rolls and fills all over the place. However, as Watts recalls, Blackmore had little problem adapting to this. "Because of the musician he was he could work round it. I remember he was so fast and quick to learn. He would do it in one or two takes but more or less get it straight off, go right through and not make a mistake."

During one of the sessions Meek became so irritated by Mitchell's flashy drumming that he stormed out of the control room armed with a shotgun: "If you don't play this right I'll blow your fucking head off!" Even though the RGM crew were used to Meek's unbalanced behaviour; throwing typewriters, tape recorders and other inanimate objects against the wall in fits of anger, this was the first indication of something much darker. Meek's outburst was fortunately nothing more than an idle threat on this occasion but for those present, the consequences could have been potentially far worse. Whether or not the incident helped to seal Blackmore's view of Meek is unclear but Watts remembers that Meek, "wanted 100 per cent and Ritchie didn't want to give that. Joe got very pissed off when Ritchie went off to Germany for about four weeks and I think their relationship went downhill after that."

Blackmore returned to Germany, along with Andersen and Evans, to back Jerry Lee Lewis during a residency at the Star Club. By now Blackmore was getting tired of the backing jobs and RGM sessions tread-mill. While he could have opted for the New Tornados gig, musically he would no doubt have felt stifled by Meek's musical direction. When the stint

---

* This information came from the sleeve notes to a Tornados compilation CD. However it must be said that when Cattini was asked about the song in 2006 he was of the view that Blackmore didn't play on it. Judging by the aural evidence Blackmore *is* on the track and Meek may well have added his overdubs at a separate session.

with Jerry Lee finished, Blackmore, Andersen and Evans formed their own trio, the Three Musketeers. Arvid Andersen: "Ritchie went to Hamburg on a search mission and flew back to London with this entrepreneur [who shall remain nameless]. This guy signed us and guaranteed our wage so Jimmy gave up his job. He paid for us to fly to Hamburg where Ritchie was already installed. This German guy had contacts in the clubs and I believe he owned a few himself. He sold second-hand things as a living."

The trio began a regimented set of rehearsals. Arvid Andersen: "Hamburg for The Musketeers was really a workshop. We rehearsed every weekday afternoon in a club with our amps and PA. Home to Ritchie meant practise. He bought a two-track tape recorder and dissected Les Paul, re-recording the guitar tracks in his own style."

As well as playing most Saturday nights in Hamburg, the Three Musketeers were also contracted to play a week at the Star Club in Bochum. Due to the backers' publicity aplomb the place was packed for their first gig. Arvid Andersen: "Bochum with its Star Club became one of our strongholds. We were sold on to other managers and often did weekly stints on a Hamburg based network. One secondary manager had some strip clubs on the Reeperbahn. Another was a lawyer anxious to break into the music business. The original idea was to turn the Musketeers into a four-piece with a black guy called Tony Cavanagh. He was a good singer but I didn't like the tone. Not rock or even soul. He could however hold a melody and was good on stage but not my cup of tea so I showed a general disinterest and he just sort of dropped out of sight. The Star Club and Top Ten audiences were great but other venues, especially outside Hamburg were still wanting people like [German bandleader] James Last.

"I never missed a gig and was rarely late but on one occasion, Ritchie was. It was Saturday night in a Hamburg suburb and the place was steaming. Ritchie got stuck somewhere so Jim and I went on with just bass and drums. Into our third number I spotted Ritchie, who had been in an accident, charging in, guitar in hand. I could see him fighting his way through the crowd still in his overcoat. In one movement he had his coat off and was plugged in. I stopped and signalled Jimmy. Without faltering, Ritchie played a barrage of notes to set the scene. He turned to me and mouthed 'car' and I went to the mic '2-3-4' and we went straight into 'Lucille.' The crowd thought it was all part of the act. We were so tuned into one another, so sure of each other we didn't have to say a word."

For Blackmore it was a time he looks back on with "very fond memories. It was the first band where I really enjoyed playing. We used to dress up as Musketeers, 'cause I always had to dress up as something, and we used to sword fence on stage. We were the first three-piece – people had never heard of three-piece bands. So we'd be playing, and all the songs we had were very fast. The big thing in Germany was that you played music for people to dance to. And they could never dance to us, so we didn't really get much work. There was a guitar player called Joe Procter – we used to copy some of his stuff. We'd open up the show with a song called 'The Plainsmen' followed by 'Yackety Sax', then we'd do 'Javes', but in the middle of the act we'd do our speciality – a really fast number – 'Flight Of The Bumble Bee.' So you can imagine the audience watching us, and there was another song called 'Sabrosa' by Chet Atkins. Everything was like that – extremely fast which was great for me but was terrible for the audience. So they used to kind of disappear and our work went down."

Previous documentation suggested that the Three Musketeers only did one gig, a story that today Andersen claims to have originated. In what was apparently the opening night of a residency at the Bochum Star Club in January '66 they were fired straight after it. Andersen, who recalls playing in Germany with the Musketeers for "eight to ten months," got extremely drunk before going on stage – so drunk that during the gig he allegedly started urinating on the audience. Needless to say this didn't endear a great deal of affection from the group's investor and their contract was terminated immediately.

When Ritchie rejoined Neil Christian & the Crusaders a few months later he told Christian about the incident: "Arvid got a bit pissed, I think it was the opening night and he started pissing over the crowd from the stage. It didn't go down well! So it opened and shut the first night! Ritchie told me about it when they came back. They had a backer there who had plenty of dough apparently. Ritchie was telling me he took them round to this big clothes shop, they got all this musketeer gear, and he paid for the whole lot. On the opening night a lot of publicity went round – the place was packed. They started and Arvid started pissing on people! Then it folded and that was that!"

Andersen's only comment on his alleged behaviour is, "The German [stint] came to an abrupt end due to an incident. Bad behaviour on my part plus the usual bundle and rumble. So I was responsible for the end of it all." If Andersen had kept himself in check events might have turned out differently. With the imminent arrival of the 'power trio' in Cream closely followed by the Jimi Hendrix Experience, the music scene was shifting to bands that emphasised the virtuosity of the musicians.

At a loose end Blackmore's love for Germany was such that he decided to stay on, managing to earn a few Deutschmarks by doing sessions for the

Polydor label at their studios in Hamburg. His memories of these sessions are hazy and the only artist he can recall working with was a female singer called Heidi.*

With no regular work coming in, Blackmore flitted between Germany and England taking whatever session work he could, including other Derek Lawrence-produced sessions for the US market – one for soul singer Ronnie Jones and another for the Soul Brothers, who featured Tony Wilson, later a member of Hot Chocolate – when the offer came through to rejoin Neil Christian. Christian was looking to put a band together to promote 'That's Nice,' a minor single in the UK but a hit in Germany. Along with Andersen, Evans and pianist Tony Marsh, Blackmore became part of the new line-up of the Crusaders, touring from April through to July. Arvid Andersen: "My first love was the band, our trio, but to keep going we just had to play [behind] other singers. It was a tightrope act. If you are carefree you can always sort yourself out but we were three guys with wives and kids."

Although the schedule included a Radio England Swinging '66 package tour of the UK[†] Christian's popularity was far greater in mainland Europe. Neil Christian: "We did France, did a bit in Spain, Germany, quite a lot in Berlin. I never forget once in Germany, this was when the border was up, we were going through the Eastern Bloc, we were coming from Berlin. We pulled into the Eastern Bloc with the Commies and in the back of the car we used to have a wop box; John Lennon gave it to me. It used to flash on and off all the time. These guards go through poking everything about with a gun and of course as they are poking this box Ritchie said 'Look out' and jumped back. That done it and we were locked up in a fucking bunker all night long, freezing cold and they took the car apart! That's his sort of humour! He used to travel in the band bus most of the time. When I used to use him on his own he'd travel with me but mainly he'd want to be with the boys. I used to do a lot of promoting in Germany myself every now and again and you needed a band to back you if you did a show so I'd just take Ritchie on his own and we'd get out there and he would just say to the group, 'This is what it is, blah, blah' and away we'd go."

---

[*]The only Heidi known to have recorded for Polydor in Germany around this time is Heidi Bachert who had a single 'Super – Boy' b/w 'Blumen Für Die' released in 1966 but it is unclear what if any involvement Blackmore had on this record.
[†]The tour – starring The Small Faces, Crispian St. Peters, Lou Christie, The Limeys and The Koobas with guest star Wayne Fontana (replaced by Dave Berry) – started at Lewisham Odeon on August 12 and ended August 25 at Southampton Gaumont.

By now it was clear that, having had a taste of his own band with the Three Musketeers Blackmore was eager to carry things further. Neil Christian: "He always knew what he wanted to do. I had no second thoughts about it because we used to talk about it. He used to pass the time talking about it and if you didn't fit the bill that was it."

After concluding the European tour with Christian, Blackmore's next live work meant a return to Continental mainland when his former band mate from the Wild Boys, Ian Broad had been entrusted with the task of recruiting a suitable backing band. Arvid Andersen: "Ian Broad showed up in London after touring Spain and Italy in a band called [I think] The Biss. Ian contacted Ritchie saying there was a stack of work in Italy where they had just discovered British bands and musicians. Ritchie called me and I went over to the Blackmore's flat in Holloway Road. We were not doing a lot at that moment and I was keeping a low profile in London as a few people were looking for me so it seemed like a good idea. 'Italy, great, let's go *now*.' Only problem was Jimmy Evans. We couldn't go with two drummers unless Ian wanted to be manager – he did not. So we settled with Jimmy because we thought we would be back in six weeks or so. Ian had come over by road so we piled into his Italian car and motored over the Alps."

As well as Blackmore and Andersen, Broad brought with him a rhythm guitarist named Billy Gray. Following on in the Sutch tradition, each member was given a nickname. As Andersen was a fan of Charles Dickens he took the name Silas Wegg (a name that Blackmore still refers to him by), Ian Broad was 'The Ram,' Billy Gray became Gilles, while Blackmore adopted the moniker of Tom Brown. With the growing use of drugs within the music business and in particular, LSD, the group was given the psychedelic name the Trip.

Arvid Andersen: "We were due for a month's residency in a club on the Adriatic. We had never played so long in one place before. 'Won't the people get fed up?' I thought. Ian set my mind at rest by pointing out that Riccione was a tourist hot spot, literally thousands of holidaymakers. There were plenty of people to fill the club with a different crowd every night. The other thing that worried me and Ritchie was over material. We were a rock 'n' roll trio not a fucking dance band. 'Don't worry,' said Ian. 'There is a house band for that. We are what is called the attraction.' When we got to the club, it was pissing down. This place was in the open air with no welcoming umbrellas. Even the chairs had been chained together in a pyramid covered with a tarpaulin so we headed for Milan. We had no money left so we sat in the car whilst Ian went knocking on the door of the recording company to get us signed up straight away, which incredibly he managed to do.

"Ian arrived spot on at midday with an advance so we went to eat then picked up the keys to our studio flat in this spanking, newly built residence with a view over the cathedral and the Piazza Del Duomo. Next day we met Gianni – the boss of the record company. Ian hadn't signed away anything too serious – we were just required to back Riki Maiocchi. He was due out on the road and needed a band. We had a couple of rehearsals and learnt his miserable songs. We did one gig. What a laugh, I wanted to put an end to it as soon as possible, you know? Thanks for the grub but really not this. So using an old tactic, I said 'Riki, we go on first, play three numbers and then I announce you with a proper build up.' So what does he do? He wanders out on stage with us. 'No Riki, go back, get off. I'll call you. It's dangerous on stage during our show – you might get a guitar on your nut.' So he left, we cranked up and let fly. The crowd were in shock. I called up Riki, he did one song, told us 'Carry on, do some more,' stood by the drummer danced, cheered, clapped his hands and tried to look as if he was enjoying himself. Later he said we will have to work something out but we never backed him again."

Blackmore's recollections were hazy when he talked about the tour in a 1971 interview: "We went to Italy about five years ago, and we were contacted by a certain Maiocchi, who was one of the best Italian singers of the time, I think. He had left Camaleonti [one of Italy's most popular beat groups at the time] and was starting a solo career, but our relationship lasted only one evening. Wegg and me had been playing together for several years and we were up to all sort of mischief. We used to jump on the amps, run like mad, and things like that … we've always been a little crazy, and we still are, I guess. Maiocchi couldn't understand our enthusiasm, or maybe he wanted to be the only one to move on stage, so we immediately gave it a miss. We played at a festival with the Casuals and Giganti, and during our set they cut off the electricity. We couldn't understand why!"

In another interview, he claimed: "I stayed in Italy for three weeks* but it was a very long period for us because we didn't have any money at the time. I remember that we were staying in one of the most expensive hotels in Milan, and we couldn't go away because we didn't have enough money to pay the bill, so one night we escaped from the window."

The November '66 issue of the Italian music magazine *Qui Giovani* ran a

* He probably meant three months – Blackmore's stay in Italy lasted from August to November.

feature on Maiocchi and the Trip which reported some of the venues the band had played: The Paip's in Milan (where the article said they had played a residency throughout October) and the Le Roi in Turin. Although little is known about this period the Trip apparently got some gigs without Maiocchi, as confirmed by Andersen. "We had our rooms paid up for one month so Ian [Broad] got out looking for work. We played the Paips but not a residency and a few other clubs until Ritchie got news from London about his impending divorce and had to get back. I was living in this girl Ella's flat, Ian went to Turin to his girlfriend's and everything was put on ice for a bit. This is when Ritchie left by train to London from Milan. I took him to the station, Strazione Centrale and gave him what I had, about 10,000 lire. It was 24 hours to Victoria Station on the Simplon Enrev."

Back in London, on November 11, alongside fellow ex-Musketeer Jim Evans, Blackmore recorded one of his last RGM sessions at '304', laying down guitar on three Glenda Collins tracks* for which he was paid a session fee of £9.00.

By now a lot of the musicians that had worked for Meek were turning their backs on him. Patrick Pink: "Once the board of trade had been on his door Joe started to go to bits after that because of the financial problems. That hurt Joe badly, nobody wanted to work for him, there was a problem getting the musicians so he was lucky to get Ritchie back."

The main financial problem that was crippling Meek involved French composer, Jean Ledrut whose claim that Meek had stolen one of his tunes for 'Telstar' resulted in Meek's royalties for the song being frozen during a lengthy court battle. But financial difficulties were only a part of it. Patrick Pink observed how the mounting pressures were affecting Meek: "He was too far gone. Joe was talking to me of suicide in late '66. He had it in his mind to kill himself, no matter what. Back then homosexual people got depressed and suicidal because they all got in a closet and were frightened. They lived in some kind of fear. Joe was talking about suicide and I laughed it off but I had known one or two people who had overdosed and died and I thought that's what Joe would probably do, that I'd go in there one day and find him dosed out. That was the common trait for homosexuals back then. It was terrible the way they used to live."

Meek was still clutching at the possibility that Blackmore might become a part of the New Tornados. "I have been trying to pinpoint the approximate date or at least month of Ritchie's session with us," says Rob Huxley.

---

* These tracks didn't emerge until being released on a Glenda Collins compilation in 1997.

Ritchie Blackmore, 1971. "I thought, 'I'm gonna show people, I'm gonna play the guitar really well.' So they would say, 'He was a terrible pupil, but he could really play the guitar.' That's exactly what they said later on… That's the motivation, to show people that you're worthy of something, you're not just an idiot." (GERARD SHEPPELL/CORBIS)

Ritchie, approximately 15 years old, with his first electric guitar – a Hofner Club 50.

(COURTESY OF FINGERSTYLE GUITAR MAG)

Ritchie's first group, The Dominators, pictured at a dance in Ealing, West London, 1960. L-R: Alan Dunklin (bass), Barry Lovegrove (rhythm guitar), Clive (surname unknown, drums), Ritchie (lead guitar).

(COURTESY BARRY LOVEGROVE).

Billy Fury and Mike Dee (front) backstage with The Jaywalkers; Ritchie (second from right) at the Dartford Granada, November 20, 1961. "What made Ritchie stand out was that he was 10 times faster than anybody else," said Nick Simper. "The Jaywalkers stood out because of him, they were just an ordinary run of the mill band... but he was the one guy."

Screaming Lord Sutch & The Savages, with Ritchie (far right). "I learned a lot of showmanship from [Sutch]. He taught me that you can go out there and act like an imbecile and people would think it's wonderful."

Onstage with Screaming Lord Sutch & The Savages, 1962 (L-R: Ritchie, Carlo Little, Rick Brown). "I was thrown in the deep end really because they were touring everywhere. Very professional band, very good musicians and I had to learn quick." (COURTESY NEIL NEWSOME)

Ritchie backing Jerry Lee Lewis at the Star Club, Hamburg, May 1963. It was a trial of nerves because, as Ritchie said, "I'd been told that 'If Jerry doesn't like you he'll give you a whack in the face!'"

The Outlaws in Germany, 1963. L-R: Ritchie, Chas Hodges (bass), Ken Lundgren (rhythm guitar) and Mick Underwood (drums). "The Outlaws tried to appeal to the male audience as opposed to girlies," said Lundgren, "trying to look as macho as possible in a Sixties context and playing really rough music; music that wasn't pretty; rock 'n' roll and rhythm and blues, we were really into that."

On board the cross channel ferry, M.V Royal Daffodil, June 1, 1963, The Outlaws were backing Jerry Lee Lewis. L–R: Mick Underwood (The Outlaws), Billy Clarke (The Atlantics), Ritchie, his girlfriend Jacqui Shirley, Jamie Lee (The Atlantics) and Barry Taylor (The Atlantics). (COURTESY NEIL NEWSOME)

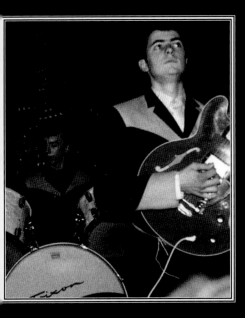

Mick Underwood and Ritchie onstage at the Star Club, Hamburg, 1963. "It was a very dynamic live scene," said Underwood. "You had to be careful but the thing with the Star Club… let's say the gangsters were frightened of the Star Club. That says it all."

(K&K ULF KRUGER OHG/REDFERNS)

Heinz and The Wild Ones, 1964. L–R: Dave Adams (organ), Ritchie, Ian Broad (drums), Brian Woods (bass), Heinz Burt (front). "Ritchie was a true perfectionist," said Woods, "but a little moody at times if things were not going his way."

The Wild Ones, pictured backstage at Longleat House, May 1964. L–R: Dave Adams, Ritchie, Ian Broad, Brian Woods. One of the band's earliest gigs backing Heinz, the bill also included The Hollies, The Searchers and headliners Billy J Kramer & The Dakotas.

Lord Caesar Sutch & The Roman Empire in full regalia, boarding the hydra-plane to Denmark (from Germany), early 1967. L–R: Matthew Fisher (organ), Tony Dangerfield (bass), Ritchie, Joel James (sax), Sutch, and Carlo Little (drums). Dangerfield: "Dave decided we'd all get changed into the gear and he'd chase us up and down the gangway." (GEMS/REDFERNS)

Deep Purple, MK I line-up, pictured on the roof of the Dorchester Hotel, London, January 3, 1969. L–R: Rod Evans (vocals), Jon Lord (organ), Ritchie, Nick Simper (bass), Ian Paice (drums). (HULTON-DEUTSCH COLLECTION/CORBIS)

Ritchie with German fiancée (and second wife) Babs Hardie, 1969. Her earnings as an exotic dancer kept him afloat during his time in Hamburg.
(JOHN MINIHAN/STRINGER/GETTY IMAGES)

Deep Purple, MK II (new recruits Ian Gillan and Roger Glover next to Ritchie) pictured with conductor Malcolm Arnold, outside EMI's offices in Manchester Square, London, September 1969, to promote Concerto For Group And Orchestra.
(KEYSTONE/STRINGER/GETTY IMAGES)

"Put a guitar in Ritchie's hand and he's the nicest guy in the world," said producer Derek Lawrence. "Get him in a room and there's nobody else, just you, he's as happy as a sand boy sitting there, with the feeling he doesn't have to say anything. But outside of that he's so unpredictable..." (JORGEN ANGEL/REDFERNS)

"I know that it must have been late in '66 when we put down the backing track and I know that I put the vocals on before Ritchie did his part and by the way, the Diamond Twins, Sonia and Sandra put down backing vocals at the same time as Ritchie put down the guitar parts. I remember this as very shortly before Joe's death so it could very well have been Ritchie's last session. When we first met Dave Watts I was in the Saxons and we had been brought up to London and had been reincarnated as the New Tornados by Joe and Dave was to be our organist. I definitely remember that Dave told us those stories of Ritchie and Mitch Mitchell being solicited by Joe to become another set of Tornados along with Dave and although I could not have been there when it happened I have no reason not to believe that this was true.

"I believe that it would have been a great group but if we look at the situation Joe really only wanted the band to be an extension of himself and was hoping to make another 'Telstar.' We know that not too long after this that Mitch went to Hendrix and Ritchie went to Purple. This to me shows that they were more into what they wanted to do as musicians than just to be a Joe Meek puppet group. Dave ended up joining the Saxons as the New Tornados and I believe that the rift that occurred between Ritchie and Joe was a direct result of this situation. Joe must have had a great liking and admiration for Ritchie. One time Joe said that he would like to get a mad guitarist for the New Tornados. It was most likely that it was Ritchie that Joe had in mind as the mad guitarist but Ritchie I'm sure had higher aspirations and probably wasn't interested. Anyway we still have Ritchie playing on 'No More You And Me' for the New Tornados first vocal A-side. It was either late '66 or maybe very early '67. Unfortunately Joe died before it could have been released, although it did get released about 25 years later on a compilation."

With the situation at RGM becoming less stable, Blackmore rejoined the Savages for a third stint, initially as additional guitarist playing alongside their then current guitar player Johnny Bedder. Just prior to Blackmore rejoining, the group had undertaken a successful Scandinavian tour, as Savages bass player Tony Dangerfield recalls, "We'd just come back from Sweden and the line-up was Johnny Bedder who had worked with me in the Thrills, Carlo [Little], and Tony Marsh on piano. Then [Ritchie] joined the band and Johnny really admired him – he was so in awe that he left! But that was the first gig I did with [Ritchie]."

By December, a new line-up of Blackmore, Little, Dangerfield, along with Matthew Fisher on organ and Joel James on saxophone underwent a name and image change to Lord Caesar Sutch and the Roman Empire.

Their first gig in Fulham was a benefit for the wife of the late Johnny Kidd, who had tragically died in a car crash near Bury that October. Nick Simper, formerly of Buddy Britten & the Regents, had been playing with the Pirates at the time of Kidd's death and was actually in the crash. Simper had always been an admirer of Blackmore's playing. "After Johnny Kidd died and I kept the Pirates on the road for a little while we fetched up on a bill with Sutch in Glasgow and Ritchie had improved no end. When I got to know Carlo, he was definitely Carlo's favourite, he always used to push Ritchie and that's when I first got to know him."

Sutch's continuing desire for ridiculous group images was losing favour with his musicians – particularly Blackmore and Dangerfield. Tony Dangerfield: "We had this photo shoot, Marble Arch in December and it's freezing cold. Dave said, 'I've got a great image coming up' and he opened up the back of this truck and there's all this Roman Empire clothes, togas and stuff and it was all cheap budget stuff, typical Dave. The helmets were all plastic, looked like they'd got a Betterware broom stuck on top. He said, 'Right get changed we've got a photo shoot' and in those days we used to backcomb our hair. Ritchie tried to be inconspicuous and Dave runs off down Oxford Street with the big axe chasing us and Ritchie tries to sneak into a shop doorway. There's Christmas shopping going on and he's standing there freezing in this fucking toga with this silly thing stuck on top of his head and we weren't into dressing up anymore. Dave thought we were going to really love it but that was a funny day. It stopped the traffic in Oxford Street."

Although the image changed the music remained the same, full of Chuck Berry numbers and Sutch's own songs, though the presentation did alter slightly according to Dangerfield. "We used to do an opening set and we didn't break the set like we did in the Savages. It would work out about an hour 15 minutes, hour and a half. We did about 20 minutes before Sutch came on."

Dangerfield and Blackmore had a shared passion for bizarre humour and large breasted women with the pair having regular competitions to see who could pull the bustiest girls. Tony Dangerfield: "We did a gig one night and the dressing room was out in the car park. I pulled this thing that was like slightly cross-eyed, glasses, knock-kneed, looked a bit like Olive Oil with Jordan's tits. And the deal was you had to screw them as well. And I was screwing her across the bonnet of this Ford Anglia on a bank and of course I'd left my handbrake off! Anyway I went back into the dressing room and there was no Ritchie. I'd got this bird with me, Matthew Fisher and Carlo was with us then. I thought 'He won't beat this,' the door opens five minutes later, the silly grin, and this thing that followed him in, it looked like a female Desperate Dan but massive tits and I was like, 'Aaah fuck!'"

At times Blackmore seemed oblivious as to what effect his warped humour had on people. Tony Dangerfield: "We were in Burnley I think and this guy invited us back. A lovely house and he was really being a nice host and I was sitting on the settee with Ritchie and this guy's wife had cooked this glorious apple pie. She was offering it around and they were really being nice to us and Ritchie just threw it up the wall! 'Out, out'."

Although at this point in his career Blackmore was basically an unknown, the prominent British guitarists who were making headlines and having hit records were very aware of him. Tony Dangerfield: "Through working with the Savages, Blackmore had got a hell of a reputation." Despite Sutch's habit of employing the best musicians, his stage act had not developed, still churning out the same madcap show he had been doing for the past six years.

The Savages would often open for one of the newer, hipper groups on the scene. Tony Dangerfield: "We did a gig at Sussex University, Brighton. Being with the Stigwood agency they put us on to support Cream. Ginger and Carlo knew each other and we shared what was a classroom as a dressing room and we pulled all the stops out that night. I'll never forget this, Ritchie walked into the dressing room and Clapton's picking his Les Paul up and Ritchie heard him say, 'Fuck it I don't know why I'm bothering going on.' Ritchie had pulled all the stops out and we got thrown off the next gigs with Cream. They had us off straight away. Ritchie knew that he was better and he proved it. Put his money where his mouth was that night. He never went on about it – 'Should be me kind of thing,' but I remember when Jimi Hendrix came over and we both went 'Fucking hell what's that!' [Ritchie] was knocked out with 'Hey Joe'."

At the beginning of 1967, Sutch and his band were booked for a return tour of the continent. Tony Dangerfield: "We went back to Sweden in January and the line-up then was myself, Ritchie, Carlo, Matt Fisher and an American sax player called Joel James. We went to Germany first and that was eventful. That was where Ritchie and myself gelled because it became commonplace after that, booking hotels, double room, always Ritchie and Tony together. We had to go over on the hydra-plane to Denmark. Dave decided we'd all get changed into the gear and he'd chase us up and down the gangway. The captain got us off and got us in the Customs Shed. The promoter hadn't arrived yet and Ritchie was eating this apple and he suddenly threw it at this customs guy. It hit him on the side of the head and Ritchie just looked the other way with that silly grin and the guy turned straight away and pointed at Matt, who is the most innocent guy in the world and they had us back up the gangplank. They wouldn't let us into the country until the promoter was there. This was in January and we were up and down that gangplank, they wouldn't let us in. Ritchie was responsible for all that."

Despite Sutch's popularity having waned in his homeland, record success on the Continent put the band on a higher level. Tony Dangerfield: "Over there we had the big limo, the business. On that tour I think a record had gone in the charts, 'Purple People Eater' and we were promoting it. The agency and the management that took us over there was from a band called the Hep Stars, two of them went on to Abba. They gave us this roadie called Arne. Half way through the tour he left. Just got out of the car and left. Basically I just stuck my arse out of the window, mooning, going through this Swedish town. I remember Arne saying, 'I have the Walker Brothers, I have Spencer Davis, no trouble, you – trouble all the time!

"Basically every night we'd be getting women in the hotels and to get them in some times ... I remember once Ritchie and I had to get this ladder across this roof to get these girls up and get them into the room. Anyway last night of the tour we were back in Stockholm and Arne has been recommissioned and he said, 'Tonight your last gig, no trouble please and that night Ritchie said, 'We've got all these women, how are we going to get them in?' We just talked to the guy on the desk and he broke the emergency thing to get the key and there must have been 16, 17 women. 'Cause the next morning nobody knows about this, and all these women were coming down the stairs!"

Come the last gig, Sutch was up to his usual stringent financial controls. Tony Dangerfield: "The night we left, Dave knew what was going on and he paid us off for that gig but he paid Ritchie short. This was typical Dave, God bless him. Ritchie said, 'That's not my full gig money, Dave' and he said, 'But you know that AA book you lost about six months ago ...' He used to count every note."

Years later, Sutch spoke proudly of what he felt Blackmore had achieved under his stewardship. "He went off and joined Deep Purple and it took off. When they did the stage shows, they said Ritchie Blackmore was taking over, because he was so visual. He was streets ahead of all the others. They could equal him maybe musically, but not visually, because he had the Screaming Lord Sutch and the Savages training. The others, they were just plain musicians."

As the Roman Empire tour was coming to an end, on February 3, 1967, eight years to the day that Buddy Holly died, dramatic events were unravelling back at Holloway Road. The recent discovery of a rent boy's torso in Suffolk in the infamous 'suitcase' murder had compounded the pressures on Joe Meek. With the police starting a process of questioning known homosexuals, Meek knew it would be only a matter of time before they contacted him and the inevitable adverse publicity was something he greatly feared. Along with all the other pressures weighing down on him and in his undoubted state of anger, fear and confusion Meek shot dead his landlady Violet Shenton after a confrontation before turning the gun on himself.

Tony Dangerfield: "When we came back from that tour, we arrived back the day after Joe had died. I stayed with Ritchie and Margrit for a while after that."

With Blackmore being on the road so much, his relationship with Margrit wasn't exactly the ideal marriage and from the comments she made to Meek biographer John Repsch, she was obviously feeling isolated and lonely. No sooner had Ritchie returned home, he was off again to Germany in April. Meanwhile, with the investigations involving Meek's suicide, Margrit and Jürgen moved to Camberley to live with Ritchie's parents.

Having left Sutch again, along with Dangerfield and Little, Blackmore rejoined Neil Christian in a new line up of the Crusaders that also included Matt Smith on piano. Christian & the Crusaders were booked for a one month tour of Germany, on the back of Christian's big German hit 'Two At A Time.' Neil Christian: "I just got them together to do this short tour with me. I had a record out in Germany and it was doing very well, first week it went to number three, then number one and we were doing all this promotional gear. We were doing some shows in Germany and live TV in Berlin, that's more or less what I can remember. We opened a club in Berlin for teenagers – that was live TV. We did one or two live TV's out there. Did one in Hamburg. Another time after we'd done this TV show we were in this restaurant to watch it on TV, this was a recorded one. We were all sitting down there, we'd had our meal and when it comes to pay for it an argument starts. I look at Ritchie and he starts laughing and Carlo and Tony were arguing over a slice of bread. So I said, 'Look let's not be silly, I'll pay for it.' 'No you fucking well won't!' and a fight suddenly ensued between the pair of them in this restaurant. I rushed out, Ritchie followed me, we got outside and they locked the doors kept them in there: all over a slice of bread. They were the silly things that happened."

After the tour had finished Blackmore and Dangerfield stayed on in Hamburg for a few more weeks of carousing at the Star Club and the Top Ten Club. One of the most popular haunts the British groups frequented was the Blockhütte, where Blackmore met Bärbel Hardie, the woman that would ultimately become his second wife. Neil Christian: "I think he first saw her in the Blockhütte then he found out where she was dancing and they took it from there. She was an 'exotic dancer.' Ritchie went for birds with big tits and she had the most massive pair of melons you'd ever seen! The Blockhütte was Ritchie's favourite hang-out. Just a restaurant bar, all seats – sitting down but if you were with the in-crowd you were there. It was where all the musicians hung out and the artists and all the top strippers in the area, they all used to accumulate there. Hamburg was over my eyes. I hadn't seen anything 'till I got there."

Although having been through one relationship with a busty German blonde, Blackmore's penchant for such women couldn't prevent him from falling for another. Bärbel was one of the top strippers in Hamburg's red light area when Blackmore met her during the Crusaders tour. Affectionately referred to as 'Babs' by all who knew her, Derek Lawrence simply recalls Babs as "big breasted and big hearted." Neil Christian: "We were going into Hamburg, I was going to do a TV show and my car broke down and we're about five miles from Hamburg, there's only me and the roadie Ronnie, plus all the gear in the car and I said to him, 'I don't know what we're going to do but you will have to get into Hamburg and see if you can get hold of someone, come out in the van and tow me in." To cut a long story short Ronnie found Babs and she paid for the guy to come out, tow us in, paid for all the repairs. I said to her 'I'm gonna do the TV but I'll be back' and I went out and did the TV and came back went into the bank and paid her but not many people would have done that. She really was a blinding girl."

Tony Dangerfield remembers the first time he met Babs. "We went out to Germany with Chris and we didn't come back, Ritchie and I stayed in Hamburg. This is when the idea for [Deep] Purple came about. We didn't want to do any more backing work. Ritchie was staying with this girl and I was in the bar with him and he said, 'When she walks in you will know which one she is.' And she walks in and that was Babs. He'd got Margi at home and now he's with Babs. We were there about three or four weeks and Ritchie's mother didn't know where he was. Margi was going to phone him and Ritchie's mum actually phoned my mum and got a number, so he said 'We'd better go back and sort this out and then come back.' We flew back and Ritchie went down to his parents and saw Margi and I was hanging about in London. He said, 'We will meet up in a week or two in The Ship [pub] in Wardour Street' but I never went back."

Dangerfield wanted to go back to being a solo artist and had a deal on the cards with Robert Stigwood. "For four or five weeks afterwards

[Ritchie] was sending me letters [from Germany] asking when am I coming back."

With Babs becoming the new woman in his life Blackmore's relationship with Margrit was to all intents and purposes over and later that year, she and Jürgen returned to Germany, where they both live to this day. However, according to Frank Allen, who later had an affair with Margrit, "She may have moved back to Germany and then returned. At that time she was staying with Ritchie's parents in Camberley where Mrs. Blackmore ran a Spar store, Watletts Stores in the Frimley Road. I believe [Margrit] also helped to run it for a while.'"*

With RGM no longer in operation, Blackmore took on other sessions whenever the opportunity arose. He retained his link with Christian and along with Jimmy Evans, Arvid Andersen and Nicky Hopkins they recorded a couple of tracks for German label Deutsche Vogue. 'My Baby Left Me,' the old Arthur Crudup song popularised by Elvis Presley, was backed with 'Yacketty Yak' a reworking of a number done with Sutch. The German-only single was not released until the following year.

Blackmore's time in Germany lasted approximately a year. As he told Pete Frame, "When The Crusaders split I stayed over in Hamburg and for the next eight months all I did was live off immoral earnings and practise the guitar."†

Ritchie moved in to Babs' flat and while she brought in the money from her nightly work at the strip joints, he stayed at home practising. In the early hours of the morning he would regularly wander down to the Star Club with his faithful Gibson and if he liked the sound of the bands that were playing he would often get up and jam. Scotsman Ricky Munro was a drummer in one of the bands that impressed Ritchie. "He came up and had a jam with the band I was in from Dundee called the Rite Tyme. We were doing a month's stint in the Star Club … We got a shock when he got up."

Blackmore was sufficiently impressed with Munro that he started putting a band together with him. Ricky Munro: "I went back to

---

* Margrit's conversation with John Repsch about Joe Meek is the only time she has given an interview. As of writing she has never spoken to the press about her relationship with Blackmore and when contacted for this book she said that due to a serious accident she was now severely disabled and would only consider talking in exchange for monetary compensation.
† Even to this day Blackmore's official website still quotes him as "living off immoral earnings."

Hamburg and formed Mandrake Root with him. It was his idea I think he was actually looking for musicians. There were a lot of guys that got tried out; he was seriously tying to put together an act. That was what was behind him going up and playing. He asked me, 'Can I come back to Germany?' and I said, 'Yeah give me a couple of weeks.' I went back and he got hold of a drum kit and we started rehearsing and getting a set off. I had nowhere to stay but he wouldn't let me sleep on his floor so I was a little bit … you know."

Among the hordes of Star Club performers, Ritchie recruited a German bass player by the name of Kurt Lungen and it's possible that Graham Waller, who had previously been in the Crusaders, may have been around for a spell on keyboards. Munro remembers the disciplined and authoritarian approach that Blackmore adopted to Mandrake Root from the outset. "Every time I went round there he said, 'This is what I practise every morning like press-ups' and he used to play 'Flight Of The Bumble Bee' note for note. He had raised frets on his guitar and he just slid his finger up and down in the proper manner and it just sounded like separate notes. When Kurt joined us Ritchie demonstrated and said, 'Can you do this?' He held his guitar in a sensual way and did this sort of wiggle. The guy couldn't do it; he'd never tried any of these things before. It was like movements he had and sex was a big thing with him but he was pretty single-minded. I can't actually remember having a laugh with him. I remember laughing at some of his patter. I thought he was a bit obsessed. I suppose he just had it in his head I'm going to make it and start making records or die in the attempt but he was far too accomplished not to do it.

"But he needed the musicians to make his dreams come alive. He spoke a lot about American black blues, he loved that. The numbers we were doing ourselves, the original ones were mainly based on things he had gleaned off these old black blues players. I was pretty sure he was very much influenced by that, a more modern equivalent. One number had to have a drum solo in it. A lot of it was just jamming and he had ideas for songs also and we just followed our noses and the ones that turned out to be quite exciting became a permanent fixture in the set list. We rehearsed at a Youth Centre or a school or something like that."

Having decided to call the band Mandrake Root, one of the first songs they came up with was an instrumental that was given the same name as the band, a tune developed by Blackmore and Munro. Ricky Munro: "I co-wrote the song I invented all the drumming and the accents and he wrote the riff. It was more of an instrumental than a vocal song." Unbeknownst to Munro, Blackmore actually got the riff from a song called 'Lost Soul' a number he had learnt from Carlo Little during his time in the Savages, written by former Savages' guitarist Bill Parkinson.

Despite some intense rehearsing Mandrake Root never got to the point of live work. Ricky Munro: "We didn't get as far as doing a gig. It was mainly original stuff. It was ideas that Blackmore had and that I had and the bass player and the other guys just sort of tagged along. It would be typical to pick on something obscure and touch it up and give it a paint job and claim it as his own. He was very much into that but he was such a good bloody musician that I can't really assassinate his character too much because I really admired him as a guitar player, which is why I went tearing back to Germany thinking great – a decent band playing progressive rock. That's why I was drawn to it so much because everybody had a free hand to ad lib and be progressive. When we started rehearsing we just knew the band was going to be great but unfortunately it didn't happen. The singer that was with us at the time was a Glaswegian guy called Johnny Law but after I left there could have been more personnel."

For decades substances had played a part in the lives of many musicians but by 1967 with the advent of psychedelia the drug culture was far more prevalent. Ricky Munro: "There were an awful lot of drugs about, speed and so on because a lot of people were staying up all night practising and you needed something to keep you awake. Babs would occasionally give me some tablets because the prostitutes and strippers used to take speed." Although most of the pills used at the time as either uppers or downers were invariably legally prescribed, it's unsure if Blackmore needed them or not because as Munro recalls: "He was very much a night person, he would come into the Star Club at about two in the morning and I think he'd just got out of bed, but everything was open all night and there was much more happening musically at night than during the day."

In the Nineties, Blackmore told one interviewer: "It's funny, when you're talking about the so-called drugs period, everyone says, 'Oh, the Sixties.' I still don't recall the Sixties as being any different to any other time. The drugs I never took. Until this day I've never taken cocaine. I want to be the only musician in the world who has not taken cocaine. That's my ambition. Okay, I drink. But LSD, cocaine, all that nonsense, I don't take, and I've never touched it – I was too nervous. I never needed LSD; it's not needed in the way that I think. I would have gone mad. I was lucky for that. I think I have had very stable parents. They did not even drink, and mainly my thoughts against drugs came from my parents."

Despite now living with Babs, Blackmore still had Margrit hanging on back in England, although he never spoke about it to Munro. "I suspected it but I never asked him because I knew he would lose his head." Although he wasn't bringing any money in, Babs' earnings kept him afloat as he told Munro, "she was the highest paid stripper in Hamburg." In the short time that Munro spent with Mandrake Root he saw enough of Blackmore's single-minded attitude to recognise his moods. "If you were of no use to him he wouldn't give you the time of day. I knew that from when I first met him. When he was auditioning for Mandrake Root I noticed how he spoke to the guys that he wasn't interested in and I thought, 'Fuck there's no need to be so horrible.' I thought this guy is definitely mercenary. I'll stick with him and maybe make some money."

The rehearsals continued for a month or two before Munro jacked it in. "I just hung around with [Ritchie] and rehearsed as long as I could and then I made myself quite ill and eventually I had to get my father to send me my fares home so I had to opt out of that, which is a pity because I missed out. He was really just poaching musicians to get his band together. I think he intended coming back to England because he had contacts in England. I think he had something going with some record company but I didn't get that far. That was due to him being unhelpful. If he'd let me sleep on his floor … I don't think he would let me because of Babs and he wanted his privacy and he didn't want any reminder that he was already married. I wasn't interested in that I just wanted a place to crash. All I can say really is that I didn't give him a chance to sack me."

Although Munro recalls Johnny Law as the singer, Matt Smith who had been with Ritchie in the Crusaders is also thought to have auditioned, but after about three months the whole thing folded and Blackmore was back to square one. Former Johnny Kidd & the Pirates bassist Nick Simper was one of the many musicians to cross paths with Blackmore during his year in Hamburg: "When I was working with Billie Davis we had Ged Peck with us who was no slouch, but Carlo was always pushing Ritchie to me. We went over to Germany with Billie and bumped into Ritchie and he was doing nothing at all. Carlo said, 'Why don't Nick and me come over. We'll live in Hamburg for a bit' because [Ritchie] was getting a reputation, just by walking up to the Star Club and sitting in with people and jamming. He could get up and blow everybody away and just walk away like the man in black, like a gunfighter. Carlo talked him into that but the only reason we didn't go was because to get it going I was going to handle the vocals, keep it a three-piece but at the time I got afflicted with this terrible tonsilitis. Even with Billie Davis I was just singing backing harmonies but I would get a sore throat and I couldn't speak for a week so there was no way I could have gone out and done 10 or 15 numbers singing so we abandoned it."

Blackmore was now excited about getting a band together with top class musicians. Nick Simper: "Keyboard player Matt Smith was out there at the time and Ritchie was talking about involving him as well." Meanwhile back in England former Searchers drummer Chris Curtis had made contact with two men who were keen to get into the music industry. John Coletta who ran an advertising agency and Tony Edwards who worked for his family textile business had agreed to put the sufficient finance in place; all Curtis needed to do was find the right musicians. Curtis' first recruit came as a direct result of moving into a flat in Fulham, where several musicians happened to be lodging. Among them was organist Jon Lord, originally from Leicester, who had recently left R 'n' B outfit the Artwoods for a musically less challenging but financially more lucrative gig as part of the Garden, the backing group for the Flowerpot Men, who were popular following their smash hit, 'Let's Go To San Francisco.'

Curtis remembered Blackmore from his days playing in Hamburg with the Searchers and tracked the guitarist down. Blackmore came back to London on the understanding that his return fare would be paid but after meeting Curtis he wasn't happy with what was proposed and quickly returned to Germany. With various telegrams flying back and forth between London and Hamburg, Blackmore decided to check the situation out again. He arrived back in London in the winter of '67 to find that "Nothing happened. I was waiting to join but nothing happened. I was in Hamburg, and had played [on the same bill] with the Searchers in '63, and remained friends with Chris Curtis. When he wanted to put a band together he sent me all these telegrams in Hamburg and called me over. I came over and it was – all very Monty Python – he was very animated and very theatrical, a bit like Hitler! I asked him, 'Who's in the band? What's the deal?' And he would go, 'The best guitarist in the world is you. You're in the band. You'll be playing second guitar.' 'So you'll be playing lead, right? Who will be playing drums?' 'I'll be playing drums.' 'Jon Lord?' 'Jon Lord will be playing organ!' And then he said, 'And I will be playing bass and vocals!' So he was playing lead guitar, drums, bass and vocals! So, when I saw Jon, I said. 'What's going on? Is he a bit [mad]?'

"So, after a while, we were playing together at this little house where Deep Purple started in – Cadogan Gardens, that's it, in South Kensington just off Sloane Street, a short walk from Sloane Square and the King's Road, one of those nondescript areas. But Chris was saying such ridiculous things it was so ludicrous with what he wanted to do. We were gonna be called the Light, initially, and whoever the biggest band was at the time – I think it was Clapton and the Cream – they were going to be opening for us. He was

97

nuts! The second time I went there the house looked like it had actually been hit by a bomb. There was rubble – no more furniture and carpets – just rubble! Someone had gone in with a pneumatic drill and drilled up every-thing. Plaster was down everywhere; then I saw some of the plaster move. It was Chris, who was sleeping on the floor. 'Ah, Ritchie, come on in. The band's great, it's all happening.' He was just full of bullshit.

Somewhat out of the blue Simper remembers meeting Blackmore upon his return to England on December 8, '67. "We had a gig down at the California [Ballroom], Dunstable and I went round to Carlo's house and Ritchie was there and he said, 'I want to come along and hear this keyboard player, I'll come along with you guys so I can hear him play.' According to someone else he was coming along to hear me play. I don't know which is the true story."

After their short time spent backing Billie Davis, Little, Peck and Simper had also taken on the gig backing the Flowerpot Men teaming up in the process with Lord who replaced the line-up's previous keyboard player. However, according to Simper, "The Flowerpot Men didn't like Ged Peck's playing and they wanted him fired and we held auditions but we couldn't find people as good as Ged Peck let alone better. Carlo was always saying we should get Ritchie because we wanted to do our own thing. When we used to go to Germany I'd go out front and sing a couple of numbers and it went down a lot better than the four singers. There was a split, us and them and the Germans liked the heaviness and when the singers came out it would kill the atmosphere. We had this feeling we had something good there and Carlo would say, 'If we had Ritchie with us that could really add that little extra ingredient' and we talked about it all the time. I don't think Jon knew anything about Ritchie other than what we told him. Chris Curtis did because he'd been to the Star Club with the Searchers and knew how good he was."

While staying at Lord's flat, Curtis had told the keyboard player about the maverick guitar player. "He told me he had this fantastic guitarist who lived in Hamburg. I thought he was German," explains Lord, "but Curtis said 'No, he's English but he loves it over there. He wouldn't come back for anyone but me.'" Blackmore recalled how it all started to come together: "Funnily enough it did take off about a week later. I met Jon – thank good-ness we kept each other's numbers – and he asked me: 'What do you feel about Chris?' 'Urm, bit of a strange guy, isn't he?' 'Eccentric? Mad?' 'Fucking mad!' So we got together and thought what are we going to do with him? We had these backers that were going to push the band; and that was when we started to go, 'Maybe we should just get him out.' So we spoke to our backers – Edwards and Coletta. They were excited about the band but thought that Chris, being a name with the Searchers …"

Curtis, who had called his enterprise Roundabout, eventually drifted out of the equation and it looked as if it was all destined to fall flat but Blackmore at least acknowledged Curtis' involvement in setting the wheels in motion. "He's a strange guy, but he's so eccentric, he's a really good bloke. Great guy. I remember him in the good days in the Star in '63. He would be standing up playing the drums, a really forceful character. A genuine rock 'n' roll character. He wasn't a showbiz character; he wasn't manufactured – and I can relate to that. I think he got into drugs and he started to get silly, unfortunately – for he did get everyone together. It was his band. For what it was worth a very important person: without Chris Curtis it would not have happened."[*]

With Edwards and Coletta committed to seeing the project through it was left to Lord to act as the lynchpin to hold everything in place. Having heard Lord and being suitably impressed Blackmore paid him a visit during a cold wintry December evening, as Lord recalled 35 years on. "He appeared at my door in a snowstorm, carrying an acoustic guitar. That night we came up with two of the songs that went on the first album, 'And The Address' and 'Mandrake Root.' It was a wonderful evening. Right away I felt that he wouldn't suffer fools gladly, but it felt right. Ritchie seemed dark, he always seemed dark."

With Blackmore now feeling that the band had potential, he contacted Bobby Woodman for the position of drummer. Woodman had a top reputation, being renowned as the first British drummer to use two bass drums. He was then working abroad, in France, backing French singer Johnny Halliday. For the bass position Blackmore contacted his former band mate Arvid Andersen, who was still living in Italy since the tour with the Trip but because he was enjoying life there, he turned down Blackmore's invitation.

In the meantime Lord approached his fellow band mate Nick Simper about the bass duties. "The first I knew about it was when we went on a tour of Holland with the Flowerpot Men," says Simper. "I always roomed with Carlo and Jon always roomed with Ged and he said, 'I've got a proposition for you. I can't talk about it now but would you room with me when we get to the hotel?' As soon as we got in the hotel room he said, 'Would you be willing to give this up?' We were earning ridiculous money and he

---

[*] Curtis died at his home after a long illness on February 28, 2005.

said, 'Suppose you had the opportunity to do your own thing with just enough money to get by on would you pack it in?' He said, 'I've been offered this proposition and it involves Ritchie Blackmore.' I said, 'It sounds good and who's in the drum chair?' He said, 'Bobby Woodman. We haven't got a singer yet, there's a guy who's been hanging around my flat who we considered, Dave Curtiss.'"

Although Curtiss*, formerly lead singer with his own backing band the Tremors, was considered, it was only in passing. Although they still needed a vocalist, Blackmore, Woodman, Lord and Simper were now ready to start rehearsing and in early 1968, Blackmore and Babs left Hamburg and headed back to England.

* No relation to Chris Curtis.

CHAPTER 5

Shades Of Deep Purple
(1968–69)

Edwards and Coletta's investment was serious enough for Blackmore to fully commit to the situation. Not only had they invested in equipment such as amplification and a Hammond organ, but they also rented an old farmhouse called Deeves Hall in South Mimms, Hertfordshire where the band would live, write and rehearse. Having returned from Germany, and with nowhere to live, Blackmore and Babs moved into Deeves Hall straight away, a week ahead of Lord, Simper and Woodman. Further investment came in the shape of a salesman Ron Hire, and with a third investor on board the three-man management company took their surname initials to form HEC Enterprises. However within the first year, Hire was imprisoned for receiving stolen goods and no doubt to avoid any undesirable publicity, his share was bought out by Edwards and Coletta.

After so many years as a backing musician, Blackmore was now in a situation that he could approach with serious intent. With Deeves Hall fully kitted out with the latest Marshall amplification, and Lord's Hammond organ in place, it was a happy time for all as Simper recalls, "We just breezed in there with all the Marshall equipment. No neighbours, so we could make as much noise as we liked; plenty of space so we didn't have to get in each other's way if we didn't want to. Close enough to town that you could be at the Speakeasy in 25 minutes, I loved it." The first tune the band worked on was the 'Mandrake Root' riff that Blackmore and Ricky Munro had toyed with a few months earlier. Lord had no reason to query its originality but Simper, who was well familiar with the London music scene recognised it immediately. "'Mandrake Root' was written by a guy called Bill Parkinson and it was called 'Lost Soul' originally. He was with Sutch before Ritchie and they used to do that as one of the opening numbers. When Ritchie took over Carlo taught him the melody note for note, sung it to him."

Vanilla Fudge, an American band from Long Island, New York, were the initial inspiration for the band's sound. Lord and Simper had seen the Fudge performing as the opening act on the Flowerpot Men tour the previous year and were blown away by their style, sound and approach, turning songs like the Supremes' 'You Keep Me Hanging On' into full blown musical epics. With the Fudge's heavy organ sound, "It was just something for Purple to latch onto, we had no common theme," explains Simper. "The whole idea of putting Purple together was to get guys together who had good reputations in the business and could deliver but we had no common theme. Bobby Woodman was Carlo Little's idol; he was the first guy to use two bass drums. But his idea was to do more of the same, but the fact that Jon Lord and I had seen the Fudge we knew we wanted to do something new."

With Blackmore being influenced by Hendrix, and also introduced to Vanilla Fudge by Lord and Simper, a common bond was struck. With highly accomplished musicians and equally important, sufficient financial backing, the platform was now set to play music that would showcase the band's musical virtuosity. Their timing was fortuitous for the days of singers and backing groups getting a 10-minute slot on a package tour were being usurped by the likes of Cream, Hendrix and other more 'progressive' groups such as the Nice.

Having spent most of the previous few years merely playing other people's music Blackmore was keen to start developing his own compositions. Nick Simper: "When we first got together it was quite often Ritchie and me in the evenings. We'd sit up … Jon would go to bed or he'd like to watch telly late at night and we just used to kick riffs around. What Ritchie used to do, and he was quite good at, he'd take a Jimi Hendrix riff and play the same notes and just try and change the time signature or the pattern. Exactly the same notes but played differently and hey, we've got a new song! We used to do that quite a lot in the evenings. Jon's real strength was putting an intro to something. He'd pluck a classical thing out and turn it round in the same way that Ritchie was turning round Hendrix riffs and make that his own. We'd say 'That sounds good, dramatic, big chords' and of course Bobby Woodman would just look at us blank. When he said, 'This is circus music' we knew we were on a hiding to nothing with him."

102

Almost from the point that the musicians entered Deeves Hall hordes of singers were being auditioned but of the many hopefuls, none impressed until Rod Evans, a young singer from a Slough based group called the Maze turned up. It was largely due to his suggestion of doing the Beatles' 'Help' in a Vanilla Fudge-styled arrangement that attracted them the most. When auditioning Evans, Blackmore remembered having seen the Maze a year or so earlier and had been impressed with their drummer Ian Paice. The first of many underhand situations occurred when the others secretly auditioned the young drummer, while Woodman went for a night out at the Speakeasy Club.

Despite the new band having no singer at the time, weeks earlier, Edwards and Coletta had pre-booked some studio time at Trident Studios in London for the purpose of recording demos they could hawk around various record companies. With the line-up only just completed in time there was little opportunity to knock a couple of tunes into shape. One number, 'Love Help Me' had already been developed before Evans and Paice joined and the night before the visit to Trident another song was worked out. Both Blackmore and Simper were interested in playing in fourths, something that the Graham Bond Organisation was renowned for. Nick Simper: "We set the pattern right from the start to do a Red Indian sound, and that's how 'Shadows' came about. We just wrote the whole thing sitting in the living room, almost acoustically, a couple of guitars, drumsticks on a cushion and we wrote the whole thing. We just started playing a fourth below to get that Indian sound. Rod was one of those guys who could create a melody out of thin air and write lyrics at the same time. I thought Ritchie was great on that session. I'd always heard him play rock 'n' roll but it was the first time I really heard him develop his own style, especially with the wah-wah. It still sounds good today."

Although Chris Curtis had already drifted out of the situation he suddenly reappeared during this first session with a view to producing it, to which Blackmore commented, "If he's producing it I'm not playing, I'm walking off." Curtis, aware that his presence wasn't appreciated, soon left. Through Lord's contacts the band had already been offered a deal by Decca Records* with Mike Vernon, who was suitably impressed just on the strength of hearing the four of them play. While Edwards and Coletta had financial clout, they had no knowledge of the music business so Blackmore called up his old friend Derek Lawrence. "He phoned me and said, 'We are

---

* Lord's previous group, The Artwoods had been signed to Decca.

putting this band together with these people who know nothing about the music business. You know lots of people, can you help us?' Those were his very words."

Through his numerous contacts in the business, Lawrence secured record deals with EMI in the UK and in America with a new label operating under the laboured name of Tetragrammaton. Lawrence touted around the two demos recorded at Trident. "I took that to Roy Featherstone, I think, at EMI and I was involved a bit with the publishers Feldman, Ben Nesbit, and an American guy Artie Mogul who used to come over here a lot as he was looking after Bob Dylan's publishing. They started Tetragrammaton with Bill Cosby's money. Artie phoned up the band and said, 'I need an act, get that skinny kid the producer who sits on the radio to do something,' which was me. And the deal was done with Deep Purple to sign with Tetragrammaton."

In return for Lawrence getting the band established with recording contracts he was handed the job of producer. Before the band was ready to record Blackmore helped Lawrence out on a session he was producing for Columbia, adding guitar to two Bob Dylan tunes, 'I Shall Be Released' and 'Down In The Flood' performed by Boz (Burrell, who later found fame as bassist with King Crimson & Bad Company).

During the weeks spent rehearsing at Deeves Hall several visitors popped by including Flintstones' vocalist Rod Freeman. Nick Simper: "I remember Rod Freeman came along to teach us 'Hush' and he said that Ian's another Johnny [Mitch] Mitchell. He couldn't play a solo at that time like Bobby Woodman could but the enthusiasm and the attack he had just lifted him above your average two bob drummer, he was something special very quickly so it clicked into place nicely."

By now Blackmore was already a dab hand at practical jokes and he was in his element at Deeves Hall, a reputedly haunted building. Blackmore and Simper indulged in many pranks at the expense of their visitors. Nick Simper: "We had these guys testing for dry rot and they kept chopping holes through walls, tiny test holes, so Ritchie and me used to put black threads through them and tie them to ornaments and cups and things. Someone would come and visit and we would say, 'Have a seat, I'll get you a beer.' We would go out and they would be sitting there. We had a piece of string and there was a rocking chair and a bit of string went through the floor into the cellar. We'd go into the cellar and tug it and people would sit there and see this chair start to rock on it's own! The favourite one was, there was a hole just behind the upright piano and we would stand all these cups on it and with a bit of string we would pull and they would start to slide along the piano. Sometimes they would fall off and smash and people would come running out saying 'You won't believe what has just happened.' We would be dead straight-faced."

Blackmore wasn't content to stop there. Nick Simper: "Ritchie took a little amp up in the servant quarters which faced down to the floor and a lead coming down to his room and he sat in bed with his wah-wah making this noise and you could hear it echo downstairs and frighten people. Of course he went too far in the end. He got an oil drum or something at the top of the stairs with a bit of rope and he tripped that. Bloody thing weighed about half a ton, nearly broke the staircase as it came crashing down. Roddy Freeman stayed one night with his girlfriend. There were loads of spare rooms and we gave him one with a nice hole cut in the wall and Ritchie got a smoke bomb and put it through the hole in the wall. Roddy's girlfriend woke up and shouted, 'The room's on fire' and they ran out starkers. Ritchie and me were crying with laughter. Ritchie would be creeping about in ice blue pyjamas."

Séances were another common occurrence at Deeves Hall. "It was something that all bands did," Simper claimed. "Johnny Kidd, Buddy Britten were all into doing that sort of stuff. I just went along with it, I didn't think anymore or less about it than other people but I was always interested in the subject. You find most musicians are when you're on the road talking about things like that. We had a go in Deeves Hall because it was reputedly haunted. We heard a lot of footsteps and funny sounds and the girl that was living there before us said it was haunted and we didn't believe her. One of her boyfriends who used to live with her had left a few items of furniture and when he came to collect them, he said, 'Have you seen it yet?' He was quite serious. 'Didn't she tell you this place is haunted?'"

Jon Lord claimed he saw a few things at Deeves Hall. The night before the photo session for what would become the cover of the band's debut album, nobody could get to sleep. Lord and Simper shared a room and were kept awake all night by a tapping noise on the window. Lord thought it was a tree branch until they realised there was no tree near the window. Nick Simper: "We heard footsteps once above the ceiling, which was very odd because there were no floorboards up there. How could they be walking across there when there were no boards? That was a bit unnerving but we all kept together most of the time, everybody was a bit frightened by it. I suggested one night we had a bit of a séance there and we all got round the table with a glass doing the Ouija and Rod Evans came running in saying the front door was open, which was strange because we didn't have a key to

105

the front door and it was always locked up. How it got open we never knew."

For Blackmore, who had shown an interest in the occult for the past five years, none of these mysterious happenings seemed out of place. In fact Blackmore displayed little emotion to situations that most people would have regarded as unusual. Nick Simper: "The first inkling I got that he was a bit strange, because he couldn't drive, was on a journey to the local shop. I was the chauffer, plus the only one in the band who had a car. The nearest place was called Shenley Stores and he was always saying, 'Would you run me up to the stores because I've got nothing to eat,' and nobody ever laid too much stuff into the refrigerator in case somebody else nicked it so we used to shop everyday and there was this terrible sharp bend, only room for one motor. As I'm going round this bend I'm sounding the horn and there's a storm brewing up. This little old guy and lady came round the other way in a Ford Anglia and I just hit them head on, there was nothing left of their car. I had a MKII Jag, which just ploughed straight through it and Ritchie never even got out of the car.

"I got out and called an ambulance because I thought this old boy was going to die, his car was totally folded in half and Ritchie just sat there and he said to me, "Is your car as badly damaged as his is?' I said, 'Well why don't you get out and have a bloody look!' He wouldn't move, just sat in the passenger seat. I was doing him a favour; I didn't want to go to Shenley Stores. I had a smashed-in wing and a bent bumper but we drove away. This poor old boy's car had to be towed away on a low loader; he had to be checked out by a doctor. I still carried on to the Shenley Stores and got his grub, not a word of thanks, nothing."

After three months of rehearsals at Deeves Hall the songs had finally come together and it was time to put them to the test in front of a live audience. Through contacts with a Danish promoter thanks to Lord's former band the Artwoods having been popular in Scandinavia, the still-unnamed band travelled to Denmark for their first gigs. The original name of Roundabout that Chris Curtis had come up with was favoured by Tony Edwards. Nick Simper: "It was on the way over that we decided the name was definitely going to be Deep Purple. We were on the boat. It was a big decision because we weren't sure about it. We were a bit embarrassed about the sound of it. Ritchie kept pushing it. I didn't mind the sound of it but it was the fact that it was the Nino Tempo, April Stevens song. I thought it was the opposite of what we were all about: dirty rock'n'roll, hard rock and if people start to identify us with some old pop song from years ago ... But everything we came up with someone had already got it and in the end out

106

of desperation, the management are still pushing us … telling the guy in Denmark we are called Roundabout. We're billed as Roundabout, and we're saying, 'We ain't Roundabout.'

"We're on the boat and we get talking to this guy – Ritchie and me and this journalist and Ritchie's giving him all the bullshit. 'Who are your biggest influences?' And he's going 'The Ted Babbage Folk Four and the Wally Thud Trio' and all this crap and the bloke is actually writing it down, 'Wally Thud, how do you spell that?" And Ritchie, dead straight face, 'T, H…' and then he said, 'What is the name of your band?' It was all a bit vague and I looked at Ritchie and he looked at me and said 'Deep Purple' and that was it. We decided there and then and Ritchie always wanted it. It was a good choice, when you saw it up in lights or in the charts."

Lord explained how the band had wrestled with numerous names beforehand. "We had a list on the wall at Deeves Hall. It was very nearly Orpheus. Concrete God we thought was a bit radical. Sugarlump was on there. One morning Deep Purple was on it. After intense interrogation it turned out that Ritchie had put it up. The reason was that it was his grand-mother's favourite song." However, as Blackmore said, "It was a song my grandmother used to play on the piano. I once saw it in print that it was the last song she ever played – but I don't think it was. She just tinkered around on the piano – but she used to play 'Deep Purple'."

The band received a rude shock when arriving in Denmark as their roadie Ian Hansford recalls, "I remember getting off the boat and they all had to get in the back of a police van, something to do with no permits. Dave Jacobson and I were the roadies and we were in our van so it didn't matter and they were all bundled in the back of this van and taken to some custom offices. I remember Jon Lord saying, 'I'm not getting in the back of that Land Rover with Alsatians!'"

The event certainly left a lasting impression on Ian Paice: "You needed a work permit and ours wasn't quite in order. We were taken from the docks to the police station in the back of a police dog van, behind the wire grill, which was a very auspicious start. When I got out, I was smelling somewhat canine."

With their permits eventually sorted out the band only got to the hotel about 5 o'clock, the evening of the first gig. Nick Simper: "Ritchie was very, very nervous, because we'd just got the act together and we used to practise in front of the mirrors, all the gyrating with the guitars like they did with the Savages, and we said it would be great if we could do it in unison, knee tremblers and playing the guitar at the same time. It wasn't easy to do and even on the boat Ritchie was suddenly getting into a bit of a panic,

'What are the chords to 'Hush,' what's the intro?' He always used to forget intros in a blind panic. You'd think he'd be all relaxed and all of a sudden it would go right out of his head and suddenly he'd think 'Christ if we're on stage and my mind is blank.' He used to get that all the time. We always used to have a couple of scotches before we went on. But he was fine, it was exciting."

The fledgling Deep Purple performed its first gig before a crowd of about 500 at the Park School in the district of Vestpoppen in Tastrup, Denmark, on April 20 1968. Nick Simper: "The curtains opened the first night; it was like a school hall but it was packed out. Obviously the pro-moter had done his work because we were nobody but he'd sold the whole thing on ex-Flowerpot Men, ex-Artwoods and we just went really over the top, completely went crazy with all the movements and the music went completely down the tube, we were hitting bum notes all over the place because we wanted to look outrageous. We wanted to go out there and just hit people right in the face but the overall impression was these guys don't take any prisoners." The amount of equipment they had squeezed onto the tiny stage prompted one reviewer to describe it as looking like "something out of a science fiction story."

The 45 minute set opened with the band's own instrumental 'And The Address' but the rest of the set relied largely on covers and followed the Vanilla Fudge influence of re-arranging a combination of familiar and less well-known songs: 'Hush', 'I'm So Glad' – an old Skip James blues that was a logical choice as Rod Evans and Ian Paice had recorded the song with their previous band and Cream also played it in concert, the Beatles' 'Help' and the Rolling Stones' 'Paint It Black,' also recently rearranged by Eric Burdon & the Animals. With Blackmore's growing admiration for Jimi Hendrix, 'Hey Joe' was the band's closing number. The only other self-penned song was 'Mandrake Root,' which would soon develop into the closing number in the band's set and remained that way for the next three years. It was also the perfect platform for Blackmore and Lord to extempo-rise with lengthy solos. Nick Simper: "It was loud and raucous and the feeling we had afterwards, we just knew after that first gig we'd got some-thing through the crowd reaction." The maximum volume left another reviewer saying: "The sound wave that penetrated the stage curtain as the band took the stage helped to confirm my association with rockets. An infernal noise ripping your ears into bloody pieces." With the promotion based largely on Lord's reputation, he was seen as the band's leader and also due to his grammar school education became spokesman for the band. He defended the use of excessive volume by saying, "I know we're loud on stage but you need to be to reach the youth of today. We're not just loud for the sake of being loud, you just have to make sure the people don't think they're at a tea party, because then they'll lose interest."

Following the first gig and despite concentrating on the visuals at the cost of bum notes, it didn't take long before Blackmore started to do more than just gyrate around the stage. Nick Simper: "Ritchie was spurred on to greater tricks then. He would take his guitar off and the Gibson would feedback like there was no tomorrow. His favourite trick was to hold the Bigsby patent tremolo arm and let the weight of the guitar swing. Once or twice he ended up holding the Bigsby and the guitar was on the floor. The screws would just rip out of the bodywork. That's why he got himself an old Telecaster and proceeded to try and smash it to pieces. He couldn't damage it; it was indestructible, quite funny. We wanted to put on a show and we did."

"There was an element of show in the way we put the band together," according to Lord. "When we first started playing live I was astonished at Ritchie's antics. He was marvellous, very balletic. Ritchie was very much a showman. He'd come out of the mid Sixties thing, the guitar behind the head, like Joe Brown."

On their return from Denmark, Deep Purple immediately went into Pye's studios at Marble Arch and over one May weekend they rattled out an entire album while Lawrence spent the Monday mixing it down. The fact that it presented no problem for them to make an album in such a short time was testimony to the abilities of the musicians involved, coupled with the fact that the material had been rehearsed for three months and knocked into shape during the Danish tour.

Nick Simper: "When we did the first sessions at the Pye Studio all we were told was you've only got if for two days but we'd come up from doing an A and B side in four hours. That's what it was like in those days so we were used to delivering. In those days you had to do it from beginning to end but we were all well practised at going into the studio and delivering our parts and getting it right first time. And nearly everything was first take on that first album. We hardly made any mistakes. We would put a track down and Derek would say, 'Maybe you could do it better boys' and we'd do it again and you'd have an alternative but then maybe the first one was the best. But we hardly ever blew it and had to start again. Usually we would do it without even a vocal guideline. You played it as live and we just knew the song. If you weren't quite sure you would write it down or Jon would score it out for you. He put the tablature down on a sheet of music paper and you knew exactly what you were doing and you'd have it on a music stand just to remind yourself. We'd all do that but basically you knew the song and where the singer was supposed to be singing. You learnt the song from beginning to end. It was basically our live show, we'd been over to Denmark and as soon as we came back they said, 'You're in the studio.' 'What are we going to do?' 'Do what you did in Denmark.' So we did. We left a few of them out, we did the ones we liked best and did nearly everything first take in 18 hours."

Working in such a quick way suited Blackmore though being something of a perfectionist he would sometimes want another stab at a solo but with so little time on offer, invariably he was overruled by Lawrence. While some critics have felt that Blackmore's work on the album was poor compared to what would follow, Lawrence begs to differ: "Ritchie always played some good solos. I mean he played ... you know, if anyone doesn't think a classic Ritchie solo is not on 'And The Address' then you know, hey! I mean somewhere there was a take that we did and no one has ever found the take, Ritchie played a Hendrix kind of thing, went into a Jeff Beck kind of thing, taking the piss ... not taking the piss, kind of admiration, respect. No idea where that is."

No band member had much in the way of composing experience and writing their own material was something of a struggle. They were all more than happy to do covers and if Ritchie wasn't coming across as well as he was capable of, again Lawrence has a theory: "A lot of the songs on the first album were covers, you're limited, you really have to keep the melody going whereas Ritchie's solos got into where the solo could melodically take off."

Once representatives from Tetragrammaton had heard the album they wanted it released as soon as possible. 'Hush' was picked to be released as a single, both in America and Britain. In June, EMI released the single on Parlophone and reviews were positive. *Record Mirror* commented that Deep Purple was a "highly talented group with percussive effects and a pounding rhythm – they are worth commending and this one could even be a first time biggie for them." The same paper even went as far as to say that it deserved to be a hit, and that the band were all proficient darts players!

Meanwhile Lawrence helped set up the first of what would be many BBC radio sessions over the next couple of years. "Because I was involved with the publishers and the record company and everything we worked out if you wanted the records played – if you did live sessions you had a chance of getting them on the play list so if a successful producer turns up at Deeves Hall and goes in and sees them and says, 'Oh, Deep Purple will do a session.'

The first Deep Purple radio session was done on June 18 at the BBC's Studio 1 in Piccadilly where the band taped three numbers; 'Hush', 'One

More Rainy Day' and 'Help' from the recently recorded album. As Simper remembers, the band got off on the wrong foot with the BBC staff from the start. "A lot of those producers just looked at us as long-haired kids coming in and most of them were middle-aged blokes, they'd be sitting there eating their sandwiches, reading the paper and the engineer would do all the work. They didn't have faders, they had these bloody great knobs big as your fist, it was almost like wearing white coats it was so antiquated. I said to this Don George could we just hear that back to see if we are in tune, 'I've put the tapes away now' and he was like insulted that I'd even asked him. We had the same with the John Peel show, Bernie Andrews. Most of them were done in one take. We used to pick whatever was needed." Although the BBC used their own engineers and producers Purple also brought Lawrence with them who had some input in a supervisory role. "I sat with the BBC engineer and said 'Bring that down, pull that up, that's the wrong sound for that.'"

With a single out and the first album imminent, a few selected gigs were done in England during the summer of '68, the first being in the upstairs function room of The Red Lion in Warrington. Roadie and Warrington native Ian Hansford arranged the gig. "We hadn't had a gig for ages and they asked me, 'Do you know anywhere to play?' I said the only place I know is my hometown so I phoned Bill Medland up who was the owner of the Lion Hotel and said any chance of a gig and he said 'Yeah.' Nick Simper: "We said 'We are a new band and we'll do it for nothing as long as we get our expenses but we must be top of the bill' and he agreed and said, 'I'll pay your gas, put you up for the night and give you a meal.'"

Once again the band went totally over the top by playing twice as loud as the other bands. Ian Hansford: "They got taken off, he cut them short because basically The Lion was dance music, Northern Soul and that didn't go down too well. Ritchie was trying to be flash with his guitar and going up and down the frets with a cymbal and then threw the cymbal on the floor and cut right through the PA leads, I do remember that!"

From the outset Blackmore was hell bent on presenting a visual performance, remembering all the tricks he had learnt from his days with Sutch and embellishing them with new visuals. Nick Simper: "We went down to Ramsgate, one of the very first gigs we did in England and [Ritchie] used to run across the stage dragging this thing with the pick-ups down across the edge of the stage getting this horrible raucous noise and bang it like a cricket bat. I remember one night there was a big pipe that ran across the ceiling and there was about an inch between that and the ceiling and he grabbed the guitar like a javelin and hurled it. The neck just forced itself in and stayed there. The bloody thing was quivering! No matter what he did to it, it just didn't seem to damage it, it still played."

Included among these first English shows was a performance at London's Roundhouse with the Rolling Stones' Mick Jagger in the audience checking out the new hopefuls. After the gig Coletta went backstage to give the band the bad news that had filtered back: Jagger was unimpressed with what he heard. Blackmore and Simper looked at one another and almost in unison replied, "It's the day he says he is impressed is when we need to be concerned."

Although Simper was the only member who owned a car, because the management wouldn't agree to his requests of paying for the running costs, HEC invested in a second hand Jaguar 420G for the band to travel around in. Nick Simper: "I used to drive to all the gigs in that and they'd be snoring away on the way back and not one person ever said thanks for getting us home safely. Ritchie would say, 'I'd like to go and see my mum and dad. I'd like to go down on Sunday.' They had a shop in Frimley, The Frimley Stores. Ritchie and Bärbel would sit in the back of the car like royalty. They did tend to treat people like skivvies a bit. One day when I picked him up he said, 'You're always smiling at me, it annoys me.' 'Have you ever thought I'm smiling because I'm pleased to see you?' Very strange."

The dark, brooding image that Blackmore cultivated throughout the next few years wasn't an act but very much a part of his character. Hansford recalls his initial impressions of 'the Man In Black' as "quite depressing at times." A bit later Hansford would often drive Blackmore to UK gigs, journeys where the roadie would have to endure the guitarist's pessimistic ramblings. "All the way up the motorway he would be going, 'I hate this bloody gig – the dressing room is this and that, and the stage is this and that' and when we got there it would be a completely different venue he was thinking of. Then he would be over the moon and I would be depressed as hell because I'd had this GBH in the ear all the way there."

Even though the early days of the band saw Blackmore as a far less dominant character than the one that would eventually emerge, Hansford's recollections from the very beginning were that, "if he didn't want to do anything he wouldn't do it. He wouldn't even consider the band, 'I'm not doing it.' As simple as that: Very selfish."

As far as musicianship was concerned Deep Purple were streets ahead of most other bands but establishing a name in their homeland was proving difficult – a situation the band blamed on poor publicity and inexperienced management. Nick Simper: "Coletta and Edwards are paying some guy 50 pounds a week, which was a lot of money then, to be our press guy. He did nothing at all. He was just a freeloader. Jon and me told them we knew this guy Keith Goodwin, he's got a proven track record he's handled big stars, Dusty Springfield and he's been in the game for 20 years, he's also an ex-musician, he knows the ropes. So they said, 'OK perhaps we should get him' so Jon and me went to see him. Meanwhile they've hired this other berk behind our backs. So we're getting no press. Even when we're creating riots in Europe there's not the slightest sniff in this country. You switch on the radio and all you are getting is Ten Years After and how great they are. Not that we had anything against Ten Years After but all you heard was 'Alvin Lee, fastest guitarist in the West.' Ritchie used to seethe – 'Fuck that, I'd blow him away with a broken arm' and took it quite personally that they were flavour of the month and we just couldn't seem to break through in our own back yard."

To try and establish Purple in Britain the band were added to the bill of the Eighth National Jazz Pop Ballads & Blues Festival at Kempton Racecourse in Sunbury.[*] Deep Purple had the opening spot on the Saturday, headlined by the Crazy World Of Arthur Brown and also including the Nice, the Jeff Beck Group and, ironically, Ten Years After. Purple's opening spot was largely ignored and Simper recalls that Chris Welch's review in *Melody Maker* didn't even mention them. "Joe Cocker came on after us. [Welch] never even acknowledged we were there. We sounded pretty dire, it did us more harm than good." As the band prepared to go on, an incident not too dissimilar to the one with Bert Weedon several years earlier occurred. Nick Simper: "Alvin Lee walked out dressed like Clint Eastwood with this poncho. Ritchie and me are farting around with the amps trying to get a sound and Alvin walked out and all the crowd knew who he was and roared. Alvin plugged in and did his greatest run and Ritchie sort of looked at him. I don't think he realised. Then Ritchie switched his guitar on and did the most blinding exercise you've ever seen and said, 'All right Alvin' and he just kind of skulked off. The crowd thought who was this guy? They didn't know who he was, he didn't get a big roar or anything. Once Ritchie got *that* attitude he was the king of the stage. He had the power there to have the crowd eating out of his hands. I think Jon felt a bit upstaged when that happened."

Even if the band didn't find favour with the critics others felt that even at this early stage Deep Purple was an impressive live act. Roger Drew, who

---

[*] Also known as the Sunbury Blues Festival.

had seen Blackmore three years earlier with Sutch in Dunstable recalls catching Purple at Sunbury by accident: "Top of the bill was the Crazy World Of Arthur Brown supported by many other bands that I have long since forgotten – except one. Apart from the main stage there were various marquees set around the site where the lesser-known bands were playing. I wandered into one as the next band was setting up, and immediately recognised the ace guitarist from that night in Dunstable. I figured that they would be worth a look so I hung around. One of my better decisions! I believe this was one of the earliest Deep Purple gigs; it may have been the first. I can't remember the details of the set but I do remember that they were sensational and I became an instant fan and have followed Ritchie's career ever since."

Elsewhere Purple attracted a more upbeat response, including a gig in Switzerland. Nick Simper: "We got asked to do a gig at the last minute. The Small Faces were on it and Dave Dee, Dozy, Beaky, Mick and Tich, and we were the unknowns, the also-rans. We caused a riot that night and smashed the place up. Dave Dee got all the publicity. It was actually in the *Melody Maker* but it was us that did it but we had such a useless press guy. It was us that got them all smashing the place up."

Having spent the previous few months in various temporary homes such as a hotel in Balcombe and another near London's Paddington Station, the management rented 13 Second Avenue in Acton, West London as a permanent base for the entire band. Living under the same roof as Blackmore, Hansford's strongest memory is of his devotion to his instrument. "He was just playing guitar all day long. Not even with an amp, just practising all day long." The modest three bedroom house had a downstairs room converted for sleeping and a large communal living room upstairs. Lord and Simper shared one room, Evans and Paice another, the two roadies took the front room while Blackmore and Babs occupied the upstairs bedroom. For the others, sharing a house wasn't a problem but the presence of Babs in such an enclosed environment wasn't ideal. While she was viewed by some as "a pain in the backside," as Hansford explains, "to be fair to her, it was all for Ritchie. She was a bit of a bossy boots but in a nice way." When Babs wasn't interfering the pair would sometimes partake in séances and when Ritchie felt the need for some exercise he would go running with Hansford. "Ritchie and I used to go jogging at night. I remember one night we had a police car following us all along the back streets and we just disappeared into the house but they followed us around one night."

EMI were curiously slow to release the album but by July Tetragrammaton had the first Deep Purple album in American stores. The record company may have been new and inexperienced but they put all their weight behind pushing Deep Purple and within days *Shades Of Deep Purple* had sold 30,000 copies. Although the band's preference was to see 'Help' pulled as the single, Tetragrammaton's overruling decision was to pay dividends. On the face of it the four and a half minute, turbo-charged cover of Joe South's 'Hush' was a brave choice but the days of radio stations ignoring any song over three minutes had been kicked into touch three years earlier with Bob Dylan's six minute 'Like A Rolling Stone' and by '68 audiences were far more receptive to lengthier tunes.* 'Hush' was soon a popular choice on the play list of West Coast stations and within the first four weeks of release, it sold a staggering 600,000 copies and was sitting at number 13 in the *Billboard* Hot 100. Despite the lack of attention in Britain, all the years of dues paying was suddenly and unexpectedly paying off. One US radio station reportedly played a track from the album every 15 minutes, while another was playing the single every hour on the hour – not bad going for a British cover version of a contemporary American song. 'Hush' eventually peaked at number four with sales exceeding well over a million. Ironically, while all attention was focused on promoting Deep Purple in the States, back in England EMI still hadn't set a release date for the album.

If EMI was slow on the uptake, Tetragrammaton was very much a driving force as Jon Lord explained at the time: "They gave us a big build up in America – but none of us expected this sort of success. The Tetra people sent over an advance of a quarter of a million dollars a few weeks ago for us to live on and use to record another album. They want to release it when we go over to America in October."

With the advance in the bag, De Lane Lea Studios in Holborn was booked for a couple of weeks in August, again with Lawrence producing. Although the band had significantly more time to record, because composing was still something that didn't come easily, roughly half the album would follow the same formula of arrangements of other artistes' songs. Blackmore was more than happy to go along with this course and one of the covers, a Neil Diamond song was a surprising but inspired choice as Simper remembers. "By the second album 'Lord Jon' is established as the leader of the band and the main musical force and Ritchie hadn't surfaced at that time as a bolshy guy who would have his own way, so he tended to

---

* That summer alone Richard Harris' six minute 'Macarthur Park and the Beatles' seven minute 'Hey Jude' tested radio formats and both became massive hits.

go with the flow. Jon wanted to do 'Kentucky Woman.' I said why don't we do it how Mitch Ryder would do it. It worked out all right."

Derek Lawrence: "In those early years it was all so exciting. You've got to remember they weren't multi-millionaires with multi-million egos. They were all doing something they loved and it was better than working for a living." Despite the band having more time on offer in which to record, they weren't given the opportunity of pre-production to work on song ideas so most of the material was written in the studio under pressure. Of the covers, another Beatles' number 'We Can Work It Out' was successfully revamped whereas Ike & Tina Turner's 'River Deep, Mountain High' was given a complete makeover and turned into a 10 minute extravaganza with Lord coming up with the idea of adding Richard Strauss' 'Also Sprach Zarathustra' as a lengthy intro. With Lord's classical upbringing and the rest of the band failing to come up with sufficient ideas, Lord incorporated classical themes elsewhere on the recordings and the ballad 'Anthem' was even given a full string quartet middle section. The album's stand out number and another that would become a huge part of Purple's stage set was the instrumental 'Wring That Neck' written in the main by Blackmore and Simper with Lord adding the E flat run. It was the first song giving an inkling of what Blackmore was capable of even though he admitted years later that it wasn't entirely original. "I'd heard a violin piece that was similar and that was where I got that idea from."

Even though Blackmore was now in a band with a full workload, he still found time to fit in session work. Lawrence had landed the job of producing the second single[*] for fresh-faced pop duo Anan whose first release earlier that year had bombed. Blackmore and his Purple colleagues were roped in more as a favour than for any necessity. Around the same time Lawrence also got Blackmore to work for another duo, Sun Dragon, who had reached number 50 for one week only with a cover of the Lemon Pipers 'Green Tambourine'.[†] For Lawrence working on sessions with Blackmore was a pleasurable experience: "Put a guitar in Ritchie's hand and he's the nicest guy in the world. Get him in a room and there's nobody else, just you, he's as happy as a sand boy sitting there, with the feeling he doesn't have to say anything. But outside of that he's so unpredictable it's a joke but in the studio he was a dream to work with apart from, you would do a take

---

[*] 'Madena' / 'Standing Still', released on Pye Records.
[†] Lawrence recorded an entire album named after the single with Blackmore's contribution on four tracks.

116

and he'd go and do it 15 times and you still go back and use his first one all the time."

On October 15 Deep Purple arrived in sunny California for their first US gigs booked as high-profile support to Cream, who were undertaking their farewell American tour. The plan had initially been for Purple to do the full 20-date tour starting on October 4 which would have netted them a handsome £80,000. However Purple didn't join the tour until the first of two nights at the LA Forum on the 18th. The night before their first gig the band appeared on *The Dating Game* TV show, adding to their already growing popularity.

Through his involvement with the Yardbirds, John Mayall's Bluesbreakers and now Cream, Eric Clapton had built up a reputation as one of, if not *the* top guitarist in Britain. It wasn't a view that Blackmore or indeed many of the other musicians on the scene necessarily agreed with. Nick Simper: "I have to agree with Ritchie when he said you can go in most pubs and see someone just as good." Clapton had already experienced sharing a bill with Blackmore when Sutch played with Cream in Brighton in late '66. Now he had to face the experience all over again. Whether or not Blackmore's presence had any affect on their attitude is unclear but Simper recalls how unfriendly the headliners were to their support band. "I thought it was a bit strange, we got to the Forum and we expected them to come up to us and say, 'How are you going?' We'd bumped into them on the road before and you've got two English bands on, 6,000 miles from home. Wouldn't it be normal just to walk in the dressing room and say 'Do you want a beer?' But no they kept well away from us. I can understand Eric Clapton not being too pleased. He must have known of Ritchie's reputation – not going to look too special following this bloke.

"I don't think the other two had any problems. The crowd were there to see them. We went out and gave it our best shot and by the third night we were on equal billing. Apparently I heard Ginger [Baker] was incensed saying, 'You can't put their name the same size as ours it's not right, we're top of the bill' and we didn't do any more after that. I remember we went down to Rodeo Drive where they had all the posh shops and a guy came in the shop and said, 'Congratulations, guys. I saw you blow Cream away last night.' I can't pretend that we didn't feel good when he said that. But we never saw anything of them."

Tetragrammaton recorded Deep Purple's performance at the first Forum show and the aural evidence suggests that Blackmore was quite subdued for the first few numbers. Lord dominated proceedings on 'Hush' and

'Mandrake Root' with Blackmore more interested in presenting a visual image on the latter. However the instrumental 'Wring That Neck' saw Blackmore pulling out the stops and throwing in a snatch of 'Jingle Bells' at the end. It was probably such antics that Cream took a dislike to but the audience responded positively which was of far greater importance. From herein Blackmore's playing seemed more self-assured and at the end of their set Purple received a rapturous response.

Even though Blackmore wasn't over enamoured with Clapton, Jimi Hendrix was a major inspiration to him. Hendrix showed up for the second night at the Forum and after the show the band was invited to a party. "That was the house where Sharon Tate got murdered as well," says Hansford. According to Simper, Hendrix was certainly impressed by the guitarist from Heston. "Hendrix admired Ritchie greatly – he told me. With [Mitch] Mitchell being a friend of mine we met at this club in New York. Hendrix came in later on and he came up to me. We were the only band to do two numbers on the *Merv Griffin* show. You only got one slot but obviously Bill Cosby pulled some strings and we got two songs on it, which was good because Ritchie forgot the intro to one of them and completely hit the wrong chords, came in totally wrong, live television as well. It's understandable if you've got half an hour before your next spot in the dressing room and complimentary beers going round, you won't be in great shape when you go out for the next bit. But Hendrix came up to me about a week later and said, 'I saw you on the *Merv Griffin* show, great band, love it. That guitarist of yours is something special'."

Cream were unhappy enough with the response Deep Purple received to get them removed from the tour but with the success of 'Hush' and further TV appearances, including a memorable guest spot on Hugh Hefner's *Playboy After Dark*,[*] interest in Deep Purple was sufficiently high that smaller headlining gigs were booked as replacements. Such was the demand that the band's touring schedule was extended to last a full three months.

By headlining smaller gigs the band was able to present a lengthier show and for Blackmore, the opportunity to showcase his ability for improvisation at last had a platform. Nick Simper: "I remember once Ritchie doing 'Wring That Neck' and going into his solo and he got to the bit where he was really doing some clever picking and some guy just bellowed out, 'You suck.' Ritchie's totally un-phased; he just starts getting faster and faster and

---

[*] Performing 'And The Address' and 'Hush' along with a hilarious 'straight' interview with Jon Lord by Hugh Hefner surrounded by a gaggle of his harem.

in the end the crowd just roared. You could tell he was thinking 'Who sucks now?' On a good night it would go on for ages."

Even if Deep Purple wasn't always winning the crowds over with their musicianship, Blackmore's experience learnt at the hands of Screaming Lord Sutch gave him plenty of options to fall back on. One night in Los Angeles, ironically with Sutch watching in the wings, Purple were getting no reaction at all from the crowd of predominantly college kids. Blackmore decided to spice things up by spearing a big hole in the ceiling and pulling the tiles out, leaving a massive, gaping hole. The more he smashed it, the more the crowd loved it.

Deep Purple's potential had yet to be realised in Britain although some within the business had already taken notice of them, including the Beatles who apparently rated the group's interpretation of 'Help' as being among the best cover versions (to date) of their songs. Such accolades were of little consequence to Blackmore, whose own talents were still being largely ignored. With the exception of Hendrix and Jeff Beck, alongside the lesser known but as equally talented Big Jim Sullivan and Albert Lee whom Blackmore highly respected, he couldn't come to terms with the media's enthusiasm for other guitarists who were at the forefront. With the music scene rapidly changing, a host of bands such as Pink Floyd, the Nice, Ten Years After and Jethro Tull were breaking down commercial barriers, and at the same time, gaining a greater degree of media coverage than Deep Purple.

Despite 'Hush' being a huge hit in America, EMI seemed generally unconcerned with promoting the band in Europe. "We did hear a rumour that someone was fired," says Simper. "Apparently someone said, 'Drop everything and just push the new Beatles' thing'."* Although 'Hush' was re-released by EMI in September at the same time *Shades Of Deep Purple* received its UK release, the promotion was still poor. Nick Simper: "People couldn't get our single. I was going in the shops myself just saying, 'Have you got 'Hush' by this new band Deep Purple.' 'We've got that by Kris Ife or we can get it you by Joe South.' 'What about Deep Purple?' 'We don't know that one.' It was pathetic they didn't have a clue. We had this big launch in Mayfair with Sir Joseph Lockwood looking at us as if we were bits of shit. The Tetragrammaton guy was saying these guys are going to be big,

---

* If Simper's statement is true, EMI would have been putting their efforts behind 'Hey Jude', the Beatles first single on their newly-formed Apple label.

they're going to be worldwide, and there's us in all our fancy clothes and big haircuts and Sir Joseph Lockwood was like, 'Have I really got to be here?' You could just feel it. They were an old man's record company. Edwards and Coletta sold us to them for next to nothing, peanuts, no promotion, bugger all."

Tetragrammaton rush released the second Deep Purple album *The Book Of Taliesyn* during the US tour and 'Kentucky Woman' proved to be another successful single release. Nick Simper: "It was a mega single, a huge hit in America. It got so much airtime, especially in Kentucky and it was a good stage number – gave Ritchie a chance to shine." The band spent the rest of 1968 in America touring from California to Kentucky, Washington to Michigan and even venturing in to Canada as demand for the band continued. Tetragrammaton tried to milk Deep Purple's current popularity for all it was worth and without the band's consent, released a third single, a heavily edited version of 'River Deep, Mountain High.'

Nick Simper: "Nobody was fighting our side at all. Edwards and Coletta were useless. They should have said no, you give our boys some time, let them go back and get their heads together and try and create some stuff. It was like you were just machines."

Deep Purple's first American tour concluded with a spate of gigs in New York at the Electric Circus, and prior to that a brace of shows at the more prestigious Fillmore East. Although 'Hush' had been a huge hit, some critics had initially seen the band as a manufactured teenybopper group, due to their sudden emergence on the scene with seemingly no pedigree. One reviewer of the Fillmore gigs went along expecting an average group performing at a lower standard than on their records but was pleasantly surprised and impressed with what he heard. Jon Lord told the press how, prior to playing the Fillmore, "everyone was telling us how really important it was to do well there. 'If you bomb out at the Fillmore,' they said, 'you're dead.' But we found this attitude a bit annoying so up we went on stage feeling slightly aggressive and tried hard not to care how important the whole thing was supposed to be. We weren't going to let ourselves be cowed by the awesome majority of the Fillmore audience. The ice was broken when Ritchie went to the front of the stage and played a very simple but fast run on his guitar – a sort of note progression that he normally uses when he's just practising. But it sounded really freaky and the audience loved it. From then on they were on our side." This somewhat arrogant attitude that the band displayed became an integral part of Deep Purple's live performances.

Despite having just completed an arduous three-month tour, Edwards and Coletta were already making plans for a return visit. Before the band flew home the pair got the band into a New York studio in an attempt to make another single. Instead of being given the opportunity to take some time out to try and create, re-group and rethink, the band tried working up another Neil Diamond song, 'Glory Road' but with little success. Nick Simper: "The Neil Diamond song was very difficult and we couldn't make it work. I know the Everly Brothers attempted it and they couldn't do it either. It was one of those songs that every time we thought we knew it and went to play it, it went wrong." Due to their involvement with Artie Mogul and his own connections with Bob Dylan, they also tried a recently written but at the time unrecorded Dylan song 'Lay Lady Lay' but it went no further than the one studio session. Dylan had written the song for the film *Midnight Cowboy* but because it wasn't completed in time Harry Nilsson's 'Everybody's Talkin'' was used instead. In fact Dylan didn't actually record it until a couple of months after Purple had toyed with it and had they per-severed with the song, the band may well have scored a coup.

At the time, Blackmore seemed happy for the band to work on covers and just went with the flow. Nick Simper: "He never came into the band throwing his weight about he seemed quite regular. He also seemed rela-tively unconcerned with the financial elements and although he was happy being in a band with some solidity behind it he appeared to have little in the way of ambition. He said, 'I've got one ambition, if I get a house like my mum and dad's out of this business, I'll be very happy.' They just lived in a little semi. He wasn't into spending vast amounts. If there were ever any questions to ask he would always put it to me, as if he was sort of nervous. Like the first accounting meeting, he said I want to know precisely what I'm worth. 'Lord Jon' picked up the sheet of paper with all these figures on and he didn't know what it meant he just tried to be Joe Cool, 'It looks fine to me.' Ritchie looks at it and goes blank. I look at it and Ritchie just said, 'Ask him, Nick'. 'Do you have a problem, Nicky?' 'Yeah I don't understand these figures, Bill. All I want to know is precisely what I'm worth.' 'You're worth precisely nothing.' We've just had a three-month tour, we've got a second album coming up, two hit singles and we're worth nothing?"

Despite the apparent wealth the band was generating, the costs of record-ing, promotion and touring ate away at their income, although the band wasn't totally unaware of the expenses. Nick Simper: "I remember Rod Evans and me saying one night, 'It's ridiculous. Coletta and Edwards are over here doing nothing for us. We're having to pay Jeff Ward to be our tour manager. What are they doing, why are they here? They're staying in the best hotels' and everybody said, 'Yeah they should go back to England and keep our name going there and in Europe.' So we're all agreed, we're going to tell them 'Yeah' and Jon Lord said, 'I couldn't say anything like that to them, they're my friends.' 'Well hopefully we're all their friends and they're our friends but it's a fact. Why do we need two guys sitting on their arses doing nothing who've got no purpose in being here except following us around on the road and spending our money?' In the end it was Rod and me who had to go and tell them."

Although Blackmore had been playing his Gibson ES335 for the past six years, he had always admired Fender Stratocasters, and many of the players he admired as a kid had used them. However in the late Fifties and early Sixties, Fenders were not easy to get hold of in England. Thanks to Hendrix's influence, the attraction with Fender for Blackmore was greater than ever. Ironically the first Stratocaster he acquired was an Eric Clapton cast-off bought from Clapton's roadie Mick Turner. "It wasn't very playable that's why Clapton gave it to Mick," says Hansford. "It was a Stratocaster body and a Telecaster neck."

Blackmore would go on to play Stratocasters almost exclusively from then on and soon become synonymous with the model. "The Strat I used belonged to Eric Clapton. I used it and I liked the sound of it; it was very sharp but impossible to play. The neck was so bowed it was really bad. It had a great sound for a wah-wah pedal because it was so sharp, but it was very difficult to play because it was so bowed. I thought it was an interesting guitar at the time, even though all the octaves were out."

Theoretically, for a guitarist of Blackmore's abilities, switching from one brand to another shouldn't have presented any problems but he claimed it took some time to adjust to the Fender, telling *Guitar Player* in 1978: "The transition was really hard. I found great difficulty in using it the first two years. With a Gibson you just race up and down, but with a Fender you have to make every note count; you have to make the note sing or otherwise it won't work. It's more rewarding because with a Gibson nobody has an identity."

The band returned home on January 3, 1969 followed by a press call on the roof of London's Dorchester Hotel, where it was announced that Blackmore and Lord had just got engaged to their respective girlfriends. Another BBC session did little to raise Purple's profile and of the few gigs they did fees were as little as £75 and even a college gig in London where they shared top billing with the Nice could only command £125. In America the band's nightly fee would range between one and three thousand dollars and there was even talk of the band's second American tour being with the Rolling Stones. Despite EMI having still not released *The*

Book Of Taliesyn much of January was spent at De Lane Lea recording material for a third release.

Despite having to fit in recording time between gigs, a greater cohesion and confidence started to shine through the ideas. More importantly, the band, and in particular, Blackmore were starting to develop as songwriters. Lawrence definitely noticed the changes. "In those days, you gigged then you were told you had three weeks to go in the studio and do the album. You start getting more free-form from Ritchie and I think you start getting more jazzy from Jon. You saw the band getting heavier, and these other things were coming out in a lot heavier, more free form way. Ritchie was the one that kind of heard that."

The third album, a mere nine months from their first, showed another step forward, with Blackmore showing greater potential than he previously had on *Shades Of …* and *The Book Of Taliesyn*. Despite being labelled producer, Lawrence considered his role to be relatively minor. "Probably the biggest thing I did with those three albums at the time was working on the sound with the engineer Barry Ainsworth. It's like if you listen to my stuff through the years you can hear my sound. But probably the biggest thing I did was saying no, about this or that part, saying it doesn't work." Certainly Lawrence never suggested or intervened with any of the musical directions. Tracks such as 'Painter', 'Why Didn't Rosemary' and 'The Bird Has Flown' showcased the heavier side of the band that Blackmore and Simper in particular were pushing for. Blackmore's solos were also showing a greater maturity and his soloing in 'Chasing Shadows' and 'Why Didn't Rosemary' were among his best to date. However the album still showed a side of the band that was at odds with Blackmore's desire to play louder and heavier; a side that leaned toward Lord's alternative agenda as he continued to throw in classical structures and styles; most notably with the harpsichord flavoured 'Blind' and the grandiose, 12-minute 'April.' The latter saw the band using a choir and string quartet, a precursor for what was soon to follow. The track was divided into three sections, the final part saw the band rocking as hard as it ever had, ending with a particularly sublime Blackmore solo.

Lawrence saw the start of a division and was left in no doubt that Blackmore considered Lord's classical leanings "got in the way of rock 'n' roll." Also publishing rights were to become an issue. "[Ritchie] didn't turn down the part in the writing. That was one of the first big arguments I think. Like Ritchie had written most of the Purple stuff and the band shared in it, then Jon did an orchestral thing and it was Jon's. I don't think that went down very well." January also saw the band making an appearance on BBC 2's *Late Night Line-Up* show. *Record Mirror* reported that "the old blues number played was written by them on the day of the show" but such information was most likely the result of a typical off the cuff Blackmore remark.

Deep Purple started their second American tour on April 1 in Tacoma, Washington – a trek that would take them though America for two solid months concluding in Buffalo, New York on May 29. An incident involving Ian Hansford, affectionately referred to as 'The Warrington Ape,' at the Wardhouse, Rhode Island nearly got them lynched. Nick Simper: "We played at a place in Rhode Island, right on the coast, a real redneck gig. I always remember it. The Warrington Ape started having trouble with this guy as soon as we got there."

Hansford recalls how he made an off the cuff remark to get the guy off his back. "It was a loading ramp and it went down about 45 degrees. There was this guy at the top with this little chopper bike and I just said off the top of my head, 'Ride down it and I'll give you five dollars' and he did and he came up and he said, 'Where's my five dollars?' and I said, 'What about the bike?' and he said, 'It's not mine' so he left it in the sea."

Hansford was blissfully unaware of the repercussions it would have for the band when the gig finished as Simper explains, "When we came out that night they're all sitting on our motor. It was like in a movie, a guy was picking his teeth with a knife, the guy on the bike, still wet, riding in circles around our car and they're just giving us a hard time. So we all get in, guitars in the boot and one guy is sitting on the bonnet, another is leaning on it. What do you reckon fellows? Ritchie just said, 'Give it the gun.' I hit the throttle so hard the car just went round and round in the sand and these guys just flew everywhere, the guy on the bike flew off and the next thing they are in their car and hitting us up the back, just like *In The Heat Of The Night* with Sidney Poitier, banging into us. We had this big V8 thing and I could see the Holiday Inn looming up on the left, we've got to get off so I signalled right and they went right with me and I suddenly went left and completely wrong-footed them and we shot into the car park of the Holiday Inn. All those guys were out of the car and in the lift before I could even turn the key. I'm getting out and getting the guitars out of the boot and these guys actually pulled up on the highway just past us saying, 'We'll get you next time, we'll kill you.' When I got in the lift I was shaking with fear, the back bumper was all bent in. The others had just got out of the car into the lift and they'd gone!"

When not being chased by rednecks, Blackmore and Lord were becoming increasingly unhappy with Rod Evans style. The emergence of Led

Zeppelin had struck a particular chord with Blackmore, who felt the band needed to shift the music into a harder direction, and along with Lord, felt that Evans wasn't the man for the job. But rather than have it out with Evans face to face, in time-honoured fashion, they just allowed the situation to evolve in a way that Lord openly admitted years later was cowardly. With Evans having helped get his fellow bandmate Paice into the band, Blackmore and Lord needed to get the drummer to go along with their plans for a majority decision. Paice sided with them and the management was duly informed. With commitments to continue the tour and concerns that Evans would walk out in the middle of it, Blackmore, Lord, Paice and the management agreed the news would go no further for the time being. With Evans blissfully unaware of the others' intentions, the tour successfully continued as normal.

On their return to England, Blackmore called up Mick Underwood, his old pal from the Outlaws, asking him if he could recommend any singers. Underwood – then drumming for Episode Six* – somewhat bizarrely suggested the group's own singer, Ian Gillan.† Mick Underwood: "Ritchie called me about needing a singer. I think we had a Radio 1 Club session coming out the following day so I said 'Have a listen to that, it's a live broadcast.' Then they came down to the next gig we did and Ritchie got up and had a little play with us but at that time only Ian was in the frame as far as I knew but of course they took Roger as well, which was rather sad for Nicky. But he wasn't in the frame, nothing was mentioned about bass players, they just wanted another singer."

With Evans still knowing nothing of his imminent departure, Gillan accepted the invitation to become Deep Purple's new singer. While Gillan suggested to his Episode Six colleague and writing partner Roger Glover that they knock up a couple of song ideas for his new band, Purple had a session booked at De Lane Lea to record a Greenaway and Cook song, 'Hallelujah.'

Although initially the plan had only been to change one member, the major attraction of the Gillan–Glover duo was their songwriting capabilities, something that up to then had been a weak spot in Deep Purple's arsenal. In the same underhand way that Bobby Woodman was dismissed

---

* Hailing from the Middlesex area, the sextet Episode Six were relatively unsuccessful in Britain – releasing eight singles for the Pye and Chapter One labels between 1966 and 1969 – but were popular on the Continent and had even performed in Beirut.
† Ironically, Gillan had originally turned down Nick Simper's invite to join the band when singers were being auditioned at Deeves Hall.

Nick Simper became the victim in an unforeseen set of circumstances. "It was only pure luck that I wasn't at the studio when Ian Gillan arrived. Sources close to the band told me that I was going to be told Gillan was joining when I arrived for the session that evening. The roadie said when he went to pick up Gillan, Glover was with him who said he was coming for the ride. We'd been in there in the morning laying down backing tracks. If I was out of the band why did they go through all the motions and expense to do that? What I was told adds up because I was told we could only have the studio in the morning and in the evening so during the afternoon we had a break and I was told Gillan was going to be brought to the studio, taught the song, complete the routine, maybe even lay the vocal down, who knows and when I got there in the evening I would be told the truth. The only reason they wanted to keep it secret was because they didn't want Rod to know and also Ian Gillan was under contract to the manager of Episode Six who would have sued Coletta for a few bob. It was all to be kept hush, hush and according to people who were in the studio that night they decided, probably after an afternoon of jamming with uncle Roger on my equipment and my guitar that this worked out rather nice."

Deep Purple were committed to several UK shows in June and through word of mouth Simper started hearing rumours that he was to be replaced. Before long he discovered the hard way when it was published in a newspaper. Evans and Simper confronted Coletta and Edwards whose only explanation was that it had been a majority decision by the other three. Clearly still hurt by the experience Simper has a view as to the thinking behind it. "It's not hard to imagine Jon and Ritchie thinking this is a good way of controlling the whole show and doing exactly what we want to do. And in one fell swoop they've got total control. They've got three yes men in the band because they've got two new guys with one guy who doesn't say boo to a goose, how easy is that? The two dominant personalities in control of the whole show. Bingo, these guys have also got loads of ideas for songs. Same time they say goodbye to Derek Lawrence and bang we're off. They told Tetragrammaton that Rod and I had been fired. Rod was in America anyway so he didn't know what was going on. He was arranging his wedding – that was a nice wedding present for him. So next thing they tell Tetragrammaton, here's the finished product, we've fired Nick and Rod and Ronnie Wood's playing bass and the guy out of Spooky Tooth was singing on it. That was to make sure that if they said that to anybody else it wouldn't lead back to Gillan and Glover. Rod was quite incensed. He made sure he got Ian Paice in the band."

In June Tetragrammaton released the band's third album, simply entitled

Deep Purple but due to a combination of the company being unable to get the album out during the tour, and record stores taking exception to the cover, sales were disappointingly lower than the previous two albums. The decision to ban the album on the strength of the cover using a mono-chrome image of part of Hieronymous Bosch's 14th century masterpiece 'The Garden Of Earthly Delights' was a peculiar one. Edwards commented: "It does seem particularly weird that in one or two of the more puritanical States they are taking exception to a painting, which has been displayed for so long in one of the greatest religious centres of the world." Banning it from open display certainly didn't help Deep Purple or Tetragrammaton at a time when every cent counted.

At least back in Britain it looked as if EMI were finally starting to address Purple's situation. EMI's A & R man Malcolm Jones suggestion that EMI needed a label to specialise in the popular 'underground' scene was greeted positively and around the same time *Deep Purple* was released in the States, EMI held a launch party at London's Roundhouse for the newly formed Harvest label. The first LP release on the label was *The Book Of Taliesyn* some nine months after it had been released in America. Within a couple of weeks of the announcement of the new label, the original line-up played its last gig at the Top Rank, Cardiff on July 4.

Deep Purple was now entering a new phase and in some respects they were starting from scratch all over again. With a new singer and bassist, a new single on the way on a new label, there was at least the prospect that Deep Purple might finally break through in their own country.

CHAPTER 6

Hallelujah! In Rock (1969–71)

The new line-up of Deep Purple made their debut on record with the Greenaway and Cook song 'Hallelujah.' Blackmore was under no illusions regarding the motivation behind the recording, telling *Record Mirror*: "Quite honestly we need to have a commercial record in Britain. We want to be known in England, so we've come out very much on the commercial side with the new record." He described 'Hallejuah' as "an in-between sort of thing" – a median between what Deep Purple normally attempted but with an added commercial imperative. Having already tasted success in America, Blackmore's downbeat attitude was already starting to surface. "You have to think commercially to be able to live. There's no point being a fantastic musician if you're starving to death. I sometimes get fed up with the whole business – conforming to the rules and going into the studio to make hit records."

Despite TV appearances to plug 'Hallelujah', by and large, the British public once again ignored a Deep Purple record. Furthermore, the groups' popularity in America was already starting to dissipate and Blackmore could have been forgiven for thinking that the whole enterprise was about to derail. With Purple unable to get noticed at home, HEC Enterprises saw the potential in combining the band with the Royal Albert Hall, the Royal Philharmonic Orchestra and one of England's most respected composer's and conductor's, Malcolm Arnold as the ideal tonic for a much needed boost. Purple managers Edwards and Coletta called Jon Lord's bluff and gave him a mere three months to compose what would ultimately become *Concerto For Group And Orchestra*.

Despite Lord's classical foundations, his ability to write rock music was limited and with the concerto plans being made public, the new writing triumvirate of Blackmore, Gillan and Glover didn't take kindly to the perception of Lord being Purple's leader and principal composer. In his typical, forthright manner, Blackmore described the event two months before it happened as, "purely a gimmick," claiming tongue-in-cheek that, "as far as I know, the RPO is interested in getting together with the group. I hear that one of the violinists has all our records."

His reluctance to be involved in the project caused a major rift with Lord. Blackmore was concerned that Lord was using Purple as a platform for his classical interests and although a lover of classical music, the heavy use of strings was at odds with the hard rock direction Blackmore was insistent on taking the band in. In his view Deep Purple had just recruited a powerfully-lunged singer with the ability to project over a loud, hard rocking sound, yet here they were dallying with an orchestra. Years later Ian Gillan commented, "First of all there was a wave of anti-*Concerto* feeling started by Ritchie and I went along with it. I saw some sense in what Ritchie was saying. He said, 'This is going to detract from what we are doing on our album; this is going to detract from the rock stuff; this is going to make people confused.'" The tensions increased when Lord occasionally missed band rehearsals and writing sessions while he toiled on his creation.

During this period, on September 16, 1969, Blackmore tied the knot for the second time to Bärbel Hardie, his girlfriend of two years, at Acton Registry Office. Although the wedding was less eventful than his first, five years earlier, it was still a slightly odd affair as Derek Lawrence recalled, "I was supposed to be the best man, I went, and no one asked me to do anything so I didn't. We ended up in a Chinese restaurant." Following the ceremony and wedding lunch, there was an evening reception where a host of musician friends such as Neil Christian and Mick Underwood were among the guests. "My wife and I both went, and there were a lot of good people at that, a nice little do," Underwood remembers.

Concerto For Group And Orchestra was instrumental in raising the UK public's awareness of Deep Purple and although Blackmore had shown little interest in the project, come the evening of the performance – September 24 – he produced some stunning playing, and in a rebellious gesture extended his solo spot during the First Movement: Moderato-Allegro. In keeping with the free-form tradition of Deep Purple, the solo was to be improvised within the space of a select number of bars, with a pre-arranged motif as the cue for Arnold to bring the orchestra back in. Lord had envisaged the solo lasting for around 60 seconds but Blackmore wanted to make his own statement that the evening was as much about rock as it was classical. He soloed for several more bars than was planned which had Arnold shuffling frantically through the score to assure himself that he had not missed his cue! Despite some raised eyebrows from the violinists, Blackmore's solo was, in Lord's eyes, "a stream of wonderful inventions," and with the aid of the Albert Hall acoustics, the recorded document gives fans a rare chance to hear him really cut it on his Gibson ES335.

Most reviewers saw the show as a great success and Purple had the opportunity of playing a half-hour set of their own material before the concerto. "Their dynamics were a delight to hear," was how one reviewer described them. Regardless of the positives that occurred from the experience, Blackmore told *Melody Maker* shortly after the concert: "Although I felt the concert was a success, it isn't the direction that we as a group are going in at all. There are two sides to the band. Jon with his training is classically influenced and my influence is rock 'n' roll."

Irrespective of his concern over what he saw as a novelty situation in combining Deep Purple with the RPO the venture worked out to the band's advantage. Although Keith Emerson of the Nice had produced a similar project (the 'Five Bridges Suite', performed a few weeks earlier at the Plumpton Festival), *Concerto* gained much greater publicity (being sponsored and broadcast on BBC TV) and helped to pave the way for a much more open-minded approach to the merging of classical and rock music. By the mid Seventies, many top rock acts were to undertake similar projects, most notably Procol Harum's collaboration with the Edmonton Symphony Orchestra and similar works by Rick Wakeman.

While *Concerto* increased Purple's popularity overnight the drawback was that many people now saw them as a band that played with an orchestra – much to Blackmore and Glover's chagrin. "The next day the papers were full of us, it really was a press explosion," Glover reflected. "Jon Lord suddenly became the main writer and main composer of the band, which really got up the noses of everybody else in the band because he wasn't the main writer or main composer, or even the leader. Ritchie in particular got very bitter about it." Roadie Ian Hansford observed, "It came across as Jon Lord was the main songwriter. I know Roger was pissed off with it. The main songwriters were Ritchie, Roger and Ian Gillan."

The friction became so intense that Lord seriously considered his position within the band. Once the situation was ironed out, he took a less prominent role, leaving Blackmore perfectly poised to take centre stage. "We'd done the orchestra thing for about a year, two years [sic], and we were a rock band," Blackmore told Neil Jeffries. "I couldn't understand why we kept playing with orchestras. It started to get up my nose because we did the first thing – it was a novelty, a band playing with an orchestra; I didn't think it was particularly good but we pulled it off. It was just a novelty. Then he wrote another one (*The Gemini Suite*). And they wanted us to do it again, and I went, 'No, no, I'm not getting involved again. I'm in a rock 'n' roll band.' In fact, I said, 'Jon, we should make a rock 'n' roll record for people at parties. It should be non-stop, hard-hitting rock 'n' roll.' I was impressed with what Zeppelin did, and said I wanted to do that kind of stuff, and if it doesn't take off we'll go and play with orchestras for the rest of our lives. I remember saying that.

"So we did it and it was *Deep Purple In Rock* which, luckily, took off. It's funny, because someone spoke to me about six months later and said, 'I always hear that record at parties.' We'd purposefully made it so it hammered along every song. There was no lull. There was no showcase of the band, which always loses that party feel. Different tempos, but the energy level was high. So it worked – and I was very pleased with *Deep Purple In Rock* because I never wanted to work with an orchestra ever again. But then *The Gemini Suite* came out and it was like, 'Oh no! The nightmare's back again.' So I said, 'No, count me out, Jon,' and I think he got Albert Lee. And Albert, being the brilliant, wonderful person he is, brilliant guitar player: 'Yeah, I'll do it. Where am I?' But I really don't care to play with orchestras."*

Following on from the *Concerto*, the new line-up (which came to be known as Deep Purple MKII) focused their attention on songwriting and gigging extensively throughout the UK and Europe. In truth they had little option, as by now Tetragrammaton was going under, and royalties owed from the sales of Purple LPs and singles weren't forthcoming. The first live shows featuring the new line-up continued with the same material that had been played with Evans and Simper but it wasn't long before new songs, worked on in rehearsals also found their way into the set. Rehearsals took place at the Hanwell Community Centre. The venue was an ideal location, within easy reach for the band and suitable for playing loud without causing a nuisance. As well as functioning as a live venue, bands could use it as a rehearsal facility. One of these was Spice, soon to achieve success after changing their name to Uriah Heep. "[The Community Centre] was really the place

---

* *The Gemini Suite* was commissioned by the BBC and performed live by Deep Purple at the Royal Festival Hall on September 17, 1970. Lord also made a studio recording of it, and it is this version, which featured Albert Lee that Blackmore declined to do.

where it all happened," as far as Heep bassist Paul Newton was concerned. "I suppose the legend came about because one day, Deep Purple rehearsed [there] at the same time as us, but that was just one day."

Blackmore was still up to his usual pranks as Hansford recalls when driving the guitarist, who was armed with a catapult and gooseberries, back to Acton from Hanwell. "I can remember him hitting this girl, who was laden with carrier bags, right in her back. She dropped her carrier bags, turned round and slapped some old man thinking he'd hit her in the back. A bit further down the road, there was a woman inside a ladies hairdresser's having her hair done. The hairdresser was inside the shop with her back to the door which was open. Ritchie hit her right in the middle of the neck! I remember him hitting three skinheads once as we were going to Fulham and he hit this skinhead on the ear. These skinheads turned round to confront who was behind them by which time we had gone past. Also we were going down two consecutive Fridays either to Bristol or Bath and I think we were going through Marlborough and this window cleaner was up his ladder and the band let fire three in one go. The following Friday the same bloke was further down the road at another house and they did him again!"

Of the new tunes that emerged, the first one the new line-up knocked up was a fast driving rocker that went through the working titles, 'Ricochet' and 'Kneel And Pray' before eventually becoming 'Speed King.' When Blackmore suggested something akin to Hendrix's 'Fire,' Glover started jamming and before long the rest joined in and the essence of what would develop into their new stage opener was in place. Another new number that was also in the set by September was 'Child In Time', a dramatic 10 minute excursion that highlighted Gillan's vocals and also gave Blackmore the opportunity to stretch out on an extended solo. In fact it had been played during the band's own set at the Albert Hall and was fast becoming the centrepiece of the new stage act.

With the band revamping their stage set with new material in just a matter of weeks, EMI belatedly released their third album *Deep Purple* in November, undoubtedly confusing new converts who discovered it featured an earlier and now defunct line-up. Despite being the strongest studio album from the Mark 1 band it paled in comparison to the live shows the band were now producing. Writing in *Melody Maker* Steve Peacock went into overdrive when reviewing Purple's show in Manchester on December 6. "No words could possibly do justice to the climax of Deep Purple's act at Manchester College of Technology on Saturday. It came at the end of a brilliant set lasting more than one and a half hours, before one of the college's largest and most appreciative audiences this year. Suddenly Blackmore

132

threw a mic stand over the stage, stepped back and went into a wild flailing solo. Simultaneously a strobe light came on focusing on the guitarist and casting the rest of the group into an eerie gleam as they crouched over their instruments, providing an electronic drone behind Blackmore's amazing solo. He danced in the strobe, weaving around and throwing his guitar all over the place again and again. The move was terrific and the spectacle was terrifying – it went on building and building with ever increasing intensity, until all the force was spent. This was a musical and visual catharsis, and it left both the group and the audience dazed and exhausted."

With Blackmore and the rest of Deep Purple knocking them for six at colleges and clubs around the country, all that was required was to transpose those performances into a studio environment to produce an album that could see the band attain the same level of popularity as their contemporaries. Whilst Lord had played a significant role in the creation of the first three albums, Blackmore took over the reins, but both Gillan and Glover also played a big part in the compositions. Glover had started writing while in Episode Six, but was now with musicians that were able to take his ideas and develop them into truly spectacular rock songs.

From the outset Blackmore stated, "If it's not dramatic or exciting it has no place on this album." A writing pattern of ideas from Blackmore and Glover became the norm, with the latter also sometimes involved with the lyrics alongside Gillan. Lord and Paice's input was variable but it was agreed from the outset that all songs would be credited as group compositions. Indeed Blackmore was very keen to get his name on the publishing credits from the moment he saw how much money Rod Evans and Jon Lord made from 'One More Rainy Day' – the B-side to the million selling 'Hush.'

By the end of the year Tetragrammaton released *Concerto For Group And Orchestra* in the States (EMI doing likewise with a UK release on Harvest) but the LP would turn out to be the last from Bill Cosby's company. Their lavish expenses and investment in unsuccessful films finally pushed the company into liquidation. Not only was HEC Enterprises owed substantial sums of money but with no American backing, what had been Deep Purple's most lucrative market was all but closed to them, albeit temporarily.

"In a way, we were a big name over there because of the single," Blackmore told Steve Peacock in an August 1970 interview for *Zig Zag* magazine, "but it was more a hindrance than a help. 'Heavy groups' just don't have hit singles and it was a real drag – we had to go around proving ourselves. We played, I suppose, underground clubs – but all the audiences were there by luck … they had not come to see us. Once we were there and played, a lot of people just wouldn't believe we were the same group. But then we were playing very 'poppy' on the record – It was the first thing we'd done and we didn't really know each other. But before people heard us, they'd just say 'Deep Purple – pop group.' We got fed up with coming back from America to find everybody saying 'Deep Purple? Who? Never heard of them.'

"It was a bringdown. We used to get the reaction from audiences in this country, but you would pick up a paper and there's all these other groups and nothing about you. We thought 'Right, we're going to stay in this country and get something going here.' I think we have now because we've done one hell of a lot of personal appearances and we're getting a bit of a reputation, but it's a weird way of doing it – going to America and making it big over there and coming back to England and starting again.

"Personally, I don't like playing in America. They're great audiences, always give you a standing ovation and things, but it's the travelling where you have to spend three months in a suitcase. I'd much rather stay here. Go home every night, go across to the continent for a week at a time. In America it's three months slogging; it's very hard, and of course the drugs scene is bad out there and you tend to get caught up in all that. The money is the main thing out there."

1970 kicked off with a gig in Paris on January 5, followed by several one-nighters throughout England, coupled with sporadic gigs and TV appearances in Holland and Germany. Touring relentlessly and building up a healthy reputation as a great live band, Blackmore was continually leaving a lasting impression as both a guitarist and showman wherever he played.

One young fan, Joe Wright remembers the impact of seeing him for the first time at Lancaster University on January 23: "The start of Purple's set found us sat on the floor about six rows from the front at stage right in front of Jon Lord's Hammond. Purple erupted on stage with 'Speed King.' Twice during the song Ritchie disappeared behind his Marshall stacks to reappear seconds later with a different coloured Strat. I had previously considered tremolo arms to be the province of 'uncool' guitarists like Hank Marvin, but had never seen one used the way that Ritchie did. I had also never heard anything as loud as this before. The Who were currently touring with *Tommy* and had a 1,000 watt PA system, but nowhere near this loud. At the end of the number there were a few seconds of stunned silence before the entire audience erupted. My thought was how on earth could they follow that? 'Child In Time' soon provided the answer. What next? The arrival on stage of a chair with a tiny Vox AC30 amp on top and Ritchie with his Gibson ES335. 20 minutes or so of 'Wring That Neck' was about to begin.

I can still see Ritchie strolling back and forth across the stage playing one handed before killing the sound by stroking the guitar down his amp."

Despite Derek Lawrence having been axed as Deep Purple's producer (they had elected to produce themselves), he remained in contact with Blackmore and booked some studio time in February to record a few songs with Tony Dangerfield. "Tony is a tremendous singer and I wanted to get something going. We went into the studio with Tony on vocals, Ritchie, Chas Hodges on bass and Ian Paice on drums. We went in to try and do three numbers … 'Who Do You Love', 'Makin' Time' – Ritchie had always loved the Creation – and 'Walk A Mile In My Shoes' but somehow it didn't work out."

Also that month, in a bid to raise their profile further, Deep Purple performed live on BBC Radio 1's new *In Concert* programme. Unlike the sessions they had previously recorded for the Beeb, this new programme was done in front of a small audience at the Paris Theatre, Lower Regent Street. Given the fact that Purple hadn't had any hit singles, and despite the meagre £80 session fee, they were fortunate to get such a prestigious booking, which only occurred when the programme's producer Jeff Griffin offered the slot to Purple after Joe Cocker cancelled at short notice. It was also the first time that most people got to hear 'Speed King' and 'Child In Time.' In the days before a thriving bootleg market existed, there was little concern with broadcasting as yet unreleased material and the show allowed Deep Purple to get across to more people in one Sunday afternoon, when it was broadcasted on February 22, than a years worth of concerts ever could.

Six days later Ritchie was the victim of theft from under his nose when one of his prized Stratocasters was stolen at Liverpool's Philharmonic Hall as a result of a rather comical incident involving Ian Hansford. "In 'Mandrake Root' when it went into the strobe lights occasionally he had an old guitar, which he would smash hell out of and if we could use it again I'd bolt it back together but this night he's at the front of the stage, he's rubbing the guitar up and down on it. It's in his hand, not round his neck – he's got the strap off and the lead came out – the jack plug. He comes running back to me and I run back to him and with these strobe lights … you know how deceiving they are – the eyes and the mind play tricks on you – and we crashed head on. We were both seeing stars and god knows what. We both had splitting headaches. By the time he'd picked up his other guitar and I'd gone to the front of the stage it had gone. People at the front of the stage must have thought it was part of the act. We had to go out looking round the streets for 20 minutes after that. I was not in favour – it was all my fault. Then we had a couple of days off before we went to Switzerland … In the meantime this kid came home with a Fender Stratocaster and one of his parents said where did you get this from and got in touch with the hall. Roger Brewer who used to help us out on a gig basis went up on the train and brought the guitar back with him and Ritchie was a happy boy when I saw him in Switzerland and apologies all round."

The pattern of touring and recording continued for the next couple of months with sessions slotted in between gigs at either IBC or De Lane Lea Studios depending on which was available. De Lane Lea, opposite Holborn tube station, was the favoured choice and had been used for the previous two albums. The assistant to De Lane Lea's engineer Barry Ainsworth on those sessions had been a young tape operator named Martin Birch, who had taken over as the chief engineer and would become an integral partner in future recordings for many years to come. In keeping with the mood of the time, Purple was slowly but surely piecing together an album that would comfortably stand alongside their contemporaries. Led Zeppelin had already made much headway and in February a new band from Birmingham had emerged with an extremely dark, heavy and powerful self-titled release called *Black Sabbath*. The recordings they were laying down were in the heavier direction Ritchie favoured.

During the sessions, Mick Underwood, then with the band Quatermass who were also signed to Harvest, sometimes popped into the studio. "We were doing the *Quatermass* album when they were doing *In Rock* but they were at De Lane Lea in Kingsway. I always had an open invite to pop down and see them. I saw them one or two times in the studio and that's where Ritchie heard that 'Black Sheep Of The Family' track 'cos I had a tape of that track and took it down and he liked that. We also did a gig together. We were supporting them and I came back in the car with them. I always had a good rapport with the guys."

In March Purple's five-date tour of Scotland concluded at Hamilton Town Hall in what was described as the towns' first 'underground' concert but sadly due to a bus strike only 500 showed up! Amid the touring sched-ule Blackmore got a phone call from his old employer Dave Sutch, inviting him to a jam at the Country Club in Hampstead, north London on April 12. "Sutch phoned me up and said, 'Do you fancy playing tomorrow night?' I agreed and I came down with Matt Fisher of Procol Harum. We just did a night of playing and I saw the recording equipment and thought, 'He's doing it again.' He said, 'Here's 500 for playing tonight' ".*

---

* The jam, that also featured Carlo Little and Keith Moon on drums, was eventually released on Sutch's album *Hands Of Jack The Ripper* in 1972.

Sutch also invited along Nick Simper. "I didn't want to do it. I had the worse cold I'd ever had, I felt really ill and I said to Dave, 'I don't think I'm going to make this gig,' but I said, 'Who's playing guitar?' I'd told him to get Albert Lee and he told me he'd got Albert Lee because he knew that a: I'd want to be there even if I had a broken leg and b: He knew if he said Ritchie was doing it I wouldn't probably show at all. And when I got there, there he is. There was Gillan and Glover skulking up the back. I wasn't up to it, I felt out of it and it didn't help seeing Ritchie there but he played pretty good. We did some numbers before Sutch came on and he was playing a blinder. He came up with the old Gibson and a little Vox amp. But he was on one side and I was on the other and that was it. We didn't speak."

A couple of months after the aborted recordings with Tony Dangerfield, Lawrence had the idea of getting a bunch of friends to play on a jam session at De Lane Lea. "I had the studio booked for three days and I thought I'll get all my mates and that's what it was. And it was funny because Ritchie was doing a gig somewhere, he said, 'I'll be back by eight o'clock I'll come over afterwards, which he did but for me it was just great fun; Ian Paice, Chas Hodges, Tony Ashton, Matt Fisher, Jim Sullivan and Albert Lee." Although Lawrence had been relieved of his role as Deep Purple's producer Blackmore had no qualms about being a part of Lawrence's session, most likely because the two guitarists he admired most in the business were also taking part. Big Jim Sullivan, who by then was working with Tom Jones, had helped set Ritchie on the path to success in the first place but Albert Lee, one of the fastest pickers around, was a much more casual acquaintance.

Albert Lee: "That's when I really got to know [Ritchie] because all of a sudden I got to know Derek and he drew all these people together and he was going on about 'Ritchie this, Ritchie that, Ritchie thinks you're great and you two have got to play together and all that' and that's how it really came about. He seemed to have unlimited studio time and he had this idea of just having a big jam with loads of guitar players. It was very easy going, no preparation at all we just kicked around ideas, and we never really worked that hard on the tracks."

The idea of three of Britain's finest guitarists playing alongside one another could potentially have been a recipe for in-fighting and ego battles but as Lee recalls, "Ritchie was kind of quiet but I guess we were all a bit tentative really because we were all with some of our peers and heroes, so there was a lot of mutual admiration. Looking back at it, my playing has always veered towards the country thing and the way he was playing back then was very different to the way I play so it was very interesting. None of us would have stepped over the other guy's feet. Everyone listened to what the other guys were doing. Of course Big Jim is the consummate professional session guy and we both looked up to him because he was the more experienced of the three of us."

Blackmore's decision to play on the Lawrence session may have served as an act of attrition for removing him as Purple's producer. He was certainly capable of remembering old mates and repaying favours. One such example occurred at Purple's gig at Dunstable Civic Hall on May 18. Once again journalist Steve Peacock, praised Purple's set, this time for a local paper. "As a band they work together with beautiful timing and understanding, and as individuals musicians they shine out among the hundreds of good musicians that are playing at the moment. Visually they all move well but Ritchie is a master of the flailing guitar dance, and his strobe-lit finale to their set defies description." The support band that evening was Wishbone Ash. According to Wishbone Ash's Martin Turner, "During the soundcheck Andy (Powell) was onstage playing his guitar when Ritchie walked on and started playing. Gradually they started speaking to each other with their guitars and there was quite a little rapport going on there. Anyway, Ritchie didn't say a word to us, but afterwards he told Derek Lawrence about us."

With another evening session for the Lawrence project occurring five days after the gig, the producer confirms this. "Ritchie had come to me one day and said 'We were playing the other day and there was this band supporting us, they're really good. I've given them your number; you should do something with them.' That was how I came to do Wishbone Ash." Lawrence then took the demo tape the band had done to a contact at MCA and Wishbone Ash were signed on the strength of it.

The Derek Lawrence sessions were concluded that same May evening with Lawrence deciding who should solo on specific tracks, with Sullivan adding his views as well. Albert Lee: "I'm sure Ritchie sat back like I did and said 'Okay I'll play now then,' we certainly looked up to Big Jim in that respect." The one exception was the lengthy instrumental track that gave the project its name. 'Bullfrog' was a joint Blackmore–Lawrence composition but due to contractual reasons Blackmore wasn't credited. In fact, none of the musicians could disclose their identities. Blackmore's pseudonym was 'Boots', which, according to Lawrence, was because he "always wore a pair of purple suede cowboy boots that he'd had made at Anello & Davide's." When the album was released in America the following year under the title *Green Bullfrog* it raised little more than casual comment in the press. A belated European release on MCA occurred in 1972 and according to

Lawrence's royalty statement the record company claimed it sold less than 500 copies.

Much more importantly *Deep Purple In Rock* – the first studio album from the MKII line-up – was released in Britain in June. Blackmore's conviction that the band's direction lay in heavier, more aggressive music was fully vindicated, as the album became both a commercial and critical success, remaining in the UK charts for over a year, peaking at number 4. If one album truly defines what Deep Purple were really all about, then *In Rock* fits the bill. From the cover pastiche of Mount Rushmore to the final notes of the album's closing track 'Hard Lovin' Man', *In Rock* was a hugely powerful statement of a fully confident band at the forefront of the heavy rock genre.

In Rock hadn't been an easy album to make. The band would have preferred to spend more time working in the studio but because of the financial problems they had been forced into continually gigging. With Tetragrammaton having gone into liquidation, its assets were bought by Warner Bros and by default they acquired Deep Purple as part of the package, totally unaware of how to place or promote them.

Although an album's worth of material had been recorded the management also wanted a single and having returned to De Lane Lea they were struggling to come up with anything tangible. Assistant engineer John Acock recalls how they all sat about in the studio unable to come up with a suitable riff and retired to a nearby pub, the Newton Arms. "Ritchie took along an acoustic in the pub and came up with a riff. Ian Paice started working out a rhythm." Eventually after several drinks they staggered back to the studio where Ian Gillan sat in the rest room and within half an hour had written some lyrics. With the tune worked out, "it was pretty much done in one take and we finished around four in the morning," recalls Acock. The song's arrangement wasn't entirely original; the riff was taken from the bass line of Rickie Nelson's 'Summertime' a tune that Nick Simper had introduced to Blackmore the year before and also owed a heavy debt to garage band the Blues Magoos' 1967 US hit, '(We Ain't Got) Nothin' Yet'. The band instantly dismissed the track as a throwaway, at best a B-side but for once the management got it right. The ability to produce a three-minute song that would find favour with the single buying public played a significant part in Purple's rise to the top. Appearances on *Top Of The Pops* and other TV shows in Britain and Europe helped 'Black Night' to become Deep Purple's first and biggest UK hit – reaching number two in September, being held off the top spot by Freda Payne's 'Band Of Gold.'

Blackmore's heavy use of adapting other composers' song ideas was to backfire with regards to 'Mandrake Root'. Initially it was the unfortunate Simper who was unwittingly in the firing line. "One day I got a very angry Bill Parkinson come round my house, a pretty fearsome guy, tall, built like a brick shithouse saying, 'You guys ripped off my number.' I said, 'I'm not even in the band now. I knew it was your song, my name's not on it. Everybody knows it's your song.' He said, 'I'm going to do something about it. Would you stand up in court and say so?' 'Well if I had to I suppose, it's the truth.' He said, 'Whatever I get I'll give you half' and I never saw Bill again. Apparently they paid him off with about £600."

A year on from the dissolution of the original line-up Blackmore commented, "We decided in America last year that although we were going down very well there was something lacking. Quite honestly Jon, Ian and I were going down well, but the other two were really just passengers. So we looked at it from a cold point of view and decided they'd have to go. Rod wasn't really our kind of style as a singer anyway. He was more of a ballad singer than an improviser." Such forthright comments are indicative of Blackmore's, at times, selfish and unthinking manner. He seemed totally unperturbed as to the effect his comments had on others, such as the odd occasion that he crossed paths with Nick Simper.

"Once when I was with Marsha Hunt [the backing band that Simper initially joined after Purple], he put his hand out and Ged Peck [Marsha Hunt's guitarist] actually stopped me hitting him. I remember he had this big tasselled suit and he came up with his guitar and just put his hand out with a smile on his face, which you didn't often see. Ged Peck just held me back – all of a sudden a red mist came down."

It seems Blackmore was eager to bury the hatchet with his old bassist. When he saw Simper's newly created band Warhorse on BBC 2's *Disco 2,* Blackmore phoned Nick up, saying "'That was the most exciting thing I've seen all year.' I think he meant it. We were talking then, he invited me over a few times. And he got Bärbel to phone up saying, 'Ritchie does not vont to lose your friendship.' I used to talk to Ritchie quite regularly. My mate Dave Wendels sometimes used to phone me up and say, 'I'm over at Ritchie's. Ritchie says do you want to pop over?' Yeah maybe I will. I kept it kind of friendly."

Shortly after the change of line-up, Blackmore and Babs, with Gillan and Paice, took a boating holiday up the River Thames. The two Ian's hired a large and sedate vessel, while the Blackmore's chose a more modern, sleek and faster craft. With the annual Henley Regatta in full flow and the riverbank adorned with 'hooray Henrys' Ritchie took great delight in circling

Paice and Gillan's boat, manoeuvring his boat as fast as possible in all directions, soaking the upper class hordes in the process. Later he moored up to explore a small island in the middle of the river. Unconcerned that the boat's engine had got entangled in tree roots he left Babs on board with their dog Strokie and wandered off. A while later, Gillan noticed Babs was getting restless and took it upon himself to dive into the river to free the boat from under the hull. The boat rapidly disappeared downstream with a panicking Babs unable to control it. At that moment Ritchie reappeared and, as Gillan recalled in his book, "she screamed "Ritchie vot I do?" The guitarist shouted back, without much enthusiasm, "Turn the wheel you soppy cow!" and promptly went back to his wanderings on the island, as Babs disappeared into the distance."

Elsewhere during the holiday, Blackmore amused himself with an air rifle he had brought along with him. Peppering the bank at various spots on the journey his behaviour was brought to the attention of the river police and he ended up appearing at Windsor Magistrate's Court. PRs today would make great capital out of such an incident involving a rock musician but HEC somehow managed to keep it out of the papers.

Having just returned from a three-gig stint in Germany, on June 12, Deep Purple played at the famous Eel Pie Island Club in Twickenham, situated in the middle of the River Thames. Although it was best suited to blues bands with less equipment than Purple used, it was still a worthwhile gig, despite the added difficulty in getting the gear to the venue via the only route, a narrow bridge. Ian Hansford: "You couldn't get the van across there. They used to have two Morris Minor Travellers. We had to put everything in them and there was only two inches either side of the bridge to drive over. We had to park one side of the bridge and ferry everything over, then the same thing after the gig." But that was only the start of the problem.

Quite often Blackmore would get annoyed during soundchecks if things weren't to his liking, as Hansford explains. "If he didn't like the sound at the rehearsal he'd get really stroppy. You couldn't get it over to him that it would be different when there were people in there. It might not be a totally good sound but at least people would soak it up. It would be echoing and bouncing all over the place but he'd really get the hump." But at the Eel Pie Club other factors were also affecting Blackmore's moods. As well as the tiny stage, there was water in the building. Ian Hansford: "When we got there it was flooded, the floor was awash. The Thames must have been really high, so he played the set in the changing room. He said to me, 'Go and put a bit more top on the amp.' I remember Jon Lord was furious, 'Get him out here.' 'It's no good Jon, if I asked him to get out here is he going to say yes?' He might have started on stage but then he disappeared, I would say, for at least three quarters of the set." What the Eel Pie crowd made of hearing five musicians but only seeing four sadly hasn't been documented. Inevitably such eccentric and stubborn behaviour didn't endear him to his band mates. "I learnt quite early on he was going to do things for himself and no one else mattered," said Glover.

While the rest of the band had moved out of the communal home in Acton, Ritchie and Babs continued to live there for a while longer. Ian Hansford: "We were there for about a year and then the owners wanted to have the upstairs of the house and I was supposed to have the remainder but Babs talked the owners out of it saying that she and Ritchie were having it and I was out the door basically." Eventually the Blackmore's also had to find accommodation elsewhere.

Ian Hansford: "When [Ritchie] left Acton he moved to his parents for a matter of weeks and then [he and Babs] bought this house in Cranford. He thought it would be better to live near the airport then he could have a couple of extra hours in bed when he was flying out somewhere." The Blackmore's moved into a semi-detached house but even though Ritchie was now starting to earn sufficient money to afford a mortgage on his own home, ready cash was still hard to come by as Derek Lawrence recalls, "I think I lent him money to buy a black leather three-piece suite."

The reviews for *In Rock* were invariably glowing; one writer commented: "Ritchie Blackmore's gutsy guitar tears its way through the album, dominating it." Another stated, "Ritchie Blackmore is not merely a fast guitarist but one with immense style and presence."

On July 4, Deep Purple headlined an all-day, open-air gig at Bedford Town's football ground, The Eyrie. The show dubbed 'Blues At The Eyrie' created quite a deal of local press coverage, though not all positive. The football club was suffering financial difficulties and had come up with the idea of hosting a rock concert to help raise club funds.

As part of the hype surrounding the gig, local newspapers were suggesting that thousands of fans from all over the country would potentially descend upon the small shire market town. Some reports suggested as many as 20,000, and as this was the golden age of the rock festival, such numbers were highly feasible. Deep Purple were by no means a household name when the concert was announced in April and with *In Rock* having only been released a matter of days before the gig; there was no surrounding publicity. The other big names on the bill were Chicken Shack and Tyrannosaurus Rex. Although poor weather on the day may have proved a

142

deterrent, only 1,250 turned up for the show. Ian Hansford: "We were only on about £125 and the promoter didn't have enough money to pay us. He was only a young guy then his older brother turned up and he only had £25 so we were still short on that. He said he didn't take enough money to pay us."

The following month Deep Purple played at Plumpton, the same festival event where they had gone down like a lead balloon two years earlier. Although they were now scheduled to headline the show, at one stage, it looked as if the whole event was going to be cancelled. Tory MP Martin Madden had brought a court action against the festival on the grounds of noise and audience behaviour at earlier festivals. Fortunately for the thousands descending on Plumpton for the August Bank Holiday weekend, the judge decreed that the injunction had been brought too late to stop the festival going ahead. Although Purple were due to perform last, progressive rockers Yes turned up late forcing Purple to take the stage first. With Blackmore determined to be the star of any show, during the closing number, 'Mandrake Root', he instructed Hansford to set fire to his amps to add to the visual spectacle as well as to upstage Yes in an effort to prevent them from performing.

Ian Hansford: "I can remember the fire and I remember Fred Munt, the Bonzo Dog Band's roadie putting it out straight away with a fire extinguisher. We got the cleaning bill for the curtains! I remember someone going through the itemised bill when the final payment came through, docking this and that. But the best fire he had was at a festival in Aachen. I poured a whole gallon of petrol on the amp and set it on fire. Flames went right up to the top of this canvas roof. Paicey was looking around and said, 'For Christ's sake!' It just went out on its own in the end but the police came inspecting the amp. We had a shell of an amp and put a battery inside it so when you switched it on the indicator light came on although that was the only thing inside it and we always had a couple of old speakers. Looking back it could have been so dangerous and a fire hazard, setting it on fire on purpose, I could have ended up in gaol. It was only done at big gigs or if they were going to be on TV."

With Purple's highly visual stage show now drawing headlines in England, the collapse of Tetragrammaton had the reverse effect in America where the band returned for a two-week tour in August. Although Warner Bros now had Deep Purple on their books, *In Rock* had yet to be released, and instead the company chose to re-issue the *Concerto* album, as its first release. Warner's also convinced the band it would be a smart idea to perform the concerto at the prestigious Hollywood Bowl with the Los

Angeles Philharmonic. Despite reservations from all members they begrudgingly played it, albeit in a shortened form but it had less of an effect on sales than had been the case in Britain. The rest of the tour was far less successful than previous Stateside trips with nightly takings significantly down.

Back in Britain, the continuing success of *In Rock* and 'Black Night' meant that Ritchie Blackmore became one of the most talked about British guitarists. His emergence occurred with perfect timing as Cream had left a void in the two years since their break-up (with Clapton now pursuing a more rootsy direction), the Jeff Beck Group had split with Beck sidelined after a serious road accident, and in September, Jimi Hendrix, the most revered guitarist of his generation, died in London. With contemporaries like Led Zeppelin and Ten Years After spending most of their time on the road in America, Blackmore's years of slogging around Britain and Germany playing as a back-up musician were now behind him.

Although Blackmore and Lord had previously clashed over the rock-orchestra divide, with their mutual understanding of classical foundations, they now combined to fully integrate classical, as well as many other musical styles into their performances. Earlier tracks such as 'Wring That Neck' and 'Mandrake Root' were often stretched out to 30 minutes or more, and while both players employed classical interjections, with much of the playing improvised, the overall approach was more akin to modern jazz. With a pounding rhythm section and Gillan's soaring vocals, Purple's music showed a level of musicianship that had rarely been seen in rock music up to that point.

Sessions for *Fireball* – the follow-up to *In Rock* – started in September 1970 at De Lane Lea. However due to the increased gigging demands, very little time was available and some nine months passed before the album's completion. Taking so long over an LP was unheard of in those days – Deep Purple had already released four studio records and one live album between September '68 and June '70, five albums in under two years – but thanks to the success of *In Rock*, they could now afford to take their time. Only one track was laid down at the first session, the country flavoured 'Anyone's Daughter,' which paid homage to country style, Blackmore-admired guitarists such as Albert Lee. "We were sitting round the studio waiting for inspiration and Ritchie just started tinkling around with that chord thing and we joined in," said Glover.

In October the band appeared on the French TV show *Pop Deux* a stunningly visual presentation that perfectly captured the Purple combination of

144

musicianship and arrogance. Although the 25 minute programme only featured edited versions of 'Mandrake Root' and 'Wring That Neck', Ritchie's
nonchalant display of playing one-handed whilst drinking a bottle of beer
with the other, perfectly embodied his insouciant spirit at the time. Within
a matter of months Purple's popularity throughout Europe increased
immeasurably. A four-date Scottish tour the same month prompted headlines of 'Purple mania.' Due to the huge demand the gig in Glasgow had
been switched from the 1,000 capacity Electric Garden to the larger
Tiffany's ballroom in Sauchiehall Street but even that wasn't big enough as
a reported 3,000 fans fought to get in to the venue. 17 police cars and vans
were called to the scene resulting in the headline '3,000 Pop Fans In Riot
At Hall Door' in the following morning's *Daily Record*.

Support act for the tour was a band called Tear Gas that included
Blackmore's former Hamburg associate Ricky Munro who recalls meeting
up with him for the first time since those days in Germany. "I actually came
across him again later on. But it was hello and goodbye … I got on with
him okay but he's a pretty private person." Blackmore's reluctance to renew
old acquaintances is another example of the way he ignored people without
giving it a second thought, even his own son. Ian Hansford: "I can remember Jürgen turning up at one gig and telling another band member to tell
him he was there but Ritchie wouldn't come and meet him."

The last gigs of the year were in Germany in December supported by the
Roy Young Band, featuring Blackmore's old mate Dave Wendels, on guitar.
The tour included a return to Hamburg and after the gigs the two men
socialised. Dave Wendels: "We had a great time in Hamburg doing all the
things musicians do: Drinking, picking up chicks. We went out together
partying, to the Top Ten Club. I'll never forget it. Some flash band got him
up there. The other player was frantically trying to play his Saturday night
licks even faster and Ritchie reduced him to a gibbering idiot. The other
guy just walked off embarrassed. Ritchie never liked that – it was the aspect
of jamming he didn't like. He couldn't just get up and play and enjoy
himself. Somebody would always want to play faster than him or show how
much better they are, which of course wasn't true for the most part."

Unhappy with trying to write songs on the road or in the studio the
band wanted to use the same approach they had done with the first album:
locked away somewhere remote without any distractions. After returning
from Germany they found a cottage in rural Devon but it turned out to be
a less than productive time, hanging around the local pub while Ritchie also
indulged in his beloved séances. One in particular involved Ian Paice's girlfriend Wendy asking Roger Glover if they could borrow his crucifix. Glover

wanted nothing to do with it and refused Wendy's request only to get an axe smashed through his bedroom door. "I leapt out of my bed and caught sight of Ritchie running down the corridor. I chased him, and he ended up in some dark corner. In my anger I picked up a chair and ripped off a leg. I'm a placid person but there I was with my hand around his throat and this chair leg raised. Ritchie's going 'Hey Roger it's me, remember I'm the guitarist.'"

The incident with the mild-mannered bass player was nothing compared to the friction that was starting to develop with Blackmore and Gillan. As Gillan admitted in his autobiography he had gone off the rails with his attitude and drinking problems. "He and Ritchie were at complete loggerheads," observed Glover, "and Ian may have got to the point where he thought, 'I'm the singer of the band – if Ritchie can behave like that so can I.' Blackmore's often selfish behaviour – not wanting to perform encores or in the case of the Eel Pie Island gig, playing offstage – annoyed Gillan. As time went on the relationship between singer and guitarist would continue on a downward spiral, but the friction was largely kept in check during the making of *Fireball*.

As 1970 drew to a close, Glover told one magazine that he hoped the album would be released by March but his comments were somewhat optimistic as by this time only a handful of tracks had been written. Of the new songs, 'I'm Alone' and 'Strange Kind Of Woman,' were coupled together and released as a single in February, while the rest of the album was still being worked on. Despite lyrics concerning a prostitute, 'Strange Kind Of Woman' became a Top 10 hit in the UK. While agreeing that all songs should be credited as group compositions it didn't take long for Blackmore to become unhappy with this arrangement.

The release of 'Strange Kind Of Woman' coincided with Purple's first official British tour: 19 dates commencing in Leeds in late January and continuing through to early March. The tour had various support bands including Heads, Hands & Feet featuring Chas Hodges and Albert Lee, who recalled, "I think we were in a hotel together and Ritchie tried to break into our room with a fire extinguisher and trash our room. I was sharing a room with Chas and I remember there were all these shenanigans going on." The tour was also notable due to Glover's ill health and at some gigs when he wasn't well enough to go back for the encore, Hodges deputised. The band's nightly fees were now in excess of £1,000 which helped to compensate for the temporary lack of funds from the American market.

Although the band were still travelling together to gigs, the Jaguar 420G had been upgraded to an even more luxurious Daimler DS420 limousine.

Long journeys were often spiced up by mischievous mayhem inevitably from Blackmore with Glover usually the hapless victim. "We actually tied Roger up in a Marshall case and we left him on the Severn Bridge," Blackmore claims. "He was the bass player – you had to do that to bass players. We went back for him later, and he was wriggling, trying to get out. We could see this wriggling Marshall thing! It's Roger Glover! We should have left him … Gillan used to sit in the back seat and was always trying to play with Roger. It was unbelievable! Roger would be sitting there, and I'd be in the front – we'd all travel together in the same car – and I'd hear this, 'Hey! Get off!' I'd look back and Gillan's going, 'Oh, just let me touch you, Roger.' Roger's going, 'Get off!' Jon would be reading a book. 'Cause Jon was there … the whole band … reading another book. Paicey would be counting the money and Gillan was actually always trying to play with him! Very strange! Until this one day … we kept hearing, 'Get off, Ian!' And I thought it was funny. But one day I looked round, and Roger's got his trousers half way down – Gillan's pulled his trousers down – and is now trying to perform oral sex … I'm like, 'What the hell is going on in here?' Of course, at this point Roger went berserk! 'Stop the car! You pervert! Get off!' I'm going, 'What the hell's going on here?' " On other occasions Glover would be stripped naked and kicked out of the car, left to fend for himself while getting to the hotel.

By now Purple's popularity had become global and in May '71 the band did their first ever tour of Australia, playing four or five shows depending on which set of accounting figures are given. Ian Hansford: "When we toured Australia, legally we only did four gigs but illegally we did five. We got cash for the last one. We did Randwick Stadium [Sydney] in the afternoon and then we even got caught up in our own traffic jam. Melbourne had sold out so quickly they said can we stick another night in and we said 'Yeah we'll do it for cash.' That was mad. We flew round the world and did five concerts in four days. I was only away from home for eight days, completely round the world. When we got to Los Angeles they gave us six hours off and a hotel room but not us – we went clubbing down the Whiskey A Go Go then straight back to the airport and on the plane again!"

A short European tour followed on from the Australian visit, including a trip to Reykjavik, the one and only time Deep Purple played in Iceland. On the flight over, the ceiling of the plane collapsed and one of the crew decided to attempt putting the wiring back in place without any instructions. Fortunately the group yelled at him to stop and the band arrived in Iceland unscathed. For Blackmore the experience determined the type of planes he was prepared to travel on in future. Ian Hansford: "We had a chartered prop plane and arrived the evening before the gig. It was strange there because in the clubs it was only non-alcoholic beers but you could buy a bottle of Scotch. Anyone taking any beer in had it confiscated at the airport – strange place."

A sign that Purple were recognised as one of the world's top bands was provided by their hotel being under virtual siege by the Icelandic fans for whom visits by bands of Purple's stature were a rare occurrence. Ian Hansford. "We had to walk up stairs, we couldn't get in the lift, there were so many people in the hotel and there was this young girl who was absolutely out of her brains. Roger and I were walking down a spiral staircase and she's staggering down the stairs and we are about four flights up. This hotel had a marble floor and she fell over the edge and I didn't want to look over because I just envisaged blood and bones but she bounced back onto the stairs on the floor below but she didn't even know it had happened she was so out of her bonce."

Recording sessions at both De Lane Lea and Olympic Studios in Barnes, south London continued to be slotted in between the band's touring commitments. By May the record companies were getting impatient, particularly in America where the band was scheduled to tour in July. Warner Bros desperately needed a new album to promote on the back of the visit but even after a solid fortnight in the studio in early June, the album still wasn't complete. Warner Bros opted to include 'Strange Kind Of Woman,' featuring a lengthier guitar fade out not on the single. In pacifying impatient fans in the UK, Gillan promised that when the album appeared there it would include this extended version of 'Strange Kind Of Woman' but this was overruled when the last track to be written and recorded, 'Demon's Eye' was favoured instead. When the LP eventually saw the light of day in Europe in September, exactly a year had passed since the sessions commenced.

The US and Canadian trek kicked off in Toronto on July 2. *In Rock* had not been released in America until late the previous year but the album hadn't take off in the same way it had in Europe. Despite the tour being the lengthiest in America since 1969, after five headlining shows, Purple had to play second fiddle to Rod Stewart and the Faces as they joined a three-act bill that also included openers Southern Comfort. However, at some gigs, despite Purple being limited to a one hour set, they often overshadowed the star attraction. Ian Hansford: "Anywhere near Detroit the Faces were enormous but go to Salt Lake City and they wouldn't let Purple off the stage. When the Faces came on people were just leaving."

Playing large venues, the tour went a long way in re-establishing Purple in America. The penultimate gig was at California's vast Long Beach Arena and for many young American rock fans it was their first introduction to Deep Purple and Ritchie Blackmore. One such fan, Mike Hill, recalls the impact they had: "All the instruments rocked away and each musician forced it to the limits. It became evident there and then that this mysterious thin man in black was rocking out, not only with the guitar in the most unlikely positions but in impossible ways no one had ever dreamed of before, not even Hendrix. During the closing number 'Mandrake Root', the guitarist emerged from the wings, then unstrapped the guitar and threw it down. Thereupon, he stood on it, actually playing music, not feedback. From our seats it appeared he was fretting with one foot and somehow picking with the other. Picking the guitar up, he proceeded to play what I can only describe as flute-like music. He then unloaded a flurry of notes that sounded like a machine gun, which taunted the organist who repeated the notes in kind…This was the greatest demonstration of creative energy output I'd ever experienced. [Ritchie] approached the mic stand and sawed the guitar back and forth on the shaft and then tied it to the stand with his shoulder strap, before slapping the machine head so that it began to spin. He left the stage and the house lights came up on an abandoned stage, the rest of the band having left during all of this. An announcer walked on, and over our grateful adulation shouted, 'From England! Deep Purple!' All about me people lauded the set; it was not only the greatest group I'd ever seen, it was the greatest entertainment ever. I sat winded; my senses had been pulverised."

Shortly after returning home, Blackmore confirmed to *NME*'s Richard Green, "The Faces pulled the crowd and we appealed to the Faces' crowd. We were prepared to be second to the Faces, but in certain places people would say 'Why are you second to the Faces?' They are very big in America. It was a very, very good tour – both for us and for the tour as a whole. We'd have to do very, very well, but at the same time they'd have to pull their fingers out to follow us. The result of the tour was the album going from 587 to 57, which helps. Obviously everyone who saw us on the tour has gone out and bought the album."

Upon the strength of *In Rock*, *Fireball* reached number one soon after release, yet the album didn't receive quite the same positive response as its predecessor. Perhaps mindful of the time that dragged from start to finish, Blackmore in particular was disappointed with the results. "There are only three tracks that I think are good – 'No No No', 'Fools' and 'Fireball' itself' ", he confessed shortly after the record's release. The other members were less damning but remained sceptical. The exception to the rule was Ian Gillan who to this day cites it as his favourite Deep Purple album.

Blackmore was already focusing on the next record. "The main thing is getting the next album done. I'm hoping the next one will be a little better," he commented in *NME* the same week that *Fireball* entered the charts. With a lack of conviction surrounding it, very little material from *Fireball* was played live during the tour designed to promote it. 'Demon's Eye' and 'Anyone's Daughter' had been included at a few shows earlier in the year and 'No No No,' 'The Mule' and the title track were included on the tour but with the exception of 'The Mule' most were soon replaced with a batch of new songs. In fact even on the way to the opening night of the tour at Portsmouth Guildhall on September 13, Blackmore came up with a new song on the coach. Several journalists had gone along with them for the ride and when one asked Ritchie how he wrote songs, he simply picked up his guitar and replied "Like this", before proceeding to play a fast riff with Ian Gillan making up lyrics off the cuff.

After working on the idea further during the soundcheck, the band opened the show with it that evening and although the lyrics would go through some revisions before being recorded, the title given to the new number remained as 'Highway Star.' Another new song written after *Fireball* had been completed was also rehearsed in time for the tour and as a blues based song, 'Lazy' replaced 'Wring That Neck' in the set. 'Wring That Neck' had been the one number on which Ritchie continued to use his Gibson 335, so this meant the guitar that his parents had bought him shortly after getting his first professional gig was retired from stage performances.[*] From this point on he chose to use Fender Stratocasters exclusively for the next 25 years. The UK tour concluded in Coventry on October 10 and two days later, Gene Vincent died. However it's highly unlikely that Vincent's former backing guitarist shed any tears.

Though commercially Purple were still on an upward curve, it could be argued that they had already peaked as a band; underlined by the tension that continued to fester between Gillan and Blackmore. In most major rock bands the singer and lead guitarist always command the most attention (e.g. The Rolling Stones – Mick Jagger & Keith Richards, The Who – Roger Daltrey & Pete Townshend, Led Zeppelin – Robert Plant & Jimmy Page, etc.). Almost from the moment Gillan had joined Deep Purple he found himself being rated among the world's top rock vocalists and Tim Rice and Andrew Lloyd-Webber picked him to sing the part of Jesus Christ in their

---

[*] Its last public appearance occurred on December 16 1971 when 'Fireball' was performed on *Top Of The Pops*.

rock opera *Jesus Christ Superstar* which certain Purple members might have felt was the ultimate example of typecasting!

On the opposite side of the coin Blackmore considered his virtuosity to be the main reason why Purple's popularity was increasing. Both parties felt they had an almost divine right to do as they pleased, as Roger Glover described, "They became two poles because the more one would do it the more the other would do it and the more one got away with it the more the other was determined he was going to get away with it."

In many respects their responses were quite similar. As an example, on an American tour around this period, Purple roadie (later Rainbow tour manager) Colin Hart had a run-in with union officials in Detroit when nailing Paice's drum kit to the acoustic rubber flooring of the venue. Sound engineer Bob Simon, whose company Tychobrae engineered the sound for many of Purple's American tours around this time recalls: "Ian Gillan found out what had happened and how Rob [Cooksey, roadie] and Colin had got 'rough housed' and so during the show, Ian Gillan walked over to me in the middle of the song and said 'How much do you want to bet me I can bust that microphone stand all over this stage?' I looked at him and said, 'I'll bet you a couple of bucks you can't.' He walked back out there and took the microphone stand and started digging big holes in that rubber flooring. Those union guys flipped out. We got Ian in the limo straight after the show and got him out of there but we still had a show to do there the next night. Next day these union guys grabbed him and took him in the dressing room with Tony Edwards there and made him sign a bunch of paperwork to say he'd pay for it. That's pretty much how they were. And Ritchie was also in to causing trouble. They [both] thought causing trouble and making a big stir would get in to the papers the next day and be the news, free publicity. Gillan was the first with that kind of action that I saw and then as Gillan kind of faded away Ritchie took over and intentionally, would not turn up for shows. We had five major riots I went through with those guys for not showing up."

With the friction between the pair not yet public knowledge, Blackmore revelled in his mean and moody public image – much of it an accurate reflection of his natural persona. Occasionally his nicer side emerged. John McCoy, who ironically later became a member of Ian Gillan's band, but was then bass player with Curtiss Maldoon, fondly recalls: "We were signed to Purple Records. We did a European tour [with Deep Purple]. Now that was a band. That was absolutely ... well ... just ... I mean I was there every single night. I was just, like, ga ga. It was so good and they weren't sort of ... huge egos between themselves. They were really a band then. I watched every night of course and ended up behind Ritchie's stacks helping their manager John Coletta to hold them up when Ritchie decided to give them a shove! When we did that 1971 European tour with Curtiss Maldoon Ritchie was the only one in the band who was nice to us! The rest of them just treated us like … basically you are the support band though we were on the same record company and had the same management … Ritchie was really nice to us. I think he got a lot of bad press."

After the success of the previous American tour, Purple returned in late October for another lengthy tour – this time headlining with nightly fees now in the region of $5–6,000. Sadly after just three shows the tour was cancelled when Gillan contracted hepatitis. While on the one hand it was a disappointment, it at least gave Blackmore and Gillan the opportunity of a few weeks apart from one another. With time now on his hands, along with Paice and Thin Lizzy's Phil Lynott, Blackmore went into the studio to experiment with the possible option of starting a new project.

Ian Hansford: "What Ritchie and Ian Paice wanted to do was a Jimi Hendrix type thing. I can't remember if it was before or after but they also had a rehearsal at Hanwell with Hamish Stuart from the Average White Band. I can vaguely remember one rehearsal at Hanwell and then once in the studio with Phil Lynott." Sadly the recordings were never finished and those who have heard them report that the results were nothing more than half-baked jams. Some sources suggest Blackmore had originally wanted to use Free's Paul Rodgers as vocalist on these sessions; such was his admiration for arguably the finest blues voice in Britain. The mercurial guitarist was focused on shifting Deep Purple into a bluesier direction and as a result, he was now viewing Gillan's singing style in a different light.

CHAPTER 7

Down The Road Of Golden Dust (1971–73)

With the exception of Ian Gillan the members of Deep Purple generally agreed that *Fireball* had been too radical and that the next album should return to a more 'down the line,' no compromise approach. They unanimously decided to break from touring to record the new album as opposed to the stop-start way the previous albums had been completed. Once Ian Paice discovered the startling difference in sound between the studio and the corridor as he wandered around banging a snare drum during the making of *Fireball*, the band wanted to take things a step further; to get as close as possible to a natural sound from all the instruments. As Roger Glover explained at the time, "Live recordings nearly always seem to have so much more vitality and excitement. Partly due to the presence of an audience which brings out an indefinable spark in the musician that doesn't exist in a 'cold' studio, and partly due to the natural acoustics in which the music is recorded." Clearly there was no way the band could set up and play in a corridor, so instead they opted to record the album on stage, making a studio album under live conditions minus an audience.

When revealing to *NME* that the record would be made in Switzerland, Blackmore was quizzed as to why. "Money! When you make a record in England, the tax people come down on you but if you make a record out of the country you're not really taxed on it." The chosen venue was the Casino in Montreux where the band had played several times and been impressed by the acoustics. With Gillan now recovered from his illness the band and entourage travelled to Switzerland in December 1971, with three weeks set aside to write and record new material prior to returning home for a break over Christmas.

On arrival, promoter and Montreux Festival organiser Claude Nobs invited the band to the final concert being held in the Casino prior to the winter shutdown, after which, the band were to take up residency to record. As all lyrically discerning rock fans will be aware, the concert, by Frank Zappa and the Mothers, was halted midway through when someone fired a flare gun into the wooden roof. Mothers' keyboard player Don Preston remembers the Casino burning down, and some of the rather bizarre connections associated with it. "On that tour, one of the promotional items had the tour dates printed on a box of matches! I thought that was kind of interesting. The other interesting thing was that four days before we played [at the Casino] and in the exact same spot when the fire started: in the middle of my solo during 'King Kong', somebody came out on stage and stopped us from playing and issued a fire warning that they had detected smoke or flames somewhere and they wanted people to vacate the building. But before they could, someone else came out and said it was okay, so we finished playing. [In Montreux] we played as we normally did and we got into 'King Kong' and my solo on mini-moog and someone threw a firecracker up into the roof, which was covered with dried palm leaves and that started a fire right up on the roof."

In his autobiography Zappa wrote, "There were between 2,500 and 3,000 kids packed into the room – well over capacity. Since more kids were outside, trying to get in, the organisers had cleverly chained the exit doors shut. When the fire began, the audience was left with two ways out: through the front door, which was pretty small, or through a plate glass window off to the side of the stage." Preston recalls that "People were starting to panic and if I remember correctly it was during the day, it was like a matinee, but I do remember people coming up on stage and grabbing these huge Orange amplifiers and they were throwing them through these plate glass windows that were along one wall, looking out to Lake Geneva, so they were breaking all the windows to get out of the room. If they hadn't had all those windows there would probably have been fatalities.

"The other thing I remember really vividly, [backing vocalist] Mark Volman had just bought a brand new hollow-bodied Gibson guitar and it got knocked over in the heat of the moment, no pun intended, and as he bent over to pick it up and take it to safety, someone's foot went right through and smashed the guitar to smithereens because people were running to get out of the place. They were getting on the stage so they could go backstage and go out one of the back doors. I remember all of us leaving the venue and going back to the hotel located on Lake Geneva so we could actually see the place burning down from our hotel and also the smoke on the water. It really was smoke on the water."

While Deep Purple had been in the audience when the fire broke out, in a BBC Radio *Guitar Great* special over a decade later, presenter Alexis Korner claimed that at the time of the incident Blackmore was trying to find a quite room backstage to take a young lady he had just acquainted. If true it would be in keeping with his general behaviour at the time although it isn't clear whether or not Blackmore was literally caught with his pants down.

Despite all the problems on his hands, Nobs found the band a new recording venue; Le Pavilion, an old concert hall where further problems ensued. The noise generated caused complaints from the locals and eventually the police were banging on the door demanding the band stop. The roadies kept the officials at bay until the track being worked on was completed. The backing track in question, the only one completed at Le Pavilion would become known as 'Smoke On The Water' featuring (arguably) the most famous rock guitar riff of all time. Eventually recording moved over to the Grand Hotel, another building closed for the winter season. The lack of padding and soundproofing enabled the sounds of the instruments to reverberate around the walls. 'Highway Star' and 'Lazy' had already been written and established in the live set and some of the other songs had been worked out so despite the difficult recording circumstances, the album came together fairly quickly. The enforced lay-off due to Gillan's illness had also helped the working environment and apart from the physical problem of having to walk through rooms, over balconies and down staircases just to hear a playback, the end results were to pay dividends.

The quality of the material produced in Switzerland was greeted with unanimous enthusiasm from the band and before long most of the songs found their way into a thoroughly revamped live show. With recording completed, Purple returned home for Christmas before another American tour kicked off on January 13 in Hollywood. The pressure from cramming 16 shows into 19 days and the long distances between cities started to tell. When Blackmore failed to show up in the hotel lobby one morning Colin Hart went to the guitarist's room only to find him in tears. "I just couldn't take any more of being pushed around from one hotel to another," Blackmore told Nina Myskow in 1980. "All I ever wanted to do was to play guitar and suddenly everything was crazy. I ended up in hospital having

155

tranquillisers pumped into me. Every time the doctor tried to ask me what was wrong all I could do was cry."

Blackmore managed to get through the tour and a round of European shows throughout February and early March. Just prior to its release the band showcased *Machine Head* the first output from their own, newly formed Purple Records label, on the BBC's *In Concert* programme in March. With the exception of 'Pictures Of Home' the entire album was played alongside 'Strange Kind Of Woman' and a rousing version of Little Richard's 'Lucille.' 'Never Before' was released as the next single but when it failed to draw the same interest as earlier efforts the song was dropped from the set immediately along with 'Maybe I'm A Leo'. With 'Highway Star' already established as the opening number, 'Lazy', 'Smoke On The Water' and 'Space Truckin'' would become integral to Deep Purple's live show from hereon.

Blackmore was more upbeat about *Machine Head* than he had been with its predecessor. "When Ian was sick we had about two months to write and it shows on this latest album." As with *Fireball*, *Machine Head* reached number one in the UK and the album found more favour among fans and critics than any of the band's previous releases – not just in Europe but in America where Deep Purple recaptured the success they had first tasted four years earlier but on an even greater level. 'Smoke On The Water' – seen as nothing more than an album track in the band's eyes – received massive amounts of airplay ensuring that it soon became the album's most popular cut in America. Purple toured the States extensively throughout the year and with the band's nightly fee now regularly commanding in excess of $10,000, they could afford to indulge themselves.

Ritchie and Bärbel moved to a larger house in Camberley, close to his parents' home in Surrey. Shortly after moving, Blackmore's former Savages cohort Tony Dangerfield got an unexpected phone call. "Ritchie had got this place just outside Virginia Water and he invited me down for the day. First mistake I made I took this German girl with me, a Page Three girl called Lola, because I thought she'd get on with Babs … He'd had an extension built, which sort of resembled the Blockhütte, with the football table. He said to me, 'How's your bass playing?' I said 'Why?' 'He said, 'We've got a tour starting and Roger's health isn't too good and could you dep for him?' I was very blasé about it but it never materialised."

Whether or not it was a factor of the band's increased popularity, for Glover, "after *Machine Head*, Ritchie became increasingly single-minded." Despite the album's success the side project with Paice and Lynott was still on Blackmore's mind. "I want to get on with my band – we all want to get on with our other interests – and I have to envisage an end to Deep Purple to stay sane. But we'll keep together for a bit yet because we're earning good money and we might as well clean up. I think we deserve it. I starved for six years, and the band has built itself a good reputation over the years."

Through a combination of selfishness, passion and determination, Blackmore felt he ruled the roost in Deep Purple and most of the band became generally subservient to his demands. The inevitable exception was Gillan who regularly sought to undermine Blackmore's dominance. Although exuberant onstage the guitarist was a far more introverted character out of the limelight compared to the gregarious singer. "I used to call him Oliver Rude, because he is very similar to Oliver Reed," Blackmore recalled in 1998. "He's a very brash individual. It wasn't just the voice. I found him very disquieting to be around. I always found myself going, 'I've got to get out of here.' We used to get reports, in '72 I suppose, a roadie would call up and say, 'If you're thinking about going for a drink in the hotel, I just thought I'd tell you Gillan's in the bar.' I'd say, 'Is it hunched shoulders?' If he said, 'Yes, *very* hunched shoulders' that meant that Ian had been in there all day and night and just wanted to blow off steam to someone. That used to bother me. Why was this guy so overbearing? Sure enough, you'd walk past and you'd look into the bar and there would be this hunched shouldered figure, looking into his beer. Of course, if you walked in and he saw you, he'd sit up and go, 'Hey!' But I'd be like, 'Yes, Ian, all right? But, er, I've got to go now.'

"You've got to know Ian to figure out what his personality is. It takes quite a while because he's a very astute man, very clever but he's got this very strange side to him, which is another side I don't like, the obnoxious side, and that doesn't often come out until you've been around him quite often. Because he's got the flattering side, the very charming side that some people see. He knows how to put the charm on; he's an intellect in his own way. He's an intelligent man. People often say that Jon Lord is the most intelligent one of us, but no – Gillan is the most intelligent. But he just used to be so coarse. I didn't like to be around the guy because I felt that he was doing things for shock value, to be talked about for the hell of it. Stories wouldn't come around naturally with Ian. He would manufacture a story, invariably, of course with no clothes on. The first 10 times it was funny, but after that ..."

For a man who in the past had defecated around a dressing room, and was dictatorial in his working methods, Blackmore's views on Gillan as "coarse" and "overbearing" would appear somewhat disingenuous. At times both men's humour and outlook seemed in tandem but neither appeared able to accept anything other than top dog status. Something would ultimately have to give.

Having already suffered a breakdown in America at the start of the year, Blackmore's health took another turn for the worse in March when, after starting a US tour with two shows at New York's Staten Island, he was struck down by the same hepatitis that affected Gillan the previous October. Under pressure from all corners to continue, after playing the next gig in Flint, Michigan as a four-piece, the band hired Spirit guitarist Randy California as a replacement. Following a couple of day's rehearsal, California played a show in Quebec City but as good as he was, without Purple's bedridden guitarist it plainly didn't work. As Glover said, "We all realised we couldn't work without Ritchie. He was such an integral part of the sound that it was impossible to carry on without him so we cancelled." Even Gillan was gracious enough to add, "I don't think it would have been right to carry on without Ritchie. They didn't carry on without me when I was ill and that had a lot to do with the decision to cancel."

When speaking to Scott Cohen for *Circus* Blackmore used his illness to explain his superstitious nature. "I won't stay in a room that adds up to 13. Like if the number of the room is 607. I noticed it when I went down with hepatitis. Two weeks before I went down with it I wasn't feeling too well and did notice the numbers on my door. I tended to add them up because I was bored and noticed that in nearly every hotel where I stayed I got a room that added up to 13."

By May Blackmore was well enough to go back on the road but special dietary requirements had to be followed as Ian Hansford recalls: "He pissed me off after we went back on tour after he had hepatitis. It was basically because of the diet. He could only eat boiled fish and boiled chicken and we ended up buying him a portable cooker and then someone had to do his shopping. And he was also on glucose which was difficult to get in America. Whereas here you can go into a chemist's and buy as many bags as you want, you couldn't do that over there because apparently it's used to dilute drugs. Basically you could only get one packet and I had to find time to get that packet and you might have three flights a day to get somewhere from one small place to another small place. I was a bit pissed off after that tour. We finished in Los Angeles and there was only me and a couple of the band going back the next day but Ritchie wasn't one of them. I had to be up at eight and he had great pleasure about four in the morning banging on my door, going 'Oh thanks for all your help this tour' and he gave me a bottle of Bacardi. I felt like smacking him over the head with it."

Blackmore's illness unwittingly brought him into contact with a little-known American band called Elf, who included among their ranks vocalist Ronald Padavonna, better known by his stage name of Ronnie James Dio. The band's roadie was Raymond D'addario: "We'd done an album and it was a really funny story because the guy who was booking Purple at the time was Ronnie's manager Bruce Payne and he set up an audition in New York City with Columbia Records for Elf. In the meantime Purple had come over to do a tour and Ritchie got hepatitis and went back to England to get healthy and they got Randy California – played one or two gigs and they said, 'Nah forget it, we're knocking it on the head until Ritchie's healthy again.' So Roger and Ian Paice come to New York City and Bruce brings them to the audition and they go, 'Whoa that band's great.' Bruce said, 'You wanna produce them?' So three weeks later in Warren, Georgia, Bruce is having Ian Paice and Roger Glover produce the band and a month later we were back touring with Purple. We did a lot of touring with them. That's how Ritchie got really familiar with Ronnie. You could tell he liked Ronnie's voice. When I first started working for them Gillan was still in the band and it was around the time when Ian and Ritchie weren't speaking."

With Blackmore back to full fitness, the tours continued throughout America for most of the summer. As befitting a Seventies rock star Ritchie enjoyed the rock 'n' roll lifestyle but eschewed the drugs in favour of the sex. His penchant for women would involve a roadie scanning the audience before a show as sound engineer Bob Simon relates: "[Ritchie] was always kind of a lonely guy so he would hook up with a chick. He'd have [Purple roadie] Ron Quinton out in the audience before the show had started. I said to Ronnie one night 'What are you doing out here man?' and he was walking around while looking and he told me one night that his deal was to find the prettiest chick with the biggest tits, and take her back to the dressing room for Ritchie. That was pretty much every night. [Ritchie] was into his women and isolated himself from the rest of the band but he had that planned. He was the star of the show. He walked up to me one day and said 'I'm right up front, I'm always up front. And then comes Gillan. Then comes Lordy and then Paicey and Glover. But I'm up in the mix all the time.' He's got it all planned out, he's got a mission; he's always on a mission. Some nights I'd just crank it up and people would walk out of there; 'Ooh my ears.' He'd be really happy with that – he told me he wanted to put them down in their seats when he was playing."

When he wasn't putting them down in their seats, during one of the '72 American tours Blackmore's passion for busty young women got the better of him, resulting in the cancellation of a gig in Roanoke, Virginia. On the evening before the show he allegedly enticed two women back to his hotel room, blissfully unaware that they were under the age of consent in Virginia. They were delighted to be dallying with an English rock star but one of them took a photo that was subsequently found by her father, as Hansford confirms, "We cancelled the gig for that reason. I think she had a Polaroid." Fortunately the Purple management got wind of the situation and Blackmore was hastily whisked out of state before the police arrived at his hotel, but without a guitarist the band had no option but to cancel that evening's show.

Deep Purple were at their commercial peak during the groupie age and some eyewitnesses report seeing Blackmore with several different girls during the course of a day. With the wives and girlfriends being left at home, the American tours in particular had a seemingly endless supply of willing females at the band's disposal as Ian Paice said, "Touring was a lot of fun then. It was a single man's game and we were all single men or at least we behaved like single men." Although they might have liked to behave like single men the fact that Gillan insisted on bringing his girlfriend Zoe Dean along caused a rift in the camp, which he openly admitted in his autobiography. "The close bonded relationship within the group began to crack when I brought Zoe with me. We started to live in separate hotels and I even took my own limo." As Zoe said herself in an interview in *Record Mirror*, "I never get bored on the road. There's always something for me to do like making phone calls." Unfortunately for the others, some of those calls would be to their partners, updating them about events on the road. "She used to come everywhere and get up people's noses – mainly Ritchie's actually," comments Hansford.

It was partly for this reason that Gillan started to travel separately. While he claims in his book this was because he was "generally playing the star part to the limit," other sources claim he was pressured into it from the rest of the band so that Zoe would be impervious to what went on. Blackmore certainly didn't want his private fun being commented on by the girlfriend of a singer of whom his respect was dwindling. Ian Hansford: "I don't know how Ian Gillan went about it but in Scotland or somewhere like that, he managed to get some poll going with Zoe as to who was the best member or musician in Deep Purple and it came out Ian Gillan and that got right up Ritchie's nose."

In July '72 Purple took a slight break to focus on writing but by the time they travelled to Rome to start work it was treated as a holiday, resulting in only one completed track that ended up on what would become *Who Do We Think We Are*. During these sessions, Blackmore continued to isolate himself as he did most of his work while the others were absent, spending time in the company of old pal Arvid Andersen who brought along his friend, Italian keyboard player Joe Vescovi.* In spite of the scorching August weather, Vescovi described the house as having been turned into a fortress, surrounded by a host of roadies, with all the doors and windows closed, and the Rolling Stones Mobile Studio parked outside the courtyard because it couldn't pass through the gate. As with *Machine Head* close circuit cameras were installed so Martin Birch could view proceedings from the recording truck, and what little work Blackmore did do was often by Birch's side and away from the rest of the group.

Slotted in between the Rome trip and tours of America, was the band's first ever visit to Japan in mid August. To mark the occasion the Japanese arm of Warner Bros wanted to record a live souvenir. Given Purple's reputation as a live act with an emphasis on improvisation, it seems strange that it took them so long to make such a recording, which would probably have never eventuated without the record company's initial suggestion. Once Purple agreed to the idea they were adamant that if it was going to be recorded then it should be done properly. To this end, Birch was employed to record three shows the band played in Osaka and Tokyo. Once the band heard the playback they were so taken aback by the quality of the recordings that what was originally planned solely for the Japanese market gained a worldwide release in December '72. With no overdubs of any kind, Glover and Paice (the other members showed little interest) selected and mixed the best of Birch's superior recordings into one of the finest live rock albums.

But no matter how great a live band Deep Purple were at this time the friction between Blackmore and Gillan was reaching breaking point. The management was doing its utmost to keep the internal bickering from the public glare and even those who worked for the band seemed unaware of the depth of enmity between singer and guitarist. Hansford first got wind that there was bad blood between the pair at the penultimate show of an American tour in Norfolk, Virginia on September 1. "I was out at the mixer and I can remember Ritchie just took his guitar off half way through a number, it was the end of the set anyway and he threw it on the floor and walked off. He didn't lay it down, just got hold of it by the neck and slammed it on the floor. I spent about 15 minutes walking round, asking 'Where's Ritchie?' Apparently he got a lift from somebody back to the hotel and when I got there I was fuming because I didn't know where he was.

---

* When approached in 2006, Andersen did not recall bringing Vescovi with him to the villa.

Apparently Ian Gillan said to him, 'Look at me, you cunt.' He was like leading it and Ritchie took umbrage to that and took his guitar off and threw it on the floor and went.

"I just said to him, 'What the hell was going on? I've been looking for you, I didn't know where you were. I didn't want to leave the gig in case you were still there.' He just said, 'I'm sorry, I've just had it with Gillan basically.' I can remember Gillan pointing at himself — that must have been when he said, 'Look at me, you cunt.' I think that was the first time I knew there was a bit of friction going on between the two of them. After that life did get a bit fraught. It was like trying to keep them apart basically. If one were getting away with one thing the other would try and get away with something else. It was just an ongoing battle." Sound engineer Bob Simon concurs with Hansford's observations. "Probably the third tour I did with them they were completely on different trips. There wasn't much socialising between them." According to Glover, "the last year I don't think Ritchie and Ian Gillan spoke one word to each other."

It was hardly conducive to making good music. In October the band travelled to the small village of Waldorf Nord near Frankfurt in another attempt to record songs for the next album. Gillan's feelings towards Blackmore were documented in 'Smooth Dancer.' Although not mentioning Blackmore directly, the metaphor 'black suede', his preferred choice of clothing at the time, left no doubt as to whom Gillan was referring. "Black suede just brings me misery" / "You can rock 'n' roll but you can never show your soul" and "Your swollen up inside with nothing but your pride" were some of the more direct attacks on Blackmore's character. Gillan also expressed a desire, "I want to be inside of you" but having failed to sufficiently analyse what made Blackmore tick, as well as his own disillusionment with Deep Purple's musical direction, Gillan informed the management of his desire to quit via a handwritten resignation letter. However, with touring commitments booked up to June '73 throughout Europe, America and Japan, he agreed to fulfil forthcoming performances over the ensuing six months.

At a gig in Holland on January 28, 1973, violence erupted among the audience on a scale never before witnessed at a Deep Purple concert. Due to the band's popularity, the venue (De Oude Rai, an old wooden cattle hall) was the only building in the city big enough to cater for the ticket demand. However the power supply was insufficient for Purple's PA set up. The band arrived late in Amsterdam from Cologne via the Trans Europe Express and after being made aware of the power problems, Purple's management threatened to withdraw them from appearing until somebody suggested feeding electricity from the Okura Hotel next door. With 12,000 crammed into the hall over an estimated 10,000 capacity, concerns over the lack of security once again threatened the cancellation of the show. Blackmore took one look at the mob, muttered "What a mess, I'm not going on stage like this" and headed back to the dressing room with the rest of the band close behind.

Consequently the band did not appear until an hour later than scheduled. Approximately 55 minutes into the show one of Blackmore's guitar strings broke at the end of a song. He threw the guitar in the air and left the stage with the rest of the band soon following.

The following day road manager Nick Dorman explained to *Veronica* magazine, "It's not just the fault of one party. The organisation was bad and there wasn't enough security. The band is partly to blame for not playing an encore. They should have known it would end in a riot. A few days ago we played in Germany. They refused to play an encore as well and the German audience wasn't too pleased either but we managed to leave without any damage. Here in Amsterdam we have a lot of damage. Quite a few things have been stolen; cables, microphones, stands, cymbals, bits of amplifiers. But the main damage is the equipment that got destroyed. Nothing was left of the drum kit; the organ doesn't function anymore and has lost quite a few keys. Blackmore's guitar is broken but then he threw it in the air. The mixing desk halfway down the hall is completely gone. Somebody poured beer in it. All the amplifiers on stage are broken. So is the lighting equipment. That's about it, I think. We have to find out how much can be repaired but we're talking probably 50–70,000 guilders worth of damage. The problem is we need the equipment in three days time in Copenhagen so we've already ordered new stuff from Marshall in London. We are insured but we probably won't get a payout because there wasn't enough security. We found those guys tucked away under the stairs! Of course it's pretty clear we will never play in Holland again."

Although the rest of the tour went off without any major hitches, it looked as if Deep Purple were going to fold completely. With Gillan leaving, the management initially hoped that the rest of the band would keep the name alive. However the whole situation was turned upside down when the original trio decided to stay together upon Blackmore's proviso that Glover be replaced. Years later he expanded on his reasoning, "I hadn't 'decided', I had gone [to the other members] 'Come on, we've got to do something.' And it was always like, 'OK, you're right – what?' I remember with Roger, I didn't want to get rid of him, *I* wanted to leave. I said, 'Paicey, we're leaving!' because I wanted to form this thing with Phil Lynott. I said

I wanted to leave and he said, 'Well, could anything persuade you to stay, because we're on to such a good thing. Why mess it up?' I said, 'No, I want to get together with Phil. Myself, you and Phil will be a great band. I want to do a bluesier thing.' I felt that Purple was getting into that armchair thing, that security thing. But I also had hesitations – and I think Phil did too because he was doing kind of well. We wanted to play together but he'd just had a hit.*

"But Paicey was reluctant to leave: 'Phil's good but don't you think we should try?' I said, 'No, I can't handle Gillan.' 'What else is the problem?' 'There's just too many changes I would make and that's not fair for me to say.' 'Well, what are the changes?' 'That doesn't matter.' I remember being hesitant about it because Roger was Mr. Nice Guy. But the next day Paicey asked, 'What exactly are the changes you would make to stay in this band?' So I went, 'Get rid of Roger … but I don't want to. He's the anchor of the band, such a nice guy. He's done nothing wrong. I would want another bass player who's bluesy. But I can't ask for that, that's why I want to leave, get out and do my own thing and hopefully you'll come with me – if not I'll get someone else.' He's going, 'If you want to get rid of Roger, we'll get rid of Roger.' 'No, that's not really fair, he's doing nothing wrong.' I had no regrets about Gillan – we both hated each other and that was it. But Roger didn't hurt anybody, why should he get sacked? But then it was, 'OK, but who's going to tell Roger?' 'We'll get the management to tell him.' 'Well if you can do that I might stay 'cos this changes everything.' I had my thing with Gillan but I wasn't going to force Roger out of the band. It was time for me to leave but Paicey talked me into it. Jon didn't know anything about it. He was reading a book, as we used to joke."

Another possible factor in Glover's removal was Blackmore's disillusionment over the five-way writing split. With Deep Purple records selling by the millions and with Gillan leaving anyway, to remove Glover from the equation gave Blackmore the chance to effectively dominate the songwriting even further. In the same underhand way that Rod Evans and Nick Simper were treated, Blackmore, Lord, and Paice started looking for a bass player, with Glover oblivious to what was being plotted.

While touring America Deep Purple had picked up on a young Midlands three-piece called Trapeze, who were signed to the Moody Blues' Threshold label. Trapeze gained little success in Britain but were making waves in

---

* 'Whisky In The Jar' by Thin Lizzy reached number six in the UK Top 10 in early 1973.

various American states. Co-conspirators Blackmore, Lord and Paice were suitably impressed with bassist-cum-vocalist Glenn Hughes, who initially had no idea they were sounding him out. "I was pretty slow to understand that because I was so young and so naïve that I just thought they liked the band. Lordy and Paicey would come one night and Ritchie would always come alone or with his wife. Maybe the third time I figured something's up here. I think it was the last time Ritchie came to see me. They'd seen me twice in LA at the Whisky, and then Ritchie came again in London and Jon again in London at the Marquee. It was then that I started to realise and I'd heard a rumour that Gillan was leaving. All along I never realised they wanted me to take Roger's place. I thought they just wanted me to be the singer."

Once Hughes realised that Glover would also be leaving the band he made another false assumption. "I'd heard a rumour that Ritchie and Ian had been doing something with Phil Lynott so I just figured they were just looking for a trio thing with an organ. Then if I remember correctly Purple were playing at the Felt Forum [in LA] for two or three nights and they had flown me in and after that concert they had a meeting the next day and asked me to replace Roger who they were about to let go. I wasn't really interested in that but the thing that swayed it for me was that they said they were going to ask or that they were really interested in getting Paul Rodgers to sing. Being in a band with Paul and singing with him was really interesting to me."

In just a few short months from when he was considering leaving Deep Purple, Blackmore was now back in the driving seat and dictating the band's future direction. Not only did he have it in mind to shift into a blues direction, something suited to Rodgers but with Hughes on board as well, Purple would have two fine vocalists, adding a further dimension with their capability of providing harmonies.

During the final months that Gillan served out his notice, Glover soon started to feel alienated. Sensing something was afoot he quizzed the management who eventually confirmed that the remaining trio were looking to replace him. Glover didn't wait to be fired and instead took the option to quit at the same time as Gillan's departure.

On the Deep Purple MK II line-up's final tour of Japan the normally disciplined Japanese audiences caused a riot during the penultimate show at Tokyo's Budokan. Although damage to the band's equipment wasn't on the scale of the Amsterdam show earlier in the year, it was caused as a direct result of Blackmore's uncompromising attitude. With the audience leaving a trail of devastation and destruction within the 13,000 seat auditorium, Bob

Simon recalls: "Finally I get back in the hotel a couple of hours later. My clothes are all torn up, I'm all bloody and I've been fighting with all these Japanese guys. As I'm getting into the elevator to go to my room, Ritchie's getting out and I said to him, after we [the crew] had just taken a good bollocking and all the equipment got busted up, 'What the fuck was that all about?' He said, 'The audience sucked. They didn't deserve an encore so fuck 'em.' He liked to see things happening."

CHAPTER 8

The Black Sheep Of The Family (1973–75)

Although Glenn Hughes agreed to take over as Deep Purple's new bassist and second vocalist, Paul Rodgers turned the band down, much to Blackmore's disappointment. Free had recently split for the second and last time, but the idea of joining Purple held little attraction for him as he was more interested in creating a new band which became Bad Company. In 1973 Rodgers was regarded as one of Britain's top rock singers and when the press heard rumours that he might unite with Purple they couldn't contain their excitement. It was a situation that Blackmore believed convinced Rodgers to turn them down. "If Paul had been interested in joining he would have. But when he saw that in *Melody Maker* he went, 'What kind of morons are these, saying I've joined their band when I haven't even made my mind up?'"

The management's presumptuous claim that they had got their man was undoubtedly a poorly-handled situation, but although the band could have continued as a four-piece with Hughes handling the vocals, Blackmore was adamant that he wanted a front person with, as he put it, a more "masculine" voice. The other two went along with his idea of introducing harmonies into the music as Lord explained at the time: "The lead singer carries the voice of the band – no pun intended. He carries the major portion of what the audience gets from the band. When Ian left it was an enormous gap to fill – we had to find the kind of singer who could carry that weight on his shoulders. So the guy we obviously thought of was Paul Rodgers."

167

While looking for a lead singer Blackmore and Hughes commenced working on new ideas, as the latter remembers: "A couple of months after joining Purple in June of 1973, after spending time with Jon and Paicey, Ritchie asked if I'd like to come down to his house. As always, the enigma that surrounded him was true; he is the 'Man In Black.' He even had a black dog, black everything! After spending time in his pub that was built in his house, we strapped our guitars on and started jamming. We got into this half-time groove in F#. The song in question was the early stage of 'Mistreated.' It was a real blast to have just the two of us, face to face, creating this fine song. Ritchie was very jovial and extremely passionate about his views on life and Deep Purple." Hughes recalls the results of the response to the Vocalist Wanted advert placed in *Melody Maker*. "There was a lot of listening to tapes at the Purple offices in Newman Street. I listened to a couple but the guys were listening to a lot more. Some of it wasn't very good but I think all along Ritchie was wanting the Paul Rodgers sound and with David's tape it was definitely that tonal quality they were looking for."

During an interview with Swedish journalist Mike Eriksson Lord recalled, "When it became known that we were looking for a new singer we were swamped with tapes. We tried to listen but we really had a hard time finding anything decent. And one day, and I swear that this is true, I picked up a tape and said 'If this isn't any good, forget it,' and it was the tape from David Coverdale."

Coverdale was plucked out of obscurity from the North East of England and despite the initial reservations the band may have had Hughes considered it was the right move. "David was under the gun because he was green and had never been on a major stage, he'd never even been recorded before properly, he was very nervous. It was a massive thing for any band to do of that stature. We could probably have got a bigger artist to join but it probably was best for Deep Purple to bring in a total unknown. It was a major thing that nobody else had done in that category that was massive."

Purple couldn't have found a greater challenge than replacing Gillan with such a total unknown. Coverdale's audition took place at Scorpio Sound in London, a process the singer remembers vividly: "Paicey and Lordy were already at the studio when I arrived. Mr. Lord was exceptionally charming and welcoming, doing his best to put me at ease whilst Ian messed around on his Ludwig drum kit. Ritchie arrived next with his wife, Babs, and their two wolfhounds whom Ritchie obviously doted on. He completely ignored me, other than a quick surreptitious look to check me out, a brief nod when we made eye contact. I told them I'd learned 'Strange Kind Of Woman' and we proceeded to 'blues' it up. Ritchie looked at me and said the way I was interpreting the song was how he'd envisaged it sounding when he wrote it."

It didn't take long for the new recruits to work out who was the dominant force in the band. Glenn Hughes: "Jon was very calm and nice and well spoken, and Paicey has always been and probably still is a very money orientated guy. Ritchie on the other hand was the artistic character, larger than life. I think him; Pagey, Beck and Clapton, after the death of Hendrix, were ruling the world as guitar players. When I stepped into that band after *Machine Head* and *Made In Japan*, he was probably the greatest live guitar player since Hendrix, so I was joining a band where I was working with *the* top guitar player and he was playing brilliantly back then."

Like Hughes Coverdale was invited to Blackmore's house for a writing session. "I quickly found out that Ritchie was the principal composer in Purple. He played me much of the basic material for what ultimately became the *Burn* album. Ritchie worked on a Revox reel-to-reel recorder. He knew how to double and triple track his song ideas, so, they were very full sounding and pleasing to the ear when he played his demos to me. Ultimately, he used to take his tape deck with him to use during live shows to create a tape delay on his guitar sound, fuelling a rumour that he wasn't actually playing live, which, of course, he was."

Initially the band considered recording the album in Germany and while in Hamburg, Ritchie showed the young and impressionable Coverdale the notorious Hamburg club scene. "I had never been in clubs anything like this and the band was treated like royalty wherever we ventured. The music the DJ's were playing sounded insanely good. I'd never heard anything like it. Ritchie told me to watch what tempos were inspiring the dancers and to apply it to how I wrote music. He was definitely an observer was ole Ritchie and I learned an immense amount from him."

The band then decamped to Clearwell Castle in Gloucestershire where they invited the press along to introduce their new lead singer, after which time was devoted in working up what were predominantly Blackmore's ideas for the album. Being a 'new boy' Hughes was subjected to Blackmore's pranks. "Ritchie was the first guy there and I was the second. On the first night it was just Ritchie and I alone with our roadies. He set up the normal thing for me, a microphone in my room and he had my room tapped and the speakers in the wardrobe making weird noises. He waited four hours until about four in the morning and got me. That's Blackmore. He's 60 now and I believe he carries a water pistol to this day!"

Hughes confirms Blackmore's desire to overthrow the five-way writing credits. "On *Burn* Ritchie wrote a lot of the music. I think he was getting

tired of other members; I shan't name names, who weren't really contributing. Let's face it; songwriting is our life's financial blood, that's where an artist
makes his serious money, the catalogue still sells. Ritchie was done with splitting it five ways that was something he discussed with me and everyone else.
He befriended me and said, 'Every man should get what he writes.' That
started on the *Burn* record. He said 'Enough is enough it's a new band, we'll
do it a little differently' and I think Ritchie was right about that."

Whereas Lord had originally been quite involved with the writing, after
the *Concerto* he had very much taken a back seat. By his own admission he
confessed: "I don't think of myself as a great rock 'n' roll writer. With a guitar
you can come up with a decent riff in minutes. You can't do that with keyboards." While playing down whether any one individual dominated Deep
Purple, Lord's comments to *Circus* revealed Blackmore's role: "It's totally
democratic. The major force in the group for the last couple of years has
been Ritchie. It's been his energy that's got us through a lot of our personal
problems."

David Coverdale: "I could sense, even then, that they all deferred to
Ritchie and most definitely didn't want to piss him off but, still, it was quite
democratic, and everyone contributed to the development of the songs."

Mindful of the friction that had been present during the making of the disappointing *Who Do We Think We Are* the band opted to return to
Montreaux – where *Machine Head* had successfully gelled – in November
'73. Although once again they had "the Rolling Stones mobile just
outside", fortunately this time around no fire "burnt the place to the
ground" and the album was recorded without any hitches. The enforced lay
off gave Blackmore time to write new songs and for the band to rehearse.
By the time they arrived in Montreux most of the ideas were already in
place. The overall sound was noticeably different with the bluesy approach
favoured and largely directed by Blackmore. The combined talents of
Hughes and Coverdale, who were also naturally inclined in that direction,
helped to shape the new songs such as 'Might Just Take Your Life', 'Sail
Away' and in particular 'Mistreated'.

The more familiar Purple style was found on the fast-driving title track
'Burn', inspired by George Gershwin's 'Fascinating Rhythm.' One night, as
Blackmore was overdubbing some guitar parts on the Bach influenced
sequence of his solo, Coverdale walked into the mobile truck to observe
him working alongside Martin Birch. "He had Martin slow the tape down
as he recorded a very high guitar piece and when they played it back at the
normal pitch Ritchie turned to me and asked me what I thought. Without

thinking I said it sounded like a bouzouki. Well, you could have sliced the atmosphere with a knife! Apparently, you do not say things like that to Ritchie and live to tell about it. After a deafening silence he told Martin to play it back again then he said, 'He's right, it does sound like a bloody bouzouki. Wipe it off!' From then on I decided to be honest with Mr. Blackmore and I think he appreciated it … for a time, anyway."

With the recordings completed the tapes were mixed at De Lane Lea Studios in London.[*] One of the first songs mixed was the seven minute blues epic 'Mistreated.' Hughes and Coverdale had recorded a dozen or so vocal tracks for the choir sequence at the song's climactic ending. Birch took the other instruments out of the mix so the pair could revel in the lush harmonies, which obviously delighted them. David Coverdale: "When Ritchie came down to hear work in progress I could hardly wait to play him the outro. Mmmm … he seemed completely underwhelmed! I couldn't understand. 'You can't hear the guitar solo for the voices,' he said without even looking at me. You could have heard a pin drop. Martin had no choice, but, to turn the Coverdale-Hughes choir down and highlight Ritchie's outro solo. I was heartbroken. We ended up burying the voices to the point where it was almost impossible to even hear the drama of the stack 'o' voices Glenn and I had spent a whole night recording. I just got up and walked out of the studio without saying anything to anyone. On reflection, he was right, of course. Ritchie was the primary composer. The Riff Merchant, his electrifying guitar playing and his unpredictable live performances were undeniably a major factor in why people flocked to Purple's shows."

Alongside the changes in the band, there were changes occurring in Blackmore's personal life. According to Hughes, Babs no longer stayed at home quite so much. "We used to call her the Swiss Alps because she had large breasts. When I joined the band she went everywhere with Ritchie, and looking back, I think she went everywhere with him because she probably didn't trust him. When she wasn't, all the shenanigans would start: these shenanigans would involve himself, his roadie and whoever because Ritchie never really hung out with us. On the Starship he had his own little booth and we never really saw him, he had his own limo and sometimes he would have two hotel rooms, one in another hotel to escape us. He just didn't want to be around.

"[Onstage] he pretty much early on let me know not to come past the

---

[*] The studio was shortly to revert back to its original name of Kingsway Studios when ironically ownership was taken over by none other than Ian Gillan.

bass drum because that was something he never allowed any one to do. I did try to on a couple of occasions and got a couple of looks. That was the most bizarre thing about Ritchie 'Don't come over my side' and that would go for everybody. You don't get near him, he hated that, he wanted that full attention."

Prior to the release of *Burn*, the new line-up played a handful of low-key European gigs just before the Christmas holidays, after which the focus was to follow on from the success of the previous line-up with larger concerts booked for America in March and April. It was also announced in February that Deep Purple would be introducing the new line-up to UK audiences in May. A group spokesman told *Melody Maker* that they were keen to play "smaller venues like the Marquee and so on and get back to the people."

Whatever size venues they would elect to play in Britain paled in significance to the huge stadiums the band performed at in America. The previous year Deep Purple had reached the zenith of their performing career when they were announced as America's number one albums selling artist, outstripping other star names such as the Rolling Stones, Pink Floyd and Led Zeppelin. Only two years previously they had supported the Faces but now they were capable of drawing huge arena and stadium crowds from New York to California and all points in between. To make the forthcoming five-week tour more comfortable a luxurious, privately owned Boeing 720 jetliner called 'Starship I' was hired at the cost of $127,000. Although the huge record sales were directly as a result of the Mk II line-up's work, for the average American fan, this appeared of little concern.

On the '74 tour Deep Purple Mk III's nightly fees now commanded between $20,000–$40,000, culminating with a headlining show at the California Jam festival at the Ontario Speedway on April 6, filmed by the ABC and watched by an estimated 400,000. The gig, which also included Emerson, Lake & Palmer, Black Sabbath, the Eagles and Earth, Wind & Fire, has gone down in Purple folklore largely due to Blackmore's notorious guitar demolition, during which he smashed his guitar into one of the cameras before instructing his roadie to explode part of the back line. Glenn Hughes: "We all loved the grandiosity of it, the larger than life aspect. We definitely sold albums after that and got a great response around the world." A stagehand threatened to sue the guitarist, claiming the explosions deafened him and with police, fire chiefs and promoters baying for the guitarist's blood, John Coletta, who managed to get Blackmore out of the county straight after the show, confirmed, "They wanted to put him in gaol there and then."

Blackmore's behaviour was the direct result of his refusing to go on stage before sunset. With the show running ahead of schedule the promoters expected Purple to appear in broad daylight incurring Blackmore's stubbornness. If other people had not done their job properly he had little tolerance for incompetence and on this occasion his apparently unreasonable behaviour was justified. Bob Simon feels that Blackmore was right to stand his ground: "I know all the angles because Pacific Presentations, who were the promoters of the gig, were partners with us at Tychobrae Sound and ABC was the overall promotional technological guys behind the gig. But when it came to the sundown thing Deep Purple was the headliner of the show, they were getting the most money, I know that, so technically they were the headliners of the show. We had a show in Arizona the next day so we had to leave early. Instead of going on in the headliners spot, to get out of the traffic and get the equipment on the aeroplanes and get out of town it was decided to let ELP end the show, so ELP tried to take advantage of the situation.

"Bruce Payne came looking for me. 'Ritchie doesn't want to come out of the dressing room until right at sunset. ELP says it is in their contract that if they have to go on late they don't even have to play and will leave right now and still get their money.' The promoters are all flipped out so they came up to me and said, 'What the fuck's going on with him? He ain't coming out 'til sunset. Well we can't delay the show it's in the contract with ELP so somehow you have got to delay the show.' So it had to be a technical malfunction on the part of the sound company then ELP would still be bound by their contract. Bruce said, 'Can you pull it off?' I said, 'I'll take care of it.' Jim Gamble was a partner of mine at Tychobrae. I said to him, 'Here's what we're going to do I'm going to pull some plugs and it will take a while for them to find out, meantime we're going to have this delay.' At first he went along with it but after a while he was plugging stuff back in as fast as I was unplugging. I got Ritchie some spare time that way. But at that point he was put in a position of non-compromise. Nobody had really thought about the sunset and the rainbow behind but that was where he was at. That should have been part of the production planning that went in beforehand but that whole California Jam thing was ill-planned. It was originally planned for 60,000 people and the last count I got on it there was close to half a million. I remember the night before when we did the soundcheck, Seb Donahoue ran out to me saying, 'You got to hurry up we got to let these people in here now. We can't even wait until tomorrow.' So it's unfair to blame Ritchie for being a stubborn shit about the whole deal."

Glenn Hughes endorses Simon's take on the event: "When the California

Jam was booked six months before we were the headliners and it was during the last two months that the promoters wanted to add another artist as a co-headliner to attract even more people. But it was still our concert, most of the receipts were coming to us and we wanted to go on at sunset and they would follow us. Of course it was the first gig in the history of rock when everything was running *ahead* of schedule. Ritchie delayed it 20 minutes by locking himself in his trailer. We would have gone on 20 minutes before but they couldn't get him out. That was why Ritchie was wearing his street clothes on the Cal Jam for the first half of the set. He's not wearing his stage clothes. He'd never done that before and he was really angry but even though he was angry we didn't know what was going to happen."

A year after the concert Blackmore gave his version of events to Cameron Crowe in *Rolling Stone*: "The Who's producer – I won't name him – came into my dressing room and demanded that we go on immediately. I had just gotten there. I just ignored him. The guy kept standing there and said we'd be off the show if I wasn't onstage by the time he counted to 30. I sat there, tuned my guitar and listened to him count out loud. He hadn't reached 15 when I had him thrown out. Forget the money we stood to lose, it was a matter of principle. Even Jon Lord came to me in the end and said, 'Look, will you go on … for the band?' I told him absolutely not and was ready to quit the band right then and there. Somebody else from ABC came in and asked me politely if I'd go onstage. I was angry, but because he was nice about it, I went on."

Of his decision to smash his guitar into one of ABC's onstage cameras, Blackmore said, "Actually I hadn't planned to go for the camera, I was out to kill this guy who gave me the countdown. I thought he'd be onstage. If he had been, you would have seen more than a smashed camera. I don't like violence, but I was raving that night. He talked to us like we were absolute shit. Anyway, I couldn't spot him so I had a go at the camera."

Following the American tour the band undertook a 22-date tour of Britain. Despite the advance reports they failed to play anywhere as small as the Marquee and because of the lack of large venues, the UK gigs were in 2–3,000 seat theatres and concert halls. In London the band chose to play three such venues rather than the cavernous Empire Pool, Wembley or Earl's Court, which they would certainly have had no problem in selling out.

Back in February it had been announced that Deep Purple had provisionally agreed to appear at a London outdoor summer festival with the Who as headliners. The *Melody Maker* report claimed that Purple had been approached directly by the Who to be part of the bill,* but when the even-tual announcement of the show, to be staged at Charlton Athletic's Football Club ground, The Valley was made, Deep Purple weren't among the line-up. That night, Purple's UK tour itinerary kicked off at Dundee's Caird Hall. The set played was the same as it had been in the States, with audiences getting a preview of 'Might Just Take Your Life', 'Lay Down, Stay Down', 'Mistreated' and 'You Fool No One' from the new album *Burn*, mixed in with a couple of old favourites, which naturally included 'Smoke On The Water.' Blackmore was on particularly fine form and having left his guitar on top of his stacks at the end of 'Space Truckin'' a rapturous Scottish crowd called them back for the now standard Mk III encore of 'Goin' Down', an old blues standard by Don Nix. During the song Blackmore used a beer can as a bottleneck and as the can was still full, the beer spilled out over his guitar, as he nonchalantly continued playing.

After the show, he elected not to be chauffeured back to the hotel. Jeff Ward, reviewing the show for *Melody Maker* reported, "Ritchie and I walked back to the hotel through side streets, scarcely anyone recognising him. 'It's like a smash and grab," he said. "If you walk back into the shop afterwards no one believes it was you who did it.'"

Support act on the UK leg was Elf, who by now had been signed to Purple's own label, bonding them closer to the Purple organisation in the process. Elf roadie Raymond D'addario recalls, "We used to play all these little theatres with orchestra pits and one of the last shows we did, Ritchie had the crew go out and get all these bags of flour and they put holes in them and pelted Elf with them. There was Ronnie trying to sing and these little bags of flour hit him and exploded. That was the first time I'd ever seen him do anything like that."

During the tour, film student Graham Hough (now a BBC cameraman) sought and obtained permission to film part of Deep Purple's show at the Lewisham Odeon and to record backstage interviews with the band. Blackmore was interviewed before a gig at Belle Vue, Manchester where for the most part he took delight in being obstructive to Terry Hardy, Graham's fellow student and the man who given the task of asking the questions. Indeed at one point he turned the tables on Hardy, questioning why he wanted to interview him anyway, when he wasn't particularly interested in Deep Purple.

During the 40 minute interview Blackmore said very little of value but

---

* A claim vehemently denied by Who employee Bill Curbishley.

did expand on his reasoning for having his own dressing room; once again with a mixture of straightforward honesty laced with more than a smattering of humour. "I have my own dressing room because I like to tune up and I like my solitude before I go on stage. I tend not to get too involved in people because to be quite honest I find a lot of people boring. I find myself boring most of the time. I always like to be the opposite; I always was at school, that's why I don't smoke. I used to find everybody at school smoking, rebellious image, so because of that I won't smoke and never have. Mind you I was probably doing other things that were just as bad if not worse. I'm still very moody, shy and very honest which a lot of people can't take. The hardest thing in this business is sincerity. Once you can fake that you're laughing."

He also expressed his dissatisfaction with the music business in general, and the treadmill of touring and recording. "I don't know if I've got the guts but I've often thought that's it, I want to leave, not the band, get out of the business, play when I feel like playing, do a record when I feel like recording that would be fantastic but you can't have it all your own way."

After the UK tour concluded, there was a period of relative inactivity that allowed him to relax. With Lord releasing two solo albums during this time, Blackmore agreed to a brief busman's holiday by playing on an Adam Faith session. Faith had been seriously injured in a car crash the previous year but had made a miraculous recovery. Although his own singing career had declined, he had been successful in his acting role in the UK TV series, *Budgie* and was also managing singer/songwriter Leo Sayer. Having signed a deal with Warner Bros for his comeback album *I Survive*, Faith wanted the introduction to the opening track ('I Survived') to simulate a car crash and specifically asked Blackmore to play the passage. "We were thinking who would be the perfect person for the piece and Ritchie was the one. What he's done is brilliant," said Faith at the time of the album's release. The only other Deep Purple activity during this period was a lone show at Southend's Kursaal Ballroom, and a festival performance in Italy. The former, a replacement for an earlier cancelled show is best remembered when a naked girl got up on stage to dance around Blackmore. No doubt he couldn't help but notice the size of her breasts before she was led off stage and what happened after the gig is pure conjecture.

While Blackmore had made clear his dissatisfaction at having to churn out albums with such alarming regularity, within a year the band were in Munich to record the follow up to *Burn*. With the songwriting credits now acknowledged on the basis of who contributed to them, Roger Glover opened up about the way the situation had been when he was still in Deep

Purple, telling *Melody Maker,* "We always credited songs as being written by the whole group, which was never the case. Most of the songs were only written by myself or Ritchie. Most of them used to come out of jams and we'd give the song to Ian who'd add all the lyrics. But we got into this thing where Jon was always seen as some sort of musical leader although he never was … in fact he contributed very little in writing. I'm glad for the new guy's sake that they decided to credit each song separately to its real composer."

If Gillan's departure had seen the removal of the major obstacle in Blackmore's single-minded vision, another musical schism soon emerged. With their confidence growing, both Coverdale and Hughes started to push their ideas forward more. With his love of black American soul and funk, Hughes, in particular, was bringing in elements that Blackmore loathed. Under normal circumstances, he would have been more forceful and stopped such developments in their tracks. But by the time Purple were in the throes of making what would become *Stormbringer* Blackmore's five-year marriage to Babs had broken down and he was going through the process of a messy divorce, summing up at the time, "There wasn't as much guitar because in a way I was going through more personal problems."

Hughes explains how he saw the guitarist change during the making of the album: "Ritchie might have been losing his grip a little. David and I were firmly implanted by '74. He didn't bring a lot of songs into *Stormbringer,* I brought a lot more and he played brilliantly on the stuff I wrote but probably midway through it he was thinking about leaving and of course we didn't have a clue about it. But I think probably through one of the songs like 'Holy Man' or 'You Can't Do It Right' he was thinking it wasn't the kind of stuff he wanted to play. It was another band and was becoming something entirely new. Ritchie was never mean. He had his own way, he just wouldn't speak or he'd send notes through his roadie and it was all childish but we were all pretty childish back then."

Blackmore's interest in Deep Purple was evidently on the wane during the making of *Stormbringer* and for the first time since 1969, tracks appeared without his name in the writing credits. It also partly explains why instead of coming up with original song ideas, he suggested the band cover 'Black Sheep Of The Family,' a favourite track of his from Quatermass' one and only self-titled 1970 album. The rest of the band refused to cover other people's material and for the first time Blackmore felt marginalised. Additionally, 'Soldier Of Fortune' a ballad that he had co-written with Coverdale was disliked by the others. "Dave and I wrote that song. It's one of my favourite songs. It's got a few of those mediaeval chords. You will be

177

surprised how difficult it was to convince the others to play that song. Jon fairly quickly said okay, but Ian and Glenn didn't want to know about it. So I said, 'I'll play your funky song if you will play mine.' So [Hughes] said as casually as possible, 'OK I'll do it.' Glenn hated that song, he thought it was shit. Ian quit after two takes as well. Not enough for him to do in that song to prove himself.' As he explained Blackmore hated Hughes' song 'Hold On' to the extent that he claims to have played the entire solo just once but with his thumb!

Although having been instrumental in bringing about the changes Blackmore was becoming seriously disillusioned with the way that the new members were steering Purple's style away from the hard rock he favoured towards soul and funk. "Glenn is a good singer, but a soul brother, a big Stevie Wonder fan. He wanted more funky things and Dave went along and even Ian started to play differently. Ian always used to be a straight rock 'n' roll drummer but all of a sudden he started to experiment with a lot of things. Very composed, very nice, very tight, very funky but no emotion. I wanted to try different scales, stuff from the 15th century. I could see that it would be the last album. I thought if it goes beyond this point then that's it for me. That's why I left, too many solo trips. I thought, 'Go ahead with your shoeshine music; I'm off.' "

Stormbringer certainly lacked the cohesion of previous Purple albums and Blackmore was quick to dismiss it, telling the press "Back to rock 'n' roll next LP" shortly after its release. Coverdale tended to agree, saying, "The next album is gonna be an out and out rocker."*

Ironically Blackmore was pondering his future at a time when Purple were now reaping the rewards. As Lord explained earlier that year, "Out of the six [years], I would say three have been financially excellent, the other three were getting out of debt, the debt that it cost to start this band." HEC Enterprises accountant Bill Reid advised the band to uproot and move to America where high earners were not burdened by the ridiculously high rates of income tax that the then current Labour Government imposed on them. The mid Seventies saw many Brits within the entertainment business emigrate to low tax destinations, including *ELP*'s Carl Palmer who told *Melody Maker*, "England is like stealing my pension when you have to pay 83% income tax."

Blackmore was the first member of Purple to leave England and initially

---

* The album that followed *Come Taste The Band* was indeed more rock orientated than *Stormbringer*.

moved to Oxnard County in California. With the amount of touring Purple did, and in particular America, the States was the logical place to be based. Up to this point he had been quite vociferous of his dislike for America but was unrepentant when journalists asked why he'd chosen to move there. "I have to, as long as the tax climate is as it is in England. If you want to make some money, England is hopeless. England is a nice country to live in, but with the present government, the trade unions led by communists ... I hope that will change some day."

Glenn Hughes: "By this point we weren't really talking to Ritchie at all – there was no communication going on at all. This is when he's firmly realised he's going, in January '75 when we all moved. Nobody hung out with each other. It was like your typical band that looks great on stage but nobody ever calls, it was just a nightmare. I never saw Ritchie or went to his house. It was just becoming five guys in the band. Ritchie just wanted to be away from what he called the 'shoeshine music' but David and I listened to black artists from Kool & the Gang to Stevie Wonder to the Ohio Players and Sly & the Family Stone. Blackmore was going more Bach orientated."

The moneymaking machine rolled on with another huge American tour at the tail end of the year, featuring Purple supported by Elf and the emerging Electric Light Orchestra. During the trek Blackmore became a victim of identity theft. An individual from Iowa, whose English accent "came and went", claimed he was Deep Purple's lead guitarist, conning several people including a family who sheltered him. After wrecking the son's Porsche he promised the boy a $1500-a-week job and re-payment for the car. Police said the impostor had ID which claimed he was Ritchie Blackmore and gave a London address. When they asked him to stay in town until his manager arrived, he hastily zoomed off in a Mercedes saying he "had to make a concert in New York." Once it was established that the real Blackmore was actually performing in San Francisco that night, the Iowa City police issued criminal charges of misrepresentation but the impostor had long since vanished.

With Blackmore's growing love for baroque music and in particular the work of Bach he approached ELO cellist Hugh McDowell to discuss the instrument. "It must have been the first concert we supported them on that tour. After the concert he started talking about how he liked the cello, and how he liked things like Pachalbel's 'Canon,' the whole style of it. I suggested I could show him a couple of lessons or at least give him ideas. At some point during the tour we found a little town and he had a bit of a go. Being very musical, with a great ear it all went very well. I don't think we

179

did a huge amount on the actual tour but sometime after we got together a few times and I gave him a couple of lessons. It might have been at his old house in the Hollywood Hills. I seem to remember going up there a couple of times and gave him lessons. He was always interested in baroque music."

McDowell also recalls the complete lack of empathy between the Purple musicians: "I remember on the tour there was very little communication with them off stage. I flew quite a lot of times with them on the Starship. They all had their own seats, their favourite seats. The whole group had a very strong routine. I saw very little communication between the members at that stage. I think they were really quite bored with each other in a sense, going through the motions."

According to D'addario, an event occurred during one gig that was the probable catalyst for Blackmore's decision to quit the band. "One night we were on stage and Ritchie came over to Ronnie and said, 'The weirdest thing just happened to me when I was doing my solo.' He did the usual bit and stopped suddenly and he heard someone in the background yell 'Rubbish' and it was Glenn. He was physically shaking when he's telling Ronnie about this and said, 'I just don't think I can do this anymore, do you want to start a band?' And Ronnie said, 'Are you kidding? He said, 'No, we'll use your band and I'll play guitar.' Then the next day all the crew were saying 'Did you hear Ritchie's starting a band with Dio?' It was really weird. The whole vibe changed on the tour."

Although by now indulging heavily in drugs Hughes empathically denies ever criticising Blackmore's playing: "I would never – stoned or boozed up. I'm not that kind of guy. When I was drunk or high I was never irreverent to people around me, only to myself. I was never disrespectful to them on a plain where it would injure them mentally or physically and I never thought he was rubbish. Most of the time Ritchie made me cry when he played and some of the time when he went out of his way to be a jackass he would do that, but I've never knocked his playing on any level."

Blackmore still desired working up his own version of the rejected 'Black Sheep Of The Family' and decided to record it as a solo single. Raymond D'addario: "In Minneapolis there were a couple of days off and [Ritchie] took Elf into a studio and they recorded a couple of tracks. It was more like a test for Ronnie before he left the band." For a B-side Blackmore asked Dio if he could write some lyrics to a tune he had written, which resulted in 'Sixteenth Century Greensleeves.' Lyrically Dio was interested in the same historical periods that Ritchie was now being drawn to and it didn't take long for the pair to discover a common ground musically. Having worked on the songs in Minneapolis, a few days later on December 12, Blackmore asked McDowell to help out with the recordings. "We were around the Florida area in Tampa. I remember he'd got these two-inch master multi-track tapes and Ronnie Dio came along. It was a day off on the tour and I put down some cello tracks. We spent a few hours there doing that. The impression I got was that he loved the instrument and the sonorities of it, a basic attraction in that sense. I think it was very much a personal interest."

Apart from spending a couple of days in the studio, women continued to play an integral role in Blackmore's road routine. By now he had employed Ian Broad, his old bandmate from the Wild Ones and the Trip as his personal roadie–cum–assistant. McDowell recalls one particularly amusing incident that Broad organised. "Ian had a role of getting them all lined up in a row. One concert in particular there was actually quite a queue of girls and they went into a shower room where they exhibited their wares for Ritchie to admire. It was all very well organised by Ian, 'OK next!' I hung out with Ritchie and Ian Broad quite a lot. I quite often went back to their hotel after concerts. There would be quite a few people going back with them. Ian used to collect quite a posse of girls together and take them back. Between Ritchie and Ian they had quite a few clever magic routines. One of them would retire to their room or whatever and you had to guess something or other and the other one would come back so they had some clever means of communicating. It was sophisticated enough to have me boggled, it was quite clever.

"Ian Broad was an absolutely ideal sideman for Ritchie. He used to actually organise a lot of 'after concert events' in a sense. He could entertain a crowd. He was quite content in that court jester role. It must have been one of the last concerts on that tour. Ian used to find his way out on stage quite a bit; I think he put on a pair of leopard skin tights and during one of Ritchie's guitar solos he was playing his guitar on Ian's arse basically. All the little adjusters and so on, on the bridge of his guitar was like ripping Ian's arse to shred. Apparently Ian was in some pain afterwards."

Whatever Blackmore's peccadilloes, when it came to his abilities as a musician, McDowell was unequivocal in the same way as most others. "I was absolutely stunned by his playing."

Although *Stormbringer* turned out to be less successful than the previous few albums, the band was still hugely popular worldwide and as 1975 began, the band jetted off to Australia for a one-off show headlining the Sunbury Festival. The gig is best remembered locally for the show overrunning with

181

Deep Purple's set finishing 40 minutes later than scheduled. While a common occurrence at festival gigs, there were accusations from some quarters that Purple had done this deliberately, because although they were headlining, it had been agreed that local up and coming band AC/DC would conclude the day's entertainment after Purple had finished their set. Because of the late finish, AC/DC didn't get to perform and a feud started between the two camps that continued for sometime. This probably explains Blackmore's later comment that he considered AC/DC to be "an all-time low in rock 'n' roll."

A relatively long break followed the Australian visit and having been re-energised from his brief collaboration with Dio, what was originally planned as a single now gave Blackmore the impetus to make a whole album. With the spare time available, he booked studio time at Musicland in Munich where *Stormbringer* had been recorded, with the view to doing a solo album. The members of Elf weren't the only ones that helped out on the recordings, as Blackmore explained, tongue-in-cheek. "There was the vicar; who used to go round blessing people. We're very religious. And also there was Shoshana on vocals, Hughie McDowell came in when he wanted a drink and he used to play cello."[*]

Shoshana's (real name Judith Feinstein) was the stage name for an American opera singer that Blackmore had met about a year earlier. "I fell in love with an American gypsy girl who was an opera singer and we lived together for a year on the beach near Malibu," he told Dante Bonutto for *Kerrang!* in 1982. Shoshana was credited when the album was released and contributed backing vocals to 'Catch The Rainbow' and an otherwise instrumental take of the Yardbirds' 'Still I'm Sad.'

Just prior to recording, Blackmore confirmed to the music press that he would be doing a solo record with Ronnie James Dio. Although he talked about being unhappy with the last Deep Purple record he refuted suggestions he was quitting for a solo career. However his disillusionment with the direction Purple were heading, coupled with his diminishing influence on the music, ultimately lead to his decision to leave and form his own band. The resulting album, *Ritchie Blackmore's Rainbow*, allowed Blackmore to explore some of the ideas formed through his love of baroque and Renaissance music. Although it was not the guitar album some expected, it contains some notable material. However as he was still a member of Deep

---

[*]When speaking to McDowell for this book he didn't recall doing any work in Munich, only for the original recordings done in the States that were subsequently shelved.

Ritchie backstage in the mid Seventies. "He had exactly the same personality before he became a success," said Ricky Munro. "He always had a high opinion of himself but unfortunately it didn't extend to him being civil. He was very difficult to get on with because you never knew when he would turn around and say 'You're sacked.'" (FIN COSTELLO/REDFERNS)

Deep Purple filming a promo clip for 'Black Night' at De Lane Lea Studios, London, 1970. The song became the band's biggest hit, reaching number two in the UK that year. (ADC/REX FEATURES)

Deep Purple MK II in 1971. L-R: Paice, Gillan, Blackmore, Glover, Lord. A war of egos between Blackmore and Gillan brought this classic line-up to an end two years later. As Glover described, "They became two poles because the more one would do it the more the other would do it and the more one got away with it the more the other was determined he was going to get away with it." (HARRY GOODWIN)

Deep Purple, MK III at a press launch at Clearwell Castle, Gloucestershire, September 1973. L-R: Blackmore, Paice, David Coverdale (vocals), Glenn Hughes (bass) and Lord. "When I stepped into [Deep Purple]," said Hughes, "Ritchie was probably the greatest live guitar player since Hendrix… he was playing brilliantly back then." (ANWAR HUSSAIN/CONTRIBUTOR/GETTY IMAGES)

Blackmore backstage with his collection of Fender Stratocasters, 1974. He started playing Strats exclusively on a UK tour in 1971 and continued to do so for the next 25 years. (FIN COSTELLO/REDFERNS)

Rainbow circa late-1975. L-R: Tony Carey (keyboards), Cozy Powell (drums), Jimmy Bain (bass), Ritchie, and vocalist Ronnie James Dio. "A lot of people say, 'Why did you leave Deep Purple?' It's because there was too much pressure and I'll never let that happen again. Same kind of success would be nice but not the same pressure. It might not get as successful, but that's okay. I want to be myself." (JORGEN ANGEL/REDFERNS)

Ritchie during the 'Rainbow Rising' tour, 1976. "[Rainbow] was a very democratic band," said Tony Carey. "The interplay developed from the first gig and it wasn't the sound of Seventies metal - it had more in common with Weather Report than Black Sabbath." (RICHARD E. AARON/FIN COSTELLO/ REDFERNS)

The infamous stage-spanning electronic Rainbow, built by a New York lighting company, See Factor. "It was nothing but grief," said Cozy Powell of the band's first US tour. "The rainbow either broke down or something happened..." (LFI)

Rainbow in 1977, L-R: Bob Daisley (bass), Dio, Powell, Blackmore and David Stone (keyboards). "We started slowing down on the third LP," said Blackmore. "I knew that we were finished then, because I couldn't talk to Ronnie any more. I suddenly saw him in a different light."
(FIN COSTELLO/REDFERNS)

Another year, another line-up: Rainbow in 1979 L-R: Blackmore, Roger Glover (bass), Don Airey (keyboards), Powell and Graham Bonnet (vocals). "Back then to have short hair wasn't the thing, it wasn't the uniform of a so-called rock singer," says Bonnet, "before a gig I went and got my hair cut, didn't say anything to anyone and I came on stage that night. I remember the look of shock on [Ritchie's] face, jaw dropping to the floor." (LFI)

Ritchie's onstage guitar maintenance, 1981. "He was a smart bloke and an aware bloke," says Bob Daisley, "but like all of us he definitely had a bit of anger in him. To play that kind of music properly you have to have a bit of spark as far as anger and aggression goes." (MICHAEL JOHANNSON

Rainbow 1980 L-R: Blackmore, singer Joe Lynn Turner, drummer Bobby Rondinelli, Glover, Airey. Joe Lynn Turner: "At the very inception he was very polite, a kind of jovial, tongue-in-cheek joker... I knew he could be a bastard. But I didn't seem to mind because he wanted what I wanted: that absolute. It had to be great."

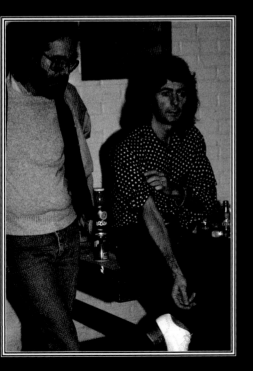

Ritchie with long-serving manager Bruce Payne. The two parted company in 1994. (MICHAEL JOHANNSON)

Ritchie with third wife, Amy Rothman, who aroused a degree of resentment from band and crew. The couple met in 1978 prior to a Rainbow show. According to Stuart Smith, "Amy told me that when she met Ritchie she was with another guy, a massive Blackmore fan. This guy said, 'Yeah, you go back and see him' and of course that was it."

(ROSS HALFIN/IDOLS)

Ritchie with cello. Thanks to his growing interest in classical music, the riff to Rainbow's
'Stargazer' originated from him practicing on the instrument as a compositional tool.
Tony Carey: "He just lugged it around and posed with it. I never heard him play a note."

Purple the album was kept under wraps and wouldn't be released for several months.

In light of his comments the other members of Purple certainly hadn't seen the writing on the wall, more than likely figuring that if Blackmore got this solo project out of his system, he would be more focused on his role in Deep Purple. A European tour was to start behind the Iron Curtain in Yugoslavia on March 16. Paice and Coverdale had agreed to meet up with Blackmore at the Arabella Haus Hotel, (Musicland Studios was situated in its basement) prior to departing for Belgrade. The *Rainbow* album was still being worked on at Musicland on the 14th when Paice and Coverdale arrived at the hotel, seemingly unaware of Blackmore's activities. With the recording complete the three then travelled to Yugoslavia to meet up with Lord and Hughes. The Yugoslavian shows were among the first by any Western rock band behind the Iron Curtain and acted as a warm-up to further gigs later in the year as well as to get the band in shape for a new album.

Blackmore had other ideas. Having now decided his future lay beyond Deep Purple, sometime during the tour he confided in Edwards and Coletta that he would be leaving at the end of it. Although the intention was to keep the news secret from the rest of the band, the truth soon became self-evident and eventually it was confirmed that Blackmore would be playing his last show with Deep Purple at the tour's end in Paris. Glenn Hughes: "It was a bit of a shock actually, although I'd never really seen it coming. I think Paicey might have. The deterioration of the band came in many forms, whether it was women, drugs, egos and obviously Ritchie's dissatisfaction with losing his musical stamp. If we were sat down in a room and discussed the musical direction of the band like people do now and been more focused we would probably have made one more record with Ritchie but nobody really spoke.

"Purple didn't go off the rails in 75; Blackmore chose to work with another singer. He wanted to make a record of more classical sounding songs. The management team in Deep Purple weren't in any way creative at all. The managers would fly to LA or Miami or wherever we were at and have meetings but it was all financial with the accountants. Blackmore pretty much ran and still will run in his own way the way he wants to play but he doesn't really communicate with people."

Never ones to miss an opportunity, and realising the future historical significance of what may have been the end of Deep Purple, the management arranged to have the last three shows recorded. The final show in Paris concluded with a very lengthy rendition of 'Highway Star' during which

183

Blackmore "broke his guitar, playing the strings with his black silk costume and his feet" according to one review. The French press had got wind of Blackmore's imminent departure but as far as one reviewer was concerned it was almost welcome. "You could have perhaps accepted an amicable split, were it not for this downfall in Paris. 'Highway Star' no longer belongs to this band of cliché givers, for whom the stage is merely a way of staying rich."

Coverdale, who changed the words to "she had big fat tits" something that the guitarist would be in favour of, bid the Parisian audience adieu with "We hope to see you again sometime in some shape or form," knowing full well it would be without Ritchie Blackmore.

CHAPTER 9

Rainbow Rising (1975–77)

With all the success Blackmore had achieved with Deep Purple over the past eight years, his belligerence, arrogance and ego were at their possible nadir. Although he had always been uncompromising, his delight in saying things that would knowingly offend knew no bounds. When talking to Cameron Crowe for *Rolling Stone* magazine, he delighted in playing up his nasty image to maximum effect. "I don't mind being thought of as a moody bastard. I'm actually a very serious person, and when I see girls coming up to me and saying, 'Why don't you smile?' I get nasty. If I'm relaxed, you see, I look like I'm miserable. That's the way it is. I'm just not laughing. I don't laugh at 'Didja hear the one about the Englishman and the Irishman?' I say 'No,' and walk away. I love to walk away halfway through a joke. God knows where that's coming from, but I love to fuck jokes up. The things that make me laugh are practical jokes. I love to turn fire extinguishers on in restaurants. That's funny to me.

"I'm very happy. I'm a contented man, but I don't go around laughing my ass off. If I'm talkin' to some scab of a flat chested and spotty lump, who comes up to me and says, 'Why don't you smile more?' I'll usually say something like, 'If you had big tits and no spots I probably would.' That's my thing. I wear black, and don't give a fuck. Certain things I will not compromise with. There are certain compromises I will make with music if I think it makes people happy. But there are certain things I won't do, like turning up for press receptions for gold records and things. Maybe I'll look back in 10 years and say, 'I was a bit knotty then,' but fuck it. I'm having a good time."

Blackmore's dark and often subtle humour invariably sailed over the heads of many, who mistook his comments as out and out arrogance. Although he was generally unconcerned with the way his comments were perceived, with some of the more outrageous ones there was no option but to take them with a pinch of salt. "I know it sounds very morbid, but if we announce that we had been killed in a plane crash, our records would just sail up. Our manager agreed that a crash would do us well, so we'll see."

On a more sober note, Blackmore explained his reasons for leaving Deep Purple in an interview recorded around August '75: "The pressure was very hard with Deep Purple because they were so big and we had to release three LPs a year, tour the world. With this band we're trying to be a lot more mellow and we are contracted to do one LP a year which is what I wanted. I want to lie on the beach and be lazy. I know there's a lot of competition but people know what they like and the music we're making is something that I like very much. I could have carried on in Deep Purple and sat back. I'm very excited about it because I'm playing music that I want to, in the time that I want to play in. I'm not pressured anymore as much as I was. This was what I was trying to get away from. A lot of people say, 'Why did you leave Deep Purple?' It's because there was too much pressure and I'll never let that happen again. Same kind of success would be nice but not the same pressure. It might not get as successful, but that's okay. I want to be myself. When I heard Ronnie sing I felt shivers down my spine. I knew I had the chance to start something new, something I could believe in."

Despite *Ritchie Blackmore's Rainbow* being emblazoned with Blackmore's own name, he was keen to produce something within the confines of a group set up. Rainbow essentially continued in the same hard rock vein as Deep Purple but with classical influences – ironically rather like the style Jon Lord had favoured circa 1969 but which Blackmore had openly resisted. In an interview done for a radio promo album, he explained: "Ronnie and I had the same interest in music which were basically medi-aeval classical roots such as Bach, actually the whole LP was inspired by Johann, who was there some of the time. And a lot of the progressions we used were classical progressions. That's not as drastic as it sounds, they're still rock progressions because I believe that Bach even in the 16th century [sic] was still playing in a way that was very relative to the way that people are playing today which is very rhythmical and we both had the same interest so we tried to incorporate these medieval parts ... We used a lot of modes instead of scales. And modes meant we used weird chords. But we found out it worked with a rock backing. We achieved this on about four tracks. And

I'm very excited about it because I've never done this before and it's turned out very well.

"All the music I play at home is either German baroque music – people like Buxtehüde, Telemann, or it's mediaeval music: English mediaeval music. I prefer things like the harpsichord, the recorder and the tambourine. Whenever I'm pissed off with the rock scene, which is quite often I just tune into Bach, play my Bach records and mediaeval music."

While singing the praises of his new writing partner and singer, Blackmore aimed a few barbs at the previous vocalists he had worked with, "Ronnie is very versatile. He sings on the single 'Love Is All,' he used to play the trumpet in an orchestra, that's why he knows so much about scales. I like working with Ronnie, he is never out of tune, he never makes mistakes: most vocalists I have worked with don't know what they are doing, they just hope it fits. With Ronnie you know it fits. He might be small but his voice isn't!"

He also expanded on his interest in particular historical eras: "Why I am so interested in medieval stuff is because my hobby is psychic research and I believe in supernatural and reincarnation. It creeps in and I think that maybe I was around in the 16th century; in fact I'm positive I was around. It's nothing drastically different from anything else but it has that flavour of the mediaeval touch which we wanted from the beginning so I'm very happy about that."

A crucial factor in the working relationship was Dio's shared love of the same *Goons*-type humour. When talking about the songs on the album, the singer said, "The track that most exemplifies the medieval music that we've been talking about is a song called 'Sixteenth Century Greensleeves,' inspired by Elvis Presley, written by Judy Garland." Blackmore interjected with "Robin Hood" before Dio continued, "I'm sorry, written by Robin Hood, but we are taking publishing on whatever Robin Hood has written since then. Anyway the song is our idea of a castle where the black knight lives. The black knight of course being Ritchie and the black knight periodically comes out of his castle and captures a young peasant maiden from the village where they're all living in squalor, brings her back to the castle: Very, very rude. And he does this over the period of 15 or 20 years ..."*

When released in August the album received a mixed response from the

---

* Blackmore told one green Australian journalist that 'Man On The Silver Mountain', the song that Dio had written loosely about God, concerned Edmund Hillary and Sherpa Tensing's expedition to the summit of Everest!

media, probably because it was a more laid-back affair than expected due to Blackmore's conscious desire to avoid comparisons with his former band. Given his criticism of the *Stormbringer* album, many were anticipating he would vent his frustration in a march harder, aggressive manner, but tracks such as 'Temple Of The King' and 'Catch The Rainbow' displayed a mellow side, carrying on from where the likes of 'Gypsy' and 'Soldier Of Fortune' had left off.

Although Blackmore's name guaranteed that Deep Purple fans would invest in the record, for just as many more, the sum of the parts was more attractive than the individuals, a fact that Ian Gillan, who had already aborted one solo effort the previous year and was in the process of putting his own band together, discovered to his cost. While electing to initially use his own name within Rainbow's title he was adamant the album should not appear on the Purple label. Although no longer a member, Blackmore was still connected to the "Purple machine" on a business level. He employed the band's US agent Bruce Payne as his new manager and much of his day-to-day affairs were still dealt with by Deep Purple (Overseas) Ltd. The company created a subsidiary named Oyster that ironically ended up also releasing Gillan's first album.[*]

Blackmore publicly adopted a similar attitude to Paul McCartney when the ex-Beatle formed Wings by claiming to be unconcerned if his new venture didn't reach the same heights as his old band. However, in being regarded as one of the top rock guitarists in the world, and with an ego to match, proving that he could succeed with his own band on his own terms was a hugely motivational factor for Blackmore. The major problem he encountered was finding musicians of an equal calibre to those he had worked with in Purple and most importantly, personalities that were compatible. For a man with singular views this was going to be a tough order.

Although the members of Elf had performed exemplarily on the record, when it came to rehearsing in preparation for live shows Blackmore adopted a hire and fire approach that would become characteristic from this point on. Over a three month period, bassist Craig Gruber, drummer Gary Driscoll and keyboard player Mickey Lee Soule were replaced, one by one. Though initially reluctant to see his band mates cast aside, Dio saw the wisdom in Blackmore's decision and by October three new musicians were

---

[*] However a single release of 'Temple Of The King' still appeared in the remote territories of New Zealand and Venezuela on the Purple label, though it's unlikely Blackmore was ever aware of the fact.

in the Rainbow line-up. The first new recruit was Scottish bassist Jimmy Bain from Harlot, who Blackmore had seen playing at London's Marquee club. Harlot's drummer was a face from Blackmore's Hamburg past, Ricky Munro. "We had a residency at the Marquee and Jimmy Bain had a message, 'Could you go and meet somebody in the pub down the road who wants to speak to you.' I went along with him because he didn't know who it was and there sitting at a table in the corner is old Blackmore and that was the end of Harlot. I was just thinking, 'The bastard's coming back to haunt me again.'

"He had exactly the same personality before he became a success. He always had a high opinion of himself but unfortunately it didn't extend to him being civil. He was very difficult to get on with because you never knew when he would turn around and say 'You're sacked.' I couldn't believe it when he came and took Jimmy Bain. He bought me a pint. I rather we'd kept our bass player because we were going to be the first band on the Rolling Stones label so all that fell through because our main song-writer had been poached. He'd been well and truly poached and promised the earth. Blackmore was so single-minded and he got there by his own means."

Both Bain and Californian keyboard player Tony Carey were virtual unknowns, but the drummer that Blackmore settled on had a higher profile, at least in Britain. Blackmore first became aware of Powell during the drummer's time with Jeff Beck's group in the early Seventies but by '75 Powell had racked up a trio of Top 20 singles under his own name for Mickie Most's RAK label.[*] At the time he joined Rainbow, Powell was one of the UK's most renowned drummers. He was also a down to earth character, treating Blackmore in the same way that he would treat anybody else. While he initially appreciated this aspect of Powell's personality, there were occasions when it would cause friction between the pair, as Blackmore described, "Cozy was a very strong character and when we disagreed we really disagreed: this man was fire. It was like fire meets fire."

On the musical side Powell was immensely solid and reliable, something Blackmore had been used to with Ian Paice. Blackmore knew exactly what he wanted and before Powell's enlistment, a considerable number of drum-mers had been auditioned. Tony Carey: "Ritchie's idea for an audition for a drummer was to play a shuffle really fast and play it for half an hour until the drummer collapsed. Not pull a grimace, not look at him, turn his back

---

[*] The most successful of these, 'Dance With The Devil' reached number three in early 1974.

to him and keep playing at this thunderous volume until the drummer went home. But Cozy could play all day and all night."

It also counted massively in his favour that Powell enjoyed pulling pranks on a scale of his kingpin and over the next five years they were to cause a spree of mayhem wherever they went. The pair fed off each other like a couple of overgrown school kids as Powell told the author a year before the drummer's tragic death, "Some of the things we got up to were just amazing, I mean really were outrageous. So in that respect we shared a lot in common."

With the line-up finalised, Rainbow set about rehearsing for their first American tour in November. Blackmore chose the Pirate Sound rehearsal facilities in Los Angeles run by former Tychobrae sound engineer Bob Simon. In his efforts to present Rainbow's stage show in a much more visual way than Deep Purple, the wooden rainbow that adorned the stage at the California Jam event had given Blackmore an idea. Bob Simon: "I remember when he was just forming Rainbow and he walked into my studio Pirate Sound and said, 'OK I want you to make a big arcing rainbow from one side of the PA to the other and all these flashing colours.'" A lighting company in New York, See Factor was commissioned to build a stage-spanning electronic rainbow, the first of its kind, containing 3,000 light bulbs operated by a portable computer. Though highly advanced for its time, it was primitive compared to today's technology.

Simon also observed a typical Blackmore 'wind-up': "When we were doing that rainbow thing, me and one of my stage engineers were driving out to Oxnard following Fergie (Ian Ferguson, Ritchie's guitar technician). We were hungry and decided to pull in to a Jack-In-The-Box drive-in. There was a car in front with these big surfer guys up at the window getting their order and Fergie and Ritchie were in the car behind them. Ritchie started honking the horn on these guys. They are looking back and he's acting all innocent and when they aren't looking he reaches over and honks the horn so all these guys are thinking it's Fergie doing it. Next thing we know these guys jump out of the car and they are ready to pull Fergie out of the car and beat him up. Me and my buddy had to get out and say 'Back off' and Ritchie is sitting in the car laughing.

"He was Johnny Practical Joker but he was Joe Serious too. When it came to the gig and playing he could be really mean. Like when we were auditioning drummers and Colin [Hart] kept having all these guys show up. I think we went through 13 drummers. I remember Ritchie sitting there and we would be playing pool and some of them would come in and start setting their drum kit up and they wouldn't even get a chance to play. He'd tell Colin to go over and tell them to pack it up and we'd just keep playing pool and wouldn't even rehearse. He was pretty mean like that."

In addition to the visuals Simon was also hired to build a sound system. As no financial limit was specified, when Simon mentioned the mounting costs had escalated to about $75,000, Blackmore simply replied, "I don't care how much it is I know you will do it the best so just do it and whatever it is, I'll pay for it. I trust you and I don't want to know about it at all."

Bob Simon: "When I was done with the equipment I got this phone call from Fergie. 'Ritchie wants you to have all the gear set up because he is going to have someone come and play on it tonight and test it out.' I had the stack of equipment set up and a brown Rolls Royce turns up and out of it pops Felix Pappalardi. I said, 'Hey Felix what's happening, man?' He said, 'I'm here to test out Ritchie's gear.' 'You're the one?' 'Yeah, he wants me to play through it and give him my opinion.' So Felix just started jamming by himself. He just played for about an hour. We all just stood around and went 'Whoa!' "

Another example of Blackmore's less appealing nature occurred when he discovered Deep Purple were also using the rehearsal facilities at Pirate Sound. Bob Simon: "That was a total nightmare for me. I was caught up in the middle. Deep Purple came in first and they were doing the same thing and I was catering for Purple and then Ritchie wanted to come in and he was right in my face. More demands, more demands. I could divide the studios in half they were so big and one band could have the day session and one could have the night session. Whoever paid the most money got the choice of the session, which was normally the night's session. And we had them like that but he didn't even want them in the same building so I moved Purple to stage three and I had Ritchie in stage four. I had my own sound system and I was splitting it half with Ritchie and half with Purple. I'd work with Purple in the day mixing them and Rainbow at night.

"Then it just got to the stage when he came up to me and said, 'You know what, you're not mixing for them anymore. You're mixing for me and they're not using any of your PA, we are using the whole PA.' I said, 'Shit, I don't care as long as someone is paying for it. Whoever pays the most can have the most.' But it got really political. The next thing I knew I had everything set up for Ritchie and Coverdale and the rest of the band are all standing behind me. 'Si, what are you doing this to us for?' I didn't want them to take it personally but they did. They thought I'd fucked them over for Ritchie and I found out later that was kind of what it was. He wanted to snuff them."

If Blackmore's actions towards his former band were an indication of his antipathy, there appeared to be no bad blood when Blackmore took Rainbow to see Deep Purple play at the Long Beach Arena early in '76. Tony Carey: "We sat in the tenth row and watched the band with Tommy Bolin. There was no problem. He said, 'You wanna go see Purple tonight?' and we all sat there in a row like school kids."

Blackmore's actions over the studio could be explained away as another case of his bloody-mindedness. Blackmore had gone on record in 1974 as saying how much he rated Tommy Bolin. As Bolin remembered, "The first time I ever met Ritchie was after I'd joined the group. And it was weird 'cos he said, 'I recommended you to the guys and I hear things are going great.' And then David Coverdale said, 'That's a bunch of balls, I recommended yer.'"

Having got the Purple gig, the young guitar player leased a house in the same Beverly Hills neighbourhood that Blackmore was then living. When speaking about Bolin to *Guitar World* in 1991, Blackmore said, "I originally heard him on Billy Cobham's *Spectrum* album and thought, 'Who is this guy?' Then I saw him on television and he looked incredible. Like Elvis Presley I knew he was gonna be big. When I heard that Purple hired him I thought it was great. He was always so humble. I remember he would always invite me out to his house in Hollywood to see his guitar. One day I went to his place. I walked in and tried to find him, but no one was around. There were no furnishings, nothing. I stayed there for 10 minutes before he finally appeared. He showed me his guitar, and the strings must have had a quarter inch of grime on them, as though he hadn't changed them in four years. I asked him when was the last time he'd changed the strings and he said very seriously, 'Gee, I don't know. Do you think I should change them?'"

While for Rainbow Blackmore had wanted someone who could play like Jon Lord, in turn Purple wanted the former James Gang guitarist Bolin to play like Blackmore – a situation Bolin wasn't entirely happy about. "At first there was a kind of restricted feeling around the group ... like, 'Here's how Ritchie played it, play it kinda like Ritchie played it. But that only lasted a while and now I don't care how Ritchie played ... I'm being sued by him so why should I care."

If the pair of them had initially got on, Bolin was named as a co-respondent in Blackmore's divorce suit against Babs along with Jeff Beck, Keith Moon, Salvador Dali and no less than 12 roadies! Although Bolin had spent time in Babs' company, he denied the allegations when speaking to *Rolling Stone* magazine: "I was in a drunken stupor for four days and I passed out at her place. She was always having these parties. I never fucked her or nothing." Glenn Hughes who was closest to Bolin within the Purple camp believes Bolin's word: "Tommy never said if he did or he didn't. I just remember him being in the lawsuit. Truly I don't think Tommy did. When people are in their disease like Tommy was there isn't a lot of sex going on, especially when you are on opiates. It's impossible to get an erection."

Rolling Stone claimed that Bolin's name was subsequently dropped from the lawsuit, but the divorce certificate categorically names him. Although Babs allegedly had extramarital liaisons, what is astonishing is that Blackmore had the gall to file for divorce on the grounds of adultery. Had his wife brought the petition, there was a good chance the list of co-respondents would far outweigh the 16 names initially cited against her. Even more preposterous was that by Deep Purple's April 1974 American tour, Blackmore was already in the company of Shoshana while still married. The divorce was not contested and another of the guitarist's domestic episodes had drawn to a close.

Asked how he got the name for his new venture Blackmore explained it was inspired by the Rainbow Bar and Grill, a popular meeting place for musicians and Hollywood celebrities that was a regular haunt for the guitarist during his years in California. Bob Simon: "The owner Tony always had the front booth reserved for Ritchie because Ritchie was Rainbow and it was some kind of advertising deal. Everybody would be in there, the Sabbath guys, the Who guys, the Eagles guys. You could pretty much walk in there and there would be some rock stars there but it wasn't like you could just get in. They had the bouncers on the door and it was pretty much just people in the business, record agents and promoters and people like that. For Ritchie they would let in all the girls that he wanted. They were lined up down the hallway, down the aisle way, through the restaurant, out the front door and out in the parking lot. All lined up to meet Ritchie. [Ian] Broady was always working on that, providing entertainment for Ritchie. Even though they were lined up to see him they weren't permanent they would just ask a couple of questions and run off and tell their other girl-friends.

"He was living good then. The guy at the Rainbow Bar and Grill made sure he got in a limo every night and the guy would always be giving him bottles of wine and champagne so we could go up there and have a good time. Ritchie would be standing up at the bar bullshitting, pouring drinks for everybody and pouring a Heineken for himself every now and then. I never saw him get wasted. He was always in control."

Tony Carey recalls the rehearsals at Pirate Sound were neither intensive nor lengthy. "We did astoundingly little. We'd play a song and learn the chords a few times, very little, like we didn't work anything out except the structure, the ending and like who solos here, it was very free-form, really progressive rock. We weren't sweet with all these harmonies and hooks and hit singles; we played songs very long sometimes because everybody was having fun basically. That was an ass-kicking jamming band. One of the unsung heroes of that band was Jimmy Bain, a fantastic bass player, who kept it going and never let up, not a second, and Cozy too because he was so confident in his playing."

As with any new project, there were several teething problems. The first few dates of the US tour had to be postponed to allow for more rehearsal time and problems with the stage set were causing headaches as well. The first show eventually took place in Canada at the Montreal Forum, a venue capable of holding around 17,000. Raymond D'addario: "It was a big ice arena in Montreal and we played to half the arena. They put the stage in the middle but they couldn't have played in a smaller place because we were trying to drag that big rainbow around."

Dio is of the belief that this was hard to take for Blackmore, something on which Tony Carey begs to differ. "I never saw Ritchie throw any ego tantrums, that wasn't his style. His style was, he'd disappear into the dressing room with a bottle of Scotch and keep it to himself, then show up on stage. He never played like a drunk but he played like Paganini a little bit, like he'd sold his soul to the devil … or to Johnnie Walker! I don't have much sympathy when I hear a story that the very first Rainbow gig in Montreal didn't sell out. We were delighted and excited to play."

Irrespective of the size of venue it was a tour that Powell remembered for all the wrong reasons. "It was nothing but grief. The rainbow either broke down or something happened, or the lighting truss collapsed on various people, and it was fraught with all sorts." The shows opened with a fast new number not included on the album but worked up at rehearsals called 'Do You Close Your Eyes?', followed by four albums tracks, 'Self Portrait', 'Sixteenth Century Greensleeves', 'Catch The Rainbow' and 'Man On The Silver Mountain.' Two other new numbers were then performed, 'Stargazer' and 'Light In The Black' before the set closed with the Yardbirds' 'Still I'm Sad.' Unlike the instrumental take on the album, this was a fully blown vocal version complete with keyboard and drum solos with Powell performing part of his solo alongside Tchaikovsky's '1812 Overture' with the added effect of pyrotechnics.

Powell's over the top approach was perfect for Blackmore's desire to not only impress with the music but to make Rainbow a total visual attraction. However in true *This Is Spinal Tap* fashion, the electronic rainbow was causing problems at most of the shows. At the Upper Darby Tower Theatre in Philadelphia on November 15 the show was delayed because of interference and after 'Sixteenth Century Greensleeves' the band had to leave the stage for three quarters of an hour while the crew tried to address the problems. Tony Carey: "At times the buzz created by the dimmers in the rainbow was louder than the band. And we needed a height of 27 feet to hang it and at some shows that didn't work. Tony Mazzucci was the lighting guy who built it and ran it, you could hear him searching for combinations of colours that could minimise the buzz."

With the tour playing to, by and large, smaller crowds than Blackmore had been accustomed the realisation dawned that the brand name was what really sold the product as Deep Purple were still drawing large audiences wherever they played.

In late '75 the band flew to Germany to rehearse for their second album. Tony Carey: "We rehearsed at an old farmhouse somewhere like Fürstenfeldbrück around Munich. We rehearsed with really tiny minimal equipment in December, freezing cold. Basically we had some riffs and Ronnie had his pad and writing lyrics and most of the time we rehearsed without Ronnie singing while he was brainstorming his demons and wizards thing." Within a short space of time together the band had developed into a formidably powerful and tight outfit. Furthermore, Blackmore and Dio's songwriting partnership was flourishing. Three new songs had already been written and premiered on the US tour and another three were written during the rehearsals. Raymond D'addario: "There was a vibe in the air. There wasn't much said but there was a lot done. The melody and the track would be in the air for a couple of days and all of a sudden Ronnie would be gone with his pen and paper and then he'd come down and basically just sing it and not spend hours doing it. They had a great writing chemistry."

By February the songs were ready to record and the album was quickly laid down at Musicland as Powell explained several years later: "I think the idea was to try and capture it as quickly as we could. I think I was there for a week, 10 days and then once all the drum tracks were done then Ronnie did the vocals, which took forever and a day. Ritchie and Ronnie used to go through quite a lot of grief trying to get that sorted out, so as soon as I'd finished my stuff I got out of there and let them get on with it. I remember it was done very quickly. It wasn't a sort of manufactured record. It was done spontaneously and the musicians' input is the way you hear it which is possibly why it's one of the better albums that we did."

Tony Carey: "In those days studios had rugs on the walls, this dead studio

Seventies sound and we definitely wanted to make a little more damage and noise. Martin Birch engineered and was a liaison for everybody's ego, a lovely guy. The guy from Musicland, the Tonmeister came in one day in an SS uniform, not the black but the brown shirt uniform with the red and black swastikas and all day his whole demeanour was 'Sieg Heil' perfectly done, he was a really funny guy he never cracked a smile, he said, 'We will do it this way.' 'A Light In The Black' and 'Stargazer' the band basically cut without me and I overdubbed the keyboards. They wanted an intro for 'Tarot Woman' so everybody left and I sat with Martin for an hour and a half and the same day we did the solos for 'A Light In The Black.' Compared to making records today it was effortless, a breeze, it was a piece of cake because we basically did what you are supposed to do when you make a record but no one does, we just went in and played the fucking thing. And Ronnie came down with his notebook and sung and it all was done. The recordings were completely spontaneous."

Despite the guitarist's reputation of being a control freak Carey insists, "He never said a word, never told me which instrument to play he said, 'Just play what you feel.' But actually sounds are one thing but playing with Ritchie is another and I played actually quite similar to Jon Lord in that I played like a second guitar player a lot to make this fat sound. I would pretty much learn his riffs and play with them. That way when he went to solo there wasn't a big hole in the music."

While in Munich, the band played an impromptu set using the resident band's gear at an ice skating rink they visited during a break from recording as Blackmore recounted in his typically dry humoured fashion to *Circus*: "Everyone was shocked at first, but most of them knew who we were – we're quite well-known in Germany – and they sat down and watched us play the 'Ice Skating Blues.' We stayed up there for an hour, and then just handed the guitars back to the band, jumped into the rink and resumed skating. It's the first time I've played in ice skates, and I must say it was enjoyable. Good fun."

Released in May, *Rainbow Rising* is considered by many to be Rainbow's finest album. Cozy Powell: "I'm certainly very proud of it. I think it was a real milestone at that time. I mean we were competing with the likes of Zeppelin and obviously the Purple sort of thing. We had to come out with something that was serious contender stuff. Ronnie was singing really well, the band was gelling pretty well."

Dio's lyrics continued in the mediaeval theme though the one notable exception, 'Starstruck,' the most commercial song on the album, had a more unusual inspiration – a French female who had been stalking Blackmore for some considerable time as he acknowledged in his usual politically incorrect manner. "'Starstruck' is all about this lump called Muriel who's been following me all around Europe for the last few years – a real lunatic. We play a concert in Paris and she'd be there and we'd fly to Lyon and she'd be at the airport waiting for our plane to arrive. One day I looked out of my window and thought I saw the bushes move in the garden. I kept watching and sure enough she'd found my house, so I set my dogs on her!"

The album's piece de résistance, 'Stargazer' was a seven-minute epic of hypnotic power and majesty. Even Blackmore was of the opinion that the track was one of his finest accomplishments. As well as being generally considered the definitive Rainbow song, it's also an important footnote in Blackmore's career as it features his first major use of slide guitar and from this point on slide featured more heavily in his playing. With Blackmore's growing interest in more traditional forms of music, the 'Stargazer' riff originated from him practicing with the cello as a compositional tool, although he wasn't adept at it. Tony Carey: "He just lugged it around and posed with it. I never heard him play a note."

"It's such a melancholy instrument," Blackmore described, "such an isolated, miserable instrument … But it was an appropriate choice for me at the time, because my girlfriend had left me and I was going through this miserable phase." Of all the women in his life, the break-up of his relationship with Shoshana was one of the most devastating. Several years later Blackmore told long-standing friend Stuart Smith why he had to finish the relationship. "She was a complete nut case. He said they'd be driving around in LA and she'd go through a red light or whatever she felt like doing and a copper would pull her over and she'd be abusive as hell to them, and while Ritchie hates authority and that sort of thing he would be cringing in his seat because an LA cop would just shoot you. [She was] very beautiful though and I know she was very important to him, very deep in his heart. But I think for his own sanity he had to break it up and get out because she was nuts. But she was a great singer."

Several years later, Blackmore spoke openly about the break-up to fortnightly UK rock magazine *Kerrang!* "It was rather chaotic because she was just embarking on a career in rock and she thought that I could help her but I couldn't. So that didn't work and we fell apart, a split that took me years and years to get over – it was the romance of my life." Their parting was the start of dark times as he admitted during the same interview, "I was so heartbroken that I thought, well, rather than go back to Britain I'll stay in Hollywood and lose myself because it's easy to be on your own there. If you're suffering from a broken heart and all this business you can just go out and have a party with the friends, it's all very plastic. Anywhere else, I think I'd have done myself in. So I stayed in Hollywood for three years after that and at Christmas time, rather than thinking of this girl I'd broken up with, I'd just lose myself in endless parties, orgies or whatever."

A Rainbow world tour was booked to kick off in the States in early June lasting through to Japan in December. Before the tour started, less than a year after Blackmore had departed, Deep Purple called it a day.* With hindsight, David Coverdale acknowledged that "Ritchie had been such a huge part of Deep Purple. Him, Jon and Ian knew each other so well that they could read one another's minds. The fact that they didn't really get on any longer didn't mean anything. But it surfaced in the arrogance in their performances, which was fantastic. They tried to blow each other away and that created great rock music."

As with most events surrounding him the news of Purple's demise probably didn't register at first with Blackmore. Nine days after Purple's last gig Blackmore unexpectedly turned up at a Sweet concert at the Santa Monica Civic Auditorium and jammed with the Glam rockers on a rendition of Free's 'All Right Now' in tribute to Paul Kossoff who had died the previous week. Blackmore was a big influence on Sweet's guitarist Andy Scott: "In the really early days when I first joined the band we used to do 'Hush' and 'Kentucky Woman', and we also did a version of 'Black Night' but these were because we were playing popular dance halls that wanted to hear not only our music but also some other music of the era. It was a generally accepted thing in less heavy bands, more commercial bands. We all wanted to play numbers like 'Speed King' and 'Flight Of The Rat', but we had to keep it down to the more commercial things. So much so that I could probably still play the "Black Night' guitar solo exactly the same as it was on the record. This shows how much of an influence Ritchie was – I used to play a Stratocaster but I also had a Gibson 335 which I used all the way through the early Sweet era."

Scott was delighted, if a little surprised, to be sharing a stage with the 'Man In Black.' "It was completely spontaneous. We had met him a couple of nights earlier, and the one thing that he'd said to our tour manager, who used to work for Deep Purple – a guy called Mick Angus – was 'You'd better let me get into the gig tonight.' Because the last time we'd played Los Angeles he hadn't been able to get into the show, because our management

---

*Their last show was at Liverpool's Empire Theatre on March 15, 1976. After overdosing on drugs and alcohol, Tommy Bolin was found dead on December 4, 1976.

at that time and the record company had virtually sold out the gig even before tickets went on sale. Ritchie said to [Mick Angus], 'I'm gonna come, and I'm gonna get in this time.' And we said, 'Of course you are!' And somebody made the joke, 'If you want to get up, put your guitar in the boot.' There was an offer to set up another stack, but I think Ritchie just said, 'Plug me into anything, I'll be alright.' And I think the only amps on my side of the stage that were available for him to plug into were the amps that I think were monitoring the synthesisers, which had a couple of horns in them, which left him with a rather loud and clear sound."

After splitting with Shoshana, there was no shortage of glamorous women in Blackmore's life including *Playboy* centrefold and rock star courtesan Bebe Buell. Tony Carey: "She was on the American tour. She was like a famous groupie, band follower, let's put it that way. Nothing cheap about her." Buell had recently ended a relationship with Todd Rundgren and fallen in love with Aerosmith's Steven Tyler but when she fell pregnant rumours abounded that Blackmore was the father. In her biography, Buell claimed Elyssa Perry [the wife of Aerosmith guitarist Joe Perry] resented her stature within the Aerosmith camp and of wanting to put doubt into Tyler's mind that he might not be the child's father. Buell wrote, "She figured she could best get to him by naming Ritchie as the rumoured daddy. Ritchie was a friend – no more – and I'd seen a show or two of his that year."*

The technical difficulties on the previous tour involving the rainbow had been sorted out. Blackmore resolved the interference problems by using a new guitar, wired so that the "middle pickup magnetically counteracts the magnetic field of the lights," as he explained at the time. "I had a special guitar built. I was getting tired of that brown Stratocaster anyway; I was getting a crummy sound out of it. I've now got a white one with a normal rosewood neck, but the electronic wiring is all low-impedance and we have all these transformers to boost my signal. So far it's worked out as long as we can keep the cords from the lights away from my amplifiers. I'm in good shape – in rehearsals we weren't doing it right, so I would get this confounded 60-cycle hum – but I think we've finally licked it. As long as I can bash it against my amplifiers I'm alright. I never used that pickup much anyway."

Press reviews on the American tour were glowing from the start: "Rainbow's performance was excellent," "Ritchie Blackmore stunned the

---

* Steven Tyler was indeed the father of Buell's child who has since gone on to fame as actress Liv Tyler.

199

crowd with a multitude of brilliant lead guitar solos throughout their entire set." "Rainbow put on a satisfying show, both audibly and visibly." "Words could not do the awesome stage rainbow justice. It has to be seen to be appreciated," were just a sample of some of the notices.

Apart from the ever present technical gremlins affecting a few shows, Blackmore produced some of his finest live performances on this tour. His solos on 'Mistreated' and 'Catch The Rainbow' in particular, would change dramatically night by night and with the latter, at times it appeared as if he was in another world, taking the music to exceptional levels with astonishing improvisations that carried on in the Deep Purple tradition. Tony Carey admired the way that Blackmore conducted the music. " 'You improvise until I do this and hold my hand up in the air.' That's the thing, when I say progressive rock, with this band it was never 'I solo for 16 bars then we go somewhere else.' It was, like, 'I'll play until I don't feel like playing anymore.' It's trial and error. You find out what works and when a solo peaks and when you tend to leave it and repeat it the next time. But if you put any four or five good musicians together and tell them to jam it's going to work and the solos are going to fit and it sounds like they've been playing together all their lives. [Rainbow] was a very democratic band. The interplay developed from the first gig and it wasn't the sound of Seventies metal – it had more in common with Weather Report than Black Sabbath."

The hand signals that Blackmore employed to let the musicians know what was required paralleled the way that Jerry Lee Lewis had directed the Outlaws over a decade earlier.

Having been well-received in the States, Rainbow's British debut, occurring August 31 at the Bristol Hippodrome, received an ecstatic review in *Melody Maker.* "Ritchie Blackmore is back and nobody sleeps when he's on. There simply aren't words strong enough to describe how loud he and his band are. But in a masochistic way it was quite a gig. It was Rainbow's first concert on British soil, and they systematically blitzed the good citizens of Bristol who crammed into the Hippodrome. Blackmore's following is quite startling, not all leftovers from the Deep Purple days, either. Fresh-faced kids not yet out of school went as barmy as their older counterparts." The entire band was individually praised but reviewer Brian Harrigan left the greatest praise for their leader: "The King of the Stage, however, was (naturally) Blackmore himself and he was in spectacular form. Nimble, witty, very composed – he is probably one of the most heroic of guitar heroes. For unrelenting pressure Rainbow are hard to beat; for professionalism they are the peak. But God knows I could have used a little subtlety in their performance. Still, they are in business to overwhelm people. I, for one, was overwhelmed."

Blackmore's arrival in London brought other musicians to check out the two shows at the Hammersmith Odeon. On opening night Colosseum II's Don Airey and National Health bassist Neil Murray showed up while the following night, Coverdale, Glover, Lord and Paice were among the audience. An open air festival appearance at Cardiff Castle on August 13 with Rainbow supporting headliners Queen was to form part of the UK tour but the band withdrew when it became apparent that the full stage show with electronic rainbow could not be logistically accommodated. With hindsight it was a wise move as continual rain ruined the day's atmosphere.*

While in London, between dates, Blackmore took the opportunity to jam during a Fabulous Poodles gig at the Speakeasy with Mott The Hoople's Ian Hunter.† Apparently both Blackmore and Hunter refused to contribute financially for the use of the gear. As a result, Poodles' song 'The Wrist' was later said to have been dedicated to the pair.

The following night at Newcastle City Hall, during the last show of the tour, Blackmore took it upon himself to sack Tony Carey in his own unorthodox manner, as the keyboard player recalls: "He fired me because I was definitely playing too much. I know that now but he came over in the middle of the set and said, 'Why don't you just leave then.' I was definitely not playing what he expected me to play. It was his band, he could have come over and said 'Play less' or 'Stick to the rulebook' but he didn't. That's not his style. I didn't even know he was unhappy he just kept it to himself. No warning! So after the gig I said, 'OK I'm gone,' took a cab back to the hotel, called the airline and [the management] said 'Oh no, you can't do that in the middle of the tour.' 'Well he's just fired me'. I was talking to Bruce on a couch in the hotel lobby not knowing Ritchie was standing right behind me and I said, 'I think he's just jealous because I play so fast' and Ritchie of course heard this and whacked me across the back of the head but like you would hit a little kid and said to me, 'You're nothing, you'll never be anything' so there was definitely an insecurity and a pride. Why should he be jealous of me? He wasn't and couldn't have been.

"On the one hand he's an absolute genius, he's got such magnetism about

* Rainbow had originally been booked to play at Cardiff's Capitol Theatre but with the announcement of the all-day event, the original show was cancelled.
† Blackmore jammed again at the Speakeasy later that week with his original mentor Screaming Lord Sutch.

him when he walks in a room – the 'man in black' and this and that – this is one person in 50 million just from his charisma and what he's got but I wouldn't care to analyse what he is. I mean Mozart was an asshole but Ritchie is definitely an important figure, he taught me a lot. Nothing you'd ever want to teach anybody because he's way too selfish, but just observing him. The big problem I had with Rainbow was the management."

When Blackmore realised he couldn't get a replacement in time, Carey was reinstated to finish Rainbow's world tour which continued in Sweden. Given the friction the previous year at the Sunbury Festival between Purple and AC/DC it was a little surprising to find the Aussie rockers chosen as support act for the European dates especially as the feud had continued with Blackmore's derogatory comments about them in the press and AC/DC denying the guitarist's request to get up and jam with them at the Marquee. Those present on the tour say there were no hard feelings between the two parties and despite AC/DC's growing popularity, Carey believes it merely acted as an incentive to Blackmore. "Back then Ritchie got a boost from that stuff. They'd come off having done a good show and he'd go on and do a better show. I don't remember him ever complaining about them."

The French leg of the tour was best remembered by Blackmore for some onstage tomfoolery: "I remember in France somewhere, the audience were so boring – it was about the third number – I got on drums, Cozy got on guitar, and we all started playing 'Peter Gunn.' The audience actually went crazy. They wouldn't clap because they thought we were awful. And then we did 'Peter Gunn' and they thought we were wonderful! Isn't that amazing? Only in France!"

The European schedule also included Holland, the first time Blackmore had returned to the country since Deep Purple's debacle in Amsterdam three years earlier. With the incident still fresh in the minds of the Dutch press, Blackmore told *Muziekkrant Oor*: "Ahhh, yes, Amsterdam, that was terrible. Everything went wrong from the start – not enough electricity. When we arrived at the venue we weren't allowed in by some guy! We said, 'We're the band!' But the guy said, 'No, you're not gonna get in.' That made us angry. When we finally got to the dressing room there wasn't any heating – it was nearly freezing. No drinks, nothing; nobody wanted to help our road crew with all kinds of problems with the equipment, etc. It wasn't the fault of the audience, they were quite stoned, 'Hey man, Cosmos.' So we took it out on the audience, which wasn't fair, 'cause it wasn't their fault. But when a band has to go on stage like we did, chilled to the bone, agitated, and having had bad promotion, you can expect problems."

When asked if he would be making up for it, Blackmore was forthright, "I play music as well as I can, but I'm not going to make up anything for anybody. If they like it, they like it; if they don't like it then they don't like it … I never look at the audience. I don't know who comes to the shows. As long as they enjoy themselves, fine, but I haven't got a clue who they are. If it's a Purple audience, fine. We are similar to Purple – that is the band of a few years ago. That's the kind of music I like to play."

November was set aside for a full-length Australian tour and as with America and Europe, Rainbow's popularity resulted in capacity shows. The first of three nights at Adelaide's Festival Theatre quickly sold out prompting an added matinee show, remembered well by Tony Carey. "Because the evening show had sold out they scheduled this matinee show at one o'clock in the afternoon and there were only about 200 people that came. I remember Bruce Payne coming behind the curtain saying, 'The audience says he's ready' and we all laughed about that. So Ritchie said 'OK it's a rehearsal.' He used to check an acoustic nylon string Spanish guitar into airplanes without a case. The most fragile thing you ever saw and it always came back whole because no one would throw it while all the equipment in flight cases would come back smashed and scratched. His guitar always came back perfect it was amazing."

Moving onto Japan Rainbow got the full red carpet treatment. Blackmore hadn't played Japan since Deep Purple Mk II's last tour in 1973 and three years on, he had achieved God-like status. Raymond D'addario: "When we first started going there it was as big as any band who toured over there, Zeppelin or anything."

Tony Carey: "There were 700 people to meet us at six in the morning when we came in from the flight from Australia. Then we had to go into the Tokyo Hilton and we had to go through the kitchen entrance like the Beatles or whatever. But being rock 'n' roll stars we were so full of ourselves we thought we deserved it. I mean it didn't seem like anything special with 200 kids in front of the hotel and they all give you little presents in Japan. There was hysteria around the band and at the concerts the people just exploded and stayed exploded the whole time."

Having already fired the keyboard player, Blackmore's dislike of Carey's showmanship manifested itself with onstage pranks including an amusing incident during the lengthy intro to 'Stargazer.' "I'm completely involved with 11 keyboards on stage doing my intellectual thing and they're all sat there with their knees crossed like *Monty Python* reading newspapers and Ronnie in a gorilla mask. There was a lot of humour around the band anyway but being an American it wasn't really humour I understood.

Ronnie's American but a complete Anglophile, he was also much older than me and had been around the Deep Purple organisation. I was pretty much the outsider with the humour. I like British humour but I didn't understand it then."

While some of the jokes were harmless fun others had a greater degree of depravity to them. Tony Carey: "One of the things he did was he'd take a shit and put it in a hotel lamp, a wall lamp, or he'd have somebody do it. I don't know if it was his shit I didn't analyse it! So you come into the hotel room and as the lamp warms up the room would stink and you couldn't figure out where the stink was coming from. It's humiliating especially when you got to call the hotel guys and say 'Hey I think there's a dead rat in the wall.' And the janitor is looking around and saying, 'Someone has taken a shit in your lamp'."

With the tour over Blackmore brought in Italian keyboard player Joe Vescovi, whom he had briefly met in 1972 through Arvid Andersen,[*] to replace Carey. Arvid Andersen: "Ritchie called me about the organist's job he was trying to fill. He had heard Joe on one of our records and seen his photo so he asked me about him. I told Ritchie he was shit hot and arranged for Joe to make a tape with some of the demos we had written and played on together as the start of the new album we were preparing before my enforced repatriation from Italy. Joe sent the tape to me and I passed it on to Ritchie."

Vescovi's material was a collection of hard rock and neoclassical pieces that impressed Blackmore who immediately phoned Vescovi and arranged for him to meet with Powell who happened to be in Italy. The two spent the day together listening to some of Vescovi's work before the drummer contacted Blackmore to give him his opinion. It was favourable as a few days later Bruce Payne contacted Vescovi and invited him to the sessions for the next Rainbow album in Los Angeles. Arvid Andersen: "Cozy was in Monte Carlo tinkering with cars so he picked up Joe in Savona and drove him to Linate Airport, Milan and flew him to L.A."

Vescovi explained how the band used to work: "Ritchie was usually the one who arrived first, then he started to improvise on some riffs, and the band followed him, jamming until Ronnie Dio [hardly ever present] started to improvise some melodies on the track. Everything was being recorded with a small Sony, and at the end of the day they listened to it together to

---

[*] Andersen had continued with the Trip, developing the group into a progressive rock band who became very popular in Italy.

get the overall effect. The rehearsals usually started at around 3 pm and lasted until about 10 pm. Then we used to go to the Rainbow Bar and Grill, the famous bar patronised by stars where I had the chance to meet personalities like Eric Clapton and Rod Stewart."

Although Blackmore initially seemed positive about the new recruit Vescovi recalls that the guitarist's outlook changed overnight. Blackmore told Vescovi that he wasn't totally convinced about his way of playing, that his musical style was too different, and that he found him too "neoclassical" and progressive. "Ritchie was knocked out but Joe blew it," is how Andersen sees it.

At first being unaware of what was going on behind the scenes Tony Carey was eventually asked back. "He fired and hired me back twice. Once after the Rising tour. I had an apartment on Sunset Strip and I knew the band was starting rehearsing and I was waiting for them to call me and they were auditioning other keyboard players. Eddie Jobson from Roxy Music had shown up at the New York show and they were in contact with him. Then Colin and Ronnie turned up at my apartment and said 'Come on down, we'll have a rehearsal. One of the nice things, it was down at Pirate Sound, and I came in to the rehearsal and they let a cassette tape play of a rehearsal they'd had with this horrible Italian organ player playing this horrible meandering terrible solo at full volume over the PA system and that was my welcome back and I heard this horrible organ player. I never met him, never saw him but I knew he had been playing with the band and I know he sucked. If he's Italy's best B3 player now I apologise."

While Blackmore acknowledged that he had made an error of judgement concerning Carey's musical ability, largely because a suitable replacement had proved difficult to find, the personality clashes between the two men would continue to deteriorate over the coming months during which the vindictive and belligerent side of Blackmore's character came further to the fore.

CHAPTER 10

Forty Days Of Cries And Moans (1977–78)

Having recorded his previous three albums there, Musicland was once again Blackmore's preferred locale for the recording of what would become *Long Live Rock 'n' Roll*. However because the studio was booked solid Powell had the task of finding an alternative venue and the Strawberry Studio, Chateau d'Herouville near Paris was settled upon. Elton John, the Bee Gees, and T. Rex were just some of the names who had previously recorded there but the fact that Blackmore's favourite band Jethro Tull had used the Chateau may well have influenced his decision.

Unlike the first two Rainbow albums, the sessions were a lengthy and sometimes painstaking affair. Prior to commencing recording in March 1977 Blackmore had not only sacked and reinstated Tony Carey but also bassist Jimmy Bain, both being re-employed on a session only basis. By the time they got to France Bain had gone for good and finding a suitable replacement proved difficult, causing the recording to stretch on and off over 10 months. Initially original bassist Craig Gruber was invited back on Dio's suggestion. Gruber only lasted a month after which, Mark Clarke, formerly of Colosseum, Uriah Heep and most recently Natural Gas joined. Clarke was not credited on the album but when interviewed by Helmut Gerlach in 1998 he confirmed, "I actually did three tracks in the studio but 'Kill The King' is the only one I can remember 'cause Ritchie wanted the bass in quarter notes and I asked, 'Why doesn't it go in sixteenth notes?' And he said, 'Can you do that?' and I said, 'Sure I can do that.' But he wanted someone to do it like that with a pick.''

Having already been in the live set, 'Kill The King' was the first song to be recorded, along with a new track 'Long Live Rock 'n' Roll' though to this day it's still unclear if Blackmore used any of Clarke's bass lines as he didn't last very long.

Cozy Powell: "I remember every time we'd do a take, the red light used to go on and he'd go, "Stop, stop, stop!' He was out of tune. I couldn't understand this, and it went on and on – about 30 takes. 'Stop, I'm out of tune.' He'd get this tuning key and go 'Ding!' What he was doing, he was getting a bit uptight, he'd bend the neck before the start of the take, just enough to put the bass out of tune. So we'd start the track and it would be all over the place. So he didn't last very long. In the end I think Ritchie did something terrible to him. I think I threw a teacup at his son, or something like that. I can't remember now. In the mist of time it's all gone a bit faded."

Although this Rainbow line-up never toured, Clarke recalls doing a couple of spontaneous gigs on both sides of the Atlantic. "I can't remember where. One of them was Los Angeles, an off the cuff gig. We also did a gig in Paris one night. We just showed up at this club, and we actually played in Paris. And there was another one, we played two songs and Ritchie smashed the guitar and then just walked off and it wasn't even his own guitar. And the guy in this band went, 'What?' I could see Ritchie's roadie paying the guy out. That's how it was with Ritchie."

Despite Blackmore's reputation Clarke had no hesitation in taking up his invitation to join the band. "You see he paid very, very well. He paid people lots of money, so he could do that. He treated people around him, the musician's fine, you know. Yeah, he's awkward to work with – I only did a few gigs – half the time he was just going to leave, he wouldn't do an encore, so he'd just leave. So he's awkward like that. And I think he thinks that's like a cool thing to do. I don't think it is and most other people don't think it is, but everybody has their own ideas and Ritchie has his own. It's fine by me."

Carey recalls a similar incident at the Chateau. "There was a French singer there and he was using one of the studios. Ritchie went over and took the guy's acoustic guitar and threw it into the fire. Uncalled for violence, childish violence. Nobody stuck a knife into anyone and I guess he gave the guy a new Stratocaster afterwards but I was bemused. You have to think how much is calculated, how much is image building. I don't think very much, I think that's just the guy. He's one in 50 million, he stands out but you take the good with the bad but fortunately he didn't have a driving licence so he didn't kill anybody."

While outsiders occasionally encountered Blackmore's childish behaviour, it was Tony Carey who was mostly on the receiving end during the months at the Chateau. The practical jokes played on him became more vicious, although Clarke recalls that the tables were sometimes turned on Blackmore. "At the Chateau the guest house is all suites and many, many famous people like Chopin stayed there. Ritchie had the room that Chopin had stayed in. It had a huge armour, so one night we tied string to the door, we covered it with shoe polish and we took it through to the window, took it outside the window and then, late one night, Cozy Powell and I put a ladder up and we pulled this string. You could hear (making eerie noise) and all the lights were on. Suddenly we could hear Ritchie going, 'What the fuck. . .' And he was convinced ghosts were there, you see. He really was convinced of it. Then he came out and pushed Cozy off the ladder."

"I caught [Cozy] coming up a ladder," Blackmore confirms. "I went into my bedroom and I heard this tapping at the window. I crept to the window, pulled back the curtains, and there was Cozy creeping up the ladder. He was gonna destroy my room. I've forgotten what I did … I went 'Boo!' or something. 'Aaagghh!' Crash! Bang! And he ran away."

Carey had become disliked enough for Blackmore and Powell to make his life a living hell. Although quite possibly embellished, Blackmore nevertheless gave a frank and astonishing account of their treatment to the author in 1998. Although he initially attributed the cause to the fact that Carey wouldn't play football, Ritchie still derives amusement from regaling the story of events that were directed at the hapless keyboard player: "I used to throw the javelin all the time – I used to throw it at school – so I used to exercise by throwing the javelin. Just take it on the road, throw it around. And then we were in France, in the studio. I'd been throwing it in the garden, and I came back to my room. There was a corridor, and a wooden door at the end. So I thought, just for the hell of it, 'I wonder if I could stick it in that door?' Nobody else was around. It went straight through the door! Of course, Tony Carey was on the other side of the door … that's how it started. 'He's trying to murder me, he's throwing javelins at me.' So then he would stay in his room. He wouldn't come out. So Cozy and I just played jokes on him.

"There was one big incredible worked-out production that we did. What happened was … He was convinced I was the devil 'cause I was the leader of the band. So I was the devil. It took us a while to get into our first track at this place, which was haunted. I suppose the fact that we played football every day for 10 days before we went into the studio didn't help to get things going … He'd keep coming down, 'When am I going to put my part on?' 'Oh, not yet, not yet.' So when he eventually got into the studio, he walked in with a pint of Jack Daniels and a keyboard under his arm. He was already loaded – you could tell. Then he slipped, and all the Jack Daniels went down the control panel. So that was the end of him! He'd completely ruined the control panel. After waiting 10 days, he came in, tripped, into the control panel … That was it! Back to his room.

"In those days you always needed a clown to pick on and he was the one we picked on. He would stay in his room and would come out at eight in the morning until three in the afternoon. We got up at three in the after-noon and worked all the way through to six or seven in the morning. So we never saw him! He used to keep his door bolted. Then he started putting up crucifixes and obtaining all these flowers. We got into his room one day when he wasn't there, and there must have been a thousand flowers, and about 25 crosses up! Because he thought the devil was coming after him. So Cozy and I thought, 'Right, let's really get him!' We thought, 'We'll scare the life out of him!' We were in this scary place to start with – nobody would actually go to the toilet alone, that's how scary it was. People would be like (timid voice), 'Anybody feel like going to the toilet?' 'Yeah, I'll go with you.' Two guys would go together … one would be looking around. It was so weird, because we were all so petrified of this place! Chopin's ghost was there. So, we used to do things to Tony's room.

"We had it worked out that we'd play the tape across the studio to make out that we were actually recording. So Tony would think that we were recording, but in actual fact we were all hiding across the courtyard waiting to get him! 'Cause we knew he would come out of his room. He would go, 'Oh, I hear them playing … I'll go and help myself to a cup of tea' But it was the 24-track we started up, with us playing. Meanwhile, I was on top of the roof with Cozy, and we got this big piece of 4 × 2 ready to smash through his bedroom window at the precise time that the lights were put out – it was synchronised. And we knew that he'd run for the door, and as he would open his door this other 4 × 2 would hit him in the head. Because it would have a piece of string tied to the door. We had it all synchronised, we were crazy! The music started up … Cozy and I were looking out of this other bedroom window. We'd got this big long battering ram so we could lean across the roof and smash his bedroom window. Now he would think the devil's coming to get him … because he could hear us playing … the lights went out, and of course he opens his door, and the string pulls and the thing hits him in the head. This is all in the darkness. But that was just one of the things we did to him.

"After that, he thought we were out to kill him. It was like he was in gaol ... the cook would go up with his food, 'cause he wouldn't eat with us – the cook would go up and forget the utensils. I'd go up with a pair of pliers and I'd heat up the knife until it was white hot, then slip it under the door ... 'Oh, thanks a lot.' Then you'd hear, 'Aaarghh!' It was things like that that got me a bad name."

"I'd forgotten about how funny some of the things were," Powell remarked when the author asked about Carey's victimisation in 1997. "They obviously weren't very funny to [Carey], but if you think that everybody in the band and crew are all trying to make your life a misery, it must have been hell for him. Poor bloke, really! We really put that guy through some real shit, I have to say ... the last time I ever saw him, he was running down the road with his suitcases in his hands after we'd tried to kill him!"

The story of Carey literally running out of the chateau late at night was independently endorsed by Blackmore and Clarke. When I spoke to Carey for this book, he gave his version of events. "I never got any grief from Ritchie on stage. He was always amazing, in his own world. He hated me personally, he was 10 years older and I was a cocky kid from California. He didn't like me at all. It was pranks in the guise of Satanism not just teasing but really nasty. I was in my room in the Chateau and a big rock came though my window splattering me with broken glass and they cut the lights at the same time and I was just scared shitless. And it was after we'd had these séances and the twelve stations of the cross were around the studio, bullshit black magic stuff. And someone, either Cozy or Ritchie, stood outside my room and lit tarot cards on fire and slipped them under my door and I thought the place was going to burn down. I called my father in California. 'Do me a favour, dad, I can't get a travel agent here, book me a ticket, next ticket out of Paris I'm coming home.' Colin tried to talk me out of it. I said, 'No I'm gone this is not fun or music. I'm a musician, why in the world am I getting this grief' but I was the youngest so pick on somebody, like this English schoolboy thing."

Powell insisted Carey's attitude was to blame for their behaviour. "The problem is that if you're dealing with guys with an English sense of humour, and I guess by that point Ritchie's and my sense of humour was pretty warped, and you're starting to come off a bit big time, which he certainly did ... We'd say, 'OK Tony, would you like to come and do a keyboard solo now?' 'Well, man, I might come down in a couple a hours if I feel like it.' It's like ... wrong! You don't do that. When Ritchie says can you come and do a keyboard solo you go and do a keyboard solo. So he kind of made a rod for his own back in that respect. He asked for it. He really did. He was a very good player, but very cocky and a bit full of himself. So he had to go. There was no way he was going to last the pace."

By August with several months of tour dates looming, the nucleus of Blackmore, Dio and Powell eventually recruited a new keyboard player, Canadian David Stone and Australian bassist Bob Daisley from Widowmaker, thereby creating the most multi-national of all Rainbow's line-ups. Daisley had been contacted by a mutual friend Dick Middleton about the possibility of joining Rainbow.

Bob Daisley: "Really the first part of the audition was meeting Ritchie and socialising a little bit because as Dick had mentioned to me Ritchie doesn't really want to audition people unless he meets them first and finds out that they are compatible as a personality because it's pointless audition-ing people and finding out they are a great player but he doesn't get on with them. So the first thing Ritchie wanted to do was have a few beers and a sit and a chat. Dick organised that with Ritchie and we just went out to the Rainbow Bar and Grill to see if we had compatible personalities and we got on okay so Ritchie said well come down and have a play."

Although Blackmore had already done much of the bass work himself on the album sessions with a tour looming numerous bassists had been consid-ered before Daisley. "They had been rehearsing and auditioning other bass players at a film studio in Hollywood, so I went down there. Ritchie put me through the paces playing wise. First of all he wanted someone who used a plectrum because it was more precise and definite and for the style of drumming that went with it so well because Cozy would play, eighths and sixteenths on his bass drum a lot and with a pick you can really lock it in and I did, so that was a natural thing. He just put me through a few things play this, play that, keep on playing this, like fast right hand stuff with the pick hand to make sure I could keep up and we played for some time – jamming and playing definite songs and at the end of it they would down tools and have a tea break and they said you are what we have been looking for so the gig is yours if you want it. The funny thing is I actually said 'I'll think about it.'

"Don't get me wrong I loved the idea of playing with Rainbow but some people tried to warn me off, you will be a hired gun, a sideman and quite often people get chewed up and spat out. Three months down the track you could be without a job. So I did think about that, I didn't mean it in a big-headed way but I was thinking about it and I phoned my wife in England and she said 'Are you out of your fucking mind? Take it!' The decision was made for me, because with Widowmaker they quite often had squabbles and punch-ups and we had a gig to do at the Whiskey A Go-Go in LA. I think Ritchie actually came to that gig and at the end of the show we were back-stage and a couple of them started off arguing again and I thought, 'I'm off. I'm going up to the Rainbow.' That was funny because Ritchie was waiting for me. He said he would be up at the Rainbow Bar and Grill just up the road from the Whiskey A Go-Go so it became symbolic then – 'I'm going up to the Rainbow.' And there was Ritchie sitting at a table and as I walked in, he actually stood up and applauded me. I was taken aback then, that was very nice, so I said count me in. Then we started rehearsals."

Not only was Blackmore insistent on getting to know any prospective new members on a personal level but he was self-conscious about his image. So much so that by now his rapidly thinning hairline had received a makeover – of little consequence to fans but of growing amusement to others. Dio recalled the mirth within the band when they first saw Blackmore's new look. "We hadn't seen each other for a month or so, we got together for the publicity shots and lo and behold – Ritchie had had a hair transplant! Cozy was beside himself – he smirked on every picture. Blackmore wouldn't come anywhere near us!"

Because of the problems in finding a stable line-up, the completion of *Long Live Rock 'n' Roll* had been held up, causing an American tour planned for August to be cancelled. Having flown in to England for final rehearsals at Shepperton studios, the planned start of the tour with four nights at the appropriate Rainbow Theatre in north London were put back to November. The tour was then scheduled to commence in Helsinki but further problems getting the equipment trucks and gear across the border in time resulted in another cancellation. Eventually the tour started two nights later in Stockholm on September 25.

This particular European tour was notable for several incidents where Blackmore's aggression backfired on him – the first occurring on October 18 at the Stadthalle, Vienna. The UK press reported that at the end of the concert the crowd surged forward and when security stepped in to hold them back their behaviour towards the crowd angered the band and scuffles broke out with punches thrown. Daisley recalls the incident in a different way. "We went on stage. I don't know what the complaints were, too loud or something happened and they put the house lights on and this prick stood right in front of Ritchie and he was being an arsehole. He stood there with his arms folded right in front of Ritchie on the stage. It wasn't a par-ticularly high stage; Ritchie was being provoked by him; this guy was being an arsehole. So Ritchie swung his foot out near him and he went to grab Ritchie's foot, then Ritchie kicked out and kicked him straight in the jaw and down he went. He wanted to press charges for assault. But we did the whole show and after the show police came backstage with sniffer dogs, wanting to arrest Ritchie for assault. They tried to smuggle Ritchie out of the gig in a flight case but I think he got sniffed out by the dogs and the police got him. We had a roadie working for us Gerry Oxford called Thee Ox and he went to gaol with Ritchie."

Raymond D'addario: "I was sitting out at the mixer watching the whole thing and it looked like the kids got up to run to the front of the stage. No trouble and the security people were really heavy and my recollection was that Ritchie had seen this security guard pummel this chick right in front of him and when the guy got close to the stage Ritchie kicked him in the head and apparently broke his jaw. But the guy turned out to be the hall manager or something heavy. We tried to sneak him out of the place in this huge road case. There were like six to eight of us trying to push this case out and they took us one by one off the case and Ox refused to get off so they came to drag him off. Then they opened up the box and took Ritchie. Ox was in gaol two or three days longer than Ritchie because he really gave them a hard time trying to divert attention from Ritchie. When they got to gaol Ox just caused as much trouble as he could with the verbal and any-thing he could to divert the Viennese police from Ritchie and onto him."

Ox's behaviour may have been honourable but it made their confine-ment behind bars much worse. Although Oxford now sadly suffers from multiple sclerosis he still remembers the dramatic events. "We were sepa-rated that evening as we got to the prison. I was terrified and wondered if we would ever get out of there. Ritchie was really scared as well." By all accounts the Austrian police were heavy-handed and while the pair anx-iously awaited news, Bruce Payne contacted the American Counsel in Vienna to try and secure their release.

It was without question the most terrifying experience in Blackmore's performing career. "We had a very fanatical audience. In the first row was a girl who totally flipped out but didn't hurt anyone. The security was made up of policemen, and one of these security guys was hitting her relentlessly with a stick, again and again. So I kicked out in his direction, hitting his face and breaking his jaw. The guy went down, and within moments all exits were blocked by policemen. During the encore I ran off stage and jumped into a flight case that a roadie had ready for me. The lights went on, cops stormed towards the backstage area, dogs barked – it was like in a film. They wanted to teach me a lesson, and it seemed as though every gun in town was in pursuit of a mass murderer. The crew told them I had run to the railway station, and my pursuers went there on motorbikes. At the same

213

time my roadies rolled me outside and just at the moment they were putting the case on to the truck two policemen came and wanted to check the contents of the case. They opened it, and a few seconds later I had won a nice stay overnight with full board. I was kept there for a full four days [sic]. I was kept from sleeping the whole time, fed the worst shit and so on. I felt like a prisoner of war, and to make it perfect I had to pay 10,000 dollars for the service."

An important show at Munich's Olympiahalle the following evening, to be simulcast by German TV station WDR for its *Rockpalast* broadcast had to be postponed until the following day and even then it was still touch and go.

Bob Daisley: "We weren't sure if Ritchie was going to show up. It was sort of on and off all the time and by the afternoon we still didn't know, then we went down to the gig and everyone said Ritchie is on his way, he will make it to the gig but he will be late. So instead of going on at our normal time of around 8.45 that night it was put back to about 11 and I think some people had to actually leave because it had gone past the public transport hours. The majority that could stay did and it went down a bomb, it was great."

Raymond D'addario: "My recollection is he came from the gaol and said, 'I'm going to the hotel and have a shower and a meal before I go to the gig'."

The Munich gig's climactic ending involved a familiar guitar smashing finale borne out of frustration and resentment than anything else. Bob Daisley: "That was him that was what he was like. He was a smart bloke and an aware bloke but like all of us he definitely had a bit of anger in him. To play that kind of music properly you have to have a bit of spark as far as anger and aggression goes." As can be seen in the broadcast, Blackmore's anger that night was more intense than usual and during the encore of 'Do You Close Your Eyes?' he swung the guitar from its lead around and around, almost decapitating fans in the front row before eventually discarding the wreckage into the audience.

The rest of the tour went off without further incident until the band reached Britain the following month. During the encore at the Liverpool Empire on November 5, Blackmore appeared upstairs in one of the boxes and proceeded to demolish his guitar, before launching the fragments into the audience. His antics and the damage caused to the ornate décor of the Victorian building resulted in Rainbow being banned from ever playing the venue again.

★ ★ ★

Although lawyers dealt with the legal procedures involving Blackmore's assault charge, the hefty fine imposed could have been better spent considering the expenses the band had racked up with the slow progress on *Long Live Rock 'n' Roll*. Returning to the Chateau in December the album was finally completed. Blackmore didn't ask Daisley to replace any of his bass parts. "He probably just wanted to get on with it. He probably thought it's what he wanted so if it's not broken don't fix it. There was an album partially recorded and they needed us [Daisley and Stone] to finish off and record so we could at least be on the album. Ritchie had played bass on some of the tracks but it did leave something to be desired in my opinion because he is a fantastic guitar player, such a great musician but as a bass player he doesn't think like a bass player, doesn't play like a bass player and that came across a bit insipid for my liking. They were basically reproducing the same notes as the guitar had done."

During the many hours of mixing there wasn't a great deal to keep the band occupied as Daisley recalls: "There were times when there was fuck all to do there, TV was in French, we were miles from any town so we used to sit in front of the fire and drink so by the end of the night we ended up legless. It was a huge fireplace you could virtually stand up in. I remember Cozy and me were building up the logs in it and one night we built it up so much that the oak beam mantle around it started to smoulder."

Above the fireplace stood a large antique radio and in one moment of boredom, Blackmore and Powell instinctively and simultaneously picked it up and threw it into the fire. Colin Hart, who happened to be walking by, saw the laughing duo dash out of the room, and immediately knew they had been up to no good. "The radio belonged to a French band who were recording there too and they would hog the living room and play crap French stuff on this radio, so Cozy and Mr. B tossed it into the fire. I stayed behind, as usual to calm them down a bit. I made a brief attempt to get the radio, but it went up like a newspaper, so I let the owner and the French deal with it. It caused quite a stir with the owner and his friends, the French mob. They left soon after that."

Bob Daisley: "Ritchie was always saying that place was haunted and this entity that he used to contact was called Baal and he was out to get him and make trouble and we had a few blackouts when we were recording and Ritchie would always say 'That's Baal.' I was always quite interested in séances; occultism, I don't mean anything negative or dark and neither was Ritchie. He didn't like that. He didn't like people who wore crosses upside down or anything satanic. He was interested in spirituality and occultism

215

but only in a positive light. Quite often we had the séances and I was pissed so it didn't get to me too much."

Blackmore recalled that whenever they tried to work at night, problems occurred with the equipment. "If we recorded on channel six the playback would be on channel 13. The 24-track machine started working on its own." Although Dio didn't share Blackmore and Powell's penchant for nasty pranks, his interest in spiritualism ended at the Chateau. "Most séances will swear at you or use bad grammar, but this one said, 'I am Baal, I create chaos. You will never leave here, don't even try.' We tried again later and the spirit asked, 'Where's Blackmore? Oh never mind, here he comes.' The door opened and in walked Ritchie! Even he turned ashen … I thought this was the last séance for me, as soon as it began, 'I am Baal, I create chaos' I was fucking out of the room!"

No matter how strong the presence of 'Baal' the album was completed and the band managed to leave the Chateau. Ironically the last song to be taped, 'Gates Of Babylon,' turned out to be the centrepiece of the album and it was also virtually the only track on the album put together with the entire band. Blackmore's guitar work is considered to be among his finest moments by many, including Swedish guitarist Yngwie Malmsteen, who cites it as his best ever. Daisley concurs with this view. "I think the solo Ritchie did over that chord progression is one of the best solos I've ever heard him do."

Even for somebody who is highly critical of and often dissatisfied with his own performances, Blackmore was rightly proud of his work on the song, telling *Guitar Player* in 1978: "I think the solo is the best I've ever done. It is the best because it's the most intricate solo, yet at the same time it's not clinical. I was well pleased with that one. It was spontaneous and also it wasn't just 24 bars of just playing on E. There were so many weird chords involved that I could go back to my old way of playing, which is just to have the chords in front of me and play the solo, whereas now every time I go into the studio to play I know exactly what the song consists of. Usually it's just two chords and I'm stale by the time I get in there. But we threw those chords around, and in fact David Stone, our keyboard player, helped a lot with that. They were strange chords – diminished, augmented – it was great. Because I love musical theory and I was well into that, I didn't have any problems with that side of it. I love playing a few augmented and diminished runs and not just the usual blues licks."

Rainbow returned to the scene of a previous triumph with a tour of Japan starting on January 11. The previous tour in '76 had seen the band play 11 shows in 15 days but the '78 tour was a massive one by any band's

216

standards. Rainbow spent nearly a month there, playing 17 gigs, including four sold out nights at the huge Budokan arena in Tokyo. Bob Daisley: "Some of the towns we went to, we couldn't go out in the streets or anything. Number one they were all Japanese and here's us being whiteys and really obvious we were not one of them and the hotels were surrounded by young fans. I don't like to mention anyone, no matter who it is, in the same breath as the Beatles because that only happened once but it was a little taste of what Beatlemania could have been like. We couldn't go out in the streets, and we couldn't walk anywhere. Anything to do with Deep Purple was huge there."

What should have gone down as a fantastic tour was overshadowed by a tragic event during a gig at the Nakajima Sports Centre – a large gymnasium type venue – in Sapporo on January 27, when a female student was killed and several others injured at the start of the show. Bob Daisley: "That was horrible and I think she was only about 16 or 17. During the gig the house lights went down our lights came on, we started playing and all the audience rushed the stage. They had those fold up chairs, and when they rushed forward she was pushed down and the chairs went on top of her. She was crushed and killed by this audience trampling over her, over these metal chairs. We didn't know anything about any incident – we just carried on with the show. That's unusual for Japanese audiences to go barmy like that because usually they're quite subdued and they sit there and clap, then they'll stop and you do the next song and they clap then they stop etc. But they went nuts and rushed the stage and we didn't have a clue it had happened.

"I got back to my hotel room and there was us on television and it was on the news. At first I just thought a channel had been there to report on the gig or show a little bit of it and then, even though it was in Japanese I knew it was not good news. Later that night I found out some young girl had been killed. It was a horrible feeling. I felt so sorry for her, someone who just goes to a concert to enjoy it and ends up losing their life. I know Ritchie was touched by it. It affected all of us but after a while either the promoters or officials or news people were sort of saying to us 'Tone your performance down a little bit and don't look like you're too aggressive or too rock 'n' roll' because of this incident."

Despite the tragedy the band adopted a stoic attitude for the remainder of the tour as Daisley explains, "I remember after a few nights instead of wearing these black pants I came out with vertically striped black and white pants on and Ritchie came over to me and said, 'I like that – it looks cheeky.' He didn't want to lose the rebelliousness and the attitude of the

217

band because of this incident. He wanted to be apologetic to the press but he didn't want it to affect the attitude or the image of the band. It was something that was no fault of the band. We didn't incite a riot or anything like that the real fault lay with the hall manager and promoters of that show who didn't secure the seating."

Raymond D'addario: "The whole mood of the tour changed after [Sapparo] drastically. It was like up to that point we were having a wonderful time and then a lot of places had extra police, mainly worried in case people got angry with the band or something like that but it was just awful. It went on for years that whole thing. We never went back to Sapporo, a lot of people didn't but it was a real pity."

The after effects of the Sapporo tragedy and Shoshana still on his mind made Blackmore decide to uproot himself from the fast lane of Los Angeles to the East Coast, where he based himself in Darian, Connecticut for about a year. He was undecided at the time on whether to continue living in America or to move elsewhere, telling Germany's *Bravo* magazine, "I wanted to live in Hamburg, but I couldn't find a house for a reasonable price. That was six months ago. The houses there are three times as expensive as here in LA. I like Germany, I feel really comfortable there and at home. As you probably know I believe in rebirth. I know I lived in Germany before in one of my earlier lives. With the help of hypnosis I want to get to the bottom of that. I'm trying to put together the pieces to find out who I was in the past."

During the Japanese tour the presence of Dio's girlfriend Wendy started to intrude on Blackmore's otherwise cordial relationship with the singer. Raymond D'addario: "We were in Japan and Ritchie went to Bruce's door and he could hear her complaining about him. He was hearing her talking and he's just figuring she's having a go at him. Then when it all finishes he hears Ronnie go 'Oh yeah' and Ritchie's thinking 'Oh my God.' She sort of made Ronnie go whacko and as much as Ritchie liked Ronnie I think he knew Wendy beforehand and he'd had as much as he could of her and at that time it seemed as if Ronnie wanted to quit and be on his own. At that time we'd moved back to the East Coast from living in Malibu and Ritchie goes and gets a nice house to live in. Ronnie went up to see him and Wendy had to have a nicer house than Ritchie and that's sort of how it went and Ritchie probably didn't have the patience to deal with it."

"When [Ronnie] got into Rainbow it was a really big deal for him and he'd split up with his wife just before that. When he first got into the band he was living in Malibu in a beautiful house on the beach and he was going places and he tried to get back together with his ex-wife but she didn't want to know."

Released in the UK on Blackmore's 33rd birthday, *Long Live Rock 'n' Roll* has gone on to be generally considered Rainbow's best album – continuing in the same vein as *Rising* but with a slightly more commercial sound. The exception was the album's closing track, 'Rainbow Eyes.' Dismissed by many at the time as a strange and out of place balled, in hindsight it was the first real example of Blackmore's liking of mediaeval music. Although the uninitiated weren't aware that he had been incorporating mediaeval modes into Rainbow compositions on previous albums, the use of flutes, recorders and violins on 'Rainbow Eyes' was a much more obvious indication. The only electric instrument on the track was guitar but it would not have sounded out of place had it been played on a lute.

As well as the "no thanks to Baal" comment, the sleeve credits acknowledged both Blackmore and Daisley's bass work but without specifying who contributed to which track. Stone was solely credited for keyboards much to Tony Carey's dismay. Carey admits that he has never listened to the finished album and in general the presence of keyboards throughout is minimal. It's more than likely that his parts were erased as there is certainly no aural evidence of keyboards on 'Rainbow Eyes' which explains the sparse sound and feeling on the track.[*]

As promotion for the album three tracks were recorded for the late night US TV show *Don Kirschner's Rock Concert*, something that Daisley recalls with a blur. "I think [the taping] was done just outside of New York and I remember us doing them during the day and I was half-cut by the time we actually did them because we had been doing run-throughs, over and over and we were sipping vodka all day."

A lengthy four-month tour started on May 9 in Tennessee but because Rainbow had failed to develop the same level of popularity as Deep Purple the first leg of the tour included several shows supporting REO Speedwagon. Bob Daisley: "It was not good, because having been in Deep Purple, one of the biggest bands in the world, and being considered a guitar god and having done so well in Europe and Japan to have to go back to America and be second on the bill to a rock pop band. But he's grown up and professional and we just got on with it. Some nights we'd blow them off

---

[*] Blackmore overdubbed a lot of slide guitar throughout the album, leading at least one reviewer to mistake the sound for keyboards.

stage and some nights it was their audience and we just lived with that. It was a challenge but we just got on with it, did it and made it the best we could. But there was never a night when we bombed, most of the time we went down really well."

It certainly didn't help Blackmore's ego to play to half-full auditoriums, as was sometimes the case when REO Speedwagon fans remained outside until their band appeared. The combination of the two groups wasn't the most ideal pairing. REO didn't like Rainbow at all and prevented them from using their full light show, including the electronic rainbow. Despite this impediment, Powell still managed to throw in the pyrotechnics during his drum solo, ensuring the explosions were as powerful as ever. Some dates included a third band No Dice whose keyboard player David Moore recalls Blackmore frequently destroying his guitar, tossing the instrument in the air in a failed attempt to lodge it in the lighting truss.

Matters weren't helped when Rainbow often fared better in reviews, one headline in *Sounds* declaring, "REO rattled by rampant Rainbow." In explaining his motivation, Blackmore told the same paper, "If you tell someone that's not very good, then they go away and come back with something really good. That's what they used to do to me on stage, because sometimes we would go on stage and I'd get a bit lazy and I wouldn't play particularly well. One night we played with REO Speedwagon I think it was. One of those bands, and I heard one of them say as were going up on stage, 'Oh, he can't play very well. He's not very good.' So, of course I felt that I'd played the best that I'd played in years that night. And the management came in and said, 'My God, you played well tonight.' And I went, 'Well, yeah, they said I couldn't play.' They're like, 'Who?' And I said, 'Well the other band. I heard them say something.' So immediately right there he thought, 'Aha, now I know what to do to get Ritchie to play better. Stir him up.' So they tried it the next night, but it didn't work the next night. They said, 'I just heard someone saying that you weren't very good.' I said, 'Oh, I know what you're doing now.' But there is something to be said about, if you put someone down, they'll come back stronger."

With the support act only allocated a one-hour slot inevitably there were occasions when Rainbow ran over time. Towards the end of the tour, the BBC recorded a show at the Omni in Atlanta, Georgia for syndication throughout American FM radio, but tempers flared when Andy Green, REO's stage manager, switched on the house lights the moment Rainbow stepped off stage. "I punched Andy Green because he put the house lights on 10 seconds after we came off the stage," Blackmore told *Circus*. "We like to keep the lights off until the 'Over The Rainbow' theme is finished playing. The lights went up and it was like, 'Now that shit is finished, we're on next.' REO is a great band and we get on with them very well, but there has been one certain person we don't get on with and he's the one that turned on the lights."

During the tour Blackmore's penchant for dismissive comments to the press, allied to the generally contemptuous way he often treated journalists backfired on him with an infamous 'Bitchy Ritchie' article that appeared in *Record Mirror* that August. Rainbow's press officer Chris Bohn had arranged for a front cover exclusive and for journalist Shelia Prophet to accompany him to the States for Rainbow's performance at a festival in Bridgeport, Connecticut. Polydor's MD of the time had other ideas and with Bohn only having been with the company a short while he ordered Dennis Munday, a more senior member of staff to accompany the journalist instead. Munday had only been dealing with the label's rock acts for the past year being more used to dealing with jazz artists.

Having arrived in New York he recounted the ensuing chain of events in an unpublished manuscript summarised as follows: "We met up with Lee Ellen Newman, Rainbow's press officer, and she informed us of our itinerary. The next day we would be driven to Bridgeport and after the gig, Sheila would be given enough time for a one on one interview with Ritchie. The rest of the day was taken up with meetings and that night we hit the town. Lee Ellen's boss Ronnie Rosenthal accompanied us, a New Yorker through and through with a broad, loud Brooklyn accent. The booze was flowing freely, and the conversation eventually came around to Ritchie. Ronnie's tongue was running away with her, and she wasn't holding back [on Blackmore's sex life]. I didn't think much to these funny stories, however, it would come back to haunt me.

"We arrived at the stadium and after being given our backstage passes we took in a couple of bands that were on the bill. Rainbow's manager Bruce Payne suddenly appeared and there seemed to be problems. We went to the backstage office where he made several phone calls, eventually explaining that the band was not going to show up. Evidently, Ritchie was unhappy with Rainbow's billing and felt they should have been higher on the bill. The fact that the bands above him were much bigger and their records outsold his didn't come into it. It started to look like the whole trip was a waste of time.

"Fortunately, a few days later, Rainbow were due to appear in Philadelphia and the interview was re-scheduled. Having been advised Rainbow would definitely turn up for the gig, we departed for the long drive to Philly. We arrived and hung out in the theatre until Rainbow went on stage. I sat ten rows from the front, and although Rainbow's manager assured me the band had turned down the volume, it was deafening. After the third number, I decided to move to the rear of the stalls but even at the back of the auditorium, it was still too loud so I decided to take in the night air, returning for the last couple of numbers. With the show over, we retreated to Ritchie's hotel for Sheila to do her interview. So far, everything seemed to be working out for the best.

"A little later, Ritchie entered the hotel accompanied by a dark haired, well-upholstered girl. She was dressed in a very tight fitting oriental dress slit down the sides, fishnet stockings, and high heels. I noticed Sheila had clocked his main squeeze and wasn't too impressed. At the time, I thought nothing of this. Much later, Ritchie reappeared and went off with Sheila to another table where it was quieter, and proceeded with the interview. I looked across from time to time and everything seemed to be going well, and I thought we'd got a result. Sheila returned and I asked if everything was OK, and she replied, 'Yes, it was great, I got everything I needed,' and with that retired to the bathroom to freshen up. Shortly after Sheila entered the bathroom, I noticed a couple of Ritchie's goons followed her in, which seemed a little strange, as the Gents was next door. The realisation began to dawn on me, all was not well, and the night might just end up in a fiasco. On her return, I noticed she was distressed, and I asked 'What happened?' She replied, 'Two men came in, grabbed a hold of me and stole the tape out of my tape recorder.'

"By now, Ritchie's manager had made an appearance and explained he was extremely pissed off with Sheila's opening question to Ritchie which related to what Ronnie had told her in New York. Bruce then mentions Ritchie would like a quiet word and we walked over to his table. Ritchie was perched on a chair, flanked by the aforementioned hairy arsed security guards and Cozy Powell. At this point, I had no idea what was going to happen and it looked like a fight could erupt at any moment. Ritchie stared at me, trying to look menacing, which was a bit difficult with the rug he was wearing. He started the interrogation and accused me of spreading rumours about the band changing personnel. A little confused I replied that I had no idea about the changes in his band. Nor did I care as he changed band members more than I changed my underpants. The grilling went on for a while until Ritchie seemed satisfied and when the meeting broke up, I breathed a sigh of relief. From the beginning of this confrontation, I knew I'd no chance against five of them, I decided, if there was going to be a fight, I'd give Ritchie a 'Glaswegian' handshake, and at least have the satisfaction of waking up next to him in the local hospital. The funny thing was he didn't mention Sheila's interview. For me, he was a strange, and a thoroughly un-likeable bloke. I knew everyone was aware of Ritchie's temperament, but at least we got an interview."

On his return to the UK Munday was required to give his manager a report on the visit. "About mid-morning, I received a call from the General Manager's secretary, who wanted to see me immediately. We discussed the trip and he asked me how things went. Naturally, I bullshitted about the interview, and told him all went well. I wasn't about to load a gun and point it at my head. Shortly after this meeting, the chickens came home to roost. The 'Bitchy Ritchie' article appeared in *Record Mirror*, and Chris Bohn popped into see me with a copy of the paper. The front cover was a facsimile of the record sleeve and I said, 'It looks great,' to which Chris replied, 'Dennis, you had better read the article before you make any more comments.' I started to read the three-page spread and as I took in Sheila's diatribe, my heart sank.

"The article graphically detailed all that had happened, every bloody gory detail. The article was supposed to be an exclusive on Rainbow and my name appeared several times. Sheila had done a real hatchet job on Ritchie, completely slaughtering him and me into the bargain. I would have to do some pretty fast-talking, and asked whether Rainbow's manager had read the article. Chris replied, 'Yes, he has.' When my boss called me in for an explanation, I pointed out that it wouldn't have mattered who had accompanied Sheila, nothing would have changed, and the article would have been written the same way. At this point, I launched my last line of defence and weakly said, 'It's better to have bad publicity than none.' He listened to my story and accepted it, but I knew I hadn't heard the end of this, and a week or so later, I was summoned back to his office, and I was relieved of all duties on Rainbow."

The debacle almost lost Polydor Rainbow's contract. According to the company's then marketing executive, George McManus: "Bruce Payne rang me and said if you don't take over this band I'm going to Mercury."

Blackmore's treatment of journalists and record company employees in such a situation was symptomatic of his general dislike for the mechanics of the music business. While many other artists accepted it as part of the game, for Blackmore the only thing that mattered was the music and on that level the American tour could be judged a success.

The "well upholstered" girl Munday referred to was Amy Rothman, a doctor's daughter from Long Island who met Blackmore prior to a show. According to Stuart Smith, "Amy told me that when she met Ritchie she was with another guy, a massive Blackmore fan. This guy who was going out with Amy said, 'Yeah you go back and see him' and of course that was it. Then she told the guy he'd like to see her and he says, 'Go out with him then!' She felt she got pushed into the relationship by her boyfriend."

While on the four-month American trek, Dio told a journalist, "After this tour there's going to be another album. I think it will be kind of the same LP as this one. It has to maintain that same sort of rock 'n' roll music."

Blackmore, however, had other ideas.

CHAPTER 11

Down To Earth (1978–80)

With another American tour behind him Blackmore considered Rainbow's future direction. His dissatisfaction with Dio, and his girlfriend which started during the sessions for *Long Live Rock 'n' Roll*, intensified. "We started slowing down on the third LP. I remember being in the studio, and Ronnie came in with Cozy – I was kneeling down in front of my amplifier, trying to get the sound right – and [Dio] poked me in the back. I'll always remember it. 'We're not standing for this!' 'What?' 'You're on the front cover of *Circus* magazine. We're not gonna be sidekicks!' I went, 'It's got nothing to do with me. I don't know if I'm on the front page of whatever you're talking about.' 'You're on the front page of *Circus* and it was going to be the three of us!' And I went, 'So it's not?' 'No, it's just you.' 'Who said this?' 'Wendy just called me.' 'Oh, right; thank you Wendy!' That was it. I knew that we were finished then, because I couldn't talk to him any more. I suddenly saw him in a different light. I saw him as this angry bitter little man. He got very bitter."

Bob Daisley had picked up that all was not well during the US tour. "There were a few hints. When the drum solo came we would all go to the side of the stage and chat about if the gig's going well and I remember a couple of times when Bruce Payne was there, Ronnie saying to him 'Looks like I could be gone soon because Ritchie's been playing weird chords.' There would be a bit in one of the songs when there was a bit of ad-libbing in the middle of it between Ritchie and Ronnie. It was just a chord progression and it used to be different every night. I think if Ritchie played weird chords and made Ronnie sing over these progressions he thought

Ritchie was having a go at him or putting him through some kind of test. Sometimes you could hear Ronnie say, 'It was weird tonight that means I could be gone, he's got it in for me.'"

Despite their writing partnership having been highly fruitful Blackmore started to express dissatisfaction with both Dio's and his own songwriting skills, wanting to steer Rainbow in a direction that the singer was at odds with. Raymond D'addario observed the way things went downhill. "It was a weird time because I'd worked for [Ronnie James Dio] for about seven or eight years but they didn't have a bass player at the time and they were auditioning this guy Clive Chaman. It was about the same time that Don Airey came in but Ronnie was being really weird. A lot of that was pumped by Wendy, she just blew his head up, but most of that was her feeding him propaganda. You could tell, they'd go in the studio and Ronnie would be sitting in a corner some place or go off. He'd listen to the music and write all the stuff down but there was no interaction at all. He would come in but you wouldn't know he was there. He'd sit in another room and listen to the band but he wouldn't sing."

In a somewhat unexpected move, Blackmore employed Roger Glover to produce, as well as contribute songs for the album. Given that he had been fundamentally responsible for removing Glover from Deep Purple, one might see this as Blackmore's grudging way of atoning for past sins, at least that was the way Glover saw it. "Somehow this was his way of saying he was wrong and my value, although he hadn't seen it at the time. He'd seen it since in the work that I'd done, in the fact that I'd kept my nose clean, that I hadn't spouted off in the press about the bastard he was, and that I'd had some success. And he had a sort of respect for me that he hitherto hadn't. This is what I felt. Whether this is true I don't know but somehow this was a redemption."

Blackmore's reluctance to communicate with Dio also meant Glover was given the thankless role of go-between. "Roger became Ritchie's conduit," says Dio, "so he came to me and told me what he wanted and said could I stop writing in such a fantasy orientated way and maybe write some love songs. My reply was no, so that was it – goodbye."

Dio's departure now left Blackmore as the only original member. As Dio commented, "I saw him go through a succession of people who wanted more from him than he was prepared to give and those people were just about banished forever from his life."

Despite Rainbow having been well received by the faithful, maintaining a steady and successful level within the European and Japanese markets, the costs of keeping the band on the road were proving substantial. Although Rainbow's record sales were healthy, this couldn't sustain the band indefinitely against the overheads and with the enterprise having been largely financed by Blackmore, the cash flow difficulties were threatening to end the band unless it could open up to a wider audience. The previous year Blackmore had said, "I'm not going to go blue in the face trying to win America" but in true contradictory fashion, he also told another journalist, "We're not going to give up until America gives up and surrenders to us."

Powell suggested Don Airey to fill the vacant keyboard position and in December '78 Airey auditioned at Blackmore's Connecticut home. "It was just me and Ritchie. There was a clavinet there and he gave me some Bach to read, then he said, 'Do you know Beethoven's 'Ode To Joy'? and I said 'Yeah' so we wrote 'Difficult To Cure' on that day although it didn't get recorded for a couple of years. The next day we went into a rehearsal studio and I did see Ronnie in the car park but that was the last I saw of him. Ritchie had a few riffs and we just kept playing around them. Over three weeks we just worked up the album. Just me, Cozy, Ritchie and a bass player called Clive Chaman but he didn't last very long, so it was just Ritchie, me and Cozy for two weeks." Having returned to London to spend Christmas Blackmore showed up at Airey's house in Finchley, saying "Do you know somewhere to rehearse? I've got this bass player."

The new bassist was Jack Green, previously of the Pretty Things, and further rehearsals occurred a few days over the Christmas period at a place called the Tunnel. Blackmore also paid a visit to an old adversary. It was totally out of the blue, as Ian Gillan recalled in his autobiography. "It was quite late at night, I went to the door, and peered into the darkness. The snow was falling. There, standing about two or three paces back, stood the guitar player with his silly pilgrim's hat." After asking him what he wanted Blackmore told him that he was looking for a singer so Gillan invited him in. Blackmore then asked Gillan if it was okay to bring Amy Rothman inside. As she wasn't with him, Gillan asked where she was. Blackmore replied at the end of the drive. Gillan appeared puzzled as to why and Blackmore explained that he was worried the singer he had forced out of Deep Purple six years before might hit him!

They spent the evening chatting and drinking before Blackmore offered Gillan the vacant singer's position in Rainbow. Gillan declined but in turn offered Blackmore the vacant guitar position in his own band. While the meeting came to a stalemate, Blackmore agreed to jam with Gillan at the Marquee a few days later. Years later, when talking to Neil Jeffries, Blackmore said he had second thoughts as to the wisdom of his decision in making contact. "We started drinking a full bottle of vodka but before I got halfway through the bottle I was thinking to myself, 'I'm not sure this is a good idea.' He's going, 'Rich. I'm so glad. I'm so fucking happy you are here.' 'Cause he's like that; he's got two sides to him. But I'm thinking, 'Fucking hell! What am I doing?'"

The introduction of Glover to produce the album had been primarily to help give Rainbow a more commercial slant and undoubtedly Blackmore's interest in wanting Gillan as lead singer could also be seen as an attempt to pull in a larger audience. Had Gillan agreed, the trio of Blackmore, Gillan and Glover would have undoubtedly sparked rumours of a full-blown Deep Purple reunion. However with Jon Lord having teamed up with David Coverdale in Whitesnake it was unclear which line-up any possible Purple reformation would have incorporated. When Marc Brans of the Deep Purple Belgian fan club jointly interviewed Lord and Coverdale a couple of weeks prior to Blackmore jamming with Gillan, Lord revealed what had been going on behind the scenes. "It was begun to be planned a year or so ago by Martini Rosso … It was Martini, a Merchant Bank and someone else wanting to finance a big concert in Ibiza and they asked our old management who asked us individually. But I honestly think that you've got six or seven different people to take care of and everyone of these people have their own career to worry about and to be concerned about and I'm more concerned with Whitesnake being correct and successful and making good music than I am with putting back something together again that's in the past anyway."

With Coverdale's band making headway, friction between the two camps inevitably surfaced with Coverdale, albeit in a light-hearted manner, referring to 'Blackmore's Raincoat.' Both Rainbow and Whitesnake had been performing 'Mistreated' on stage and journalists invariably tried to stoke up controversy as to who actually had the most claim to the song. Although it was Blackmore's music and Coverdale's lyrics this didn't stop Blackmore stirring things up by commenting that Coverdale's involvement was minimal. In the Brans interview Coverdale retorted that "Blackmore's full of shit," while Lord commented, "That's very unfair of Ritchie because it's so much David's song."

Whatever the rewards of a Purple reunion might have been, all the talk amounted to nothing – for now.

Still without a singer Rainbow returned to Connecticut in the New Year but Jack Green failed to gel with either Powell or Airey. "We went back to Darien and rehearsed with Jack Green but it was pretty woeful," recalls Airey. "Then we went to the Chateau [Pelly De Cornfield in Southern

France] and I don't think Jack played a note of bass all the time we were there." With just three musicians and a producer, Blackmore tried to keep Green on board but the others were all opposed to him.* In a scene reminiscent of Deep Purple's tenure at Deeves Hall in '68, hordes of vocalists arrived at the Chateau to audition. Among the singers they tried was Pete Goalby of Trapeze but it was eventually decided he wasn't right for the band.

In keeping with Blackmore's love of old and supposedly haunted buildings the alternative Chateau was an ideal location. Raymond D'addario: "It was a great place but a really weird Chateau. My most vivid memory was that I never saw anything live on the ground like cats, dogs, birds, nothing. It was as though they avoided the place like the plague. The first night we were there I tried to use the telephone late at night and I heard this blood-curdling scream. What in the world was that? It sounded like a baby screaming or a cat and everyone heard it and the next day they were all talking about it and came to find out it was Ritchie. He used to have this tape recorder and he'd put these sounds on it and hide it and leave blank spaces on the tape so you could hear this awful noise and everyone would go and try and find it and of course 20 minutes later it would go off again. That's why the singer left. He was just scared shitless and took off. So we were sitting there with no singer and Bob Adcock would send singers from England and Colin and me would be going to Geneva Airport picking them up."

Blackmore and Powell were up to their usual pranks with new boy Airey being the target of many of them: "I was sleeping in the chapel and they convinced me my room was haunted. It was a spooky room, and I was starting to get freaked out and I went in there and I thought I heard a noise, I drew the curtains and there was a monk standing there. I just ran for my bloody life. I slept on the couch for a couple of days and then Ritchie said, 'I've a few ideas on tape I want to play you' and they were all these screams and shouts and sound effects and I went, 'You bastards!' I said, 'Who was the monk then?' 'Who do you think?' 'Cozy?' 'Right!' "

Unlike Tony Carey, Airey took the pranks in good spirit, recalling, "It was a very nice atmosphere, it was actually a nice little family unit with the road crew and we used to play party games and my wife came over. It was in the depths of winter but it was all right. [Ritchie] could be a bit odd at times.

---

* Despite the fact that Jack Green didn't work out, Blackmore later played on 'I Call, No Answer' a track on Green's RCA solo album *Humanesque*, recorded in April and May 1980.

He's difficult to deal with. He's so focused that he can't see the wood for the trees sometimes."

The first few weeks were relatively unproductive and more time was spent playing games than making music. Blackmore wanted to set up a snooker tournament but most of the band and crew were more interested in table tennis for which Amy Rothman was very much the ringleader. Blackmore refused to partake. Don Airey: "We used to work all day and he didn't play Ping-Pong and I think he felt left out because it got quite exciting!" The table tennis tournament became highly competitive with Rothman and Airey ending up as finalists. She emerged the winnner but most were willing the keyboard player on as Rothman caused a certain amount of resentment.

D'addario endorses the band and crew's feelings about her: "One of the first things that happened was that Amy decided she had some musical opinions and Don just went mental being a classically trained musician and all, and here's this woman … and he just went mental about that. She would be saying stuff she'd heard Ritchie say, but she didn't necessarily know what it meant. Someone in her family was a concert cellist so it wasn't as if she had come from a country and western thing. She wasn't a dummy, but she could be a bit pretentious and I think that's what struck Don more than anything, she was telling him what to play or what was wrong."

Such was the bizarre nature of events at the Chateau, Blackmore kept a diary, recalling in 1998. "I wrote a whole sketch on this, which I still have. It's very boring to anybody who wasn't there. But we were in this incredible castle – again! To make a change we were in a castle and we never got any work done. The first day, we found out that the singer we had recruited for the job couldn't sing above a top A. So that killed any song so we sent him away. We were auditioning other singers and it was costing $2,000 a day for the mobile studio that was already there. So we were in a castle spending a fortune and we didn't have a singer. Singers were flying into Geneva, coming to the castle – being driven to the castle by Colin who would go through customs every day, going in and out. And the people were going, 'What are you doing?' Eventually it was, 'Hello, Mr. Hart, go on through.' And he'd bring in another singer. We always came down for breakfast at one o'clock in the afternoon, and there'd always be a new guy sitting at the breakfast table.

"Once we had this Italian waiter who was a singer. He actually joined another band who became popular; I can't remember their name. He looked like a wrestler! He was the new singer that we were gonna try out that day. We'd always go through 'Mistreated' as it's a hard song to sing. Here we go

230

again. 'Ready Cozy?' The guy sings the first line in an extremely feeble voice. I just doubled up laughing! He was absolutely dreadful. But he looked like the Incredible Hulk. 'How can we tell this guy he's awful?' I did the manly thing, 'Oh, I've just got to go and do something. I'll be back.' Cozy's now playing on his own with Don. I always remember running away, seeing Cozy holding his stomach and trying to play. It was so funny. Everybody used to get so brought down if you mentioned recording. Everybody was into their own thing. 'We're going to record today.' 'Oh, but we don't have a singer. We'll do it tomorrow.' Any excuse to get around it …"

Blackmore's happy memories of the Chateau include an elaborate prank on Glover that backfired. "I had to share a bathroom with Roger. And he would always go into the bathroom and I'd hear him. This one night, 'Let's play a trick on him … wait until he goes to the bathroom.' And I had this big long pipe – about 15 feet – that I was going to wedge in between the door and the wall, so that he couldn't get into his own room. I heard him go into the bathroom. 'Right!' I ran out, picked up the pipe, ran down to his bedroom, burst open the door … I was going to wedge it against the door so he couldn't get in. And suddenly, I looked over to the bed and Roger's sitting on the bed. He's reading a book! And he looked up. I went, 'Oh! Right!' and I went back out of the room again with the pipe. And … the way Roger tells it is very funny. He said, "I was just sitting there, and all of a sudden I saw the end of a pipe come into the room! Christ! I know this place is haunted, but a pipe …' And then he saw me at the end of the pipe. Of course, I came in, then straight out again. "Oh! Wrong room!" What happened was he'd come out of the bathroom and I thought he was going in. I got it wrong. Of course, I tried to pretend … I was very cool. 'Oh, Roger … I'm just …'"

The band eventually discovered their new vocalist as a fortuitous result of one of Powell's quiz games. Don Airey: "It was just Cozy playing his 'Guess the single.' He had all these tapes and you'd hear a millisecond of it, then a bit more and one night we heard Marbles' 'Only One Woman.' So it was, 'What happened to that guy? Wonder where he is' and that's how we found Graham [Bonnet]." Glover was delegated to hunt Bonnet down as the singer explains, "I think at that time Roger Glover was working with a friend of mine Micky Moody who was in a band called Snafu. Roger called Micky up and through him he got to my manager. I had to go out and listen to Rainbow albums and learn my party piece which was 'Mistreated.' That was my audition song. So I went over there and did that thing and they offered me the job."

231

Airey recalls the relief when Bonnet started to sing, "He sung 'Mistreated' which he'd never heard before and he didn't know who Ritchie was and he got the gig in three syllables. 'I've been Mis …' Ritchie looked up and he had the gig. We'd found our singer."

Despite being offered the job Bonnet had reservations. "I wasn't sure about doing it to be honest with you. I thought, 'I'm not sure if I like this music' because I was into a completely different thing. Not that it wasn't great but it wasn't really what I had done. I felt a bit nervous about it. But anyway I basically got the job and it was probably one of the best moves I've ever made I think."

Blackmore recalled there being something not quite right about Bonnet's appointment. "We'd been told, 'This guy [who used to be] in Marbles … he's the best, he's fantastic!' We got hold of him, tracked him down … Roger's talking to the producer, 'Do you know Graham Bonnet? What's he like in the studio?' 'Brilliant!' 'As a guy?' 'Fantastic!' 'So what's the catch? Can he sing above a top C?' 'Oh yeah. He can sing an F sharp above a top C.' Roger could sense that there was something missing. The producer at the other end in London's going, 'He's a great … great singer …' Roger was waiting for the 'but' … except the guy didn't say it."

Once the backing tracks had been completed a problem arose when it was time for Bonnet to lay down his vocals as Blackmore explains, "We started recording and Graham's going, 'I can't sing.' I'm going, 'Why not?' 'I have to be in a studio.' We're going, 'But we're in a castle in the middle of France, it's fantastic! The ambience is unbelievable. You can't sing?' He's going, 'No. I've got to be in the studio.' This guy couldn't sing in a castle – he had to be in a dirty little studio somewhere before he could sing! Then that got out of control. 'I'm not feeling too well today.' We're going, 'We'll do it tomorrow.' Then the next day came then the next and the next, and it went on and on and on … We used to ask Graham how he was, 'Hey, Graham, how are you doing?' 'Oh, I feel a bit strange.' 'Do you?' 'Yeah, I feel really weird today.' 'Oh. Why's that?' 'I don't know, I just feel weird.' Colin would go, 'Have you eaten?' And he'd go, 'That's it! I'm hungry!' He actually said that in Denmark. And then he gets in the restaurant and apparently he sits there and … he's a vegetarian but apparently he doesn't like vegetables! [Colin] goes 'What do you want?' 'I want a beer.' They give him a beer. 'Well … I want an omelette.' And if they take more than two minutes to bring the omelette, he goes, 'I'm not hungry any more … don't want it.' So he has more beers, and that's the end of his meal. That was Graham! So he fitted in really well with everybody and everything else."

Bonnet explains his dissatisfaction at not working in a proper studio. "I hate being stuck in the middle of nowhere with nothing to do when, if it's not a good day, in a real studio you can at least go out into the street and you see other people instead of just the people you are working with. But there were the guys and their wives and that was it. Where do you escape to just relax? There was nowhere, just a little village. I remember Roger Glover put me in this Chateau in the dining room or whatever it was and we tried to do vocals in this room ... I don't know it just didn't work. It wasn't right and we didn't know what we were doing. We had no songs as such, just grasping at straws and it really needed to be done in the office so to speak instead of the middle of the countryside. I can't explain it, I just love to be in a proper work area and this just didn't feel right to me. But as soon as we went into a studio then it started to happen."

With a small fortune having already been spent on recording, Bonnet and Glover flew back to the States to record vocals at Kingdom Sound Studios in Syosset, Long Island and finally *Down To Earth* was completed. Although a hard record to make, the album reaped greater rewards than previous Rainbow albums when released in August 1979, displaying the more commercial edge that Blackmore had striven for and which Glover had largely helped shape. Russ Ballard's 'Since You Been Gone' was extracted as the first single, peaking at number 5 in the UK charts, vindicating Blackmore's decision to take the band in a more commercial direction, though the new sound disappointed some established fans and certain band members.

Cozy Powell was uncomfortable with 'Since You Been Gone' in particular. "I remember well the first time I heard it, Bruce Payne played it to me at the office in New York and he said, 'What do you think about this track?' I said, 'Great! It sounds really good.' It was done by a girl band ... Clout and then he said, 'Well, we're thinking of doing it for Rainbow.' I said, 'You must be kidding ... no way is this a Rainbow track, it's a pop song!' Anyway, it went backwards and forwards, and Roger liked it and he wanted to do it. Maybe perhaps Ritchie wasn't even sure that he liked it or whether he didn't, but he agreed to do it, and I just said, 'This is ridiculous. ... we should never be doing these kind of songs. We are Rainbow, we are leaders in our field of music.' In the end I said, 'I'll play it, but I'll play it once and that's all.'

"So I did play it and yes, it did come out, but I mean it wasn't that I didn't like the song – I didn't like it for Rainbow. I thought we were going too far over. I thought the fans would say, 'What's this?' It's obviously a very commercial song and as it happened it turned out to be a big hit. It's a great song, no doubt about it. It's just ... you can see why after having done stuff like 'Stargazer' and 'Gates Of Babylon,' suddenly you do 'Since You Been Gone.' It's like ... are you sure? Obviously Roger's influence was much more commercial. And at that time that was one of the reasons why I decided that if Ritchie was going to go along that road, it's probably better if I move off and go and do something else … so that was basically it."

Although Airey contributed much to the songwriting on *Down To Earth* his name was conspicuous by its absence in the credits. "There was a huge input from me and it's still a bone of contention that I didn't get credited. I brought it up at the time but I think the band was in such a precarious state, maybe [Ritchie] had his publishing collateralised, I don't know, but he said, 'We'll see you right on the next album, which they did to an extent.'

Rainbow still hadn't sufficiently cracked America and another US tour supporting Blue Oyster Cult kicked off in September 1979. It wasn't the happiest of tours according to Don Airey. "It just seemed hard going, Ritchie was having some problems with things, I don't know what they were. I think he was having problems financially and became very withdrawn but the band was terrific. It was so full on and of course it was all going on in England, we had a hit there yet we were in America."

The tour saw a shortened hour-long set based around the new album including 'Eyes Of The World', 'All Night Long', 'Love's No Friend', and 'Lost In Hollywood.' Truncated versions of previous stage favourites 'Man On The Silver Mountain,' 'Long Live Rock 'n' Roll', 'Catch The Rainbow' and an instrumental revisiting of 'Kill The King' were also performed. With the Dio era now over a fresh approach was adopted from all angles. Even the electronic Rainbow was put into retirement. Raymond D'addario: "To this day I think the reason we stopped using it was because Ritchie got intimidated by it. People would just sit there and watch this thing forever. It was like they would look at that and not look at the band."

The tour included an infamous show at Richfield Coliseum in Cleveland, Ohio, a gig that has previously been documented as being abandoned due to crowd trouble. Airey paints a truer picture of what went on that evening: "It was abandoned because of band trouble. Ritchie and me had a fight on stage so the set got abandoned. He went off and the rest of the band eventually followed. It wasn't very good but it sorted a lot of problems actually. We shook hands the next day and I never thought anymore about it, neither did he. It got mentioned in the papers that I threw quite a good right hook!"

The lead-up to it was a disagreement between Airey and Blackmore which the keyboard player holds himself responsible for, but to this day is still too ashamed to discuss. Raymond D'addario: "That night and for whatever reason I can't remember but Ritchie was behind his amps playing and

234

Don came over and yelled at him, told him he was unprofessional or something and when Cozy was playing his drum solo Ritchie went over and kicked Don in the rear end and told him, 'Don't talk to me that way again'."

On tour in Europe the band booked time at Copenhagen's Sweet Silence Studios to record a B-side for 'All Night Long', the follow up to 'Since You Been Gone.' The result was one of Blackmore's finest recorded moments, 'Weiss Heim' a glorious instrumental that took the name of his then current home for its title.* It was knocked out in a couple of hours as Don Airey recalls, "It was just a tune Ritchie had and we developed it very quickly and the bit at the end, where I played the Bach Prelude was just spontaneous, I just went into it but it's an extraordinary piece." 'Weiss Heim' was a perfect example of Blackmore working at his best when things are fresh and spontaneous. As Glover said, "I like to see Ritchie just open up and let loose. Sometimes when he's tuning up he plays the most brilliant things, then when he actually comes to solo they're not there."

Don Airey: "That's the way he likes to work. I think he was frustrated a lot of the time. I think he expected to come out of Purple and just get more players and it would just be like Purple. But getting good players is very difficult. I was always prepared to get right behind him and that was tricky for him because he didn't have to tell me anything. So he resented me in a way for that. He thought I was laughing at him sometimes, which I never was. He has difficulty with people because of this raw, nerve of talent, he's so creative and life's not easy for him. I don't think he's ever comfortable with anything because he's always looking for something new. It's his talent and the other side of it, what it does to his personality."

Airey's comments eloquently sum up the situation Blackmore faced in Rainbow. The constant turn around of musicians was a standing joke in the industry and the role of keyboard player was certainly the most precarious. On no less than five occasions Blackmore had asked Jon Lord to join Rainbow as Lord himself revealed to Swedish journalist Mike Eriksson in May 1981: "I really don't want to be a background musician and I wouldn't even be sure that I had a job because he fires people more often than he changes his underwear. You would never know who would be in the band; who you would socialise with. Because it wouldn't be with Ritchie, you never see him. It could be Freddie Mercury."

---

* Blackmore's short-lived stay in Connecticut ended with a move to Long Island in early '79. As consolation for not moving to Germany he called his new house 'Weiss Heim' (White Home).

By this time Blackmore had also developed a fondness for the music of Swedish pop sensation Abba. Stuart Smith: "He was a massive Abba fan he played it all the time, to the point where I'd take the cassette out and hide it – I was fed up of hearing it." Blackmore casually mentioned his desire to work with vocalist Agnetha Fältskog but as far as Smith was concerned it really was nothing more than that. "I remember hearing that in the press. I don't know if it ever happened. I think it might have been something he probably said and it got out but I really don't think it was anything he pursued in any way really. I think it was just an off-the-cuff remark."

However those within the Rainbow organisation definitely saw it as more than an off-the-cuff remark. Don Airey: "[Agnetha] came down to a soundcheck in Stockholm. Cozy and me were playing something and she walked in and there was consternation, she was so beautiful. I think they had a meeting the next day; it was going to be Rainbow with Agnetha, we were going to do an album with her. I remember it well because there was a Russian ice skating troupe and it was their day off so we took over the ice rink but all the Russians came down to watch and they were standing around with Russian hats on so I started playing 'Kalinka' and they all started dancing and that's when Agnetha Fältskog walked in and everything stopped."

In 1988, backstage before a gig in Cologne, Blackmore confirmed to the author that the respective artists' management companies were in contact but nothing further materialised. Either Fältskog's management didn't take it seriously or the thought of teaming up with one of the world's greatest exponents of hard rock guitar wasn't to her liking. Sadly as a result, what could have been an unusual and fascinating collaboration never materialised.

The last date of the European tour was in Munich where promoter Erik Thomsen struck on the idea of having 10,000 Ping-Pong balls suspended above the audience in a net to be released at the end of the main set. When returning for the encore as Airey recalls, "There were Ping-Pong balls bouncing on the stage everywhere, a highly surreal moment."

By this time a renaissance in traditional hard rock was emerging with a glut of new bands referred to under the banner of 'the New Wave of British Heavy Metal'. The movement was not only beneficial to Rainbow, who now had two Top 10 hits to their credit but Gillan and Whitesnake were also rapidly rising in popularity with a degree of competition developing between the bands. As Whitesnake guitarist Bernie Marsden commented, "If they can get to number six, we'll try and get to five; sell out the Hammersmith Odeon quicker than they can. There was a lot of that going down and I think David loved it because he knew it would get up Ritchie's nose." Having spouted off in a derogatory manor about Blackmore and Rainbow in the press Coverdale had the gall to attend the Munich show. Backstage he continued with his tirade, commenting how terrible he thought the gig was and that the audience had pelted the band with Ping-Pong balls which needless to say did not go down well.

Don Airey: "Ritchie read a bunch of stuff that Coverdale had said about him and for whatever reason David needed to say it, which Ritchie couldn't understand because he'd got the guy into Purple to begin with. Nobody else [in Deep Purple] wanted to deal with him but it was only Ritchie who said we can get rid of his glasses and he sings great. And he was really offended that the guy was going around slagging him off. I don't think he'd ever had a beef with David in Purple. Glenn was really the one that made him itch. So he hears this thing that he's coming to the gig and he said, 'I don't want him in the show.' And I think it was Ozzie Hoppe, I don't know if Ozzie was managing [Ritchie] at the time, who said, 'You can't keep him out, he can buy a ticket just like anyone else' so Ritchie goes 'Fine let him buy a ticket but I don't want to see him backstage.' So [David] comes backstage, Eric goes, 'What's he doing here?' Somebody said, 'He's here to see Cozy,' so Ritchie goes into Cozy's dressing room and says, 'Is Coverdale here to see you?' and Cozy said, 'No it's nothing to do with me man.' So Ritchie went outside, swung Coverdale around and punched him and that started it."

Raymond D'addario: "I'm on stage with Colin and the lighting guy Tony and by the time we got there they're in a brawl so we got to break it up and the best part was watching Coverdale thump Erik Thomsen. Eric got his head in the way! And Coverdale is pummelling him. Coverdale's girlfriend at the time is jumping on Ritchie and I'm trying to pull her off and him off Coverdale."

Blackmore gave his own account to Neil Jeffries in 1995: "I had a lot of faith in David Coverdale when he first came to the band. Paicey discovered him; he played me his tape and I said, 'This guy is great, who is he?' 'It's David Coverdale.' 'OK, let's get him down.' Coverdale was the guy that I always went towards in the band, more so than Glenn. I always found Glenn a really nice guy, but I didn't like his vocals. I was always very pro-David Coverdale until I left and got my own thing together and for some reason he took it so personally. It's almost like I'd slept with his mother or something. He got this really nasty shit with me, for years! 'Oh, Ritchie slag slag slag.' Everything was about slagging me off. I thought, 'What did I do? Just because I left the band, went off with Ronnie, did the Rainbow thing? He

237

has Deep Purple; what was the problem with him?' I could never understand what his problem was.

"I'd had it with him knocking me; I'd had about four years of this fucking shit in the press. He'd be asked, 'David, what's your new LP like?' and he'd say, 'It's better than Rainbow's.' It was always like that! Out of the blue, for no reason. So I used to read this stuff and wonder 'What's wrong with this guy? Why's he always picking on me?' So I started getting antsy towards him. Then this girl who was running the show said, 'Oh, David might come tonight.' 'David who?' 'David Coverdale.' So I was like, 'Just keep him away from me. If David Coverdale wants to come and see the show I want him to pay and be in the audience, I don't want him back here.' So I told that to the girl and she said, 'Of course.' I said, 'Don't you even think about bringing him backstage, because I'll lose it if I see him' – after all this bullshit that he'd been saying about me. Sure enough, what happens? I come offstage and go into the dressing room. It was a really good show. I'm there, coming down, and Cozy comes in, 'Hey! Seen who's out there?' 'Out where?' Cozy was brilliant at stirring. 'Coverdale! He's in the corridor!' 'Coverdale is in the corridor? Why?' 'He's backstage, drinking our Scotch, and he's putting the show down.' 'He's putting the show down?' 'He just said what kind of pantomime was that? Quote.' Cozy knew that was enough to get me going. So I'm going, 'Where is he?'

"Sure enough, he was in the corridor, up against the wall talking to some girl, doing his grand pose [affects upper crust accent]: 'Of course, I usually drink only the very best brandy.' So pompous! I went up to him and said, 'What the fuck are you doing here? Roadies! Get this guy out. I don't want him here sipping our drinks saying, 'What kind of shit was that?' With that, I grabbed him by the collar – he's quite tall – and went 'Out!' He lunged at me, missed, and we fell to the floor, wrestling – at the feet of the guys in Queen. The drummer Roger Taylor and the bass player were there, drinking away, but looking straight ahead while we're grovelling away on the floor. … 'You fucking so and so' 'Fuck you.' I look up to see Roger Taylor just casually talking to his girlfriend, very nonchalantly. So my plan was – if I'd wanted to whack [Coverdale], I would've whacked him – but I wanted him thrown out. Then he started throwing punches at me and I thought, 'OK we're into fighting.' So they pulled us apart and the promoter Erik Thomsen is going, 'Calm down! Calm down! Are you okay?' But as soon as they let us go I went, wham! Hit him straight in the fucking head! With that, Coverdale ran back to get his own back – but punched Eric in the face. So I didn't get anything, and that was that. But the whole point was that could have all been stopped had this girl listened to me."

The Rainbow show moved on to Britain where most of the concerts quickly sold out with public interest high thanks to the hit singles. With the tour opening in Newcastle Blackmore's preoccupation with Rainbow's personal grooming was causing concern regarding the short-haired Bonnet. "I said 'Graham – your hair's too short. The people that follow us like long hair.' 'I used to have long hair.' 'Okay, but you don't have long hair any more – it's very short and you look like a cabaret singer. Can you please grow your hair?' 'I cut it off.' By the time we were in Newcastle we actually had Colin Hart on his door to make sure he didn't go out to get his hair cut. It was actually getting down to the back of his collar, and it was just beginning to be acceptable. Otherwise we'd have been crucified because we'd gone out on stage with our new singer who had short hair. They're gonna hate that! You know what he did? He jumped out of the window, ran off and had a haircut! So it came to show time, we went on stage and I'm looking at the back of his head – like a military-style haircut – and Colin was saying, 'Can you believe it? He got out of the back window to have his hair cut!' I was so close to taking my guitar off and going 'whack' across the back of his head. I was so angry! I'm so glad I didn't. But I was being pushed there … I was really being pushed."

Blackmore's description of events is a perfect example of his abilty to embellish stories. Bonnet recalls he certainly didn't have a guard at his door nor did he sneak out of a window. "I remember that day; my hair to me was like a bloody mess; it was all over the place. If you've got short hair you have short hair. Now people shave their heads and that's kind of cool now, but back then to have short hair wasn't the thing, it wasn't the uniform of a so-called rock singer, but yeah before a gig I went and got my hair cut, didn't say anything to anyone and I came on stage that night. I remember the look of shock on [Ritchie's] face, jaw dropping to the floor."

More drama occurred at the Wembley Arena gig on February 29. After completing the main set, Blackmore refused to come back on. Some stories claim it was due to the poor audience reaction to Powell's drum solo but the disgruntled audience rioted in protest at the short appearance; throwing chairs at the equipment on stage and generally dismantling other parts of the auditorium causing thousands of pounds worth of damage. Rumours that Ian Gillan was there, ready to appear during the encore appear to be unfounded as neither Airey or Polydor marketing executive George McManus recall his presence backstage. All Airey remembers were accountants saying, "In a year's time this will be seen as a masterstroke."

George McManus: "I remember Wembley, they were *the* band at the time and the whole band wanted to do an encore and guess what, Ritchie wouldn't. He just said, 'Fuck it I've done my bit I'm not doing anymore.' The rest of the band was prepared to but he just threw a wobbler and the rest of the band said, 'Fucking cunt, we had the whole of the audience on their feet screaming for more.' Don Airey was certainly disappointed by Blackmore's behaviour. "It's not as if you've got another appointment. You're there, you're not going anywhere else, why not go back on stage?"

Raymond D'addario: "Ritchie came back to Cozy at the end of the set and Cozy said something to him like 'I'm pooped' or something. I think Cozy was back there breathing hard and Cozy never really said he didn't want to do an encore just that he was winded or something and Ritchie went, 'Oh fine we won't do an encore then' and just walked away."Whether or not Blackmore felt any guilt is unclear but the following night a much lengthier show was performed complete with a dramatic guitar sacrifice.

In a strange twist, just a few days after Gillan's rumoured presence at Wembley, Blackmore turned up at a Gillan gig at the Rainbow Theatre. By now the singer's band included Blackmore's former Dominators and Outlaws bandmate Mick Underwood: "When he turned up there. I wondered what he wanted because I know what he's like. What are you doing here?" Underwood hadn't seen Blackmore for several years and rightly surmised that he was there for a reason, which the guitarist openly admitted a few months later: "I'm very interested in getting together with Ian Gillan because I think he's got a lot to offer. He's always been an honest bloke who's stuck to his guns."

Part of Blackmore's desire to recruit Gillan was an awareness that some fans weren't taking to the shorthaired Bonnet and the new-look Rainbow's UK performances had met with mixed reactions from both fans and journalists alike.

Just prior to commencing Rainbow's first tour of Japan since the 1978 Sapporo tragedy, Blackmore gave an interview to Nina Myskow in *The Sun*, Britain's biggest selling national newspaper, which included some frank admissions about his personal life of the very type the paper thrives on. Talking about his relationship with Amy Rothman, he remarked, "Anyone who can stick with me for more than six months, I admire. Amy copes very well with me. She's very straight, very understanding." Despite having been with Rothman for two years by that point, Blackmore was quoted: "I love women, I love seducing them. I couldn't begin to count the number of girls I've slept with. 1 own up to taking every advantage. Using girls then dumping them. I've paid for it though with all the diseases I've picked up along with them."

Despite the uncertainties over Bonnet, Rainbow's six-date Japanese tour saw Blackmore's most loyal fans take to the new line-up unreservedly. A typical Japanese set-list included 'Eyes Of The World,' 'Love's No Friend,' 'Since You Been Gone,' 'Man On The Silver Mountain,' 'Catch The Rainbow,' 'Lost In Hollywood-Ode To Joy,' 'All Night Long,' 'Will You Love Me Tomorrow,' and a medley of 'Long Live Rock 'n' Roll' and 'Kill The King.' Carole King's 'Will You Love Me Tomorrow,' (a 1960 hit for the Shirelles) was an old track from Bonnet's past that was introduced into the set at Blackmore's suggestion. Several of the Japanese dates were officially recorded with the intention of a future live release, along with a live version of 'Will You Love Me Tomorrow' recorded one night after a gig and which, according to Rainbow biographer Roy Davies, was seriously mooted as a possible single.

Meanwhile back in Britain, Paul Loasby, who had supervised the promotion of the last UK tour and was then in the throes of setting up his own company approached Rainbow's management with a proposal for them to headline an inaugural day-long summer festival, dedicated specifically to the New Wave of British Heavy Metal bands. Blackmore and Payne readily agreed as Ritchie recalled, "My manager rang me up and told me that there had been talk of a big, outdoor festival in Britain and would I be interested in doing it. Obviously we then went into more detail but I stressed that I wouldn't do it unless the conditions were right for the kids. So many of these outdoor events are okay on paper but they're never practically viable. Eventually we worked out the whole idea for the show and that we'd get in a special sound and light system that would be big enough for the amount of people expected to turn up."

Although early preparations were delayed after objections from police and local residents over fears of congestion, noise and potential lawlessness, the event was confirmed by the local authorities for Saturday, August 16, 1980 at Donington Park, Leicestershire. It would seem that Powell had some influence on the venue chosen, being one of Britain's major motor circuits as Airey claims, "Cozy wanted to do it at a racing circuit so we picked Donington." It was to be the first time the racetrack had been used to stage a rock concert, and seemed an ideal venue, as it was used to both dealing with large crowds and had the necessary amenities. Its proximity to the M1 motorway provided easy access.

Loasby came up with the idea of billing it as 'The Monsters Of Rock' Festival, assembling a balanced mix of British and international hard rock including Judas Priest, Saxon, US acts Touch, and Riot, Canada's April Wine, and Germany's the Scorpions.

With plans to record the concert and an audience of 50,000 anticipated,

241

Blackmore naturally wanted to ensure Rainbow was well prepared for the event. For three warm-up shows in Scandinavia between August 8–10 several changes were made to the set. 'Stargazer' was re-introduced but in a much shorter version than had been performed on the Rising tour in 1976. The open-air gig in Malmö on the 9th was interrupted by heavy rain and during Airey's keyboard solo Blackmore decided not to go back on stage so instead the band departed for the hotel.

After five years in Rainbow Powell's disaffection with the band's direction finally come to a head and Donington was announced as his swansong. Having played an important part in Rainbow's success, for many fans Powell's departure signified a major turning point. A few hours before going on stage, Richard Skinner interviewed Powell for BBC Radio 1's Saturday afternoon rock show: "The band has been very successful for the last five years and Ritchie and I have had our differences in the past as you probably know. I wouldn't say we've had a lot of differences about the last year but I wasn't particularly happy with the last album. I thought it was a bit too commercial. But that's all been aired in the press so I won't go on about it now but they're just about to start recording another new album but I want to do something different.

"I've been with the band for five years. I've figured it's time … if I'm going to leave I might as well leave at a gig like this. I'm sure Ritchie's sick and tired of me moaning and groaning at him so I'll give him the chance to get somebody else in so he can moan and groan at somebody else. Half way through the last American tour we had a little bit of a contretemps, and I said enough is enough. I knocked it on the head then and I told him then I'll be leaving after the European and Japanese dates but I don't think they took me seriously. So it was only a couple of weeks ago that they realised I was serious. So here we are today, the last gig: Donington racecourse – couldn't be better."

Efforts were made to install a state-of-the-art quadraphonic sound system which had performed impressively during rehearsals the week before the festival. However, at the same time as a Judas Priest soundcheck just days before the event, a test of Powell's pyrotechnics for the local council safety officers resulted in an explosion heard some three miles away that blew out all the P.A and caused £18,000 worth of damage to Priest's set-up. As understated as ever, Powell played the incident down: "They – Priest – were not too pleased – there was a lot of swearing going on!" Some last minute telephone calls and another PA was rushed to the site in the nick of time.

Don Airey: "We arrived on the Thursday and this deluge had opened and there was so much mud it was incredible. Then Cozy was trying out his explosives and he blew the PA out of the park really. So that was a bit of a disaster so anyway, come the day there was still mud but it didn't rain."

The day itself dawned hot, bright and sunny and a crowd of over 35,000 was officially reported, though this may have been to satisfy fire regulations as unofficial estimates put the gathering at more than 50,000. Blackmore had hinted to the press that some surprises were in store. However plans to fly him on a high wire over the heads of the audience during the show were abandoned when the hoist machine failed.[*]

In response to Powell's imminent departure, Blackmore had wasted no time in finding a replacement in Bobby Rondinelli who flew in from New York to catch the show. As Rondinelli explains, some were of the opinion that his presence was not a good idea. "It was kind of silly because they didn't want me to run into Cozy. He was leaving anyway and I knew he knew I was there. It was like wherever he goes, 'Oh go the other way.' I really felt like a dummy. I just wanted to go up and say, 'Hi how are you doing?' you know. We became friends later, but I was at that gig because they wanted me to see the band live, which I'd already done in the States anyway."

Rainbow biographer Roy Davies wrote: "After a lengthy 90 minute wait the exquisite expectation built by the slowly burning intro of 'Eyes Of The World' never failed to raise the hairs on the neck; about as impressive an opener for a festival headliner as you could get. It was immediately clear the mix was now all over the place, though by the time of the slow blues that is 'Love's No Friend' it was slowly improving. The song had on the prior tour inspired Blackmore to his most emotive work, and the night itself was no exception, recalling memories of his solo flights on 'Mistreated' during the Dio era. A nice touch was Ritchie's subtle mimicking on guitar of Bonnet's vocal line."

Even though the 100 minute performance wasn't Rainbow's best, as a spectacle it was special. For all the trouble taken with the much vaunted P.A. system it only seemed to work well for the few thousand crammed down the front, anything above the slightest breeze carrying off the sound for the remainder of the crowd. But minor criticisms apart, the day was deemed an overwhelming success. Don Airey: "It was an amazing thing. There were

---

[*] Fans arriving at the adjacent campsite early enough to catch Rainbow's lengthy sound-check/dress rehearsal heard a live work-out of 'Weiss Heim' that regrettably never made the set.

some very memorable performances by different bands. April Wine were outstanding. Scorpions were good. Judas Priest were thrilling, and I think Rainbow that day were just extraordinary."

Although losing money on the event Loasby seemed happy with the outcome: "It was a great day, the show Rainbow put on is still one of the best headlining performances at Donny ... the first of its kind and a terrible risk." It also gave Loasby the impetus to organise another festival the following year and within a few years Donington became the annual event for the UK hard rock fraternity, superseding the rival Reading festival.

With the show being recorded and filmed there was the potential of additional capital to be gained and an album from the event, masterminded by Payne was released, but as it compiled tracks from all the acts, only two of Rainbow's songs were included. The film, undertaken by one of Thames Talent's companies, Green Back Films, has to this day never been released, but a half hour of highlights was edited together and broadcast on BBC TV shortly after the event. Although continuity was forsaken – the set was edited to start with the familiar tones of 'All Night Long' – the broadcast featuring Blackmore's explosive guitar and amp demolition helped raise interest in Rainbow in a similar way that *Concerto For Group And Orchestra* had helped Deep Purple's public profile 11 years earlier.

As Blackmore acknowledged a lot changed for Rainbow shortly after the Monsters of Rock Festival, "I enjoyed that. In fact it was up until that point that I was happy. Then suddenly I realised that something was wrong but I couldn't figure out what it was. For a while I thought that it was me. Things weren't gelling and I must admit I had grave doubts about Donington with so many people coming. There seemed to be no sense of direction. Fortunately Donington turned out to be a lot better than some of the other gigs we'd played at the time – maybe I was just a lot more drunk than usual. Afterwards I came to the conclusion that there was no rapport between Graham and myself and that Rainbow was simply five professionals out there going down well and being accepted for that reason."

For Bonnet Donington was undoubtedly the highlight of his time with Rainbow and a fitting finale, for shortly after, he too departed the band: "Something I will never forget. I've said this over and over again, it was the first time I think about it that my whole family was in the audience for one thing, but it was the most magical day. It was horrible because Cozy was leaving. I remember after the gig we sat up until ... I don't know we didn't go to bed that night. We stayed in a hotel in Leicester and said goodbye to Cozy and everybody cried and it was like the best day ever. It's something

I'm really proud of, what a band. What a fucking band! I think that was the best line up with Cozy playing drums and everything."

The final word on the festival comes from a music press interview Blackmore gave shortly after the event. "I was really surprised and pleasantly surprised by Donington, I thought the whole show went really well, because the whole thing could have really collapsed, it was such a big production. I was quite surprised by the press reaction. But then I thought about it and decided we were due for a slagging. I read a few letters from fans and judging by the things they were saying it didn't seem like the reviewers were at the same gig, but obviously they had it in for us before they even went. I liked it and although I'm always interested in what the critics have to say, it's my opinion that counts in the end to me, and I thought it was really good."

Blackmore, who was often seen in 1980 wearing a badge that declared "Everyone's entitled to my opinion," might have dismissed the press' take on events, but after reading out *Melody Maker*'s panning of the gig to Bruce Payne, Rainbow's UK publicist Jennie Halsall was sacked on the spot.

Reflecting back on his five years with Rainbow Cozy Powell told the author in 1997: "I thought the *Down To Earth* album was good in some [places]. I have mixed feelings about that. Some of the tracks I thought were great. I went on record as saying that I thought the last great guitar solo that Ritchie played in my era was 'Gates Of Babylon', and after that he hadn't really kind of ... it was almost like he got bored with it. Perhaps he had. Perhaps he needed to go in a different direction. Ritchie's the kind of guy that one night he'll play absolutely brilliantly and the other night he won't be bothered, and if he's not in the mood he won't play particularly that great, and he won't go on and do an encore. That's Ritchie, and that's why Ritchie's Ritchie."

CHAPTER 12

The End Of The Rainbow
(1980–84)

Despite Rainbow's transformation from underground band to radio friendly outfit with videos played on *Top Of The Pops*, and mentions in such unlikely magazines as *Smash Hits*, criticism was never far from the surface although sell-out accusations didn't concern Blackmore one iota. "I just thought we needed a little bit of rejuvenation, a bit of a push on the commercial end, 'cause we were getting a little bit too heavy and underground. Hendrix once said that everybody likes to hear their music being played on a jukebox when they walk into a place. 'Since You Been Gone' gave us a push into the commercial area, but we quickly followed it up with 'All Night Long', which was to say, 'Well we know we can do it with our own songs as well.' As long as you don't go overboard and appear on the [British DJ] Tony Blackburn show every week there's nothing wrong with doing it. It's not a compromise, you just have to appreciate that some people aren't as musically aware as others and you can't go round educating everybody all the time."

Some critics in particular were irate at Glover's overtly sexist lyrics to 'All Night Long'. When Blackmore did a *Sounds* interview a month after Donington he appeared on the publication's front cover, dressed in stockings and suspenders. For those who had criticised Rainbow's sexism Blackmore explained that dressing up was his way of saying that he "can just as easily be one of the girls." While the headline "Blackmore In New 'Black Stockings' Sexism Outrage" and photos might have been a publicity stunt

246

the article focused on the new album Rainbow were recording at Sweet Silence studios in Copenhagen.

Having recorded 'Weiss Heim' there earlier in the year, the guitar sound on that recording impressed Blackmore enough to warrant a return. "This one's going to be much heavier, it's more of a party LP. We've kept all the tempos up and so far we haven't got one slow song on it because I believe people want to be in an up mood. There's too much going on politically, the environment is so down, I don't think people need to be reminded of any-thing like that. I'm also beginning to lose my classical influences, although I have and always will have that influence within me, I'm not as obsessed with it like I was a couple of years back. For about four years I wouldn't listen to anything except classical, nowadays I find myself turning it off and listening to heavy rock which I find refreshing.

"With classical music, it's got to the stage where I'm not trying to push it on people anymore. I think the older you get, the more you become inter-ested in it because it's a delicate type of music and you have to mature as a person to appreciate it. But I'm kind of un–maturing these days. I'm going through a phase where I'm listening to a lot more rock and roll and I'm pleased because I was beginning to wonder if I was losing my interest in it. At one point all I would play was heavy baroque music, weirdo music, a lot of church music … maybe I was seeking refuge from something … I don't know. At the moment I'm turned on by playing heavy rock and that's why this album is going to be more up."

Blackmore's growing dissatisfaction with Bonnet was mirrored by the singer's lack of interest in the new material. Graham Bonnet: "The rehearsals were very unproductive for the next album and nothing was happening in rehearsals. Everybody was bored with each other, Cozy had left the band, Bobby Rondinelli came in playing drums and rehearsals were basically, 'Well I don't think I want to be here, shall we go to the pub or something?' Not quite like that, but basically that. There was one song that was written for us by Russ Ballard, 'I Surrender', and that was the only song there was, a whole song as such. Ritchie would come to rehearsals and play his bass pedals, stand there and do his thing and look around and say, 'Have you got any ideas?' Don and I played something to him one day. He said, 'No I don't like that.' 'Oh all right then. OK, so what shall we do, is the pub open?' It was very unproductive. It was an unhappy time too, because Cozy wasn't there, we were all kind of friends and it seemed to break up the family a little bit. I started to record 'I Surrender' and put down some backing vocals and I thought, 'I'm not enjoying this anymore, this is not fun' and I went back to Los Angeles and they called me up and said, 'Why have you gone back home?' I said, 'I don't want to do it anymore.'

"That's when they said, 'How about if you sing the songs that you like on this album, the tracks you like to sing, we'll get another guy to sing the other ones whatever they may be' and I said, 'Well that's not really going to work, you don't have two singers in a band. It's like having two guitar players. Can you imagine what that would be like? I don't think that will work, I don't want to do that.' Because I had in my mind that maybe I could do something by myself at this point. So that was it. I left. I wasn't fired, I left."

"I don't like everything to be hunky dory, rock and roll is not supposed to be nice," said Blackmore. "I don't think a band is a band unless you have aggravation. I get satisfaction out of Rainbow because I keep it moving and people come and they go, to me new blood gives me energy. I only change members so that people can say. 'Oh that's it Blackmore has really fucked himself this time,' and I need people to say that, because it gives me the edge that I need. I'm not a callous person but I feel if someone has to be taken away, then it has to be done. I'm not going to sustain a band so they become like Deep Purple. I got out of Purple because I felt we were getting stale and I found with certain personnel of Rainbow that we got stale again. I like to be rejuvenated; it's almost a vampire like thing. I feed on the blood of musicians passing through and when the blood's dried up I get rid of them! I'm not looking for the perfect band; I'm looking for a band I really get off playing with … and it's difficult. Not because I'm a perfectionist but I am damn fussy, I suppose."

On the plus side, for the musicians who came and went, having been a member of Rainbow raised their profile. In the case of Bonnet a solo deal was signed on the strength of his recent involvement. His first album featured assistance from Cozy Powell and Jon Lord, who offered his opinions of Blackmore's hire and fire approach. "I will never understand why he had to change it. Cozy Powell was a great drummer and Graham Bonnet is an amazing singer. I considered that band to be a very good one. He should have kept it. I just did some work for Graham's solo album and he told me that the problem with Ritchie was that he kept telling him how to sing all the time. He changes the band, but not the music. But I don't want you to think that I have anything against Ritchie, that's not true … I find him very hard to work with but I like him. I also have great respect for his talent, but it hasn't moved in the last five years. He plays pretty much what he played back in 1975 but in my opinion not as good. And I think I know why. He doesn't have to fight anymore. The moment he encounters another opinion, he changes the band. So the energy might get lost in that situation. He just avoids conflict now, like the one he had with me in Deep Purple. I wasn't about to let him have all the spotlight and that resulted in all the duels that we had, which became a trademark for Deep Purple. He doesn't have that now in Rainbow. The only guy that used to be like that in Rainbow was Cozy Powell."

After Bonnet departed the fifth Rainbow album was worked on with the four remaining musicians. Bobby Rondinelli: "We finished all the music in about five weeks or so and I think *Difficult To Cure* is a pretty good record and we did it without a singer." When it came to Blackmore putting the guitar solos down, there was a simple method employed as Rondinelli explains: "He was very quick and he would usually do a bunch of leads for a song then Roger would pick out the bits he thought were good and play them back to Ritchie at a later time and he said yes or no. It all went pretty fast considering back in that day we would make records in five or six weeks. Some records take years to make and I think those records still hold up … It was never like a big party in the studio that's for sure. I wasn't always there so I really couldn't say but there were never like some sessions when a lot of people come in. It was never like that when I was in the band. For the most part it was Ritchie and Roger and an engineer back then. I was around sometimes when [Ritchie] did the [solos] because sometimes we were stuck in the middle of nowhere for weeks at a time."

With most of the backing tracks recorded the band needed a singer. Rainbow's new front man was discovered in the same way that Rondinelli had got the gig. "When we went back to the States, Ritchie said to the same guy that introduced me to him, 'We need a singer now' … and this guy Barry Ambrosio said 'I know this guy Joe'."

Down on his luck at the time, Joe Lynn Turner was living in New York City, going to various auditions when one day he received an unexpected call. At first Turner thought it was a prank: "Barry Ambrosio introduced himself but he didn't introduce himself as Blackmore's personal [assistant], he just said 'Hi I'm Barry, I'm a big fan of yours' and he's asking me all kinds of questions and sooner or later he gets round to 'Do you like Rainbow?' 'Well yeah I'm familiar with *Rainbow Rising*' but to be perfectly honest with you I was into completely other genres of music. I was studying jazz guitar and I was into more like the Eagles and stuff like that and then he finally says, 'Well I'm sitting next to Ritchie Blackmore and he wants to speak to you' and I'm like, 'Yeah right' and he says 'Honestly I am' and I said, 'This has got to be some kind of joke, you seem like a nice enough guy but cut the bullshit.' And he says, 'Alright you don't believe me, here he is' and he puts him on and here comes this guy with an English accent and he's telling me, 'I'm a big fan of yours' and I said, 'What do you mean, who are you?' He said, 'No, this is Ritchie Blackmore' and I'm like, 'Yeah right' and he says, 'No really' and he had difficulty convincing me at first and then he said, 'Well here's the bottom line, we're looking for a new singer and your name came up, you've got a great voice, I like your style, would you be interested in auditioning?'

So I said 'Well yeah', and at that point I probably believed he was Ritchie Blackmore and either way I needed a gig so I'd go anywhere at this point to get a gig and I went out on the train to Syosset, Long Island, to a place called Kingdom Sound Studios and I walked in and of course there's Roger Glover and Ritchie and some very black haired, big breasted woman [who was] Amy, Bruce Payne was there and Colin Hart. Immediately with just a few 'Hello's' and this and that I went into the studio and they started throwing tracks at me, like 'See what you can do with these tracks' and some of the tracks of course didn't have any words or melodies. They told me to just 'flabber dabber' it and see what I came up with. In my guitar bag, I kept some notebooks and lyrics and just started singing some of them over this. There was a lot of head nodding behind the glass and then they pulled out this song 'I Surrender' with huge backing vocals on it, and it was Graham Bonnet actually. I kind of sang the song more my style and they really liked it and the next thing I know I was redoing all the backing tracks, and Ritchie comes in with a bottle of Heineken in each hand, passes me one and says 'Do you want to join the band?' and I was like, 'Fuck yeah, I'm in,' so he said, 'Welcome to the band, get to work.' The next thing I knew I was doing all the backing tracks over again, singing 'I Surrender' again, and the rest is kind of history."

Turner stayed in Syosset until he completed his vocals over the existing tracks. Blackmore took to the new singer immediately, primarily because of his ability to write, something of a prerequisite. Although Turner was familiar with Blackmore's reputation, initially what he experienced was quite the opposite. "At the very inception he was very polite, a kind of jovial, tongue-in-cheek joker. Later, in the weeks that followed, he was very particular but also very complimentary. I was working really hard and he was very complimentary about my effort and so on and so forth. I knew he could be a bastard. But I didn't seem to mind because he wanted what I wanted: That absolute. It had to be great. I think that prevailed throughout our relationship because a lot of people had trouble with Blackmore, including myself, personal and professional but not in the sense that we weren't seeing eye-to-eye as far as the music. The music came first and if you sucked and tried to get away with something that was second rate he was all over you. He would just fight to the end."

Being the new boy, Turner's initiation via one of Blackmore's practical jokes occurred while Rainbow were back in Denmark putting the finishing touches to the album: "I came back with this bird, after drinking one night in the bar and the next thing I know I get a knock at the door and Ian Broad who was Ritchie's assistant at the time, he's like knocking on the door. 'Joe, you gotta give me my passport it's in your jacket' and all this and I'm like talking through the door now; 'Ian, I wouldn't even lend you a fucking jacket, never mind that your passport's in the jacket.' 'No you've got to open the door.' Meanwhile I've got the bird sitting in the bed naked, ready to go and I'm like, 'Hey I'm busy here,' and he's like, 'Joe if you don't open the fucking door I'll break it down.' So I'm now like. 'Ok Ian, settle down!' It's like two, three o'clock in the morning. I open the door and the next thing I know he busts through the door and in come two beautiful girls, Bobby Rondinelli in a bathrobe, bottles of wine, swinging dick an' all and Ritchie with an acoustic guitar playing 'English Country Garden.' And I'm fucking looking at this – what a zoo. This is a circus and the girl's in bed just going 'Joe vot is zis?' And I'm like 'What do you guys want?' Ritchie keeps playing and Bobby's pouring wine all around and the girls were obviously these gorgeous hookers or something and Ian starts to throw everything out of the window. No personal belongings but he would just pick things up all around the room and throw them out of the window. Rip curtains off the wall, throw them out of the window, go into the bathroom, rip the shower curtains, roll them up in one big lump throw them out of the window, and I'm just going, 'I ain't paying for this shit.'

"I'm running in the hallway, knocking on Colin Hart's door, going, 'Colin, you gotta see this.' He's going 'Fuck off I'm not working for you right now. Nine o'clock comes too early, fuck off.' I'm running back in; I'm taking pictures of this stuff, going 'I can prove I didn't do this,' because the room was just trashed. So now we are all drinking and it settles down. Then they take my mattress! I'm really going to need that right? And they pull it down the hallway and throw it into an elevator, pushed the button and that was the last we'd ever see of it. Meanwhile they're dragging me for a bit and I'm getting rug burns because I'm in my 'skivvies' and it was hilarious, so I ran back into my room and locked the door. The sun is coming up and this girl is just looking at me going, 'Joe, what are we going to do now?' There is a shred of a box spring and we're lying on that and a bit of curtain covering us to try and get some sleep. I couldn't sleep much and I wake up and I'm hung over and I go down stairs and I said, 'Excuse me I need to see the

251

manager.' The manager comes out and he says, 'Good morning.' And this is a John Cleese type if ever you've seen one. He's all cheery, a big tall guy, and I said, 'I think you gotta come up here and see this room,' so he says, 'What's the problem?' 'I can't explain it, just come up.'

"So there's dead silence in the elevator and I'm hung over, feeling fucking awful and I'm going, 'Oh my god, what is going to happen?' We get in the room, and he looks about and he goes [nonchalantly] 'Oh yeah' and I'm looking at him wide eyed and he looks around and he said, 'You should have seen Bob Marley's room – there was shit all over the wall.' He said 'We can fix this up in a week, this isn't bad.' Then he says, 'By the way,' and he hands me an envelope and says, 'Here you go, Mr. Turner it's all been paid for by Mr Blackmore.' I open it up and there's a note from Ritchie saying, 'Welcome to the band, mate.' And that was my initiation! They had another room ready for me. They moved me right into another room, very classy, very nice. I saw the guys at breakfast and I saw Don Airey and Don's very reserved; he's reading his newspapers and he asks, 'Sleep well?' And I go, 'No I didn't sleep well at all,' and he says, 'Neither did I. All fucking night there was shit coming past my window' and I go, 'That was my room!'"

Difficult To Cure was released in February '81 and 'I Surrender' gave Rainbow their biggest ever UK chart success, peaking at number three. Despite already having scored a hit with one of his songs, Blackmore wasn't particularly enamoured with the new Russ Ballard composition as Airey recalls, "All I can remember is he didn't like 'I Surrender' but I thought it was great and Bruce Payne said, 'Get it recorded it's going to be a hit' so I just went in with Bobby and Roger and we just did an arrangement and Ritchie said, 'I can't be bothered to learn it.' I'd spent three hours doing something, creating my own thing and the roadies put a chorus over the top of it and Ritchie heard it and said, 'Maybe I will learn it.'"

Praying Mantis, one of the bands that had sprung up from the 'New Wave Of British Heavy Metal' were originally in the running to release 'I Surrender' and a degree of bitterness crept in when Rainbow, being the bigger name, were given the nod to record it. In a *Sounds* interview, Mantis drummer Dave Potts was diplomatic about the whole affair: "Originally, [Mantis' manager] Bob Keen came up with the idea of using the song for a single. I mean, we all really liked the idea but, unfortunately, so did Ritchie Blackmore. He realises that he still needs hit singles, I'm sure. 'Since You Been Gone' worked for Rainbow after all. Really everything works on a business level and you have to make an allowance for the business side of things if you're going to survive as a band." Praying Mantis instead wrote 'Cheated' which contained the lyric: "The colours in the rainbow they've all turned blue" as a direct response to the incident.

Difficult To Cure pleased devotees of Blackmore's guitar work with two excellent instrumentals. 'Maybe Next Time' followed in a similar vein to 'Weiss Heim' and the title was also translated into German* while 'Difficult To Cure,' concluding the album, was actually an adaptation of 'Ode To Joy' from Beethoven's Ninth Symphony. In an interview at the time, Blackmore tantalisingly hinted that more in the same vein was to follow. "Maybe next year I'll record an instrumental LP of all the songs I've accumulated over the last couple of years. They're all slow songs, there's not too much rock in it … it's just a different side. It's a side I've never really wanted to show 'cause I never really had it."

The new look Rainbow embarked on a three-month American tour, kicking off in February '81 while 'I Surrender' was regularly being played on UK radio. "Although I live in America, I think that Europeans are much more knowledgeable when it comes to bands," Blackmore was quoted before the tour began. "On the whole the bands that are more famous in Europe are better bands, they mean more and are saying more. In America you have to put yourself in a glossy little package and present the whole thing properly. You have to have the record company a hundred per cent behind you and you have to pay people this and give cocaine to other people. I get to the stage where I say 'I'm sorry I can't be bothered with that.' If it means doing that I'd rather remain an unknown idiot, I'm not going to those limits. If the guitar doesn't say it, well, tough."

One notable event from the US tour saw the writing of 'Jealous Lover' one of Rainbow's most popular songs from this time. Joe Lynn Turner: "We were in Minneapolis, St Paul the twin cities Minnesota having a bit of rest and relaxation for a couple of days because the tour was gruelling. We were definitely hitting the charts on the radio and it was all great. We rented out the Orpheum Theatre and the Rolling Stones mobile unit, which is kind of indicative of a complete circle with the whole 'Smoke On The Water' thing. We were going to do a B-side for the 'Can't Happen Here' single. Ritchie had given me a riff a week before and I was writing the lyrics and everything was set and I was ready to go and on the day he pulls this other lick out on me and I'm like, 'What the hell's that?' He goes, 'This is the one we're

---

* Although Blackmore's less than perfect command of the language resulted in the expression being grammatically incorrect. It was subsequently altered on reissues of the album.

doing' and I'm like, 'This isn't the one I wrote,' he said, 'Yes it is … well it doesn't matter.' I said, 'What do you mean it doesn't matter?' He said, 'Well one lick's as good as the next!' And I'm like, 'This isn't the one I wrote the words to come on. I've got a song here and not a song there.' He said, 'Well this is the one we're fucking doing so you'd better get it together.'

"I was like holy shit! It was a good lick but I was like 'Man what am I going to do with this?' So I thought back to two nights before and I had this huge row with my girlfriend who was just accusing me of everything on the road and I wasn't so naughty at that point because I hadn't had enough time. I just felt it was a complete abomination of our relationship so I wrote this lyric 'Jealous Lover' in about five minutes complete with 'eyes of green, seas of red' and all this kind of thing. And it just came to me very quickly, laid down the vocal in one, possibly one and a half takes where I fixed up a couple of lines and that was it. And we never looked back. The next thing we know this 'Jealous Lover' song just came through everything and became bigger than the A-side."

While undoubtedly catchy but with a riff lifted directly from Little Richard's 'The Girl Can't Help It' 'Can't Happen Here' fared less well than 'I Surrender.' Among the instrumentals and heavier numbers on *Difficult To Cure* was 'Magic,' a tune written by Brian Moran, a friend of Blackmore's. Given that it was the most pop orientated commercial tune Rainbow ever recorded, and with Blackmore's stated desire for commercial success, in hindsight it's surprising that it wasn't chosen as the follow-up single.

The day 'Jealous Lover' was recorded was made all the more memorable as it also coincided with Ritchie's 36th birthday, in itself a source of amusement for the rest of the band, and in particular Joe Lynn Turner. "What happens is its Ritchie's birthday and I remember [Eric] Clapton in a wheelchair and [his then wife] Patti pushing him. We're all in the hallway [of the Radisson Hotel] and we've got the cake and we're going up to his room singing 'Happy birthday.' He opens the door and he just looks at us and says, 'Fuck off' and slams the door. Then we all went to the bar and got smashed. We all had cakes and presents and I know Clapton had bought him this little ducky on a stick like a child's toy and when you would blow the ducky it's little wings would flap and go 'quack, quack, quack.' [Ritchie] was in a bad mood because earlier in the day he'd lost his guitar. They'd put it in the boot, because he wanted to leave early, he always wanted to leave early before the band – never wanted to travel with the band. Apparently he put it in the boot of a cab and when they got out at the hotel he just gets out and goes in, him and his girlfriend and they left it in the fucking boot. So it was really a big loss, one of his favourite guitars. They might have recovered it, I think Colin Hart stayed on it, he was very good at that kind of stuff and I think he came back with it."

The birthday present from Clapton is still something that Rondinelli can't help but recall with mirth: "Eric was in some hospital getting some treatment but he came to the show the next day and on Ritchie's birthday he got him a wooden duck. It was like a toy duck and you pull on a string and the feathers and the legs move and you wheel it and Ritchie was walking around for a couple of days pulling this duck because his friend Eric gave it to him. It was pretty funny. It's a very bizarre thing but what does Eric Clapton buy Ritchie Blackmore for his birthday? Maybe a duck! If it was a shirt or something nobody would talk about it thirty years later!"

Just as Rainbow's popularity was at an all-time high, the 'Deep Purple to reform' rumours raised their head. The stillborn event planned for '78 didn't deter journalists and fans from speculating on further developments. While being interviewed for *Sounds* in 1980, Blackmore had hinted at unfinished business. "I think a lot of American people are thick 'cause Rainbow, Whitesnake whatever, we do things in the same vein that Purple did, but unless it's got the name stamped on it, they shy away from it. Maybe it's because we were one of those bands that disappeared when we didn't have to."

Around the time of Rainbow's Donington concert, news filtered through of the 'new Deep Purple' playing concerts in Mexico which had many fans scratching their heads. It soon emerged that original vocalist Rod Evans had taken it upon himself to reactivate the name with a group of anonymous musicians and even managed to arrange some gigs at the enormous Long Beach Arena in California. Ritchie seemed generally unconcerned by the scam, "I think it did annoy me for about a day, I was just reading the interview with Rod Evans in *Sounds* and he hasn't changed, he's a really nice guy, there's no malice intended. He probably wanted to make some money out of it, which he felt he might not have done in the beginning. But that's all over and now the lawyers are in and that's been stopped."

The one thing this farce highlighted was that simply putting Deep Purple on concert posters, regardless of the musicians involved was certainly an indication that to many the name was still hugely marketable. Sales of Deep Purple's back catalogue were still healthy and compilations and previously unreleased concert recordings were being released at regular intervals. A TV advertised greatest hits LP *Deepest Purple* even reached number one in the British album charts in July '80. Whatever the individual members might have felt about their former band they couldn't deny its popularity was still strong. The potentially huge box office business that a proper Deep Purple reformation could attract was certainly of great interest within the music industry and although Blackmore appeared indifferent he was shrewd enough to appreciate the idea's commercial potential.

"When we originally talked about the Purple reunion, it seemed just like a fun idea," Blackmore said. "Now it seems a lot of politics will be involved." When asked how he could separate the two, he gave the clearest indication yet that something might eventuate. "I shall just keep myself isolated from the people I don't want to be with and keep in touch with the people I want to see, which is the band. As long as the band feel that they want to play then that's all right. I'm not going to push it; I know the line up I want to see playing. But I've seen so much fuss go down in the last six months it's beginning to bore me and it must be boring to the public. It was just an idea I thought of for nostalgia's sake, now everybody's getting too serious. Initially it was to get back together for a month, no records would be made, just a one-off."

When asked who was responsible for the reunion rumours in May '81, Jon Lord told journalist Mike Eriksson: "Nothing has emerged from this band [Whitesnake]. I mean, David, Ian and myself have even publicly declared that we are not interested in reforming Deep Purple and that we don't want people to think that it comes from us. But maybe a certain guitarist that has a habit of wearing funny black hats and lives in Connecticut … maybe the rumours are coming from Connecticut? I really don't want to see a reunion for the wrong reasons. The only thing I have heard so far is people saying, 'Hey, we are going to make a lot of money … lots and lots of money.' But I have made enough. I'm not a millionaire, but my life is okay. I live a comfortable life and I enjoy myself in Whitesnake. I don't want to see Whitesnake killed off just … and I don't want to play those songs anymore. It would be like taking a step back and that doesn't interest me."

On May 16, four days after Rainbow's US tour concluded, Blackmore married his girlfriend of three years standing, Amy Rothman. Turner attended the ceremony, contributing a wedding present of an old English style mosaic tray, but this didn't mean he wasn't still the butt of Blackmore's practical jokes. One of the most memorable occurred a month after the wedding, while on the road in Europe. "The best thing we did to [Turner] was in [Colmar] France. We played this miserable outdoor gig. And, of course, France being so organised, there wasn't a roof. So it's now raining, and people are sitting in the rain watching us. There were only about 800 people in a 3000-seater arena. And it was such a miserable event. I didn't even bother changing. I remember thinking, 'I'm gonna hate this ... I hate France ... I hate being here ... just don't wanna play!' Playing away ... Joe does his part, where he usually gets the audience going, and we back off a little bit, then we come back. So what we did was ... he starts handclapping, doing his improvisation bit. So I said to the others, 'Come on, we're going, we're leaving!' So we go off the stage, and Joe's on his own but doesn't know he's on his own, doing this clapping to the audience, going, 'Yeah, yeah, yeah.' And they're sitting there in the rain, glum faces with no expression ... nothing!

"So we're now off stage, we get down into the orchestra pit and there's all these vegetables – perfect! We picked up all these tomatoes. Now Joe is singing to the audience, but he can't really see because the lights are on him. We then started throwing the tomatoes at him. The audience meanwhile didn't know what was happening. Joe didn't know it was us in the orchestra pit, throwing things. Now he starts swearing at the audience, 'You bastards! You French bastards!' And he's picking up tomatoes, and throwing tomatoes at the audience, who are going, 'We're not gonna take this!' They now start to throw things at him and it's still raining! Then Joe goes, 'Oh! It's the band!' It was too late then! He had the whole audience in an uproar. To see his face ... smack! I loved that! That was hilarious."

Although Rondinelli took part in the prank his view was that, "Ritchie wasn't in a good mood that day, didn't get dressed up for the show. It was cruel but effective I guess. It was dark down there so at first [Joe] didn't know where it was coming from. It was a vicious joke, we shouldn't have done it but it was fun."

Although Blackmore was usually behind such incidents, Ian Broad could often match him. Joe Lynn Turner: "The 'drunken hurricane' as we called him. I'll never forget him up in Calgary, I don't know how this happened but I was in the lobby mailing some letters, we had all checked in before Ritchie and all of a sudden I see Ian Broad driving a Jaguar E Type and he pulls into the hotel, because it had these doors that were electronic and they pulled back and he drove right in and said, 'Have you got a room for Mr Blackmore?!'"

While Blackmore enjoyed dishing it out Turner soon learnt that this was solely a one-way arrangement: "We tried one time to really play a trick on [Ritchie] and he didn't fare very well. He didn't like the tricks Ian played back on him. He could appreciate it when people would at least attempt it, but if they really worked and it got him he would feel embarrassed and angry so we learnt to just back off of that. What happens is that once you are able to take it you are kind of in the band and that's alright and things slow down.'"

To Turner's relief the events at Colmar weren't repeated and the European leg concluded in Spain. Support act for the tour was up and coming NWOBHM band Def Leppard, but for the penultimate show in Madrid UFO were also added to the bill as openers. With three bands playing, Blackmore was adamant he didn't want to be on stage after midnight so the running order was switched with Def Leppard taking the stage last, playing to a significantly smaller crowd as most people left after Rainbow's performance.

With Wembley Arena out of bounds following the debacle the previous year, two nights at the Hammersmith Odeon and two at the Rainbow Theatre were scheduled to satisfy the demand. Polydor's George McManus caught one of the shows and was confronted with more than he had anticipated. "I turned up at the Rainbow Theatre and I thought I'd do my record company job, knock on the door and say 'Hello Ritchie.' I knocked on Ritchie's door and he's in the middle of the room surrounded by candles: he was completely in the dark and the whole dressing room was completely covered in candles. He was having a séance I just said, 'Good gig Ritchie' and I ran like fuck, basically saying to myself, 'I'll do my record company job but I don't want to get into a séance.'"

Even though as an Abba fan Blackmore had been unable to secure the services of Agnetha Fältskog the previous year, towards the end of the European tour, he introduced a similar set up by bringing a blonde and brunette backing singer into Rainbow for live gigs, debuting at Newcastle City Hall. Joe Lynn Turner: "Actually they were Benny Hill Girls, Dee [Beale] and Lin [Robinson], great singers and they were terrific. I think the real heavy metal heads were against it because they were girls. He loved orchestras and he loved the harmonies, a very musical person." Don Airey thought differently. "It was a disaster. I just couldn't believe it. It didn't sound right, the whole thing was falling apart. I think he was just trying to shore up a very shaky edifice."

After the tour concluded in Japan the flight back to America was broken up by a show in Hawaii. The stop over was primarily treated as a well-earned break at one of Blackmore's favourite holiday destinations. Even though it wasn't listed on the general tour itinerary approximately 4,000 witnessed the show. Bobby Rondinelli: "It was pretty strange because we were using rental gear, which we really never did. That's the only time in Rainbow I can ever remember us not using our own stuff."

It also turned out to be Don Airey's last gig, which he vividly recalls,

"After two numbers Ritchie walked off and took the rest of the band with him, pointing to me to hold the fort while he got his amp fixed. So I did a solo and there was nobody there, I couldn't see any of the band, any of the crew. Just me on stage and I played for 25 minutes. Every trick in the book, *Hawaii Five-O*, 'Hawaiian Love Chant,' Little Richard stuff trying to keep it going, desperately looking round. Eventually I thought the show's over and I walked off. I went back to the hotel and they were all sitting at the bar looking pretty pleased with themselves and I said to Colin, 'Get me out of here' and I got the first flight out in the morning and that was the last I saw of them."

With the tour concluded a break followed before work commenced on the next album. Joe Lynn Turner: "I'll never forget a Halloween party at Weiss Heim, all the house rigged. I mean it was unbelievable ... [Ritchie] told me, people are fucking nosey and the house is huge and I know they're going to be looking into things. He would leave doors cracked open and when you looked through the door you would see a perfectly set up shadow of a man hanging by a rope or something, and he'd fix that all. Another time when you were standing at the bar and looked to your right outside the window or to the back yard you would see this light with skulls and things and he had a button under the bar that he could activate. He had the whole house rigged it was phenomenal. It was fucking unbelievable, one of the best Halloween parties I've ever been to because everyone was in full get up costume and the whole house was just a full house of horrors and he really spared no expense."

In December, Le Studio in Morin Heights, Canada was the chosen recording venue for Rainbow's new album. The facility was highly regarded; Rush recorded *Permanent Waves* and *Moving Pictures* there, as had the Police with *Ghost In The Machine*. Airey's replacement was an American, David Rosenthal, fresh out of Music College. Once again a new recruit was asked to contribute with the songwriting but was told he would not receive a full writing credit. Despite his young age Rosenthal was more on the ball than some of Rainbow's previous musicians and he arranged for his lawyer to deal with the situation.

The recording of *Straight Between The Eyes* is largely remembered by the entire band for the harsh weather conditions, something that Blackmore made full use of upon receiving the letter from Rosenthal's lawyer. Bobby Rondinelli: "As a practical joke Ritchie decided to take all [Rosenthal's] furniture out of his room and put it out in the cold, in the snow. The next morning at breakfast Dave was shivering because it took all night for his room to thaw out, and he brought everything back into the room on his own. That was a vicious one."

Despite the darker psychological edge to some of Blackmore's practical jokes Rondinelli is quick to defend his ex-employer. "Most of them were fun, nobody got hurt. It wasn't like you put broken glass in someone's shoes or something. It's harmless stuff. You're in a big band now, you get the initiation. I think it's just busting somebody's chops because you can get away with it and it's funny. I mean I'm sure there have been worse things done. It's not like these things when people can get killed. It's all good fun. And most of it you look back at and say that was funny."

Released in June '82 *Straight Between The Eyes* saw Rainbow lean even further towards an American AOR sound. The ballad 'Stone Cold' and in particular 'Power' were hugely popular on American FM radio but as a result, they tested the loyalty of older fans who still yearned for the Ronnie Dio era style of underground, mystical rock that Rainbow was founded on. Indeed when Turner joined, Blackmore had forewarned him of the responses he could expect. "He said you are going to get a lot of flak. As I recall it, the general sentiment was some of these idiots are not even going to budge. They're immovable, you're gonna get a lot of flak about the Dio thing but just carry on, just know that we're in this together and this is what we want to do and for every Dio fan we drop we get two new fans. And that was the truth, literally. For example they never had any women at the concerts.

"So everyone loved that including the crew – it was thank God we have girls in the audience now, we could compete … well not with the likes of Def Leppard or Bon Jovi but we had some nice looking girls coming, so we were reaching a wider audience in the sense that we weren't just this 'metal head' sound. We had a bit more dimension and we were talking about everything from the paranormal to very street value type rock 'n' roll. It was very more about social political stuff as opposed to the 'Gates Of Babylon' or something. So we were a bit more current in that respect. That is what was happening. If you look back, something that a journalist had said that's important here, that era of Rainbow literally defined melodic hard rock. A lot of people took the nod from Rainbow. Even though we were sort of not as huge as some of the bands we definitely defined a style, where it was still hard rock underneath it but we had the melodies and the harmonies and things like that. So I thought that was quite a comment that we defined melodic hard rock."

With the introduction of MTV in 1981, giving American audiences wall-to-wall TV music coverage and by the early Eighties the cable channel was *the* major promotional outlet. Even though Blackmore felt uncomfortable with the prospect of having to make videos, he accepted it as a necessary marketing tool. At least some of his dry humour was given the chance to shine through on the ridiculous promo for the album's opening cut 'Death Alley Driver.' Blackmore was dressed in his usual black, with top hat, depicting the character portrayed in the song's lyrics, "death is in the back seat of a big old black sedan," attempting to look as menacing as possible with Amy disguised in a flat cap, driving the vehicle in question.

With Rainbow now making greater inroads into the American mainstream, the band toured there relentlessly from early May through to late August. The set lists were now largely built around the newer material with only one song from the Dio era, 'Long Live Rock 'n' Roll' retained, while Blackmore's signature Purple tune, 'Smoke On The Water' was thrown in for the encores. Taking advantage of the growing popularity of home video, one of the last shows on the tour in San Antonio, Texas on August 18 was shot for Rainbow's first commercially released concert film.

Tours of Japan and Europe rounded the year off. Rob Fodder who would later become Blackmore's personal assistant remembers the gig in Brussels. "A few friends and myself went on one of those organised coach trips to see Rainbow in Brussels. Halfway through 'Spotlight Kid' someone threw a flashcube from a camera and it hit Ritchie on the left hand. He immediately stopped and walked offstage. There was about a 15 minute break and Cookie [Ritchie's tech] came out to the mic and said that they were trying to get the band back on, but if it happened again, there would be no coming back. The lights went down and the band tore into 'Miss Mistreated' with Ritchie looking particularly fired up. On the ferry back to England, there was some Scottish guy, very drunk boasting of how he threw the flashcube. By the end of the crossing, he was bound, gagged and locked in one of the ferry's toilets and the çoaches left without him. God knows how many Channel crossings he made before they discovered him. When I told the story to Ritchie many years later, he just had that evil grin on his face that said 'Good.' "

The tour finished with a couple of shows in Spain with UFO supporting. When UFO bassist Pete Way apparently caught sight of Blackmore at the hotel dressed in monogrammed pyjamas he was reported to have commented, "A legend was shattered that night."

By the end of the year, Ian Gillan announced the end of his band and rumours that Turner, Rondinelli and Rosenthal were being given their notices as a possible Purple reunion now looked imminent didn't ring true as far as Turner remembers: "I think there was some undercurrent of that, like there was this talk about it that we were disbanding or something and I remember I got a call saying, 'No you're in and we're going to do this and we're going to do that.' I never really felt it because I didn't really dwell on it."

The departure of Rondinelli has been cited elsewhere as being instigated by Joe Lynn Turner, due to Turner's growing stature within the band but the singer is adamant he played no part in the process. "I don't recall being the responsible party. The only way that I may have facilitated that departure was the fact that Ritchie was off him. To be quite fair I had my negative points as well. Bobby was doing what we called 'dropping sandwiches.' He'd start the soundcheck on drums and everything would be great and during performances he would lose energy. Ritchie was looking at me going, 'He's just falling down now.' Bobby was gone before I even had time to say goodbye. So I can't say I was instrumental in that and I hope he doesn't ever think that and maybe this book will clear that up. I could understand why Ritchie was off him but I didn't make that decision nor did I go up to Ritchie and say get rid of Bobby."

Although a new drummer was brought in, making the follow up to *Straight Between The Eyes* was problematic. Joe Lynn Turner: "We were again in Sweet Silence and we spent, I don't know how many reels of tape trying to get the basic tracks right. This was in the days of big reels of tape. We had got six reels full and not one track was a keeper. They were all flawed. All just dipping in time, so at this point we are spending tons of money and not making any progress. I was absolutely livid. Plus I felt I had written, well not only myself, the band had written some great songs and this guy was not doing them justice. And I refused … I didn't like this new drummer from the beginning. I just felt this is the wrong direction to go in. [Ritchie] needed someone who was really going to fucking bring us up. If we're getting rid of Bobby we need to get someone who is absolutely amazing.

"So here we are in Copenhagen – no keepers, spending all kinds of money, six huge fat reels of tape, nothing on them but crap. My songs were being completed, I figured they were my songs, At this point I'm getting very territorial and we've got a brilliant album here. I'm not going to let them be destroyed with this fucking drummer. He shall remain nameless, it's not worth bringing up his name to slag somebody off. And I said, 'I know somebody who is amazing.' They said 'Who?', I said, 'This guy named Chuck Bürgi, he's a good friend of mine and I've played with him before and I'm telling you right now if we get him over here, lock, stock and

A pensive looking Ritchie in the early Eighties. Cozy Powell: "Ritchie's the kind of guy that one night he'll play absolutely brilliantly and the other night he won't be bothered, and if he's not in the mood he won't play particularly that great, and he won't go on and do an encore. That's Ritchie, and that's why Ritchie's Ritchie." (MICHAEL JOHANSSON/IDOLS)

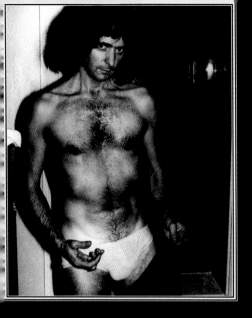

Keeping it brief, 1980. "I like to be
rejuvenated," said Ritchie, "it's almost
a vampire like thing. I feed on the blood
of musicians passing through and when
the blood's dried up, I get rid of them!"

(ROSS HALFIN/IDOLS)

What a drag – Ritchie answers charges
of sexism ("[I] can just as easily be one
of the girls") with a photo shoot for
Sounds newspaper in September 1980.
Bobby Rondinelli helps him adjust.

(ROSS HALFIN/IDOLS)

Ritchie with his estranged son Jürgen in the mid-Eighties. Following in the footsteps
of his father, Jürgen now pursues a musical career in Germany. (ROSS HALFIN/IDOLS)

Perfect Strangers: Deep Purple MK II reform in 1984. L-R: Lord, Gillan, Paice, Blackmore, Glover. The reformation was promoted with the slogan, "Destiny brought them together again." Years later, Blackmore openly admitted destiny should have been replaced by cold hard cash.
(COURTESY OF THE BEDFORD JOURNAL)

Onstage during Deep Purple's 'House Of Blue Light' tour in 1987. "Ritchie started getting cranky again," said Ian Gillan, "and I could see the nervousness creeping into everyone's eyes…"
(MICHAEL JOHANNSON/IDOLS)

Ritchie avoids facing his masked adversary Ian Gillan, 1987. Blackmore forced Gillan's sacking the following year. "Ritchie's like a terrier or pit-bull," described Jon Lord. "He gets hold of something and won't let go. He has a vision of what he wants, and he'll fight and fight until he gets what he wants." (MICHAEL JOHANNSON/IDOLS)

Deep Purple pictured backstage in Germany, 1993. Gillan (far right) had been reinstated against Blackmore's wishes. "If we didn't get to the dressing room in time," says Rob Fodder, "Gillan would say, 'Ritchie you were brilliant tonight, that's the best I've ever seen you play...' and inside I think Ritchie was cringing." (MICHAEL JOHANSSON/IDOLS)

Ritchie onstage with the last incarnation of Rainbow, Belgium, July 1996. "If they don't want to hear anymore I'll go hey and knock it on the head," he told Neil Jeffries, "because this next project I'm very excited about because it's a big change. It's completely different from the hard rock thing." (MARC BRANS)

The lifelong football fanatic on a pitch in Munich, Germany. "I love to exercise, kick a

Ritchie pictured at the Normandie Inn, Long Island, NY, during an interview with Alan Whitman and the author, May 2, 1998.

With personal and professional partner, Candice Night. "We hit it off on so many levels that we became friends very quickly," Blackmore said in 1998. "The romantic moment was six months after we first met when we got to really know each other. Then I knew she was the only one for me." (NEIL DAVIES)

Onstage in the UK with Blackmore's Night, 2001. "This is the path I hope to be on for the rest of my days. I haven't forgotten rock 'n' roll, and I do like to turn up the volume and play but that can wait for a while." (STEVE MILLS)

Ritchie and Candice, April 2002. "It was almost like the weight of the world was lifted off [Ritchie's] shoulders, said Raymond D'addario, "and he could just relax and do what he wanted to do. He doesn't have to compete he can just play music, doesn't have to argue with the singer, any of that stuff, just play music." (OLA BERGMAN/IDOLS)

Hamburg, Germany, July 2005. "When I saw the Blackmore's Night stage backdrop it reminded me of a Christmas panto," says Julian Dawson. "I had the feeling he really loved the music he was playing... and was determined to educate his audience to his new direction." (ACTION PRESS/REX

The devil incarnate? "[Ritchie's] presence looms over practically everything," says Roger Glover. "He's searching for something that turns him on and I don't think he knows what it is. He's a brilliant guitarist, one of those odd people that God pointed a finger at and said, 'You are going to have something that nobody else has got.' Maybe he can't handle how gifted he is..."

barrel, just bring him over here, sight unseen, he's gonna play the shit out of these tracks" and that's exactly how it happened. Bruce Payne was with me on this one, so he said, 'OK I'll convince everybody we're going to do this." We got Bürgi over there, they shipped over his small kit and he played like a motherfucker and Ritchie loves him to this day."

On *Bent Out Of Shape* Blackmore got closest to achieving the right balance of hard rock and commercial pop. One of the standout tracks was 'Street Of Dreams'. Joe Lynn Turner: "I had a good day that day, it was a good vocal performance and the song came to me literally in a dream and I woke up and wrote the lyrics. It was all very mystical and at that point Blackmore and I were doing all kinds of black arts and we were deep into the paranormal and he pulled me into the kitchen as I remember it. There was a huge storm happening outside, lightning, thunder, wind and rain and we loved it because all that electro magnetic energy that comes off the weather affects everyone whether they know it or not. Anyway he said to me, 'I can't play the fucking solo' and I said why and he said, 'Because the vocal's just intimidating." I said, 'What do you mean?' He said 'It's fucking brilliant, it's perfect, you've hit every part where you should.' I said, 'Ritch just get the fuck in there and do what you do, make a memorable solo.' Because he wasn't just like the sort of guitarist that would just jerk off all over the track, he was very meticulous about it; he wanted to play for the song which really separates him from Malmsteen and other guitarists. He was more song orientated.

"The interesting thing about the weather was we both heard this huge snap and it was actually the lightning hitting the rod on the top of the roof and with that everything blacked out including all the studio and the videos went down in the lounge and everybody was 'Hey what the hell?!' and we just looked at each other and went 'That's a sign.' And he went back in when the power was restored, which was only minutes later really and played the most brilliant solo and to this day I can still sing the solo. Gorgeous. And that's the way he approached things, he really wanted it to be for the song. He's not one of these hot dogs that has this huge ego about 'I'm the fastest guitarist' and all that crap. He's not that. He can play that crap if he wants but he's very song orientated, very melodic, he really believes in melody."

In a *Sounds* interview with Gary Bushell in September 1983, Blackmore commented positively about *Bent Out Of Shape*: "I think it's very good, it's got a lot of substance. I'm very pleased with the way my writing's going." He expanded about some of the album's songs on including the instrumental 'Anybody There': "The song's based on Bach's 'Prelude In C.' It's got no middle eight and no chorus. The chord structure goes for 28 bars and then repeats so it's very unlike the usual rock song. There's no catch line, just non-stop continuity. 300 years ago they would have accepted that, now bands only go 12 or 14 bars before they get into the hook. I initially called it 'Doomed' … 'Desperate Heart' was the only solo I did in the States. I'd done a solo in Copenhagen and wasn't happy with it, so I redid it in New York – the studio sound was so good it really inspired me. 'Firedance' is a really complicated riff. I have to tune the bass string down to bottom D every time I play it, so I have to do the solo on five strings instead of six … I want everyone to know how difficult it is for me!"

When not on the road Blackmore would regularly join in with bar bands in his locality as he told Mick Wall, "I play in a club here in Long Island a lot, a place called Sparks just down the road; it's a Heavy Metal club. If there's ever a really simple three chord blues I'll jump up with the band and play a bit. I get into a lot of fights over the football table though." Although Blackmore liked to embellish a story, in this case, what appeared to be a throwaway comment had some truth to it as Artie Hoar remembers: "I met Ritchie back in 1983 in a bar in Huntington, Long Island called Sparks. There was no one in the bar at the time except the bartender and me; I was waiting for some friends to show up. I knew it was Ritchie Blackmore when he walked in. He was all in black with snakeskin boots; if you didn't know who he was, you knew he was somebody, he had a certain aura. Ritchie walked in and asked me to play fusball (table football). Two other guys came in and asked us to play doubles, so, I was on Ritchie's team and a big fight broke out because the other guys said that Rich was cheating. Punches started flying. As far as black eyes went, it was the other guys who walked out with them, not us. Ritchie could fight. That was my first experience with Ritchie Blackmore. From that time on, we played soccer, went ghost hunting, and I was caretaker of his house while he was on tour. I went to work for him in 1987."

As for the ghost stories, Hoar has one particularly vivid memory: "I was in his house one time, on Long Island, and as I walked out of the living room, Rich was coming down the hallway and a ball of light shot down the hall. I rubbed my eyes because I could not believe what I just saw, and Rich asked me if I saw what he saw. This is just one of the ghost incidences."

The European tour designed to promote *Bent Out Of Shape* kicked off in the UK, with support by former Runaways' guitarist Lita Ford, briefly an old flame of Blackmore's from around the time he was living in Hollywood in the mid Seventies. Evidence of the band's tight performances was provided by the first of two nights at St. David's Hall, Cardiff being recorded for US radio broadcast, with a couple of the tracks released on the B-side to the 12″ single of 'Can't Let You Go.' Often during UK tours, Blackmore would catch up with pals from his early days in the business. During this trip Blackmore agreed to jam with Jackie Lynton's band at the New Golden Lion, Fulham. For such impromptu gigs the guitarist wasn't concerned with payment but as Lynton remembers he always had a couple of specific requirements: "A bottle of whisky and a blonde with big tits."

Although the band wasn't to know it at the time, *Bent Out Of Shape* would become Rainbow's swan song. Perhaps one more album in the same direction and they might well have finally attained the breakthrough in America that Blackmore craved for. Despite having gained a loyal following over the past eight years, their achievements didn't come close to eclipsing the success of Deep Purple.

By now Bruce Payne was busy masterminding their reformation but before this could happen, Rainbow played three farewell shows in Japan in March '84. For the final gig at the Budokan, Blackmore decided to use an orchestra for a full blown version of Beethoven's Ninth. Rosenthal worked on the orchestral arrangements and inspired by the event Blackmore produced a spellbinding intro. Fortunately the entire concert was videotaped for a Japanese only release, and although to this day the film has never been released outside of Japan, Beethoven's Ninth was used on the Rainbow compilation video *The Final Cut* serving as a sharp reminder to anyone who might have doubted Blackmore's guitar skills. These last shows in Japan were a fitting way for Rainbow to bow out and Joe Lynn Turner was proud of the spectacle. "Of course, [Ritchie] wanted to do the 'Ode To Joy' thing and really make a display of it and put it on video and it was just an incredible moment. Even standing off stage watching I was so exhilarated seeing this orchestra that Dave Rosenthal had written the parts for and it was just a wonderful musical situation that we created. So you had to be very proud of it. That was brilliant."

Rainbow's dissolution wasn't the only one to occur in Blackmore's life at this time. His marriage to Amy Rothman turned out to be a relatively short-lived affair and on his return home from Japan he started to suspect she might be seeing someone else. While he was away touring Amy would normally hang around with his circle of friends that included Stuart Smith. "There was this guy she was hanging around with – a young guy, I saw it, there was nothing in public going on but it was obvious they were pretty close, and of course Ritchie sensed something when he got home and asked me and I was the one who had to tell him 'I think something's going on' and we followed her in a car, and he found out and divorced her. She was really going for a lot and it was a female judge and apparently her comment was this girl thinks she's married to Elton John because she was trying to get millions." Once again Blackmore had taken the chauvinistic attitude that it was okay for him to play around but unacceptable for his partner to do the same. As Smith says, "He's the old school man, the man can do what he wants and the woman must stay at home."

Divorces involving wealthy individuals can often prove to be expensive and while it isn't clear just how costly Blackmore's split from his third wife was, Turner certainly felt that Blackmore's divorce could well have influenced his decision to become part of the Deep Purple reunion. "I think there was a pretty big settlement and the next thing you know he's got to fill up the coffers. I think it was part of a big pull as well. It's hard to deny that. People are human and in this world today it's a necessary evil." Smith, who was very close to Blackmore around this time, begs to differ: "I don't think so, he was still playing to sold-out houses in the States. 'Street Of Dreams' was on the MTV charts. He seemed reasonably happy with the settlement. I don't think it was that costly for him. Plus he had millions put away from his Deep Purple days and the royalties were pouring in of course. 'Smoke On The Water' must still pay him a good rate … just on that song $25 a day at least, just in royalties on radio sales."

Following his third divorce, Blackmore initially sought out his old flame Shoshana, who was still very much on his mind. Stuart Smith: "I remember once when he and Amy had broken up I was going out with this girl Denise and I had to drive, Ritchie hadn't got his driving licence at the time. Shoshana had a band and was playing in Rhode Island and he said did I want to go out and see her. I don't know what it was, because she was married I think, but the three of us went out, I drove of course – we went out to Rhode Island and saw her play and I remember we stayed in a hotel that night and she was meant to be giving him a ride back to the hotel and they disappeared for a while … who knows, say no more!"

With Blackmore once again a single man he suddenly realised he had no one to drive him around. Incredibly, despite owning cars for several years he had never learnt to drive and had always relied on others to take him where he wanted to go. According to Smith, Ritchie's inability to drive was an amusement to many. "One night we went out to see The Hollies at My Father's Place and we went backstage, and they said 'Hey Ritchie, are you still travelling everywhere on the bus?' It was just so funny. When he and Amy broke up he'd be calling me up, 'Can you come over and give me a ride to the supermarket.' I said, 'Why don't you let me teach you how to drive – it will open up a whole new world for you.' Supermarkets, post offices, bars, you can travel on your own. He was very quick once he got his confidence with it.

"The day we were going up to see Shoshana, he'd bought this Mercedes and Denise and I pulled up in my car into the drive. I'd been teaching him to drive in his driveway then in parking lots at night when no one was around. As I pull up into the driveway Ritchie is in the Mercedes with the door open and his foot in the gravel of the drive. He's driving it up and down the driveway with the door open and his foot in it. I said, 'Ritchie what are you doing?' He said, 'Well I'm practising driving.' 'Yeah but what's the foot here in the gravel?' He said, 'Well if it gets away from me I can stop it!' For someone who is incredibly intelligent he can be so dumb. 'Ritchie this is a 380bhp car, how are you going to stop it with your foot?' He thinks it's like a bike. 'It's a 380bhp Mercedes Ritchie that's what the brake pedal's for.' I wouldn't mind if it was a stick but it was an automatic for Christ sake. But that was one of the things that totally endeared him to me. I thought you've got to love him."

At the age of 39, not only was Blackmore finally learning to drive (although it would still be several years before he actually got his licence) but in early '84, while staying in Chattanooga, Tennessee he met Tammy Williams a beautiful young woman who was working at his hotel, and who just so happened to be busty and blonde. Like the reformation of Deep Purple, it was the start of another partnership that would last for several years.

CHAPTER 13

Back In The Hungry Days (1984–89)

The news that the classic Deep Purple Mk II line-up were reuniting pleased the majority of Blackmore's fans. While his loyal fan base had stuck by him, many diehards struggled to accept the way he had shifted Rainbow's music. A decade on Blackmore was unrepentant: "I was very impressed with Abba at the time and I always wanted to write something around the way they could write. I wanted to play that melodic, majestic, regal pop. I wanted to appeal to people. You have to relate to people, so I was trying to, that was a challenge: I want the postman to whistle this on his bicycle."

The lure of easy money in the shape of Purple's reunion guaranteed one thing: financial security. Although the PR people promoted the reformation with the slogan: "Destiny brought them together again," years later, Blackmore openly admitted destiny should have been reworded to cold hard cash: "It was money, purely money. The manager called me up and said that there was a lot of money in this. 'How much?' 'OK, I'll do it.' I shouldn't have done it, but I did." When first committing to it, the five members were in agreement that it shouldn't be purely a nostalgia trip so the intention of producing new work that could stand up alongside the older albums was a major inspiration to all involved.

Rumours that Blackmore insisted that they all got into good physical shape were partly true as he alluded to Sylvie Simmons in *Sounds*, "When I first got back together with the rest of the lads, I knew the music would always be there, but there were obviously a few things that were very apparent that had to be slightly changed or changed dramatically. It was, 'Well lads, if we're going to get back together we can't turn out like five old men, we have to get down and discipline ourselves a little bit.' Discipline is the important word, I think. I like to lead a semi-disciplined life, and rock and roll is not wining and dining and just drinking. You can't go onstage looking like a fat elephant – or you can; Leslie West has proved that! I never actually said to them, 'You have to go to a health farm and slim down' but I think they got the impression I might have said that. I gave them the evil eye or something, but I didn't actually say anything."

In a blaze of publicity Deep Purple signed a highly lucrative deal with Polygram; Mercury Records in America, and Polydor for the rest of the world. The deal was co-ordinated by Polygram's Bill Levenson in New York and George McManus in London, but as far as the latter can remember, despite the working relationship with Rainbow and the fact that Bruce Payne was now the manager of Deep Purple it wasn't guaranteed that Polygram would get the deal. "I remember Bruce saying to me on the phone, words to the effect of, "If you guys don't get in quick there are a lots of other labels interested as well, which must have been EMI in the UK and Warners in America." The deal was reported to be a $10 million advance in lieu of future recordings but McManus, although not privy to the exact details of the contract, isn't convinced that the reports were accurate. "I can't imagine $10 million in 1984. That's a lot of dosh, even for then but it would have been a sizeable advance they had to recoup by selling records. The deal was done in America with my support. I have no idea what it was but it would have been a big advance because good God you're getting Deep Purple. It would obviously have been a fair old whack and Bruce was a very good manager and he would have done a very good deal at the time."

With the band working on what was effectively the follow-up to *Who Do We Think We Are* they chose the relatively rural location of Stowe, Vermont. Rehearsals started on May 1 at The Bass Lodge, an old house owned by the Von Trapp family and after a month the songs had been knocked into shape and because of the location initial reports half-seriously suggested the new album would be called *The Sound Of Music*. "Ritchie jokingly said we should call [it] *At Last The 1974 Album*," said Lord. "We didn't want to sound like 1974, we wanted to sound like 1984; current without throwing away any identity we might have. And as for sounding like Foreigner or American AOR, no way we wanted to sound like that either. But when it all came down to it, and without sounding smug, it was so easy." In keeping

269

with the tradition of recording in less than conventional studio surround-ings, the band wanted to make the album at the Lodge but State authorities refused so a mansion called Horizons was chosen instead. Recording com-menced on July 10.

Whatever had occurred in the intervening years one constant remained: Blackmore was still the main creative force, something that Lord openly acknowledged at the time. "All the major writing came from Ritchie. He must have a stockpile of things he'd been saving because he's come up with some classic material, and anything that I had didn't even come close to that so I didn't put it forward. I want this to be just so good that I'm not going to foist a piece of second-rate material on the band just because I want to get publishing money. I'm sounding like a goody two shoes and I'm not – the halo's going to slip in a minute and strangle me. I'm just telling you the truth. Ian and Roger wrote the words, but I think Ian Paice and I will be represented on a couple of songs, and the lion's portion is Ritchie. I'm paying him a huge compliment here because he deserves it: this particular band couldn't exist in my book without Ritchie; he's the absolute kingpin – the kind of music he writes, the kind of guitar he plays, is essential for it to work."

For the band's rehearsal base, Blackmore chose the unlikely setting of Bedford on the suggestion of his assistant Stuart Smith, who had previously lived in the area and suggested the town as an ideal, anonymous location that would keep the press at bay. While working on the mixing of what became *Perfect Strangers* at Tennessee Ton Studios in Hamburg, Blackmore and Smith came over to England to check out potential venues and settled on St. Peter's Hall. The old building had recently been taken over by a local Italian businessman to use as a private establishment called La Mamma's Club and for a couple of weeks in October '84, prior to the world tour, Deep Purple selected the Antico room to rehearse in.*

There was generally a good feeling within the band at the time; as an example, Blackmore had dinner at Gillan's house nearby. But even during this honeymoon period his lack of tolerance for indiscipline set the tone. As Smith remembers: "The first day of rehearsal was set for two o'clock so Ritchie turns up bang on two and a half hour later one of the others

---

* The timber walled building seen in the 'Perfect Strangers' video is this very place. A film crew spent some time there with the view to making a documentary, but to date nothing apart from the footage used in the video has ever seen the light of day.

wanders in, then another half hour, someone else, then 45 minutes later another strolls in. I can't remember the exact order but I think Paicey might have been the last, so by about 4.30 the last one wanders in and all that time Ritchie has just been sat there, doodling around. The minute everyone had arrived Ritchie turned round to Colin and said, 'What time is rehearsal tomorrow?' And Colin said, 'Same time, two o'clock" so Ritchie said, 'Right, see you all then,' packed up his guitar and walked out, so they were bang on time the next day."

When not rehearsing the band spent much time in the nearby Ship pub, and it was here where the author's first encounter with Blackmore took place. On entering the pub on that first evening, the guitarist was sitting with Bruce Payne and considering Blackmore's difficult reputation, the author eventually plucked up the courage and sat next to them. After offering a greeting, he asked Blackmore "What brings you to Bedford?" He replied by saying it's where his manager came from. Knowing that Payne was American, the author assumed it was a typical off the cuff remark, perhaps as a way of getting rid of him. Undeterred he tried breaking the ice by suggesting Blackmore's hat (placed on the seat next to him) looked like it belonged to Lord Blackadder. Blackmore looked somewhat puzzled by that remark, seeing as *Blackadder* was a British television programme. Initially he seemed fairly uncommunicative until the subject of his favourite band Jethro Tull was mentioned and then he started to open up. At one point Payne was resting his foot on a stool while chatting to someone. Blackmore mischievously placed Payne's drink strategically by the back of his foot, so as soon as he moved, it would crash to the ground: a typical Blackmore antic of the type the author had read so much about.

The pub was relatively empty but at one point amongst the chat, without looking at anybody Blackmore said quietly, "I think all forms of conversation should be banned." In trying to establish whether the guitarist was something of a joker and not really the doom–laden merchant portrayed in the press, the author dug his elbow into Blackmore's side and said, "Just living up to the image eh?" Blackmore turned, and started laughing.

By this point the band had already been in town for over a week and the press were now aware of where they were hiding out. Interviews had been arranged including Radio 1's Tommy Vance, and that evening the band took it in turns to talk in the rehearsal hall. However Blackmore had initially suggested they should come over to the Ship, hardly the best environment in which to conduct a radio interview. Eventually he agreed to talk later that evening at the local Moat House Hotel where the rest of the band was staying. In typical Blackmore fashion he had chosen to stay away from the others at a more secluded, traditional hotel, on the outskirts of town.

During an arranged football game the following afternoon, the guitarist lived up to his image by deliberately pushing a young lad off the ball with so much force that the boy fell to the ground! There was no referee and no one seemed to have the courage to cry 'foul' and challenge him. It was a case of Blackmore the Bully and perhaps mirrored similar actions that he claimed occurred during his days at Heston Senior School.

That evening Blackmore had been invited to jam at another pub, The George and Dragon, with a local band Los Marbles whom he joined on the old Elmore James blues standard 'It Hurts Me Too', taking over a white Stratocaster from ex-Tobruk member Steve Woodward, an old friend of Stuart Smith's. Woodward recalls that Blackmore seemed uncomfortable with the set-up at first and spent a few seconds maltreating the amp while generally cleaning the sound up. "It surprised me just how clean he played, relying on the tone of the guitar and amp rather than any pedals or effect. I remember not a word was said between us, just a smile as I handed the guitar over and a smile and nod from him as he handed it back at the end of the number. I think I was relieved that he didn't do his full stage act, and I got it back in one piece! It was an honour to see a musician I had long admired and whose playing was a big influence on me in my early years get up and play my guitar so well. My one regret is that because of that, I didn't get to jam with him."

The Deep Purple reunion tour kicked off on the other side of the world in Western Australia. Even before the first gig at the Perth Entertainment Centre, Blackmore managed to get into the local newspapers for the wrong reasons. Accompanied by Stuart Smith, he had arrived in Perth via a gruelling 20-hour flight from New York via Honolulu and Sydney. Stuart Smith: "We landed in Sydney spent a couple of days there then we went to Perth and checked into the Sheraton. We said, 'Can we have somewhere quiet, we don't want to be woken up in the morning, we're up late, we're musicians' so they put us on the top floor. Of course they neglected to tell us they had this construction starting up at seven in the morning and we'd been out partying until three and then they had jackhammers going off. It was horrible and we went down and complained. There were these signs up all around the hotel that said 'For your convenience' about the construction crew, like they're doing us a favour by renovating the hotel. It was made up like a flyer for a band. So Ritchie drew out this thing 'For your inconvenience,' but it was like a Monty Python thing saying 'Enjoy being woken up by jackhammers at seven o'clock in the morning' and he somehow got the hotel staff to photocopy about 50 of these things and he went and stuck them up all over the hotel. It got funnier from there.

"So we said, 'Look it's not fair there are no other rooms in the hotel for us, we want this to stop, at least to a reasonable hour' and it didn't. That's when one night we got to this local music store, we'd met these guys at the show and they came and played soccer, they owned a music store and they brought a drum kit and amplifiers into this hotel room. We booked a room in the middle of the hotel under the name Mr. J. Sessions. The idea was at three o'clock in the morning we were going to wake everyone up and see how the hotel liked dealing with that because they were *our* hours. A bit selfish when you look back on it but at the time it was hilarious. So three o'clock in the morning comes and we'd all been out getting plastered with girls. I was playing guitar, Ritchie was playing bass and there was a drummer and we started a rock 'n' roll thing at 3:15 in the morning and we said to the road crew who were in there with us don't let anyone in. After a couple of minutes of this the door is like coming off its hinges and Charlie the guy who was on the road crew opened the door and the biggest guy we had ever seen in our lives, just dressed in jeans comes in and muscles all over the place and just looked at Ritchie and me and said, 'I hear one more note and you're dead!' So we shut the hell up of course, this guy was huge, and it turned out this was Alfie [O'Leary, Eric Clapton's then bodyguard]. We didn't know it.

"Everyone said we had done it to wake Eric up but apparently Eric was in the room next door and we didn't know this and he was playing a show that night. He sent Alfie through and he didn't know it was us. Of course in the morning, two days later we were checking out and saw Alfie down there. Ritchie was always good about that. He went up to him and said, 'We've got to apologise about this.' Alfie said 'Don't tell me about it, I know, I was woken up by the construction as well.' So it ended well but it was not aimed at Eric. I was the one who called the journalist in. We had met at the show the night before and said 'Do you want to come in on this?'" Although the threat from Clapton's man was enough for Blackmore to quit playing, they had managed to wake up half the hotel's guests, resulting in a jammed switchboard and the appearance of security guards, a typical Blackmore stunt designed for maximum effect.

Evidence that the Purple tour was a financial success was borne out by all 50,000 tickets for the band's show in Auckland, New Zealand selling in a day. Among the highlights of the Australasian leg was the appearance of Lord's friend George Harrison at Sydney's Entertainment Centre on

December 13. Harrison, introduced by Gillan as "Arnold Grove from Liverpool," joined the band on stage for an encore of Little Richard's 'Lucille.'

Moving on to America Purple comfortably slotted back into the same level of popularity they had achieved a decade earlier, second only to Bruce Springsteen in gross income. The set played was a pretty even split between the *Perfect Strangers* album ('Knocking At Your Back Door,' 'Nobody's Home,' 'A Gypsy's Kiss,' 'Under The Gun' and the title track) alongside the expected classics ('Highway Star,' 'Strange Kind Of Woman,' 'Child In Time,' 'Lazy' and 'Space Truckin'') with 'Smoke On The Water,' 'Speed King' and 'Black Night' acting as the encores.

In addition, 'Difficult To Cure,' (Rainbow's 'Ode To Joy' adaptation) was used as the platform for Lord's solo spot but was also a clear indication as to who was the main decision maker on the choice of songs. "I'm so used to manipulating a band, as with Rainbow, that I tend to be very domineering with my thoughts," was the way Blackmore explained it to Mick Wall. "So I said, 'I think this is a good a repertoire,' and Roger looked at it and thought it was good, but wanted to add another number, I think it was 'Mary Long' … We don't do it, see what I mean? And Jon was happy to go along with the set because I think Jon was just very nervous about the whole thing anyway and not particularly into the repertoire, more just to show how it was all going to sound after so many years. Luckily, everybody feels happy about all the numbers that we play on stage which is good because sometimes, most times, there's always one or two numbers you don't like playing."

Following an equally successful trek to Japan, UK fans had to wait until June 22nd for their first chance to see the reformed Purple in action. Their one and only concert was the all-day, open-air festival held at Knebworth Park. Despite being at the height of summer it turned out to be one of the wettest June days on record. With the gig having to be performed in pouring rain, Blackmore played the entire show in his Wellington boots! On a musical level the show proved to be a success and with the media interest surrounding the reunion, the BBC took the opportunity to record and later broadcast many of the day's performances including Deep Purple. According to George McManus Purple's fee for the gig was substantial. "I don't think Paul Loasby would want to admit he went bust over the whole thing because he paid them so much money. He would have paid them a fortune. Whatever deal went down didn't work out." As with all day events there were also the scheduling problems, as McManus recalls. "I remember Meat Loaf was over running and Bruce said, 'I'm going to get that fat bastard off the stage quick. To hell with Meat Loaf, my band is going on so get him off quick.'"

Following the success of the first Purple tour and album, a somewhat surprising move was the release of a Rainbow compilation *Finyl Vinyl*. George McManus: "Because Rainbow had finished but they were so successful, and there was great interest in Japan at the time. I remember Bruce ringing me and I said how does Ritchie feel about this, he said, 'He's very behind this because he's very proud of Rainbow and he's very happy for this record to come out'." Not only did the project have Blackmore's full support, but he was also actively involved with it. His executive producer credit was a way of acknowledging his decision to go back and redo guitar parts he wasn't happy with on the original recordings. Blackmore added an entirely new solo to 'Man On The Silver Mountain' and some additional slide work to the superb live rendition of 'Beethoven's Ninth' from the last Rainbow concert. The fact that there were overdubs was not exactly publicised as McManus explains, "Bruce told me, 'Don't tell anybody. A lot of it's quite good but Ritchie's going to overdub some of the stuff on it. Although it's *Finyl Vinyl* live it's not as live as he wants it to be'."

Whether or not the Rainbow album was a contractual obligation, it distracted Purple from focusing on a follow-up to *Perfect Strangers*. Having issued a compilation (*What I Did On My Vacation*) Gillan's record company Virgin were now after a new album. Even though Blackmore had spent time on the Rainbow project he didn't view Gillan's diversion in the same light. "It's bothering me a lot to be quite honest," he told Mick Wall. "I don't think he should. He's obliged to one because of Richard Branson and Virgin Records. I think it's a very unwise move to make but he's stuck in a corner, he has to fulfil the contractual things he signed before we got together, and I get uptight about the whole thing. We're having about three or four months off and I want it to be time off, nobody should be doing anything. I don't want anybody in the group doing a solo LP because you must take time to relax; then you can come up with good ideas for the next Purple album but if you're in the studio every five minutes that's not going to help the LP that's coming next. I've always believed in that, it's always been my philosophy to keep out of the studio as much as I can so that when I do go in something really good will come of it."

With Gillan having to focus on writing tracks for his album so soon into the reunion there was already clear evidence of familiar divisions creeping in and the conflicts that had originally split the classic Purple line-up in 1973 soon reared their ugly heads. Returning to Stowe in Vermont in May '86, the sessions for what would become *The House Of Blue Light* were far more strained. "Roger and I did a lot of preparation, only to find Ritchie wasn't interested in listening," said Gillan. "It's hard to deal with that sort of thing and I didn't. Suggestions and half-worked ideas were strangled, but so long as Ritchie was happy with the guitar parts, the lads were happy. I wasn't and said so. But let's not blame everything on Ritchie ... I was a wanker too. I couldn't deal with Blackmore at all. Ritchie started getting cranky again, and I could see the nervousness creeping into everyone's eyes ..."

A classic example was the song 'Mitzi Dupree.' With Gillan and Glover having worked out a rough demo, Blackmore wasn't interested in the song and even though he added guitar to it, he refused to partake any further so the original unfinished recording is what made it to the album. Like 'Smooth Dancer' 14 years earlier, the album's opening cut 'Bad Attitude' was inspired by Blackmore, although the tone was far less vicious. With Blackmore having resided in America for the past 12 years, Gillan took umbrage at the Americanisation of his every day speech. "I hate posey expressions, I wish people could talk properly. When we reformed, Ritchie and I were playing football and we had a row on the pitch, which ended in me telling him to piss off. So he turned round and said, 'There's no need to cop an attitude' and I said, 'What do you mean, cop an attitude? Can't you speak English?' That theme just kind of developed and ['Bad Attitude'] attacks that kinda thing."

With the release of *The House Of Blue Light* in January '87 the cracks started to show, although the band were united in their general dislike of the album. A couple of years after its release Lord told *Modern Keyboard* magazine, "The management and record company said, 'It's time to do the next album, guys.' We made the massive mistake of trying to make our music current. We discovered that people didn't want us to do that. They wanted us to do what we do best. We're Deep Purple – loud, proud, pure and simple." Purple had tried updating their sound and Glover's glossy, Eighties-style production generally didn't find favour with fans or critics to anywhere near the extent that *Perfect Strangers* had. Glover himself commented, "Making *The House Of Blue Light* was a struggle between the musicians and it kinda shows on the album. You can hear flashes of brilliance, but it doesn't really hold together as an album." The record company was also disappointed with the results as McManus recalls, "The follow up to *Perfect Strangers* was always going to be the acid test ... We had a Top 10 record with the first one but then it was never quite as big as I thought it should have been. I mean it was Deep Purple, it was a blue chip name if you like and I was quite surprised. *House Of Blue Light* was number 10 and that was it, it was very quick and it was gone."

Raymond D'addario: "The whole first year and a half was pretty good. When they went to do the second album you could tell that there started to be more things going on. Ian had been working on a record of his own for a long time and he would still be working on that when they were trying to work on [*House Of Blue Light*]. But even then there was a lot of friction. With that first record everything fell into place but with the second one I think the first studio we went to we could only stay there for a couple of weeks so that wasn't working out so we went back to Vermont and we didn't have any place to go. For the first six weeks or so we really didn't do any work we just went around looking for a place to record. But you could tell that everybody had different attitudes after the first tour. They'd made money and done a really big tour for the first time in a long time. They were really hungry with the first one, the music was great, and you could tell they were really hungry, they played great and they wanted it. The second one you could tell they'd done a huge world tour made lots of money. It wasn't like they were fat cats sitting back but that edge didn't seem as necessary as it had a year and a half before. But at the same time, Ritchie was, he lived for that. 'Where's the energy, where's the aggression?' That's the kind of impression I got."

The tour that followed was also the platform for Deep Purple's next project: as the band was first and foremost renowned for its live performances the idea (from Payne) of a live album made perfect sense. In the years of Purple's inactivity there had been various live archive releases of varying degrees of worth, that eager fans invariably lapped up. Deep Purple's reputation in the early Seventies was significantly enhanced by the release of *Made In Japan*, and Payne was of the belief that with their collective extra years of experience the band could equal if not better this landmark live album. As such, several shows throughout Europe and America were recorded.

Although the tour only focused on these territories, it did include the previously untapped Iron Curtain countries, kicking off in Hungary. Although not quite as successful in commercial terms as the previous tour, it was nevertheless ample proof that Purple was still a force to be reckoned with and the frictions from the studio didn't follow them to the stage. Artie Hoar who accompanied Blackmore on the tour learnt a handy travel tip. "Never fall asleep when Ritch is behind you. I was on a plane going to Yugoslavia. I fell asleep and when I awoke, there were hundreds of pieces of tape in my hair. My doorknobs in the hotel and toothbrush had garlic oil on them, and the ceiling fan had eggs hidden

277

on top of the blades so you can imagine the mess! He was a real joker and a lot of fun."

The European tour included a date at the huge indoor Palais Omnisport De Bercy arena in Paris, to be filmed by the BBC. George McManus flew over to help co-ordinate the operation. "*Whistle Test* was going to film Deep Purple which for the record company was great – Deep Purple on TV. So we turn up and Bruce came to me and said, 'We're not going to get any TV here.' I said, 'Jesus Christ, Bruce, I'll be fired. I've got a whole crew from *Whistle Test* here." He said, 'Ian's very pissed off because [BBC presenter] Andy Kershaw said they were doing it for the money.'*

"I was shitting myself because I had a Polydor budget to fly *Whistle Test* over to France because if we get this band on TV to a younger generation we're going to sell three times as many records, but Gillan threw a wobbler so I'm there with this TV crew trying to film Deep Purple without Ian Gillan knowing." The author was present at this show and recalls entering the venue via the backstage area an hour or so before the gig was due to start and saw the *Whistle Test* crew, still unsure whether or not they would be allowed to film. Eventually Colin Hart informed them that Gillan had allowed them to film just one number from the soundboard area using only one camera, but that they were free to film the encore. There seemed a mixture of relief and disappointment among the BBC crew. Purple put on a good show and after the closing notes of 'Space Truckin'', being aware of the backstage shenanigans and as the *Whistle Test* cameras moved into place, the author sensed there might not be an encore. Blackmore was usually the culprit in such cases but in this instance, Gillan decided not to reappear, his way of sticking two fingers up to the BBC.

Raymond D'addario saw a different perspective to Gillan's actions: "That place is huge and they would finish a song and the people were clapping and we were on the stage and it was like, 'You don't like it?' Because it was so dead you just couldn't hear and Gillan was really pissed off. He was saying, 'What the fuck's wrong?' He was just incensed, he did not understand. We'd go, 'Look don't listen they are all standing there clapping. It's quiet because this place is so huge.' But Ian just said, 'No, fucking arseholes, fucking French, I'm not having anything to do with it.' And Ritchie went, 'I think they're right, look at them I think they are enjoying themselves' and

---

*The incident between Gillan and Kershaw had occurred three years earlier when Gillan and Lord appeared on *Whistle Test* talking about the reunion. Kershaw spent most of the interview questioning their motivation as being purely financial.

he said, 'Well I'm going to go out and play' but Gillan didn't want to know and the rest of the band were like 'He's not going to go out and play by himself" but [Ritchie] and the drum roadie played!"

Sure enough Blackmore walked back on stage followed by one of the roadies who took his place behind Paice's drum kit. The guitarist started cranking out the 'Smoke On The Water' riff, then stopped, held his arms out and looked around as if to say, 'Where are they?' After a brief lie down at the front of the stage, thanking the crowd, and shaking hands with the front row he then walked off. It was without doubt one of the most bizarre situations ever witnessed at a Purple show; the only time that Blackmore turned out to be the only one to do an encore, though sadly so brief it seemed hardly worth it, except that he wanted to prove a point.

McManus was relieved that the BBC crew at least got some film to take back to England, but was taken aback when Payne told him, "Ritchie's going to do an interview and I said, 'You're joking.' I couldn't believe that he would actually speak to anybody." For that moment Blackmore became Purple's spokesman when the *Whistle Test* team managed to capture a few words in the empty arena. He was surprisingly diplomatic about the encore, saying, "Rock 'n' roll is built on an edge, that's why sometimes I won't do an encore and sometimes the band will. But I refuse to be a robot. I'm a very emotional kind of person and very sensitive. Sometimes I don't play an encore because I don't feel that I want to if I don't think the audience is channelling in on something I want to think about. But tonight I wanted to do an encore so the rest of the band didn't, so it made a good change!"

Blackmore's wry humour probably went over the heads of most who saw the interview but at the same time his comments could be seen as a way of distancing himself from the rest of the band – something that continued over the coming years. By the time the tour rolled into London the more familiar scenario returned. At the second of two shows at Wembley Arena the guitarist declined to appear for the encore of 'Smoke On The Water', resulting in a watered-down rendition with Lord left to carry the entire number on Hammond Organ.

Surprisingly, he did return to perform on the encores during the American leg of the tour at Phoenix, Arizona on May 30, 1987, despite being in considerable pain from a broken finger after tossing his guitar in the air during 'Space Truckin'' and misjudging the catch. X-rays showed that the damage to his finger was such that no way could he continue playing for the foreseeable future and the rest of the tour had to be cancelled. It was a considerable blow to the band as Glover said, "I went to the hotel that night knowing Ritchie had gone to the hospital to have his finger checked out. I woke up the next morning to find no tour and a ticket home. That was so utterly depressing. I didn't even get to say goodbye to the crew."

Raymond D'addario: "It was a big tour and we were just getting started and I know that hurt him a lot. That album did what it did but it certainly didn't do what *Perfect Strangers* did. It didn't help, America's fickle like that, you can only wait so long and I don't think they went back for a long time after that. It was like they never had a chance in America after that happened. After that tour got cancelled we never really had another big tour in America. I remember that after that, whatever we were doing in the States was never as big as what we were doing in Europe."

The break at least gave Blackmore some time to spend at home. By 1987 he was living back in Connecticut in a house named 'Baskerville Hall' after the Sherlock Holmes story. That same year, while spending time in a castle in Germany, he encountered a group of musicians Des Geyers Schwarzer Haufen (later abbreviated to the more manageable Geyers) playing medieval and renaissance music, that had a lasting impact on him. In an interview for British rock magazine *Kerrang!* he spoke of his passion. "My fantasy is to form a band – a medieval band playing Renaissance music, 1550's Tielman Susato stuff. I have a good 16th Century repertoire; all I've got to do is find the other players!"

Once Blackmore's finger had healed Purple slotted in a few shows throughout Europe in September and October, with several again being recorded for the proposed live album. By February '88 the band convened at Hook Manor in Oxfordshire to wade through the tapes and select the best performances. At least that was the intention. When the author spoke to Blackmore shortly after the album's release he explained, "We would get to a situation where say four of us would be happy with a performance only, for example, for Ian Paice to say he wasn't happy with the drums, so it would be scrapped and it would go on like that. After a couple of days of this I'd had enough and left them to it."

Ironically a year earlier Blackmore had shown sufficient interest in the live Rainbow release to overdub guitar parts, but now he couldn't even be bothered to approve the performances that would be on the finished product. Deep Purple had generally taken a lasséz faire attitude to live albums so in retrospect the situation was not unusual.

Glover was left to compile most of *Nobody's Perfect*; splicing some tracks from more than one show and shortening versions of others. Many saw this as a strange decision given that there had been a sufficient amount of recorded performances available to produce a strong live document. The album also included a version of 'Hush' done 'live' in the studio during the mixing. The final product's ironic title reflected the record company's huge disappointment. George McManus: "When they came in with that live album I remember having a meeting upstairs with all the Polydor people and I couldn't wait to get out of the room to be honest. I had to bullshit Bruce and say it was fantastic when we all knew it wasn't. Bruce had got the whole company together; press, promotion and everybody else and said, 'This is the new Deep Purple live album,' and I hadn't heard it then. And I remember sitting around with everybody and people couldn't wait to get out of the room because they all thought, 'Fuck me, what's this?' because it was supposed to be *the* Deep Purple live album. It was not what the record company expected. We expected a real storm-busting album to replace every Deep Purple live album, which is impossible to do, but that was the theory, that was Bruce's theory, that this was going to do it and it didn't. Bruce thought this was going to take over from the legendary *Made In Japan* but it actually didn't do that well. Bruce thought it would be the definitive live Purple album."

Deep Purple hosted a press event to launch *Nobody's Perfect* at Frankenstein Castle in Frankfurt, organised and paid for by Polydor Germany. The venue was chosen by Blackmore, whose love of castles and mediaeval imagery appeared to become more intense with each passing year. His desire to present the whole thing as a mediaeval event was at odds with the whole Deep Purple image, and Lord declined to take part, as he told Chris Welch, "I wouldn't dress up in mediaeval gear. That's more Blackmore's territory." The others however, did join in the fun, all resplendently dressed in period costume. To add to the atmosphere, a host of typically activities, such as archery, were included. Blackmore also invited Des Geyers Schwarzer Haufen, whom he had now befriended, to play at the event. Among the journalists and media presenters in attendance was Tommy Vance who hosted a one-hour special on his BBC Radio 1 *Friday Night Rock* show as part of the album's promotion.

However the promotion could not disguise the fact that the album got a general thumbs down from the press and Gillan admitted some while later that it was an inferior version of 'Made In Japan' – the record it tried to imitate. Accordingly resulting sales were disappointing and the record company was left to lick its wounds. George McManus: "It all petered out quite quickly but the financial aspects were dealt with by the American company because they paid the money. They would be more aware of it than we were and because the live album didn't sell, people at Polydor more or less said, 'That's it. We've had a couple of albums, the live album didn't sell, and goodnight that's it.' And whatever excitement there was initially, dissipated. It was that live album. 'If that's what Deep Purple are doing these days, if that's what they regard as a live album then there's no future for us'."

Polygram was fast becoming disillusioned with the less than expected returns on their investment. George McManus: "The advance was obviously substantial and the record company had put out three albums. In general with a band if you're half a million away from recuperating with any band you say, 'Sorry lads, we've had a go and we're half a million in the red and even if we make another record we won't recoup it.' That's the generality of it. I'm not a hundred percent sure that happened with Deep Purple but it may have been a contributory factor. They would have paid such a huge advance that the first one worked in America but it was such a huge excitement and they didn't maintain it and that was maybe paralleled in the UK as well. Even though we got a number five and a Top 10 record it never really clicked as big as I thought it should have.

"Rainbow had Top 10 singles and were on the radio all the time and they had got a whole new audience of kids who weren't even sure who was in the band. In the whole record industry, despite these days singles only selling about two dozen to get to number one, it's still the biggest thing. If you get a hit single you get across to a huge audience. I'm sure many of the people who bought 'Since You Been Gone' had no idea Ritchie was in the band."

While many older fans were initially excited by the prospect of the reunion, before long some felt that Deep Purple in the Eighties didn't fit the times as they had a decade earlier. Having built their reputation on lengthy improvisations now out of vogue, Purple had tried updating their sound, particularly with *The House Of Blue Light,* but this too hadn't worked to their advantage. Divisions within the band and with the record company as to how they should progress continued to cause problems. Gillan for one wanted Purple to stretch out and become more adventurous by going for a big production in a state of the art studio. Blackmore and Lord were particularly opposed to this and were generally of the opinion that Deep Purple did things its own way by not following trends or compromising.

On the live front the poor showing of *Nobody's Perfect* subsequently had a knock-on effect with ticket sales. Following a rare warm-up club gig in Hammerjacks, Baltimore on August 11, only one of the original 20-plus dates of a North American tour, commencing in Saratoga at the end of July and continuing through to September, went ahead. The Giants Stadium, New Jersey gig saw Purple sharing a bill with unlikely bedfellows,

Aerosmith and Guns N' Roses. Despite the cancellation of the rest of the tour Lord showed bravado when saying, "There were 80,000 people there, it was lovely, I'm glad to say our drawing power hasn't diminished and that we can still be counted among the Top 5 rock bands." In truth the other bands, in particular Guns N' Roses, were riding high following the huge success of their first album released the previous year and were arguably a bigger draw in America at the time than Deep Purple. With plenty of empty spaces in the gig diary a rather hastily arranged tour of Europe, where sales of the album had been generally healthier, occurred. However even some of these European dates got cancelled and all that remained were a few Italian shows, four German dates and one in Copenhagen.

The set that had been rehearsed for the US gigs was stripped back to a concise hour and a half, with shorter solos and tracks such as 'Space Truckin'' cut down to five minutes. Ironically, despite the ill-received live album and Blackmore and Gillan's relationship once again deteriorating, the band was still firing on all cylinders. The author witnessed two of the gigs; the first in Kassel saw the band on top form with no indications that things were not exactly fine and dandy behind the scenes. The following night in Cologne Blackmore revealed why, in his view, the previous night's performance had been so impressive: "We were just pissed," explaining that, due to his intoxicated state, he couldn't remember the intro to Beethoven's Ninth.[*] Afterwards the band were very upbeat about their future with Lord telling the author of his excitement over the next studio recording with four songs already having been written including one of his own. But as with everything connected to Deep Purple nothing was straightforward.

With the friction still confined behind closed doors, Deep Purple and Polygram were also at the end of their road. "I don't think our band and Polygram saw eye to eye anymore. They didn't give us the feeling they still thought Deep Purple was a current band," Lord explained shortly after the split. With some of the staff at Polygram moving over to the German conglomerate BMG, Payne brokered a new deal. 1989 had been earmarked as the year the band would take a break from touring, for reasons again explained by Lord. "We want to make sure this album is right because we've got a new record company, an important album to make and we need to concentrate." Despite the problems between Blackmore and Gillan, it seemed that the band was on its way to putting the next record together.

---

[*] Evident for anyone who has heard a recording of the show with Blackmore playing around the riff for ages before finally launching into the piece.

"There are six semi-completed and a further half dozen in a rough state," said Lord.

The decision on where to record the next album couldn't be agreed upon. Because of diminished sales in the American market, Blackmore favoured a more commercial melodic approach in keeping with latter day Rainbow while Gillan wanted a quirkier, more off the wall direction allied to a big production and in April, during a planning meeting, he demanded they record in a proper New York studio. Blackmore's loathing of recording studios in general was supported by Lord whose now infamous quote, "The idea of recording in New York fills me with dread" met with derision from the singer. Things came to a head when Blackmore requested a session without Gillan present.

Raymond D'addario: "You almost thought that Ian wanted to be kicked out. That's the impression I got. I was living in the same house as him and I remember either the night they kicked him out or he quit, coming back from having a meeting with them and [Gillan] said he thought he'd fucked things up. That was all he said. But he was a lot like Ritchie: he had to do things his way whether they were right or wrong. Because after [the first time] he left Purple he went out and did the Ian Gillan Band and after the first [Purple reunion] tour I always got the impression that's what he wanted to do. It just seemed like the slightest thing could make him, not be dis-agreeable, but bottom out or whatever."

Artie Hoar: "I was there when Gillan got fired. We were in Vermont and Deep Purple was rehearsing. Rich and all of the other band members (except for Roger) went home without telling Gillan that he was going to be replaced. I left with Rich so I guess Roger told him he was out."

Blackmore had been the ringleader in forcing Gillan into a corner although at the time the rest of the band publicly backed his decision. "Ritchie's like a terrier or pit-bull," described Lord. "He gets hold of some-thing and won't let go. He has a vision of what he wants, and he'll fight and fight until he gets what he wants. He's rarely wrong, and if he is wrong, he'll admit it with utmost graciousness. Until he's proven wrong, he won't budge. I love him the way he is."

BMG had also been stung; having signed the classic MKII Deep Purple line-up they found their key investment had lost its recognised vocalist and unable to produce an album.

No sooner had Gillan's sacking been announced, the singer was back working on a project ironically featuring his recent sparring partner. On December 10, 1988, the horrendous Armenian earthquake disaster had left over 45,000 dead and half a million people homeless. Several people in the music business were spurred into staging a huge charity concert in Moscow and Deep Purple were mentioned alongside such incongruous names as UB40, Bonnie Tyler and Joe Cocker. Originally planned for February '89, and then put back to May with talk of satellite link-ups around the world, the ambitious project never got off the ground. Given the disharmony within Deep Purple at the time, it's unlikely they would have been in a position to commit to such an event anyway.

Instead, a charity record was proposed and the track chosen for the all-star recording was 'Smoke On The Water'. Guests musicians such as Paul Rodgers, Dave Gilmour, Brian May, Roger Taylor, Alex Lifeson, Chris Squire and Bruce Dickinson gathered at Metropolis Studios in Chiswick, West London on July 8. There was talk that Lord and Blackmore would participate, but in the event, only Blackmore agreed to do it. "I was asked if I would like to play on it, and I thought it was a great idea to do a charity project; one of the things that stirred me up was that Paul Rodgers was singing on it, and I've always been a fan of his." Despite knowing that Blackmore would be present, Gillan invited himself to perform on the track as it was his song. Any possibility that he and Blackmore might bump into one another was eliminated when the latter insisted on doing his parts last after everyone else had left the studio.

Despite Purple's dipping popularity, the remaining four elected to carry on under the name. With no particular candidate in mind several months were spent auditioning potential singers. Artie Hoar: "In Connecticut, Ritch was around most of the time and we just played soccer, went out to bars to check out different bands, and kept our ears open for a good singer for the band."

While in New York, Deep Purple arranged a charity football match against a Long Island radio station. After the game, a young blonde Candice Isralow who worked for the station was among the congregated crowd. As Blackmore was so enamoured with her beauty he despatched one of the Purple road crew to catch up with her to extend an invitation for the 18-year old to have a drink with him later that evening. They instantly clicked and discovered they shared many common interests, particularly in the spiritual realm. "We talked for hours," Blackmore recalled in 1998. "We hit it off on so many levels that we became friends very quickly. The romantic moment was six months after we first met when we got to really know each other. Then I knew she was the only one for me."

Born on May 8, 1971 in Hauppage, Long Island, Isralow was some 26 years younger than Blackmore. Driven by her parents, she took singing and

285

acting lessons from the age of four until she was 12, when she started modelling and also studied piano for a few years. At some point during her
modelling days Candice adopted the surname of Night and at 18 went to
college studying communications, which led to her work at the radio
station. For Blackmore, the next few months brought major decisions to
ponder over, both professionally and personally.

CHAPTER 14

The Battle Rages On And On ... (1990–93)

Several singers had been auditioned to replace Gillan in Deep Purple but none were deemed suitable. Two who came closest to getting the gig were Jimi Jamieson and Terry Brock. Jamieson, vocalist with Survivor was apparently offered the job but turned it down after being advised by his management it would be a bad career move. Brock, a much less well-known singer from a Scottish band Strangeways had also impressed but rumours of a clash between Blackmore and Brock resulting in the singer walking out are as yet unsubstantiated. Eventually Blackmore suggested they try out Joe Lynn Turner though initially the others were opposed to the latter day Rainbow singer. However Turner was eventually contacted.

"I got a phone call from Colin Hart and he said, 'Do you want to come up to Vermont and audition for Purple?' Because I had heard they had a friend of mine from New York, Terry Brock who was going to be the singer and I love Terry, Terry's great. And we are still friends to this day and we joke about it. Whether or not I was lucky or whether it was a curse. So I was like flabbergasted and he said, 'Rent a car, we'll pick up the tab, drive up to Vermont 4–5 hours and we're at such and such'. This was in the middle of winter in a ski resort and it was an old country club and of course they're in the bar rehearsing and it smelt of cigarettes and stale beer. I remember walking in and they were set up at the far end. As soon as Ritchie saw me he started the 'Hey Joe' signature riff from Hendrix and I just walked over to the mic and started singing it. We had a fantastic jam with everyone playing their hearts out. After that settled down that's when I got introduced to Jon Lord and Ian Paice because I'd never met them really. Then we started to go through things and Jon said 'I've got something here' and he started the keyboard intro and the next thing you know it turned into 'The Cut Runs Deep' and that same exact vocal line 'What about the heartache? What about the emptiness inside?' were exactly the first two lines I sang and that went right into the song, just off the top of the head again. Of course Roger and I evolved it later and I never forget that experience and they all sat around and said, 'You've got the job man. You've just got all the stuff that's right' and Ritchie and Roger were just nodding their heads saying, 'We told you we knew that he would fit in perfectly'."

Having spent four years in Rainbow, for Turner, the set-up in Purple wasn't a great deal different. "It was very similar. Ritchie would mostly lead it. You all looked at Ritchie and he started something up and Jon would chime in and Paicey would pick it up and so on, so it was pretty much the same kind of pattern. Ritchie was obviously the leader and it was well known. It's not Purple without Ritchie, he's the cornerstone, he's the riffmeister, he was the one that gave them that sound."

Although it was apparent that Blackmore was the musical instigator, the other musicians were not exactly hired hands and it didn't take long for a scenario to develop. Joe Lynn Turner: "There were certainly more people pulling on you – 'Here's Ritchie and Joe again from Rainbow and they're stealing the show and it's becoming Deep Rainbow.' They didn't like that at all, Roger and those guys. Roger kind of had some pals now so he sided with Paicey and Lord. I mean I can remember Jon was saying 'Love Conquers All' was shit and it wasn't a good song and I said, 'If you play it right I'm gonna sing the hell out of it and it's going to be a great power ballad so just shut the fuck up and get started.' Ritchie just turned on his stool and laughed and tried to hide his laughter. He'd wanted to say that to Jon for years. And at that point I guess I had overstepped my place but I was frustrated musically because here's the thing … Jon would never write and he'd be sitting there drinking his glass of wine reading his book listening to classical music and he wouldn't write and then he'd accuse us of being the biggest part of this Purple thing and we tried to include him.

"So I could never understand that dynamic. You want somebody's energy in it, you want somebody's input and creativity yet they're reluctant and they're not doing it. He was the most brilliant keyboard player I've ever seen. It's like Ritchie says 'It's not what Jon Lord plays it's what he doesn't play.' He's fucking brilliant. I think he was a fish out of water and he didn't want anyone to know."

Ironically, considering Gillan's insistence on Deep Purple recording in a proper recording facility, the bulk of *Slaves And Masters* was made at Greg Rike Productions in Orlando, Florida. The album drew a mixed response with some inevitably dismissing it as sounding more like Rainbow than Deep Purple. While in Rainbow Turner had his critics and these same dissenters now aired their disapproval at his involvement with Purple. Blackmore seemed nonplussed at this but it nevertheless drove a wedge between him and the other band members. Some fans felt some form of betrayal particularly when, at the time of the band's reformation five years earlier, Blackmore had told journalists that in the event of one of the classic MKII line-up departing he didn't think it would be right to continue. Because Blackmore had been the one behind Gillan's removal, although the other three didn't exactly oppose him, once again his reputation was called into question.

The 1991 tour to promote *Slaves And Masters* equally tested the loyalty of Blackmore's fan base. Not surprisingly the warm-up shows with the new line-up took place out of the media glare in the former Eastern Bloc, namely Ostrava, Czechoslovakia; Budapest, Hungary and Zagreb, Yugoslavia. Because this was a market that had been mostly starved of Western rock music, the controversy over band personnel was largely irrelevant. Another of the things that Gillan had argued over – the inflexibility of the set-list – was now seen to though the opening number, 'Burn' from the Coverdale-Hughes era was almost certainly a number Gillan would have refused to sing. The set-lists actually altered quite a bit as the tour progressed with six out of the nine tracks from *Slaves And Masters* being played at varying stages. One of the stand out tracks from the album, 'Wicked Ways', was dropped after a few shows. Joe Lynn Turner: "[Ritchie] would say, 'Well it's an epic type of number.' For us it was fantastic to play but I think the audience reaction was quite good but we wanted to get on to the meat and potatoes type stuff like 'Cut Runs Deep.' But I recall it was always Ritchie's decision. He would say, 'Could we not do this one tonight and can we kind of phase this out and this in and so on' because we were constantly trying to search and find things that were going to work. At one point we also went back and did a bunch of old stuff and had a blast doing it."

The tour moved on to France and Germany, where the shows were also greeted favourably. Although Turner recalls a good spirit within the band at this point, Blackmore invariably kept himself to himself, with a degree of tension never far from the surface between the others. "Maybe we told each other how we felt a little too much. I mean sometimes that happens when familiarity breeds contempt and I think that in ways, looking back I could have probably tempered my attitude a bit, and they could have tempered theirs. That's all said and done and water under the bridge. It's a love-hate relationship in a band that's worse than a girlfriend or a wife or any of that. Maybe you're not having sex with the guys thankfully but you still have that relationship where it's lovers and again that's exactly what it's about, so the tensions and everything you say can be taken out of context, misconstrued. Guys don't forget things like when I told Jon to shut up and play it right."

Like Germany Sweden was a major stronghold for Deep Purple but on March 1 at the Isstadion in Stockholm, the band played one of the most lacklustre shows of their career. Joe Lynn Turner: "I don't know what happened but there are moments when there's nothing coming from the band, nothing coming from the audience and that does happen. Unfortunately that happened in Stockholm, which was one of the big markets and of course you can feel it much greater when you are all psyched up for a show and you run into a bad night. It's better when you do it in a little one horse town, but it wasn't, it was Stockholm and I don't think the band had the energy, the audience was just kind of numb and cold and there was no fire and I think that scared Ritchie. I think that frightened him into a reality of 'Well that's it for me' and I think it was a lot of the other things that were starting to build up as well. Obviously he didn't quit at that point, so you have to understand these things do happen and you want to be at your best and you're not – you're at your worst."

After the show Blackmore told Payne of his intentions. "It was the worst concert I've ever done. When we played Stockholm with Joe that was really awful. I couldn't blame Joe, it was everything; it was horrendous. We just lost it; nothing, it all fell flat. I wanted to leave that night, I felt like giving the money back to the audience. I went back to the hotel and got our manager and said, 'I don't know if I want to stay in the band. After tonight it's all over.' And we stayed up for hours. I was sulking about the whole thing and the next night we played Gothenburg and we played a lot better."

During the UK tour Purple played four nights at Hammersmith Odeon, and the author caught the third of these shows. Sitting in his dressing room before the show, Blackmore appeared happy with the way the tour was going and got up to his usual schoolboy antics. Support act, all-female metal band Vixen had several stink bombs thrown in their direction from the wings, with the remainder awaiting the girls in their dressing room. Rob Fodder was Blackmore's personal assistant during the 'Slaves And Masters' tour: "At one show there was an area right at the front of the stage, next to the PA, set aside for disabled fans in wheelchairs. Not only were they in direct line with the PA but they probably only had a partial view of the stage. Before the encore Ritchie said to me, 'Get them up on stage.' There was about four or five of them, and they weren't light guys! I had to get Jim [Manngard, guitar roadie] and one by one we carted them up these stairs. They must have wondered what was going on and we put them on the stage on Ritchie's side in front of his stacks. They closed with 'Smoke On The Water' and they were wheeling backwards and forwards with the music!"

During the US leg, the band played at New York's Radio City Music Hall. "Ritchie didn't like the dressing room that had been set aside for him and wanted to be in the basement area," explains Fodder. "They rigged up a temporary dressing room down there. It was funny because this girl fainted during the show and the first aid crew took her down there and laid her out on a stretcher. When she came round Ritchie was looking over her. I'm surprised she didn't faint again!"

For Blackmore the road offered light relief from the continuing turmoil in his personal life. His relationship with long-term girlfriend Tammy Williams was under strain, and as Purple continued the second, and what would ultimately be the final leg of the 'Slaves And Masters' tour he was in a quandary whether to commit to a relationship with Candice on his return. As the band toured Brazil in August, and Poland, Greece and Israel the following month, their relationship flourished with the smitten guitarist sending several postcards back from these locations.

Deep Purple played four nights in Sao Paulo, two at the Ginasiodo Ibirapuera, and two at the Olympia. At one of the Brazilian shows, Ian Paice cocked up the intro to the opener 'Burn.' Blackmore would always sit behind the amps and give Paice the nod when he was ready to start, but on this occasion the drummer started hitting the cymbals but then looked across to Blackmore realising he wasn't ready. Lip reading Paice's response of "Oh fuck", Fodder describes Blackmore as "warming up, guitar off and Paicey has just gone into it. Ritchie wasn't too happy and just joined in with the song." In another example of always wanting to have the last laugh, during Lord's solo spot later in the set, Blackmore used the opportunity for a toilet break and headed back to the dressing room with Fodder. Blackmore cracked open some beers and as they both sat there relaxing Fodder noticed Lord's solo was about to end and the next song, 'Knocking At Your Back Door' was due to start. "I said, 'Are you going to go back?' And he said, 'Yeah in a minute.' When I kept reminding him he quickly changed the subject.

"Eventually Jon starts playing the song's intro with Ritchie relaxed in the dressing room with his feet up. At this juncture Bruce Payne and Colin Hart walk by the open dressing room and do a double take to convince themselves of what they have just seen. 'Are you okay, Ritchie?' Colin asks. 'Yes I'm fine.' 'You sure there's nothing wrong?' 'No, I'm fine, I never did like this fucking song.'" Unfazed Ritchie remained in the dressing room during the entire song as the rest of the band muddled its way through it, minus the sound of his Stratocaster.

With the tour over and with some time off, Blackmore agreed to play a rather obscure session for French singer Laurent Voulzy in 1992. "My management at the time contacted me and they sent me the tape. I went into a studio in Connecticut where I was living then did my tracks there." He contributed guitar to one track, 'Guitare Héraut' on Voulzy's album *Caché Derriére*. Around the same time Blackmore once again moved back to Long Island, naming his new home Minstrel Hall.

When the band commenced writing sessions for what would be the follow-up to *Slaves And Masters*, the very same dilemmas that had dogged Deep Purple since the '84 reunion came to the fore. Turner felt that new ideas and a new slant was required in order to make Deep Purple relevant in the Nineties, something that Paice and Lord in particular found impossible to accept: "All of a sudden I stepped in and take this legacy of this legendary band and I'm now a part of it and they felt as if they were giving away the candy store. They felt I didn't deserve this yet I thought I was pulling my weight by writing good songs and singing all this other stuff but they didn't see it that way. And I couldn't understand why – a work ethic that was very strong and motivated and they didn't respect it or consider it and all they wanted was Gillan, Gillan, Gillan. I said, 'Look I can't replace him but at the same time you could at least get on with what we have.' We did make a great album and the second one was going to be even better as far as the tracks that I have. I still have a lot of those tracks. A song called 'Stroke Of Midnight' was a real kind of dirgey Zeppelin track, a bluesy, heavy riff.

"You see another thing that was happening was that because we wanted to elevate the band, Jim Peterik from Survivor and 38 Special, he wrote all these great songs, we called Jim in to co-write some stuff, just flying with the material. Jim was such a great writer. Roger was of two minds, one he liked it and the second he was siding with Paicey and Lordy so it was really just a mess at that point and I just remembered getting to an impasse where we just weren't seeing eye to eye about anything."

Glover, Lord and Paice were of the opinion that Turner's style clashed with theirs as Paice summed up: "He comes from an American pop background and we've come from a European rock 'n' roll background." Normally Lord, by his own admission had "gone with the flow" but for what seemed like the first time, the three united and gave Blackmore an ultimatum.

Joe Lynn Turner: "I remember the call coming in. I'd gone to visit my family down in New Jersey from Woodstock. I got the call saying 'You're out of the band' and I was relieved. I remember not even feeling sad about it. I was just relieved that I'm done with this. It was just overwhelming my whole life at that point. And I really just wanted out because it was all about just cattiness and jealousy and envy and bad negative things. There was a big power struggle going on, they felt like they had this interloper of sorts. The first year they were all for me, the second year they were seeing it as Ritchie and Joe, we were getting a lot of crossover with Rainbow fans. People are weird, man, egos are fragile for some people and it took its toll."

Although Blackmore had a soft spot for Turner, a couple of years later after the singer's dismissal he admitted to Swedish journalist Anders Tegner, "[Joe] always wanted to copy other bands and we don't even listen to other bands. He was always coming to sessions saying. 'Motley Crue do this …' and we were saying, 'Who? What are you talking about?' He's caught up in the now. I think he referred to Jon Lord actually … this is a good quote: 'You're yesterday and I'm tomorrow.' So now when I see Jon, I say 'Hello Mr. Yesterday!'"

Glover, Lord and Paice worked on getting Gillan reinstated, but Blackmore had his heart set on Mike DiMeo, vocalist with American band Riot. "I was given Ritchie's address by a friend of mine who told me that he was looking for a singer. Somehow he told me that Joe wasn't in the band and he told me to send something to him. I sent him some things when he was still living in Connecticut, just a couple of songs on a cassette I'd done with Riot. He was very taken by a cover of 'Whiter Shade Of Pale' and he called me up two days later, as soon as he got it and told me how much he liked it and said he wanted me to go into a studio with him. So I went into a studio in Connecticut with him and Roger. I worked mainly with Roger on a couple of songs. The songs I worked on had different lyrics and melodies but they were eventually recorded as 'The Battle Rages On.'

As far as DiMeo recalls all the backing tracks had been completed. "The tracks that I sang on had lead solos and they sounded finished. Looking back on it I spent a day in the studio with Roger and we worked on these songs and I did some backing vocals on this track that I sang lead on. Basically I sung the songs maybe one or twice. This was just so they could get an idea of my voice and I think more so than that, it was really Roger trying to give

Ritchie a little of what he wanted, showing that he was at least giving me a listen. I don't think there was ever really a time when the band was going to go with anyone but Ian Gillan.

"The next day their manager Bruce called me up and said, 'The situation is Ritchie wants you in Purple' and his words were 'He has a tendency in getting things he wants but there's going to be a little bit of' ... I was 22 years old at the time and I think the guys were generally around 48 years old and I think there was a little hesitancy because of my age and also because they were getting pressure from the record company at the time because it was the 25th anniversary and they wanted to reunite the MKII band."

During the time DiMeo spent in the studio, Blackmore typically left Glover to deal with the situation while he sat in the studio's lounge area with Payne. In 2002 Glover recalled, "Sometime before 1993 Ritchie did want to try out a singer and he and I went into a studio in Norwalk, Connecticut to see what he sounded like. I wrote a few lyrics and he sang over the backing track to what would later be called 'One Man's Meat'. It was called '24 Hours' and although it was okay, it wasn't too great. At least I wasn't convinced enough to pursue it any further. Ritchie really liked him however. I didn't know that he was in Quiet Riot [sic] and I don't know what was said between them." As well as being given the role of middle man, Glover had flown to England to spend three days working in the studio with Gillan. In a 1995 US magazine interview, Glover said, "I had two cassettes, one with Ian Gillan on it, and the other with this guy. There was no comparison."

Both camps dug their heels in. Blackmore was still holding out for DiMeo while Glover, along with Lord and Paice, was adamant that Gillan should be rehired. Although DiMeo was still occupied with his band Riot, "after a month or two I would say to Ritch ... I wasn't trying to pressure him but I was trying to find out what was going on. One time he told me that Jon had said something like 'I'm not going to get on stage with a 23 year old guy' or something to that affect. And Ritchie seemed to be, 'What difference does it make as long as the guy sounds good.' I respect him for trying. I was hoping that the situation was going to work out but I had a feeling at the time that it was a little bit ill-fated. What happened was BMG said they wouldn't release the record or something if it wasn't the original line-up, that's what I eventually got but it took three or four months of me sitting around waiting to hear what was going on. Eventually when I did have a talk to Ritchie he told me the record company really wanted to release the record with the original line-up for the 25th anniversary. I assume that something made him do it and I don't think his heart was really in it at the time. The only information I got at the end when it was apparent I wasn't going to do it was from Ritchie himself. I don't remember him being happy, let's put it that way."

Joe Lynn Turner: "The story is that Ritchie held out for months and months and they were trying to find other singers besides Gillan but nobody was cutting it. Finally BMG came in – 'We'll offer Ritchie like a couple of million dollars if you get Gillan back in, then you can start Rainbow over again.' And if you look back in history that's what happened, they came out with that album, he wasn't even talking to Gillan."

By late 1992 when Gillan rejoined, the record was way behind schedule which required him to write new lyrics while recording vocals over the existing tracks in a Munich studio. Having completed his parts on the album, Blackmore left Glover to work with Gillan. It was the first time Deep Purple had made a record without the entire band in the studio at the same time. "They'd finished all their bits," said Gillan. "Ritchie turned up. We went out to dinner a couple of times; he had a couple of games of football and went home. Jon Lord turned up – same thing without the football. Ian Paice showed up for a day." It was also the first time the band had elected to use an outside producer in the shape of Thom Panunzio. "I was in this club in Florida and I heard this track by Joan Jett," said Blackmore. "It had a very big sound to it and it was done by Panunzio, and it was so loud so I thought maybe we should use him."

The aptly named *The Battle Rages On* was released in July 1993, with powerful, hard-riffing numbers like 'Nasty Piece Of Work', 'Ramshackle Man' and the title track recapturing Purple's sound from the early Seventies but brought up to date with a modern production. One of the standout tracks was 'Anya,' which saw Blackmore using acoustic guitar for the intro.

Glover recalled the aggravation he went through as co-producer to get the finished results: "We had written the song but didn't have an intro. One afternoon Jon played an intro and when Ritchie walked in that night he asked, 'What's that?' 'That's the intro.' 'Nah, shit.' 'What now?' I thought. 'Is there an acoustic guitar nearby?' Ritchie asked. The studio belonged to Peter Maffay and there was an acoustic guitar. Ritchie doodled around and I said I liked it and why didn't he go ahead and we'd see what the result would be. He played and played, at least for 40 minutes and no words were exchanged in the control room. He played whatever entered his mind, stopped, thought about it, went on playing and meanwhile the tape kept rolling.

"The next day in the studio Jon asked me what Ritchie thought of his intro. 'He didn't want to have anything to do with it, but he did some guitar parts and now I have this idea.' For four hours I went through all the things Ritchie had done in those 40 minutes and chose three or four pieces. Those I fed into the computer in a distinct order and proposed Jon to work around his intro from the previous day and to fit it in with the guitar parts. That's the story of the 'Anya' intro, which cost me almost a complete day of work. It was cutting and pasting instead of live, but I think it turned out very well."

'One Man's Meat' is often cited as the weakest track on the album, utilising the 'L.A Connection' riff from Rainbow's *Long Live Rock 'n' Roll* album that had also been revamped for 'Tite Squeeze' on *Straight Between The Eyes*. Blackmore resurrected the riff for the third time on this track originally written with Turner, entitled 'Stroke Of Midnight'.

Although a vast improvement musically and production wise on the previous two efforts, most were of the opinion that *The Battle Rages On* fell short of expectation. Blackmore certainly had mixed feelings about it, saying that the original recordings with Turner were vastly superior – in particular the original versions of what became 'One Man's Meat' and 'Time To Kill.'"That was shaping up to being a good LP without the vocals – if you heard just the backing tracks they sounded really good. Then when the vocals got put on …" It was evident Blackmore had lost all interest in Gillan's style and being at loggerheads with the rest of the band and the fan's demands, he was in a no win situation.

Shortly after completing *The Battle Rages On*, Blackmore and Gillan both agreed to be (separately) interviewed by Swedish journalist, Anders Tegner, for the television show *Metall Magasinet*. In his interview Blackmore openly admitted the behind the scenes conflicts: "The rest of the band wanted Ian in. It was not my idea, I wanted to bring somebody else in but I was voted out. The other three said let's get Ian back. I said I'll go along with it and see what happens."

In other interviews from the time, Gillan was equally candid: "Maybe in a few years time we'll be sitting here asking, 'What was the reason for the last break-up?' We'll put it to the test on the road. It depends how well the tour goes down and that depends on the guitar player. He is, as you know, an unusual sort of person. He's not only cancelled almost everything to do with the launch of this record,[*] he's not even heard the songs yet. But those

---

[*] The only promotional press item for *The Battle Rages On* was a jigsaw featuring cartoon drawings of the group!

kind of eccentricities are all part of the game. The bottom line is the man can play.

"I wonder what prank he's up to next, what huge obstacle he is going to put in our path next? If we can't get around it, that will be the end of the band again. But if we can climb over it or smash our way through it, then we will proceed."

Inevitably the ensuing 25th anniversary tour was going to be potentially confrontational. Gillan told Tegner, "I'm going to travel separately, I'm going to have my own dressing room, and I'm going to see [Blackmore] for two hours a day as we walk on stage. If I see him just looking down to the ground as he does sometimes, I'll just get on with it."

"Although none of us will ever be the best of friends offstage, it's an explosive gelling of individuals, which hits the button on stage and record," Blackmore diplomatically told *Raw* magazine. Considering that at this stage the two had spent virtually no time together since Gillan's return, the mutual feelings of animosity were already threatening to boil over.

Before the tour began it was announced that Deep Purple were to receive a Nordoff Robbins Silver Clef lifetime achievement award at a prestigious London ceremony. Gillan, Glover, Paice and Lord arrived in London with Blackmore agreeing to fly over on Concorde from New York in time for the ceremony, tying in the visit with a planned Thames boating holiday. Rob Fodder booked a vessel only to find out after an angry call from Paice that Blackmore had changed his mind at the last minute, claiming to have an ear infection that prevented him from flying. With the organisers adamant that the whole band had to appear in person a last minute alteration was made and the Bee Gees received the award instead.

The justifiably annoyed members made public their feelings, particularly Glover. "I was thinking of going to the launch to yell out a protest. We had all really been looking forward to getting our award." The band had yet to appear on stage since Gillan's return and Blackmore's actions were already causing problems. When asked the reason for his no-show, he responded in typically cynical fashion, "We were only going to get an award for turning up!" In Fodder's words, "I don't think he really cares that much, but I know that I would be pissed off! He turned down awards, much to the annoyance of the other Deep Purple members. With reference to the choices he made, I think his record speaks for itself. He would make a decision on something, which would seem questionable, but always had this uncanny knack of working out for the best in the end."

Matters weren't improved when the proposed American tour was cancelled. Despite an official explanation claiming that the dates were being put back to follow the album's release, in reality poor ticket sales was closer to the truth. The Eighties had seen a boom in the heavy rock market but a downturn had started by the early Nineties. Purple's strongest markets of Europe and Japan thus became the only dates on the 'world tour,' but when the first date in Turkey was cancelled due to the political situation in that country, the Greek shows were pulled as well.

On September 21, the band convened in Bregenz, Austria for rehearsals that were filmed and recorded by MTV for its *Headbangers Ball* show. Gillan and Glover were also interviewed and Glover, ever the eternal optimist, suggested the tour "would go a long way to cementing the good feeling within the band again." Only time would tell how accurate his prophecy would be.

After a full run-through at the venue the day before, the first gig on the 37 show, '25th Anniversary' tour got under way at the Palaghiaccio in Rome. It didn't take long for reports to filter back that the friction between Gillan and Ritchie was manifesting itself on stage. At the Italian shows 'Strange Kind Of Woman' was performed during the encore and on previous tours during the guitar/vocal duet they would often break into an impromptu performance of 'Jesus Christ Superstar,' a song that Gillan had sung in the original cast recording. However on this tour every time he started to sing it, Blackmore completely ignored him and refused to play along. Not surprisingly it was dropped from the show as the band moved throughout the rest of Europe.

After the initial bout of reunion touring back in 1984/85, some critics accused Purple of going through the motions but thanks to the onstage tension no such criticisms could be made during the '93 tour. Without doubt Blackmore was the catalyst. His natural gift for unpredictable improvisation took the shows to heights not seen or heard since the halcyon days of the early Seventies. In addition it looked as if he had a point to make, not least to Gillan.

Rob Fodder: "Those initial shows they were talking [to each other] but I don't know if Ritchie was embarrassed with the way Gillan was talking. He was ass licking a bit. After the show we would run to the dressing room and lock the door because we knew that Gillan would be banging on the door. If we didn't get to the dressing room in time Gillan would go up to him and say, 'Ritchie you were brilliant tonight, that's the best I've ever seen you play,' you're really on form' and inside I think Ritchie was cringing. But after a while we would leg it, and shut it and not answer the door. I think he got the message after a few shows."

When the author spoke to Gillan on Purple's 1996 UK tour the singer confirmed that he would go out of his way to compliment Blackmore after the shows. On one occasion he said something along the lines of 'You were really cool tonight' and that Blackmore's response was, 'Cool? I didn't think anyone used that word anymore.'

At times the music was so dynamic that it was almost as if Blackmore was trying to blow the rest of the band – or at least Gillan – off the stage. In doing so, the whole band seemed to feed off the passion that Blackmore was putting into his playing. Lord in particular was playing with so much more commitment than he had on previous tours, as Lord stated shortly after the tour, "The shows were done at an energy level and ability level I've rarely seen attained before. I think we played as well as we've ever played." Because of the hype surrounding the anniversary the thought of journalists having to eat their words might have been at the back of their minds. Although the set list didn't deviate, except the occasional change in the encores, the way the band played each night certainly made it seem as if different songs were continually being played. Blackmore would often throw in brief renditions of various songs from Purple's past plus a few classical tunes. At some shows, a bit of 'Rat Bat Blue', 'The Mule' or 'Wring That Neck' would be thrown in, other times he would start to play 'In The Hall Of The Mountain King.' On a couple of occasions the whole band joined in for a couple of minutes before getting back into the planned song.

The author caught up with the tour in Cologne, and in the afternoon Blackmore and his entourage organised a five-a-side football match within the large Sports Hall. Blackmore was wearing a Liverpool shirt who were being sponsored at the time by a company called Candy, the name of his new girlfriend. For a change the author played in the opposition's team and at one point in the game decided to shield the ball to determine whether Blackmore could execute a fair tackle. Unable to get the ball, he started kicking the author calling him a bastard and after the game, told him "You play a weird game, you hold onto the ball for too long." The experiment confirmed Blackmore's highly competitive, stubborn nature, even in a casual game of football.

Later Gillan arrived and headed straight to his dressing room. With one of the crew already mentioning how bad the tension was between Gillan and Blackmore it was no surprise that the singer didn't look happy. Fodder recalls a brief verbal exchange from around this time. "In Germany Gillan came up to Ritchie in the bar at the hotel and said, 'I've got a new way of shaping my voice, it's not going to suffer during the tour.' So Ritchie said, 'Oh really? So you won't come up to me and say, 'No 'Child In Time' tonight?' 'No that's my song. I'll never come up to you and say that.' But he did in Cologne, but Ritchie still played it."

The bad feeling wasn't soothed by the guitarist instructing Fodder to attach lyrics to Gillan's mic stand. "Ritchie was getting fed up with Gillan forgetting the lyrics to some of the songs. In the dressing room before the show, Ritchie asked me if I knew the words to the track 'The Battle Rages On', which I did and then he told me to write them out on sheets of A4, which we had taped together. My instructions were to tape them to Gillan's mic stand, just as the lights went down and the intro tape started. Gillan walked out, noticed the lyrics, tore them from the stand and threw them away. He didn't look too impressed!"

It set the scene for the whole gig. During Blackmore's solo in 'Knocking At Your Back Door,' Gillan carried on singing and as Fodder recalls, "During this show I noticed that Gillan would stand in front of Ritchie and jump up and down as he was soloing. However, Gillan hadn't noticed that Ritchie had switched his guitar in 'Smoke On The Water' and proceeded to trash it within inches of Gillan's feet, causing Ian to jump out of the way!"

As the tour progressed Blackmore's desire to deliberately antagonise Gillan became increasingly obvious. Rob Fodder: "Whilst driving in Germany, Ritchie pulled a tape from his bag and put it in the player. The intro to 'One Man's Meat' started, but this was actually the 'Stroke Of Midnight' demo with Joe Lynn Turner on vocals. It had a great bluesy sound to it and just flowed a lot better. Ritchie contemplated giving it to the sound guy to play just before DP came on stage." Each night the performances ranged from very good to sublime with the best shows being Munich and Stuttgart. Luckily both were recorded for a live album, *Come Hell Or High Water*,[*] released the following year. After the Munich show Glover told the author, "We always know if it's going to be a good show when Paicey starts the intro to 'Highway Star' and Ritchie starts doodling over the top of it."

At Stuttgart (the last German show) Blackmore played an incredible improvised solo in 'Anya' and as the song finally concluded nearly 15 minutes later the whole band stood applauding — something the author had never witnessed before or since. Blackmore had also developed a quiet, melodic preamble to 'Smoke On The Water' and by the time of this gig he had taken it to new heights, playing around with the melody for what seemed like ages. Despite the friction within the band, musically this was as good as Purple could ever hope for.

---

[*] Only parts of the Stuttgart gig were used, plus one song from Birmingham.

The tour then moved on to France and Switzerland. Rob Fodder: "Air France had gone on strike, so we had to charter a plane to take us from Paris to Zurich. There was so much weight from the band, entourage and the luggage that we had to leave the stewardess behind. We just helped ourselves to rolls and champagne during the flight. We also flew from Geneva to Innsbruck. Unfortunately the airline had mislaid Roger's bag, but promised to deliver it to the hotel when it had been recovered. Later that night the band decided to go out on the town for dinner and drinks, but Ritchie, Candy and I stayed in the hotel bar. An airline rep arrived with Roger's bag and Ritchie looked at me with a mischievous look on his face. Instantly we both had the same idea of 'claiming' Roger's bag on his behalf. We put the bag in my room and just happened to forget to tell Roger about it for a day or so. He wasn't amused."

Although Blackmore and Gillan rarely crossed paths, Blackmore took the opportunity to play a prank on his adversary in Austria. Rob Fodder: "It was a weird hotel because the doors opened out from the room. We'd noticed that the maids would come round and bang twice on the door and enter the room. We heard Gillan ranting. The maid entered his room and he was bollock naked or something and chased her out of the room. So Ritchie and me got her trolley. It had all the soaps, shampoos, towels and that stuff and we put it in front of his door and started banging the door. Ritchie's run into his room, I've run down the stairs. Ian's opened the door which hit the trolley and knocked everything everywhere."

Despite the positive reviews, Gillan's unprofessional habit of forgetting lyrics and the actual quality of his voice was something Blackmore found increasingly difficult to tolerate. Raymond D'addario: "Ritchie stopped speaking when Ian couldn't sing and he tried to contact Bruce and Bruce wouldn't take his calls, he wouldn't answer the phone, he wouldn't call him back. So Ritchie spent that whole tour just fuming and Bruce wouldn't talk to him. He was just travelling around with Rob and he was pretty isolated sending faxes to Bruce and he'd never hear back from him. Ian was awful, his voice was shot, he had a really hard time and he'd be on the stage singing, Ritchie would stop playing and Ian's voice would be there just hanging in the air. And especially if he came over to Ritchie's side of the stage he'd just stop playing and Ian would go nuts. He could hear how he sounded. He was never big on monitors because he didn't want to hear himself but his voice was croaky. He'd go out and drink all night having a great time and he was sick the next day."

Gillan naturally saw things completely differently: "[Ritchie] was putting himself out on a limb and distancing himself more and more. You could see the fury was building up. I can't say I didn't take a small amount of pleasure out of it." A decade later, in an interview for *Metro*, Gillan recalled, "When we were on the road I'd say, 'Hello Ritchie. How you doing? Nice one, mate, great solo tonight,' and he'd never utter a word to me. He'd turn his back. He basically could not cope with the fact that he was not in complete control. So it caused him to become a little unsettled."

The Prague show marked Candice Night's debut vocal performance, providing backing vocals during Beethoven's Ninth, though off stage and down in the mix. More significantly, with her encouragement, Blackmore told Fodder he was leaving the band. "I remember being in the car going back to the hotel after the Prague show and Ritchie turned to me and said, 'I want you to be one of the first to know, I'm quitting the band.' He looked as though a ton of weight had been lifted from his shoulders."

When arriving at the hotel Blackmore wanted to get hold of a typewriter to formally transcribe his resignation but as one could not be found he resorted to a hand written message and called Colin Hart to his room to deliver the news. Hart had the job of telling the others who had convened in the bar area. Apparently as Hart read out Blackmore's decision to quit at the end of the European tour from the scrappy piece of paper there was a stony silence and looks of shock. Glover's belief that the tour would go a long way in papering over the cracks in the band was not the case.

Raymond D'addario: "What I remember most is they've got a humungous tour of Japan after this and cries of 'We're going to sue him.' I kind of got the impression they were glad. On that tour it was Ian who had most of the problems – his voice was shot. It didn't take a rocket scientist to see that but I always got the impression the band was more angry with Ritchie than with Ian and I could never understand why. Granted beforehand he said it would probably end up like this but I always got the impression they were angry at him and all he was doing was not talking. Bruce was not talking to him, he wasn't talking to Ian, who's he going to talk to?"

As the band flew to Belgium, Blackmore was up to his usual tricks as Fodder recalls: "On the plane going to Brussels, Ritchie had decided to play a prank by disappearing. We eluded our pick up at the airport, jumped in a taxi and went to a totally different hotel. The management had no idea where we were or even if we were in the country and it seemed that there was much relief when we did contact them the next day." In Holland the bitterness between Blackmore and Gillan reached new depths when according to some eyewitnesses the singer apparently went for the guitarist with his mic stand. The actuality was not quite that way but during 'Smoke On The Water', Gillan continued singing during the guitar solo. When it came to the crowd participation part towards the end, with Gillan in full flow and encouraging the audience to sing, Blackmore went to the front of the stage and proceeded to play his bass pedals loudly and discordantly. At this point Gillan took hold of his mic stand and gestured as if he was going to throw it at Blackmore, but nothing more than that.

This particular petulant act could be attributed to what had occurred earlier that day as Fodder explains: "Before the show at Rotterdam, Ritchie had found out that Mr Udo, the Japanese promoter, had not been informed that Ritchie had quit and would not be performing in Japan. So he took out the Japanese work visa from his passport [along with mine] and tore them up in front of Bruce to show that he meant it and that there was no going back.* He then phoned Mr Udo personally, apologised that he wouldn't be going and told him the news. Obviously, the crew knew that something was going down and Ritchie wanted them to know that there was a possibility that the Japanese dates would get pulled because then they could look for other work instead of just being dumped at the last minute."

By the time of the first UK show, no formal announcement had been made so it appeared to be business as usual during the first date at Manchester's Apollo, with the band producing a professional show with no signs of in-fighting. The next concert, the first of two nights at London's Brixton Academy, started off agreeably but Blackmore appeared to quickly lose interest. The next day he was involved in a football match in Fulham's Hurlingham Park against a team of journalists from *Kerrang!* magazine and after the match he told a few fans present the show that night would be better. Once again Purple was firing with intensity, Blackmore directing the band, extending songs at will. Even the press couldn't help but review the band favourably although there was a downside. Rob Fodder: "At the second Brixton show, Ritchie had slipped because of the dry ice used during 'Highway Star' and had severely damaged his ankle. A doctor was called before the NEC gig; he strapped up the injury and actually advised that they should cancel the show."

Despite this, the final UK show at Birmingham's NEC went ahead as planned. It was also being filmed for a possible video release though

---

* Blackmore's personal fee for the six Japanese dates pencilled in for early December was reportedly $150,000 a night. To turn down almost a million dollars for one week's work reveals the extent of his disillusionment.

Blackmore had been more in favour of capturing one of the earlier German shows, pointing out that Gillan's voice would be in better shape. The film company was insistent on filming the tour's final night so Blackmore consented on the understanding that no cameras be allowed on stage. After the house lights dimmed, Paice's familiar drumbeat hailed the beginning of 'Highway Star.' However something seemed afoot as the intro continued for longer than usual and after a while it was apparent Blackmore was nowhere to be seen. Eventually the other four decided to launch into the number. Come the guitar solo and Blackmore eventually appeared on stage, during which he picked up a glass of water from atop the keyboards and hurled it at a camera stage right. As Gillan was just in front of the camera, banging away at his conga drums, it seemed to many as if it was being aimed at him but Blackmore's accuracy ensured the camera got a soaking. The guitarist continued to wander on and off stage during the opening two numbers but there was no more drama, although disappointingly some numbers, particularly the outstanding 'Anya,' were kept to a bare minimum.

In light of this it's ironic that Blackmore should accuse Gillan of a "lack of professionalism." To this day the camera soaking is still one of the most talked about incidents in Blackmore's career and fan forums on the Internet regularly discuss the motives and reasons behind it. The man himself merely reiterates that he had instructed no cameras to be on stage: "The incident was in no way directed towards any member of the band, certainly not towards the audience. I had already made my mind up to leave Deep Purple for reasons of my own. I was told by my management that BMG wanted to film the show at the NEC. I agreed to this providing there would be no cameramen on the side of the stage, (I find they put me off my performance; many of you that are paying your hard earned money should not have to put up with this). I would have thought I had made my point clear enough at the California Jam. I was quite categorically told, 'Don't worry Ritchie, they won't be there.' As the intro to 'Highway Star' started I walked out only to trip over one right in my way. I pushed him off the stage – he should never have been on in the first place – then I told the people working for us to get him off the stage. At this point they snuck him around to the other side, which, had they done this in the first place wouldn't have bothered me, but by then my temper was up, I threw the water. It is a very nerve wracking experience to play a show like this. I feel I have earned the right to have a set-up which will enable me to give my best to everybody."

Rob Fodder: "I went to tell Ritchie that the intro tape was playing and that he had a couple of minutes, and he told me to get the cameras offstage. I went back on stage and told a cameraman who was between Roger and

Jon that he'd better move offstage. He then proceeded to break down his camera and move off. I went back to get Ritchie and we walked to the stage. When we got there, we saw that the cameraman hadn't left at all. Ritchie calmly turned around and walked back to the dressing room. I ran back on stage and told the cameraman again [in not very friendly terms] that if he didn't get off, he'd be risking the show. Again I went to the dressing room to let Ritchie know that there weren't any cameras on stage. By this time the band were well into 'Highway Star.' Ritchie walked out on stage and joined the band. Then he noticed that the cameraman had just moved in to the shadows behind Jon, he picked up the water by the keyboard and threw it at the camera, not Gillan, not Jon, or even the band members wives, but definitely at the camera. Not many people know that in between 'Highway Star' and 'Black Night', Ritchie ran behind the amps with a beer and soaked the cameraman again as he was wiping his equipment. Ritchie blames management for the whole thing, as he had stipulated that there weren't to be any cameras on stage."

Backstage after the show Glover was livid with what had gone on, informing the author:"I can't tell you now but one day I will write a book, it will be a proper book, not like Ian's book, with all the shit in, and what went on tonight will be explained." Stories abound that the rest of the band believed Blackmore manufactured the situation as he had just been handed a solo contract from BMG; his way of saying "I don't need you guys anymore."

After the Birmingham show the news leaked out of Blackmore's imminent departure. Had the whole enterprise dissipated two or three years earlier most fans could have accepted it a lot easier but on a good night the band could still cut it. The way in which Deep Purple MKII finally imploded was seen by some as an example of Blackmore's worst character trait as Paice said, "It breaks my heart. Every three to four years there's this self-destruct mechanism that goes off."

The tour concluded with four concerts in Scandinavia, all continuing in the previous high standard. At the penultimate gig in Oslo, during a particularly aggressive 'Smoke On The Water,' Blackmore trashed his guitar for the last time and left it to reverberate as the band left the stage. After the final show in Helsinki he stayed on stage for a little while longer to shake hands with the first row and then headed back to the hotel. Ever the diplomat, only Paice spoke to Blackmore back at the hotel, saying, "I think you are making a mistake but I wish you all the best anyway." Once the dust had settled, Lord later commented, "He's an utterly difficult man to deal with but I wouldn't swap any of the times I had with him," before pausing to add, "a couple of odd ones when I ran off stage and wanted to punch his lights out."

Blackmore's departure was never intended to signal the end of Deep Purple and although the initial reaction was one of doom the band continued with Joe Satriani deputising for a few months, followed by a more permanent replacement in Steve Morse. While most of the crew remained, Blackmore retained his guitar technician, Jim Manngard, P.A. Rob Fodder and production manager Raymond D'addario.

The decade of being reunited with Deep Purple had generated a financial comfort zone that could have enabled Blackmore to rest on his laurels. But the old hunger to create something different was still there.

CHAPTER 15

Rainbow Rising – Again (1994–97)

In 1994, Blackmore also broke away from long-term manager Bruce Payne and his company Thames Talent and signed a new deal with Legend Artists Management run by Joe Boyland who also set up a new publishing deal while handling the messy business that resulted from the breakaway. According to Boyland, Blackmore also signed a multi-album, multi-million deal with BMG.

For his next venture Blackmore initially wanted to get away from the Rainbow tag, calling the band Rainbow Moon (citing Moon as his grandmother's surname!) However BMG pressured him to stick with the more commercially viable brand name. With the entire band consisting of new faces it could hardly be construed as a reunion. "I really didn't want to call it Rainbow," told *Guitarist* magazine in 1996. "But the record label assured me that I had fans who would buy the record if it was by a band that was related to me. Hence Rainbow."

Raymond D'addario: "Back in the early days it was a band. When Ronnie and Cozy were there they had authority but with the last band it was Ritchie's band and he hired people to be in it basically."

The new-look Rainbow was mainly American and of the four musicians recruited, ex-Warlock keyboard player Paul Morris had originally auditioned when David Rosenthal was taken on in the early Eighties. The others; drummer John O. Reilly, former Virgin Steele bassist Rob DiMartino and former Praying Mantis/Midnight Blue vocalist Doogie

White were all entirely new faces. For White, a Scottish Blackmore fan, it was a dream opportunity to front a band led by the guitarist he cited as his greatest musical influence. It was thanks to Candice Night that he landed the job after she had listened to a tape among the many that Blackmore had received over the years from hopeful musicians.

Having closely followed Blackmore's career White was fully conversant with his considerable back catalogue, and more importantly, his reputation. White soon saw the ruthless side of this when Blackmore became disillusioned with DiMartino. Instead of politely informing the bassist he was no longer required he chose a more humiliating way as White recalls, "I don't think [Ritchie] particularly liked his girlfriend. Then Rob threw a big party at his house for joining the band. I think Ritchie just thought he was getting a bit above himself so early on." Blackmore then proceeded to put greater demands on DiMartino during rehearsals that the bassist was unable to meet. "Ritchie would say to him, 'Do it like this.' 'I can't.' He got more nervous and went outside to smoke and of course when he came back in he was stinking of smoke and Ritchie would be [deliberately] coughing." It continued until DiMartino finally broke. "Rob said to me, 'Let's go down to the local pub, I'll buy you dinner and we'll get drunk because I'm going home tomorrow I'm not putting up with this shit.' Rather than just say to the guy 'It's not working, you're not playing it properly' that was Ritchie's way of doing it."

While treating DiMartino with contempt, Blackmore was the complete opposite with White: "He instilled confidence. When I watched him take Rob DiMartino apart he would come up and say, 'You did very well then.' He would build your confidence. 'That's good, keep doing that.' So you got more confident. We jammed for days and we recorded everything. There must be hours and hours of jams and he's got it all because he didn't want anything getting out. He was pissed of with the sessions from *Slaves And Masters* getting out. When Rob DiMartino was leaving he had Jim go through his bags to make sure he hadn't nicked any tapes: its just paranoia. He always thinks someone is out to get him and he won't be told, and you can't defend yourself against someone like that. We were looking to replace the bass player, and Paul Morris had this mate, and we all went to a club. Candy was there, sitting on a stool drinking and Ritchie and I have had a couple of beers and Ritchie came over and said, 'What did you say to Candy then?' I said 'Nothing.' And he said, 'You did.' We left it for the rest of the night and he came up to me and said, 'Sorry it was another Doogie who told her this thing.'"

Greg Smith was brought in as replacement for DiMartino and with the line-up complete, the band rehearsed for what would become the new Rainbow album.

Doogie White: "We went to Cold Spring in upstate New York for six weeks in autumn '94. That was the best of times. We played music everyday for six weeks and I taped every moment. I was never as happy as that time. I never had any run-in's with him except one time we were jamming. It was a really good jam and we were doing this vocal guitar thing. He was going up and I was going up, it was really rocking and he hit this note. I said, 'Ah fuck off, I can't sing that.' He just took the guitar off, put it on the seat and walked away. I was like, 'Oh my God, what have I done? Should I just pack my bags now?' He never said anything and in the morning it was soccer time and I was shitting bricks. I was talking to Paul Morris. 'What am I going to do? He's going to send me home because I swore at him.' I took him to one side and said, 'Look I'm really sorry with my use of language with you last night' and he said, 'I never noticed anything' and I was like, 'You bastard!' That was the first time he got me. He was making a point. Not that he wouldn't come and speak to me about it but that he knew I would get what the drift was."

Blackmore spoke about the rehearsals shortly after they were completed: "We went into this big house in upstate New York. We lived together and we just broke the music up there. John O. Reilly, who used to play drums in Long Island, I heard about him and was particularly interested in his time keeping. It was very steady. He's not a showy type of drummer; he is more of a timekeeper, which I think is very important. It's very hard to find a drummer in these times that plays in time. So to me it's the first thing a drummer should be able to do. But it's very hard to find a drummer."

Having played in bands full of top class musicians Blackmore's comments suggest he was struggling to find musicians of the calibre he expected. Doogie White heard stories of his regular dissatisfaction with drummers and their lack of time-keeping. "If you speak to any of the drummers who have worked with him, with the exception of Bürgi he says they are all out of time. There was another guy who came in. I don't know whether he auditioned for Rainbow or not before John O. Reilly. But I remember being told that he had said to Ritchie 'It's not me that's out of time, your time-keeping isn't any good.' That was a 'You can just pack up your drums and leave now' situation."

Ensconced in the bleak and cold surroundings of upstate New York, recording started on January 7, 1995. Doogie White: "We would all get together at about midday and Ritchie would start jamming. We would all join in and the idea would develop. If the rest of the band were jamming and Ritchie came in he would not participate and wait till we stopped, which was almost immediately and begin whatever idea he had. All the musical input was via Ritchie. I was left very much to my own devices to cultivate a melody and lyric as he went through the song with the band. I would be recording everything because it became apparent that ideas were worked on and then lost because we had moved on to something else. We had a break for dinner around 7 pm and stop when the wine ran out around 1 am. Other days we would play football. We started off just throwing ideas together, jamming for hours but as we went on and we had certain songs, he became more focused on the kind of more melodic tunes that he wanted."

Pat Regan, who had worked as an engineer on Deep Purple's *The Battle Rages On* and *Come Hell Or High Water*, was brought in to produce the album. "[Pat] did some live stuff and I liked him with Purple," said Blackmore. "I heard some of his other stuff he's had recorded. He is a great musician. He knows how to oversee a band. It's the first time I've worked with a producer. I usually worked with just Roger Glover or somebody that's just a mixer. He helped me a lot, because he knew how to correct Doogie and to keep Doogie in line. Sometimes I wouldn't know what to tell Doogie, how to approach a song and how to sing it best. He came in very handy. I tend to write an arrangement and then do the music. I make sure that the song is gonna work but then I don't stick with it. I tend to go off for a walk. Then it's good to have someone who stays and carries on with my train of thought."

Blackmore aimed to capture as live a sound as possible. "I'm used to having the microphone six feet from my cabinet. Pat recorded me with the microphone very close with hardly any echo. When I first heard it, I didn't like it. But he said, that the closer it is mic'd the more beef, more meaty the sound, more heavy. And it's true. I liked the guitar having echo on it. I don't like my guitar to be too loud. I play loud but I like to be mixed in with the band. A lot of people said, 'We can't hear your guitar!' But I didn't want it too loud. I like the guitar to be in context."

Doogie White: "Of course Ritchie decided that the sound in the lounge area below my bedroom where I worked was just perfect for his rhythm guitar parts on a couple of songs and I had 400 watts of Marshall blasting for eight hours during the night." As far as White is concerned Regan's production was too glossy. "We were doing the album and I got a phone call saying you need to get a publishing deal. The management then phoned me up and said, 'No you need to sign with Ritchie's publishing and why are you taking so long on the vocals? That's 23 days. We think that you are doing this so you can stay and get more wages. I went to Ritchie and said, 'I've just got a call from the management. They think I'm deliberately holding up the recording of the album.' This was just before his birthday and we were due to fly home on the 19th of April, so I said, 'You pay me up to the 19th and you won't need to pay me again if that's what you think is going on here.' He went, 'I know it's not you that's holding up this record.' There were times I was really friendly with Pat but there were times when I could have strangled him because he wanted it absolutely perfect and I didn't think that was what we should have been doing. If you can go in and record *Rainbow Rising* in two weeks, come on!"

Although it was a far less democratic process than the original Rainbow had been, in truth the new musicians, with the exception of White weren't writers. Even though Blackmore was open to song ideas that White brought in he appeared to have specific reasons for not using some of them. "We did a song that was one of the songs I gave him on the demo tape called 'Until Tomorrow,' which was a Midnight Blue, slow bluesy, in a sort of generically Whitesnake kind of way.

After three months in the studio *Stranger In Us All* was completed. According to White, "Only two I can remember that were recorded from these sessions did not make the record. They were 'Rich Cheese Salad' Ritchie's ballad … get it? And 'Wrong Side Of Morning' which was a reworking of an old Midnight Blue song called 'Until Tomorrow'. It was felt that we should only record songs that would be on the record so that, as has happened in the past, the record companies can't release reissues with songs that the band or artist felt were not appropriate in the first place."

The album included a couple of remakes; the Yardbirds' 'Still I'm Sad' that had been done as an instrumental on the first Rainbow album and 'In The Hall Of The Mountain King', the Grieg composition Blackmore had first heard courtesy of Nero & the Gladiators back in 1960, recording his own version of it for Derek Lawrence in 1965 and playing it at shows on the last Purple tour. Candice contributed lyrics and backing vocals to several songs including the stand-out track 'Ariel,' which Blackmore originally ear-marked for an acoustic project he was considering.

With a revitalised Rainbow occupying his time and thoughts, Blackmore turned down an invitation to appear in a Deep Purple edition of the BBC 2 TV series *Rock Family Trees*. Virtually all the past and present Purple members took part and despite his non-appearance Blackmore still came across as the central figure. Roger Glover: "His presence looms over practi-cally everything. He's searching for something that turns him on and I don't think he knows what it is. He's a brilliant guitarist, one of these odd people that God pointed a finger at and said, 'You are going to have something that nobody else has got.' He's got that otherworldly quality. So much so that it's almost to the point that it destroys him. Maybe he can't handle how gifted he is, maybe that's why he is weird."

Shortly before Rainbow went back on the road in September 1995, the story emerged that Reilly sustained an injury playing football so a replacement drummer was found in Chuck Bürgi (who at the time had just spent four years in Blue Oyster Cult). Although happy with the finished album, Blackmore was already showing signs of despondency, telling Neil Jeffries: "I'll see how the Rainbow thing goes, depending on whether people want to hear any more Rainbow. I'll leave it up to the audience. I'm finding it harder and harder to be inspired by just playing loud. I'd rather just sit down with a guitar and play."

Stranger In Us All was released in Japan that same month and in Europe in October to a mixed response. Grunge and alternative rock acts like Nirvana had driven out traditional heavy rock bands, particularly in America but in Europe and especially Japan, the new-look Rainbow was still capable of filling 5,000 capacity venues, in some cases the same, larger places that Purple had played. The live set consisted of several songs from the new album, mixed with several numbers from the earlier line-ups, along with Purple's 'Perfect Strangers' and 'Burn.'

After four days of dress rehearsal in Denmark the new-look Rainbow played their first gig in Helsinki, Finland – ironically the city where Blackmore had played his final show with Deep Purple two years earlier. During the first few gigs White got carried away in his enthusiasm at being on stage with his hero. When it came to Blackmore's guitar solo during opening number 'Spotlight Kid,' the singer announced, "on the guitar Ritchie Blackmore.""I remember him coming to me after that and saying, 'Don't introduce me Doogie, people know who I am.'"

By and large the tour was a great success and in trademark fashion there was the occasional show without an encore. Doogie White: "He pulled the Brussels encore because he and Candy had a fight in the hotel but nobody knew that, she was supposedly ill but they'd had a bust-up." In Hanover the band played in an old U-Boat factory that had been converted into the Music Hall; one of the more unusual venues where in another part of the building next door, a rave was taking place. "We'd finished our set and everyone was leaving and the house lights went on and he started playing 'Black Night.' Everybody rushed back on. I'd got my trousers off. We did 'Black Night' and then we finished. Backstage you could hear this rave music and you couldn't go anywhere. This is where he and Rob were very creative together so Rob told someone to turn the rave music off for at least half an hour so we had complete silence with all these folk freaking out in the rave club."

The tour included some highly memorable shows, including Düsseldorf, filmed and broadcast by German TV and a truly standout show at the first of a brace of gigs at Hammersmith, the only UK gigs on the tour. Blackmore has often admitted he doesn't enjoy London shows, which in his view are normally overrun by journalists, waiting to put the knife in, plus the usual array of backstage liggers. However on this occasion he pulled out all the stops in a three-hour performance that included improvised versions of 'Mistreated' and 'Rainbow Eyes.'

Doogie White: "He could pull out a gig like that when he really wanted to. Although I know he will deny it, he did that because my family and my father were there, and I know he did that for me because I witnessed him do exactly the same thing for Greg Smith when his wife and family were at a gig. He pulled out a blinding show, and was very gracious and fun. But that was the side I saw most of. I never saw the bad tempers and the mood-iness because by the time it was all falling apart he was isolated from every-body."

This Hammersmith show is best remembered by all those who attended for a 'fan' taking it upon himself to liberate Blackmore's guitar from the front of the stage after he had laid it there to feedback at the end of the main set. However the culprit didn't get far and was persuaded to bring the guitar back to the stage. It was a highly surreal sight as he walked down the aisle with Blackmore's Stratocaster above his head but even more bizarre was the fact that his actions were rewarded with an after show pass.

Midway through the tour problems were developing with Rainbow's tour manager that to this day Doogie White still finds extraordinary. "We had a tour manager, and he and his wife were Jewish and they converted to Christianity. This is going to sound like one of these made up stories and if I read it I would think it was made up. With this guy no one was allowed backstage: 'You can't have any guests backstage, no one is allowed on the bus.' But there was one time when we were in Germany and we wanted to go and play football. It was a Sunday, nowhere was open and I said, 'You need to get the car for Ritchie, you need to get it now.' He said, 'It's not time to go yet, he'll go with the rest of us' and Ritchie heard this. That was the guy's last hurrah. Joe Boyland had flown in to see how the tour was going because Ritchie wasn't getting on with this guy. Joe had come in to calm the situation down and have this guy and his wife removed. She was sup-posed to be the co-production manager and one of her jobs was to do the laundry but she wouldn't do the underwear because it was against her beliefs. What's the point of having someone do your laundry for you if you've got to end up going to the launderette yourself?!

"We were in the Stuttgart Intercontinental and this guy has been fired. Joe stayed until we got Harald Kohl in who was brilliant. He had worked with Metallica and Garbage. Then something happened and Joe came to me and said, 'Will you speak to Ritchie he's just fired me.' 'What do you want me to do?' 'Tell him it's a mistake!' I couldn't get involved."

With the departure of Boyland, Blackmore was briefly without a manager. He first offered the job to his assistant Rob Fodder but with Fodder having no experience and knowing full well how demanding Blackmore could be, he turned down the offer. He then offered the job to Candice's mother, Carole who, perhaps as a way of distancing herself from the family association adopted the surname Stevens as her professional moniker. Stevens also had no previous experience in management, be it rock 'n' roll or any other industry, as her job was a school teacher. To outside observers it was a most unusual move on Blackmore's part.

Raymond D'addario: "Carole didn't know the business as well as a manager who had done it all his life. She was taking guidance from Ritchie. What I always found with Ritchie – you've got to be careful to do what he means and not necessarily what he says. There's always a fine line knowing what he wants and you can do it the right way or the wrong way. Carole didn't know anything other than Ritchie saying 'Do this' and she didn't know if that was how to do it or how not to do it. What toes to step on and what toes not to step on. Because Ritchie said do this she would do it, it didn't matter what it was. You need to get this done but there are ways of getting it done so it was hard for me to deal with her that way. I always found it really easy to deal with Ritchie because I felt that when he said something I understood what he meant. She was so inexperienced that instead of doing something the easy way she would do it the hard or awkward way. Ritchie's not a businessman he's a musician."

In that respect Stevens couldn't be blamed for any shortfalls that arose. Apart from the matter of song publishing Blackmore had never shown any real interest in the business side of things. To some extent he hadn't needed to, but his misplaced trust and lack of business acumen had occasionally backfired on him.

Directly after the European tour, Rainbow moved on to Japan where nine gigs were played between the 11th and 23rd December, with venue capacities holding between 5–10,000. Blackmore was now in a position to pull in even more money, creaming off the lion's share of the box office takings and merchandise sales while the rest of the band were simply paid a wage.

Doogie White: "The change in the band came in Japan when Candy and I went to see the Eagles and they came on dressed down and opened with 'Hotel California.' Where do you go after that if you are the Eagles? She obviously went back to Ritchie and told him, so that next night [at the NK Hall, Tokyo Bay] he came on with a cut up T-shirt and we did 'Smoke On The Water' third song in. That was the last gig from that tour."

During the first few months of '96 Blackmore spent time working up demos for six songs with Candice for an acoustic album, provisionally titled *Medieval Moons And Gypsy Dances*. After being invited to make a contribution to a Shadows tribute album, along with Pat Regan and Candice, he recorded an interpretation of 'Apache' using slide guitar at Creative Sound Studios on Long Island.

Following the success of the first tour, Rainbow went back on the road in late June with nine dates in the relatively untapped markets of South America with a show in Chile, two in Argentina and six in Brazil. Knowing full well that White was a big fan of the older material Ritchie offered him the option of doing 'Hunting Humans' from *Stranger In Us All* or 'Mistreated' which the band had toyed with on the previous tour. Needless to say, White chose the latter. After concluding the South American tour in Rio De Janeiro, a mix of European outdoor festival shows and indoor gigs followed. Candice had been sparingly used to provide vocals to the closing section of 'Ariel' from the side of the stage on the previous tour, but now her boyfriend appeared intent on pushing her further into the spotlight. Doogie White: "When it came to the next European tour they were going to take photographs of us at the first gig, which was a big festival gig and interview us and he would only do it if Candy was in the photographs and if Candy was going to be interviewed. That was when it all started to fall apart."

During the tour, Blackmore recorded one of the most unusual and surprising sessions he has ever done. Fifties crooner Pat Boone had agreed to the rather bizarre novelty idea of an album of heavy rock songs by the likes of Metallica and Black Sabbath arranged to suit his style. Among them was a version of 'Smoke On The Water' arranged Latin style, which worked surprisingly well. Blackmore was asked to contribute to the song and to the utter surprise of many he agreed. "I've always looked up to Pat Boone; I listened to him in the Fifties, when I was going to school, and when I was asked to play on one of his modern recordings, I considered it an honour. It's great to be able to play on an album by someone who inspired you

315

when you were growing up. But it's amazing how some people are so narrow minded in their thinking. If someone has long hair or has a leather jacket, they're automatically a villain. That kind of bigotry has been around for years, and it's sad."

Blackmore also said later that his main motivation was because his father was a fan and would have been pleased to see his son on a Pat Boone record although he could never have imagined that the crooner would be singing a song written by his own son. With the backing tapes shipped to Europe, after a show in Vienna, Blackmore went into a local studio and rattled off a solo that was more reminiscent of Carlos Santana than his own distinctive style.

Blackmore's interest in the paranormal had not diminished over the years. Rob Fodder remembers being involved in a particularly bizarre séance. "We were in a castle in Austria and had been out for dinner. Candy put letters around the table and we found that the glass moved easily around the table and we were straight in. This girl gave us her name, age, and said that she died in an accident first off and gave us the name of the boat. We dragged it out of her that she was murdered but she wouldn't give the murderer's name. After so long with your hand on the glass your arm starts to ache and the glass was going round the letters that quick. Ritchie said, 'I'm going to have to take my hand off and you shout out the letters as we hit them and we'll break the sentences up.' We then decided to have a break and turned the glass up and Ritchie said it was a good connection. There was this old wardrobe and we were chatting away and suddenly the wardrobe went bang like a drum and it was empty. We all jumped and Ritchie said, 'Is that you Rosemary?' And it went bang again. He said 'Don't worry we will be with you in a minute' and we turned the glass up and started again. In the end it got really tiring and he said, 'It's been great contacting you and chatting with you.'

"It was right by my bedroom where we held this séance, then there was another two rooms and [Ritchie and Candice] were in the far end. The next night [Ritchie] got this dental floss and put it on my lamp and ran it all the way along to his room and said, 'If you hear anything in the night just give it a tug and I'll come and try and take some photos.' When I woke up in the morning I saw the slack in this dental floss slowly being pulled and I quickly untied it from this lamp and got a piece of paper and wrote 'Help me!' on it and tied it on the end and watched it go all the way through these rooms. I heard him get hold of it and burst into laughter. Of course he was waiting for the crash with the lamp on the floor to wake me up. The next night we had Candy's brother there. He was a sceptic, just playing around and the

316

atmosphere changed. We had the girl to start with but then it changed and we had this other spirit come through. Ritchie again was taking notes. I took my hand off and it was just Candy and her brother and he just asked a stupid question and it spelt out D-E-A-O. It was a totally different vibe and the spirit spelt out 'Don't mock' and I thought here we go. And Candy goes "oh it's Ronnie Dio" and the glass went straight off the table! That's when I said 'Enough is enough'."

Even without spiritual intervention the three-week tour had its fair share of ups and downs. At a gig in Bremen on August 2, after a fine version of 'Temple Of The King', Blackmore fell off the back of the stage. "He fell off the stage and landed on his head," says White. "I just remember saying, 'Where the fuck is he?' At the back of the stage there was a curtain and he thought there was more stage behind it but there wasn't – just a 12 foot drop and I was singing away and Raymond is saying, 'Stop, Ritchie's fallen off the stage,' and he's tangled up in all this scaffolding. I announced, 'If you speak English tell your German mates, Ritchie's fallen off the back of the stage and we'll take 10 minutes to see if he's alright and we'll be back.' He had a shot of Johnnie Walker and he was fine after that."

Rob Fodder: "He was lucky because he could have really hurt himself. He was a bit shaken and it was lucky the guitar didn't get smashed up."

The following night's gig involved a 450-mile trip south to the small German spa town of Bad Wörishofen. According to Fodder, the local promoter was trying to find ways to cancel the gig only hours before it was due to start. "I don't think the ticket sales were that good and it was quite a big venue. He said, 'If you don't want to do it don't worry, we can pull the show.' We were going from one promoter in the north to another in the south. The plan was that the band would go overnight on the bus whereas we would fly from Amsterdam and from there to Munich. We got to the airport and Candy realised she had left her passport on the tour bus. I went up to Customs and Immigration and explained we wanted to go out and come back in. They phoned up Amsterdam airport and said they would let us do it. Then Ritchie realised the first plane we were going on was a prop and he doesn't like props and wouldn't go on it. So now we were in the shit because we had to get down to Munich. I phoned the local promoter and said 'Don't send a driver to Munich I'll let you know what the plans are.' That's when he said about if we wanted to cancel it. 'No we don't.'

"Luckily I had a Lufthansa timetable and I worked out we could fly from Bremen to Frankfurt and there was a 30 minute slot to get a flight to Munich and it was our only chance. I explained everything to the promoter and told him to have a car ready at Munich airport. But he was saying it could take three hours to get from the airport to Bad Wörishofen." On arrival at Munich airport there was no car to collect them but undeterred Blackmore, Candice and Fodder took a 70 mile taxi journey to their destination. "We were there in about 45 minutes and we saw the promoter and I just said to him pay the taxi."

Despite Bad Wörishofen being a town that attracted pensioners and rheumatic sufferers, Blackmore had no intention of cancelling. Twice during the show the PA cut out completely, leaving the band to flounder along in the large hall with nothing but Chuck Bürgi's drums audible. Eventually Ritchie walked up to the mic and apologised to the fans. "I've heard some bad PA systems but this is the worst system we have ever worked with. Thanks for listening. You're great. Just bear with us as this sound is so awful but you're great." Rather than walk off, Blackmore perversely chose the opposite, determined to keep going under the adverse conditions and even ended up doing a four-song encore.

The final gig in Copenhagen involved a run-in between guitarist and singer. Doogie White: "We were headlining to 15,000 people at an outdoor festival. [Ritchie] cut my monitors at the front of the stage so I couldn't hear anything. I went over to Raymond and said, 'What the fuck?!' 'He told me to do it!' So I stood at the side fills, right in front of Ritchie, then he cut them as well. All I could hear was the band. After the show he came up to me and said, 'So what was all that out of tune singing for?' I said, 'Well you cut my monitors.' He grabbed me by the throat and said, 'You're not a singer, you're a fucking monkey' and he slammed me against the wall. It was the last gig of the tour and I don't know what was going down but I said, 'I'll take that as my P45, and he said, 'Take it anyway you like.' As I was leaving I was signing things as 'Doogie White, ex-Rainbow.' By the time we had driven back from Copenhagen, Carole was on the phone. I said, 'He just threw me against the wall so I figured that was his way of saying he doesn't want me anymore.' 'No, no it will all be fine.' And it was, we went over and did the American tour, and I said we can't carry on until I know what the fuck that was all about. He said, 'You tried to hug me!' I said, 'Nah I didn't, let's just forget it.' He said, 'Yeah, if I didn't want you in the band I could have Ronnie Dio or Joe Lynn Turner or anyone. I want you to be the singer for now'."

Rainbow's American tour in 1997 involved a two-month tour of small clubs, commencing on February 20 in New Jersey and concluding on the West Coast in California on March 19. Rob Fodder: "I was surprised with some of the venue sizes, but it seemed the norm for the rock circuit at that time. However, most of the venues had a capacity of over 1,500 and up to

3,000 in some cases. Ritchie didn't seem concerned about the smaller club venues. He just went on stage and did the business."

The tour almost didn't happen at all as Doogie White explains: "The phone rang at about four o'clock in the morning, and it was Ritchie's management on the phone … 'The tour's cancelled. Chuck Bürgi's left the band … we're gonna sue him …' he's this, he's that. And so I tried to calm Carole down. I said, 'You know, we can sort this out. There's still four weeks to go before the tour.' There were only about two weeks, actually! Two weeks before the tour. 'Get another drummer!' So I phoned Chuck, and he said, 'Look, man, we'd been promised so much work with Ritchie over the previous year that never materialised. I've been offered a job that's gonna see me right through this year and also probably next year.' So I wished him good luck." Perhaps out of a sense of guilt Bürgi recommended John Micelli, who was then working for Meat Loaf.

Doogie White: "I turned up for rehearsals – they had rehearsals for a week before I got in. I went in and had two days' rehearsal. Micelli had never heard Rainbow or Deep Purple! He was a rock fan, but he'd never heard them. It was a difficult situation for John to come into, nine days before we were due to start the first gig. He and the great Greg Smith worked like crazy to get it all into shape. John is more in the Cozy Powell vein. He isn't jazzy, like Bürgi was. So it changed the whole swing in the band. I thought he was good for the band."

The obstacles leading up to the tour didn't bode well, but this didn't seem to bother White: "I had never toured in America so I was fired up. We had had it postponed in '96 and had been six months off the road so it was great to be back. Of course because Chuck quit it was not the best of starts. Only Raymond and I were there at rehearsals to unload the truck as the rest of the crew were delayed because of bad weather. But Raymond and I just mucked in and got it done.

"We fired the sound guy early on. The sound was killing us. It got so bad, Ritchie was all for calling the whole thing off in Rhode Island, three gigs in. I sat with him after the show for quite a while and managed to convince him that if we got a new guy on sound, we would be business as usual. We had to dig deep during those first shows, as it was impossible to hear a thing. Add to this John Micelli being in the band for five minutes. We were under rehearsed and it took a few shows to get into gear. Eventually we got rid of this sound guy, and we got an excellent engineer called Tim Lawrence. Great sound engineer.

"We were right in the middle of the grunge explosion and classic rock was not doing as good business as it had done or indeed is doing now. The

319

shows were all sell-outs and we did the best we could given the dodgy rigs and monitor systems. It wasn't Europe or Japan that's for sure but the audiences still came and made a lot of noise." The smaller venues provided some security issues as Fodder recalls: "In Schaumberg, it wasn't until I saw the venue that I noticed that there was no stage door. So, to get Ritchie into the venue, we had a few security guys stand around him, covered him with a coat and walked him straight through the bar."

As far as White was concerned the incident in Copenhagen between he and Blackmore had all been forgotten – but not entirely, as it turned out: "He saw how much it annoyed me so now he knew what he could do to get me. I hardly had any monitors and I sung really badly on that [American] tour. He would always fuck with you. He'd go in and trash your bed or your room: 'Did you sleep well last night?' 'Well you know you let off the bat alarm, you know you put a Hoover in my room and kept switching it on, otherwise I slept very well.' The kind of things he used to do. He would put a tape under Paul Morris' bed with a two hour cassette in it and there would be 59 minutes of the tape with nothing and then this blood-curdling scream for about five seconds, then nothing. Paul would be completely freaked out. [Ritchie] shampooed my bed with all his shavings from his beard. I jumped in my bed and it was like 'Oh no!' So I went into the bathroom to have a shower and all the towels are in the bath filled with water: nasty but funny though.

"It was all part of the 'I'm in Ritchie Blackmore's band and he's playing tricks on me, isn't it brilliant?' I never felt there was any malice in what he did. Even when he threw a meat clever at my door because he was up so everybody else had to be up and he threw a tin of cat food and it hit the door and I completely ignored it. When I got up in the morning there was a meat clever stuck in my door and three tins of cat food lying on the floor. I just left it like that."

Apart from the sound problems, the American tour was beset with illness and the entire band appeared to contract some mysterious virus. Doogie White: "Just as we were gathering momentum, Greg got sick and then I got sick. Pretty soon we were all ill. I lost the middle section of the tour. I have no memory of it at all: a combination of the sickness and the medication. My voice was shot to bits. Ritchie was flying between gigs. We were on the bus, so the illness just kept going round and round. The air conditioning in the hotels did not help either. But there were lighter moments and some good shows but other things were starting to get in the way. We soldiered on ... Ritchie got it ... So we were all ill! Ritchie said to me, 'I've never had anything like that in my life before.' It was totally devastating."

Rob Fodder: "It didn't start off the best of tours. Everyone was sick at sometime or another and it wasn't until we hit the sunnier climes of Albuquerque that our moods picked up. Amazing what a bit of sun can do. Pat Boone was present at one of the shows in LA and Ritchie wanted to invite him up to sing 'Smoke On The Water.' Unfortunately, or perhaps fortunately, Pat had left by then."

Apart from these few moments of fun, the tour had been less successful than the '95 and '96 shows and the band was fragmenting. Blackmore had already suggested *Stranger In Us All* could well be the last Rainbow album. In an interview with Neil Jeffries he stated: "If they don't want to hear anymore I'll go hey and knock it on the head because this next project I'm very excited about because it's a big change. It's completely different from the hard rock thing." Blackmore was referring to the acoustic album he and Candice had written and recorded after *Stranger In Us All* and before the American tour, under the project name of Blackmore's Night.

Doogie White: "Ritchie was wanting to go out and do his Blackmore's Night thing, but had some kind of obligation to try and promote the *Stranger In Us All* album in America. He was bringing people on the bus and playing the Blackmore's Night album. My agenda was still the same – I was enjoying being the singer in Ritchie's band. And Paul was trying to be as glamorous as ever he could be, and fuck as many women as he could. And Micelli was saying, 'Fuck – is it the bridge next?' And so it really just wasn't working."

The reviews the author's own publication *More Black Than Purple* received from US fans suggested the inspiration was still there but for many of them, it was the first time they had seen Blackmore live for many years so by and large it was a case of preaching to the converted. Doogie White: "Ritchie raised his game yet again. Whether the band was as good as it had been in 1995/96 is debatable, but he played brilliantly because he knew that he was gonna have to cover for everybody else, 'cause we were all so ill. There was a suggestion early on in the tour that at the end he would take a break from the band and concentrate on 'Candy's album' as he called it. But on the bus, when we were on our way to the airport after our final show in the USA in Palo Alto, he said, 'I'm going to do Candy's album and tour it and then we will go back into the studio and do another record.' This lifted my spirits a wee bit as I had not had a good tour due to illness and might have the chance to redeem myself – if one can redeem themselves in Ritchie's eyes'."

* * *

321

The Blackmore's Night album *Shadow Of The Moon* was released by BMG in Japan on April 23 and proved to be an instant success, selling 100,000 units in its first two weeks, quickly reaching number 14 in the national *Billboard* chart. It was certainly the most radical recording Blackmore had done, combining the medieval and renaissance sounds he was so enamoured with alongside more traditional pop and folk styles. As an indication of how comfortable Blackmore was with the project, he agreed to make a documentary style video for BMG Japan, which included three performance clips and an interview at his home that gave fans a rare glimpse into his otherwise private domain. Apart from discussing the album, Blackmore can also be seen in his music room talking about his guitar collection, something it would be hard to imagine him agreeing to during Deep Purple and Rainbow's heyday.

In light of Blackmore's current preoccupation it was surprising that a European Rainbow tour was lined up so shortly after the US dates, to include Russia, Greece and Poland. Two dates were confirmed for the latter country at the Arena in Poznan on May 10, and the following day at the Spodek, Katowice. The promoter even had posters printed up for these gigs but for reasons never fully explained the tour was pulled with the exception of the final gig headlining the second night of the two-day Esbjerg Festival on May 31.

The first (Friday) night was headlined by Blackmore favourites Jethro Tull while the opening act on the Saturday bill was the Peter Green Splinter Group, who at the time included Cozy Powell. The author happened to be on the same flight over as Green's band and Powell told him that he hadn't seen Blackmore for several years and was looking forward to hopefully meeting up with him over the weekend to relive old memories. By pure coincidence the two ended up staying at the same hotel and were happy to see one another again, spending hours reminiscing. They also discussed and agreed that Powell would jam with Rainbow on the final encore number of 'Smoke On The Water' the following evening.

On meeting Blackmore that first night it was apparent to the author that he was fixated on Blackmore's Night as the first thing he asked was, "Have you heard the new album?" enquiring if he had spotted the melodies of Flemish Renaissance composer Tielman Susato. To all outside appearances Blackmore was treating the Rainbow gig as a mere side issue. Due to the strict curfews placed upon the festival organisers, the plan to finish with 'Smoke On The Water' had to be abandoned. However Powell was insistent on planting the seed for a possible future collaboration. Rob Fodder: "Cozy came up to me at the Esbjerg show and asked me to tell Ritchie that 'if he was up for it,' so was Cozy. I think that Ritchie knew that a reunion could have been possible, but maybe saw it as a backward step."

As the band came off stage at the end of the show, new contracts were given to them to sign, which among other things would have allegedly resulted in a reduction in wages. Doogie White: "I remember my final conversation with him. I said, 'Look I speak English, you speak English if you've got a problem come to me because I can't deal with Carole,' because Carole wouldn't talk to you; there was no negotiation. She just talked to you like you were an imbecile or a school kid. He turned round to me and said, 'Carole is my right hand man [sic]. If you don't like it you can fuck off.' And they were the very last words we ever spoke. I didn't expect him to come and talk to me. I was just trying to get him to speak to his management and ask them to stop being so unreasonable."

This partly explained why other European shows pencilled in for later in the year didn't eventuate. "The band was over after Esbjerg. I won't bore you with the details it was just business stuff," White continues. "People have speculated about what happened but they are generally wide of the mark. If Ritchie knew what was being done in his name, then he showed no indication that he cared. There was no room to negotiate with management. It was take it or leave it so I quit after I got back. Believe me I tried to contact anyone who would talk with me and no one would. Ritchie was on a promo tour for Blackmore's Night so there was no way to speak with him. I will always be grateful to Ritchie for taking a chance on me. He believed and I believed and we worked well together, did a pretty good album and played some amazing shows. The only problem was that he stopped believing!"

The contract issue could well have been Blackmore's deliberately oblique way of ending Rainbow, knowing full well the members wouldn't accept what was on offer. With *Shadow Of The Moon* selling well in Japan, if he was looking for the catalyst to move away from heavy rock to predominantly acoustic music, then he had found it. Whether or not it was the right move from either a critical or a long term financial standpoint seemed not to matter. Blackmore was on the verge of making the most radical change in his career.

CHAPTER 16

Play Minstrel Play
(1997–2000)

By the late summer of 1997 *Shadow Of The Moon* had been released throughout Europe and was generally well received by the usually cynical music press. Although the album centred on melodies from Renaissance composers, in particular Tielman Susato, it certainly covered a wider gamut of styles than many expected. Nor was it entirely acoustic, electric guitar featured on a few tracks. One of the album's strongest songs, 'Play Minstrel Play', based around a Pierre Attaingnant melody, featured Jethro Tull's Ian Anderson on flute. Although his style would have been out of place on a Deep Purple or Rainbow record, it fitted neatly into Blackmore's Night.

Shortly after playing on the track, Anderson spoke about it to Dave Rees for the Jethro Tull fanzine *New Day*: "He sent me a tape a few weeks ago, and asked me to play on an album that he's making of medieval music. So he sent the tape with a guide track, I played it and sent it back to him, and just said, 'Good luck,' you know, 'Thanks for asking me to do it and I hope it goes well.' I thought no more about it until a few weeks later when customs at Heathrow called me to say there was a strange package there for me. 'We had to open it and it appears to be a very large hand gun from a Mr. Blackmore!' Ritchie's idea of a gift for playing on his album was a thumping great shooter, which was not the most sensitive thing in the wake of

Dunblane …* Eventually I managed to get it out of customs and into safe keeping. Not in my home alas because doubtless the new laws would prevent me from keeping it even as a souvenir. But it was a nice thought … that's Ritchie you see. It could have been … well, anything, knowing Ritchie!"

Candice Night told Mark Welch for *More Black Than Purple*: "We ran into [Ian] on May 31 in Esbjerg, Denmark and afterwards we met up with him. And it was really funny, because in the room backstage talking with Ian, Ritchie was thanking him for basically playing on our album and doing an amazing job. And Ian just looked at me and said, 'You know, you've brought out the pussycat in Ritchie!' which was so cute to hear him say that. So now Ritchie's favourite story when he talks to journalists about Ian Anderson is, 'Oh, Candice brought out the pussycat in me, according to Ian Anderson.'"

At this juncture it wasn't clear if Rainbow had been put on hold or had dissolved. The uncertainty was made more confusing with a cover feature in the May issue of Japan's *Burrn!* magazine. The first publicity photos of Blackmore's Night included Rainbow's Greg Smith on acoustic bass, Paul Morris on keyboards and a new face, Jessie Haynes on additional acoustic guitar. At this point Blackmore's Night was still a recording project only and it's unlikely that Blackmore had given a great deal of thought as to who would make up any touring ensemble, so Smith and Morris were probably drafted into the photo shoot for convenience. Jessie Haynes: "My memory is foggy on this one. I do remember that photo shoot being very short notice for everyone involved. And on that night I also remember talking to Greg and Paul about playing together in the new band. I think it was shortly after that that Ritchie decided not to use them."

Plans for a band to be put together were already emerging. Jessie Haynes: "I remember meeting [Ritchie and Candice] for dinner the day after they arrived home from the last tour. They were totally exhausted but wanted to get moving with plans for rehearsals. They told me that they brought the current Rainbow to an end." However in an interview with Hans van den Heuvel for Dutch magazine *Oor*, published in August 1997, Blackmore suggested that Rainbow wasn't finished. "Rainbow is put on the back burner at the moment. I will replace the singer, bass player and the keyboard player. I don't have names yet of new people. We're talking February, March next year. I just had enough of having to play very loud all the time. On a big

---

* On March 13, 1996, unemployed former shopkeeper Thomas Hamilton opened fire on a class at Dunblane School in Scotland, killing 15 schoolchildren and a teacher before killing himself.

stage it doesn't make any difference, but it's difficult to hear things in perspective when you are blasting away in a small room at rehearsals. A Marshall is like a Ferrari. When you turn it down it loses its power. At least my eardrums are very thankful for this new CD."

He also spoke of the possibility of reuniting with Ronnie Dio. "There aren't a lot of old wounds. Ronnie's departure from Rainbow was so quick there wasn't time to create big wounds. One moment we were playing together, next moment we weren't. I don't think I will work on a permanent basis with Ronnie. But I'm toying with the idea to do a short tour with him, followed by a live album."*

Blackmore's Night seemed to bring the sense of contentment he had been looking for. Having worked for the guitarist for over two decades, Raymond D'addario saw the change. "It was almost like the weight of the world was lifted off [Ritchie's] shoulders and he could just relax and do what he wanted to do. He doesn't have to compete, he can just play music, doesn't have to argue with the singer, any of that stuff, just play music."

In an interview with James Jensen for *Acoustic Musician* magazine, Blackmore reaffirmed: "This is the path I hope to be on for the rest of my days. I haven't forgotten rock 'n' roll, and I do like to turn up the volume and play, but that can wait for a while. This is very exciting and a real challenge as the music is much more rigid than rock, with many set melodies and one of my weak points is remembering melodies note for note. I am used to inferring the melody and improvising, but with the Renaissance stuff you have to stick very much to the line so it is a challenge, but an exciting one."

On June 1, the day after Rainbow played the Esbjerg Festival, Blackmore, Night and Fodder drove to Germany for a promotional tour for *Shadow Of The Moon* co-ordinated to tie in with the album's release the following day via the European Record Company, Edel.

Rob Fodder: "The Blackmore's Night promo tour was just Germany, Spain and France. We stayed in a couple of castles in Germany, grandiose hotels in Barcelona and Madrid and a airport hotel in Paris [due to a mix up] but found a fantastic medieval farmhouse location just outside CDG Airport for the interviews. Journalists would come to wherever we were

---

* An offer to Blackmore and Dio to reactivate the Rainbow name for a one-off Japanese concert with Cozy Powell foundered when Blackmore reportedly wanted the lionshare of the earnings.

and pose their questions to Ritchie and Candy. Although Carole had stipulated that no questions were to be asked about Rainbow or Deep Purple, Ritchie had no problem in answering them. There were two live radio interviews in Barcelona and Madrid. Before leaving the hotel in Madrid for the radio station, Ritchie wanted to have a glass of wine to calm the nerves. We waited and waited at the bar for ages and eventually got a bottle of Rioja to drink during the interview. The radio station had allowed a select number of fans to come into the station and meet Ritchie. He had a little chat with each of them and gave out *Shadow Of The Moon* promo shirts."

Regardless of his own long-held desire to indulge in Renaissance music, Blackmore attributed the switch to his girlfriend. "For the last 20 years people would say to me 'Do an acoustic thing,' and I went 'Why? Everybody is doing an acoustic thing.' Especially the last 10 years – everything was unplugged. That got a little bit too fashionable to me. And now that it is not fashionable to be unplugged, I'm unplugged. But I've wanted it for the last 20 years, and I have been playing this at home for 20, 25 years. I think Candy is the one who brought it out in me to actually put it on record. I would never have actually done this record had it not been for her singing at home, and bringing some of these ideas to fruition with her interpretation."

During the promotion Blackmore talked about live performances for later in the year, possibly in castles but when the dates were announced they were traditional concert style venues. On returning to Long Island, he and Candice started rehearsing along with Haynes: "I arrived for the first time at the front door of Minstrel Hall and was greeted by Ritchie, who informed me 'You're early.' He made sure I knew that he didn't like that, because then he'd feel like he had to 'entertain' me. That's my first memory of arriving at their home. The rest of the afternoon was great. Playing with someone of Ritchie's talent for the first time was really wonderful. I felt like it was almost effortless, because he was so smooth. I remember playing 'Renaissance Faire' and writing down the chords and coming up with ideas for backgrounds in 'Magical World' and how Candy and I just kept smiling at each other because our voices blended so well.

"We sat in the sunroom upstairs, overlooking the water. The view is still vivid in my mind. The songs were so pretty, in their rawest form. It was just the three of us back then at the very beginning of a new project. 'Shadow Of The Moon' was one of my favourites from the beginning and 'Play Minstrel Play', which we played at the next rehearsal in their basement, which is actually a very cosy bar. That's where we had rehearsals as the band began to grow."

Originally the plan was for Haynes to double up on rhythm guitar and bass, with Joseph James playing keyboards and John O. Reilly (from *Stranger In Us All*) on percussion. In the end Haynes stuck with rhythm when Argentinean Mick Cervino was drafted in on bass. Like Doogie White, Cervino was a life-long Blackmore fan and as a means of soliciting future work, had sent a video of himself performing Bach pieces on bass, from his home in California.

Mick Cervino: "Initially the audition was done by mail, I was asked to learn and submit recordings of a few songs from *Shadow Of The Moon*. Then Ritchie, through Carole Stevens, would suggest more of this and less of that, asking me to re-record them and send them overnight, along with a few more songs from the same album. I sent overnight tapes almost daily for about three weeks! By that time I had learnt all of it. Finally, I was asked to go to Long Island for the audition in person, which consisted of going through most of the album's songs. At the audition in Ritchie's house were Jessie Haynes, John O. Reilly, Joe James, Candice Night and Ritchie. We played acoustically in the living room, very quite. It was very pleasant and the atmosphere was very friendly and professional. That evening Carole, Candice and Ritchie took me out to dinner. Ritchie and I had a toast and he said, 'You're in.' When I arrived into the picture the project was already on the way. I had never met or spoken to Ritchie before then.

"The whole experience was unbelievable, everyone knew how much playing next to Ritchie meant to me and they made me feel very welcome. It certainly was one of the best times of my life. Working with Ritchie is a unique experience. By following Ritchie's career for about 25 years and by reading everything I could about him, and the people he has worked with, I had a pretty good idea of what to expect when I came in, even though it is different from what many people think of him. The minute he notices you're not giving 110% you can be sure you won't have a very comfortable time rehearsing or performing. He makes sure everybody works hard or you don't belong there. I think that in this particular phase of his career, he is perhaps more meticulous about the music than he must have been in the past, because Blackmore's Night is very close to his heart in more than one way. I am still fascinated with the man, his personality and musical genius continues to amaze me."

With rehearsals complete, September dates for Spain, Germany, Denmark, Russia and Finland were to be followed by a Japanese tour in November. Shortly after the announcement came the news that the last three European shows in Russia and Finland had been cancelled. Worse was to follow when on September 9 Carole Stevens confirmed that the entire European tour had been postponed. Blackmore was suffering a recurrence of the finger injury sustained back in '87 while on stage with Deep Purple and his doctor stated, quite categorically, that he should not play guitar for at least three weeks. A memo was sent to the promoters along with a copy of the doctor's report and despite some cynics speculating that it was a cover-up because of Blackmore getting cold feet, the hand injury was legitimate.

Consequently, the Japanese shows became the first gigs for Blackmore's Night, debuting in Tokyo on November 2. "The people in Japan are real gems," says Haynes. "They treated us like royalty." Inevitably the opening night's 100-minute show, excepting of 'Wish You Were Here' and 'Ocean Gypsy,' was largely based around *Shadow Of The Moon*, opening with the title track. The set included a new song, 'Under A Violet Moon,' a surprise choice in Joan Osborne's 'St. Teresa' with the rest of the show made up of Rainbow songs, 'Temple Of The King', 'Sixteenth Century Greensleeves', 'Ariel', 'Still I'm Sad' and 'Difficult To Cure.' The ease with which Ritchie slotted into performing the acoustic based music was self-evident from his performance, but for those brought up on a diet of Deep Purple and Rainbow it seemed unusual to hear him perform this different style of music featuring a female on vocals. With no previous professional experience Candice was far less assured; failing to project her voice sufficiently. Perhaps to compensate, during the encore, a rousing 'Writing On The Wall,' Blackmore let loose with a brilliantly improvised Purple-style solo.

Mick Cervino: "Our first show was in Tokyo in front of 5,000 people. During the shows we played unrehearsed bits of old Purple and Rainbow tunes which I personally knew well. It seemed Ritchie was keeping everyone on their toes, testing each one of us with a new and different challenge night after night. I knew how demanding he could be by reading about him all my life, so I was ready for it and I enjoyed the challenge very much."

The rearranged European dates lost some of the shows on the original itinerary. In a fax to *More Black Than Purple*, Carole Stevens explained that "the only shows being done this time will be four in Spain and five in Germany." As for the UK being ignored, Stevens pointed out, "Ritchie, Candice and I want very much to play in England, Scotland and Wales. Unfortunately the response to the CD is not that good. Edel UK has told me that it has set up sample CD listening posts at the best independent record stores. We are very frustrated by their lack of promotion and advertising. I have informed Edel Hamburg about the lack of promotion being done in the UK but the UK office seems to tell them they are doing a lot of work. It is a shame that a legendary guitarist like Ritchie, who created a masterpiece of music in *Shadow Of The Moon* cannot get proper recognition in his home country, while the rest of the world applauds."

The last of the four Spanish gigs in Granada was cancelled when Candice took ill with food poisoning but Blackmore and the rest of the band tried to compensate at least a small number of the potential audience when they performed an impromptu show at their hotel. As in Japan apart from performing most of the 'Shadow Of The Moon' material, a few Rainbow and Purple songs were included during the European shows. Cervino is of the opinion that Blackmore's decision to rely on some of his back catalogue was not borne out of necessity: "There was never a shortage of Blackmore's Night songs to play live. Even though he never actually explained why we would play Rainbow or Purple songs, I think it's only reasonable to expect some of his old songs in the live set." Audiences were delighted when Blackmore reverted to his Stratocaster for the encores that invariably included 'Smoke On The Water' or 'Black Night', sounding somewhat unusual with female vocals. Because of their struggle to remember the words, both Candice and Haynes had the lyrics displayed on their monitors. While the instrumentals from *Shadow Of The Moon* brought out some of his best playing, it was also fascinating to hear impressive acoustic interpretations of 'Ariel' and 'Temple Of The King.'

Prior to the tour moving on to Germany, a journalist asked Blackmore if he would be meeting up with his son, but his reply indicated that despite maturing years the relationship hadn't strengthened. "I don't even know where he lives. I believe that he lives in the Hamburg area but I have no contact with him." The planned shows in German castles failed to materialise, so instead Blackmore's Night played in conventional theatres, with the exception of the Berlin show in a church. The author's first experience of seeing Blackmore's Night was the opening German show in Stuttgart and was surprised to find that it was much more mainstream and rock orientated than envisaged.

For Germany, the support act was singer/songwriter, Julian Dawson. "I was signed to BMG records at the time and my German agency did their best to put me in front of as many audiences as possible to help promote my CDs. When they offered me a support with Ritchie Blackmore I took it, as I was curious to see what it was actually like to be canned off a stage [my music being very far from heavy metal]. Ritchie's fearsome reputation preceded him too, but I was hoping for an interview for my Nicky Hopkins biography so I turned up to the first show in Stuttgart, considerably nervous. The first show proved to be a pattern that held throughout the dates. The audience of Purple fans had grown older and seemed to take to me and my music right away. I sold more CDs than on any other support tour I'd ever done. When I saw the Blackmore's Night stage backdrop it reminded me of a Christmas panto. Seeing Ritchie and the band in tights confirmed my worst expectations of the music: Robin Hood meets Spinal Tap [I thought]. Ritchie's total commitment to what he was doing and obvious enjoyment of it very quickly changed my mind. I had the feeling he really loved the music he was playing, was relieved to be away from the pressures of being part of Deep Purple and was determined to educate his audience to his new direction."

However Dawson couldn't help but observe that even though Blackmore seemed far less confrontational than at any time in the past, his behaviour wasn't necessarily mirrored by all of the entourage. "He had entrusted tour management to Candice's mum, whose complete inexperience led to some tensions with the crew and agency." But at least Dawson's presence had a positive effect. "When I got backstage, though he never socialised very much, he was never less than charming to me and seemed to have mellowed considerably. I was playing a small German-made Lakewood guitar. He took a shine to the look and sound of it and in Mainz I was able to hook him up with the manufacturer. I believe he now owns at least three of their custom-built guitars."

Whether Blackmore initially intended his new project to run alongside Rainbow is still unclear but he had finally broken away from the stranglehold of heavy rock. Mick Cervino: "When I first spoke to Carole Stevens she mentioned the Blackmore's Night project as a one album thing. By the end of the year [1997] Ritchie would be reforming Rainbow with a new line up, which could include me as his bass player." With a successful tour and *Shadow Of The Moon* satisfying Blackmore and certain critics, Blackmore's transformation from guitar hero to wandering minstrel became complete. Although some fans struggled to accept this change of direction, within the space of a few months, Blackmore had turned his entire career on its head.

Meanwhile tragedy occurred in England on April 5 1998 when Cozy Powell lost his life in a car accident on the M4 close to his home in Wiltshire. Although he and Blackmore had sometimes had an explosive relationship, a message of condolence and tribute was posted on Blackmore's website: "The news of his death has been a great shock to us all. He will always remain with us; his friendship always valued, and his music immortalised."

Blackmore was working at an astonishing pace and *Shadow Of The Moon*

331

had barely been released when he was already talking about a follow-up. "We have already written about 11 songs for the next CD. The new things I have written have a much more Russian or ethnic feel with gypsy dances, a little more 'up' than this record, which is more romantic ballads." However the long drawn out process that resulted in *Under A Violet Moon* caused more than a few headaches. Blackmore appointed keyboard player Joe James to produce it and initially all went well but the working relationship soon became strained. Although Blackmore shared much of the instrumentation between himself and James, Cervino was also requested to provide bass. "I arrived at Ritchie's house a few days before Joe took off. Joe was very tired, edgy, and looking forward to finishing the *Under A Violet Moon* project as soon as possible. I guess there were some differences of interpretation of what he was expected to do, for how long and for how much. There were a lot of tense moments during some of the sessions laying down Candice's vocals as well as with some of Ritchie's guitar takes."

For Cervino, it was the first opportunity he had to work in the studio with his hero. "Some of these sessions were precious to me, Ritchie warming up on the Strat prior to recording. ... I was in heaven. However they were somewhat ruined for me by Joe's eye-rolling motions and discontent. I woke up one morning and Joe had left. There was a message on Ritchie's answering machine saying he had the tapes. The message said other stuff that I'd rather not get into for ethical reasons. I believe Joe's and Ritchie's lawyers came to an agreement in the end. I never heard anything from Joe since."

Although Blackmore's Night had been established as a live band it wasn't deemed necessary to use all the musicians for recording. Mick Cervino: "To me Blackmore's Night has never been a 'band,' it is Ritchie's and Candice's project. When they record sometimes it makes more sense to have the producer or themselves play most instruments. A drum machine keeps perfect tempo, shows up on time, doesn't have ego problems, etc. Yes, it saves time and money. During the early sessions of *Under A Violet Moon* I had recorded about six of the songs, but after going through multiple producers and because of Ritchie constantly changing his mind on tempos, arrangements, keys and mood swings, there was not much left from the initial recordings. By the end of the final sessions, about a year later with Jeff Glixman as producer, I recorded two more songs, even though I think I was mentioned on only one."

With Blackmore having managed to recover the tapes from James, Roy McDonald was brought in to help iron out the mess and Glixman [who had produced Kansas] eventually took the producer's chair for some of the recordings. It was evident that the album was not going to be ready in time for the next European tour planned to start in September '98. If the album was causing problems, more drama was to occur during preparations for the tour. Blackmore drafted in an additional musician in the shape of violinist Rachael Birkin, who had previously worked with Peter Gabriel, plus a new keyboard player Adam Forgione and drummer Kevin Dunne. With the scaling down of his workload and only touring for a few weeks per year, not all the band were full time musicians and any notion of retainers was well and truly a thing of the past.

Shortly before the band was due to fly to Europe, Dunne informed Stevens that due to other work commitments, he wouldn't be able to commit to the tour, throwing her and Blackmore into a panic as they searched for a replacement. Mick Cervino: "If I remember correctly, Kevin had a day job as a percussion instructor, which provided him with steady financial security. He told us he could manage to leave his job to do the tour and then come back, but as it turned out his boss did not allow it. Ritchie and I auditioned Mike Sorrentino; he passed the audition only to tell us he was not available at that time." Roy McDonald suggested Alex Alexander who was drafted in with the possibility of only three days rehearsal.

Mick Cervino: "The thought of cancelling the tour was there, until Alex came along. Alex's style of playing was very different from Kevin's, so it took a bit of time to get used to it and to gel rhythmically. There was some hesitation about doing the tour, but fortunately Alex pulled it off and everything worked out splendidly well."

For Alexander, the rehearsals were arduous and extremely pressurised. "I was friends with the engineer and they needed somebody who could play hand drums and drums so he thought of me. The rehearsals were in this place in Long Island and [Ritchie] wanted to use the electronic kit. I was trying to get him to let me use a full acoustic kit but he didn't want to do that because he wanted to keep the volumes down. I tried to show him I could do it and I could play the whole show with brushes if he needed me to and I remember playing ridiculously quiet and him even pushing me further down. So I ended up using the electronic kit and then he wanted everything right. He wanted every little thing right. He wanted the tempos right and the accents, everything to be perfect so after the first rehearsal I got a call from Carole 'If you don't get everything exactly right then you're gonna be fired.'

"So I stayed up with Mick all night and we went through ... there were no charts so I didn't really know what I was getting wrong so I had to watch the video of the live show and see what it was that was missing and I wrote it all out. Mick stayed up with me all night and the next day we went to

333

rehearsal and I did the best I could and then he was happier. Then we did another rehearsal and when we got to Europe he called another rehearsal in and he kept telling me he thought the tempos were moving. And I knew he was going to do that so I was playing with a metronome. I was playing entire songs with the metronome and I showed him that the tempos were not moving. Then he told me he thought the batteries were down. The metronome must be slowing down. Then he finally conceded everything was right. Even in Europe he was questioning tempos."

With the tour looming Ritchie explained part of the motivation for his current activities: "One of the reasons I left Deep Purple was I didn't want to tour very much. They want to tour for the rest of their lives every day of the week. I'm not saying they have bad home lives even though that was rumoured. These guys want to be on the road all the time. When I was with them, I said I just don't want to be on the road that much. I want time to think, time to feel, feel a tree or something. I don't want to be on a plane going somewhere all the time. But with Blackmore's Night we tour three to four months a year at the most. And that way we can play the best dates and be at our best. We're not too tired; I was always too tired in Purple. Within two or three weeks on the road I was completely exhausted. It was like a matter of survival. The music did not matter anymore. It was can I get through another night? I'm absolutely exhausted. So with this band we choose our times, and we're playing castles, we're playing all the places we want to play. Much more relaxed. So we can give one hundred percent. That I think is very important.

"This is my music. This is something I've been wanting to do for 25 years. I was in a castle called Schloß Gotzenburg and I met a band called Des Geyers Schwarzer Haufen. They were minstrels that seemed to come out of the woods. They came to this castle and just played with so much inspiration. To me I thought 'That's what I want to do.' These are real musicians. They believe in what they're doing. There's no light show. There's no big PA system. Just four guys and they're playing their hearts out. And they weren't making much money, but there was this unanimous kind of harmony that they had, and today I'm still inspired by them. Excellent band. And that's what gives me a kick up the behind. I went, 'I have to do that.' I want to go around playing castles. I want to be in the environment that I want to be. I want to be playing the music I want to play. I don't want to play the music the management or the promoter tells me will make money. I want to be doing what I want to do. And this is why I'm playing castles."

The tour kicked off with a brace of shows in Greece before moving on to the more familiar territory of Germany. Before opening night at Fürth, a special show had been arranged for Schloß Eggersberg on September 28 that has subsequently set the pattern for most of Blackmore's German tours since. The gig was designed as a low-key private event, limited to a 100 capacity, supposedly for a select group of fans 'in the know' with a buffet which helped to add to the atmosphere. Given the exclusive nature of the event it was rather surprising that the full details were posted on the official Blackmore website a week beforehand. Fearful of the possible consequences of several hundred people turning up, the castle's proprietor employed security guards for the evening. Although these were primarily, in the event of people showing up without tickets, they were also there to search for recording equipment due to Blackmore's growing annoyance at bootlegging. The heavy-handed approach seemed grossly over the top for an event of this nature. Not only did the security guards use metal detectors but they were also fully armed.

The concert was held in a small theatre on the top floor of the castle and Blackmore acknowledged his heritage, as he did for the whole tour, by draping his amps with the Welsh flag. The stage was no more than two foot high and with such a small sound system it was definitely among the quietest Blackmore show's ever played. Everything could be heard, including his foot tapping.

As the weather the following morning was quite glorious, a group of guests (including the author) sat out on the terrace. When pieces of toast landed nearby it was no surprise to see Blackmore offloading parts of his breakfast from his third floor room. That afternoon a soccer match was organised but when Blackmore's side were being beaten by the opposition he suggested that he and the author should change sides without telling the other players. There was much bemusement as Mark Welch, the then editor of *More Black Than Purple,* passed the ball to the author who proceeded to attack the opposite goal, with Blackmore in full support in his customary position on the wing.

During the two-day stay at the Castle, Haynes had been suffering with an ailment, something that Blackmore took great interest in. Ironically in an interview only a few months before he'd remarked: "I would like to be a doctor. I love medicine. When something is wrong with a person, I love to find out what it is." He was keen to try and diagnose Haynes' problem and listened intently to what Welch (a qualified surgeon) had to say on the subject. As Candice remarked, "All the books we have in our library at home are about the paranormal and all this medical stuff, nearly all the medical books ever written. If you came in and told him that you had a headache, Ritchie would ask, 'Where is the headache, what kind, please describe what it feels like?' And then he would look it up in the book and tell you exactly what was wrong. It's great!"

Under A Violet Moon was eventually released in Japan in April '99, followed soon after in Europe. The lyrics to the title track were partly written by Blackmore, the only time to date he has tried his hand at such. The Violet Moon title was created from his late mother's first name, and grandmother's surname. As part of the usual round of promotional interviews Blackmore spoke about the problems they had encountered making it. "I'm not really nervous about the record because the record will do whatever it should do. I feel good about the record. It took us quite a while to do it. It took us a year, which is a long time for us. It usually is three months, but it started with … the producer we had in the beginning decided to leave after three months. He couldn't take the pressure. So that's okay. You just get another producer or go somewhere else. We went to another studio. His notes weren't very clear, so all the other producers couldn't understand where the hell any of the tracks were because the track sheets weren't very clear. So we had a bit of a problem in that area. It was quite nerve-wracking every time we went to a new studio to try and find the instruments that we knew were there. I'd say, 'Well I know there's a cello on track 14.' And they'd say, 'I don't think so. It's not there now.' And I'm like, 'My God! But we have a trumpet.' And I used to say, 'No, there shouldn't be a trumpet on there at all.'

"All the preparation was what took a long time. I mean Candy will be very quick when she does the vocals. She'll take probably two hours at most. I usually take a day to do my part. But it was all the preparation, buzzes and hums and synching up things because we did it all on computer and nothing synched up. So that was a mess. Actually one of the songs we sent to Germany for our German friends, Des Geyers Schwarzer Haufen. They played on one of the tracks and they couldn't sync the track up with their machine either. So it seemed it was just bad news."

Under A Violet Moon continued where *Shadow Of The Moon* left off but if anything it was less commercial, utilising songs from different European traditions such as 'Past Times With Good Company', which history tells us was written by Henry XIII or the flamenco flavoured 'Spanish Nights.' The Stratocaster was only used on one song, 'Gone With The Wind' that was based on a piece from a Russian composer. The song's introduction also has a striking resemblance to Europe's 'The Final Countdown', something that some interviewers quizzed Ritchie on. "Yes, I love that song by Europe. I always liked that band very much. What it is, is it's those beginning chords, D minor, B flat, C, A major. As soon as you put in those three chords, you have to be very careful what notes you hit because anything will sound like 'The Final Countdown.' We actually changed the intro because it sounded too much like 'Final Countdown.' But sometimes when you're writing music it's hard not to be, one of my favourite records is 'Final Countdown.' Let's say as Top 20 records, 'Final Countdown' would have been one of them. And it's hard to ... maybe another one of them would be 'Whiter Shade Of Pale,' which was almost 'Spirit Of The Sea.' It had that same Bach descending bass line. So you can't help but be kind of ... I don't listen to much music. I tend to want to make music rather than listen to it. But you can't help but be involved in it and take from it in certain things."

The album also contained some fine instrumentals, including the lush 'Beyond The Sunset' and 'Durch den Wald zum Bachhaus.' "I want to give back to Germany what it's given to me and inspired me in my music. Whenever I had an instrumental, I found myself saying, 'Oh, I wonder what I should call this?' And I was so taken by the Germanic way of life I thought, 'Maybe I should say it in German. Why should it have to be in English?' The Germans are always so understanding of English, they're always speaking English. No one ever speaks German when they go to Germany because they're too arrogant. 'Well, how come you don't understand me when I'm talking?' 'Well, why don't you speak German?' And I wanted to give something back. I wanted something to be in another language.

"And of course Germany is very close to me through a reincarnation thing. I think it is that. And I started calling my instrumentals German titles, although I always got the spelling slightly wrong, or the phrasing, just a little bit wrong. I was often told by the Scorpions, "that Weiss Heim is not Weiss Heim, it's Weisses Heim." And I'd always have one letter wrong because of my German. In the end it almost became a little trademark. Ritchie's speaking German but there's a slight mistake. And even to this day with 'Durch den Wald zum Bachhaus,' I had trouble with that because Bachhaus is one word. I thought it was two words. It was Bach's house. 'No, it's Bachhaus.' There was a time, I had this instrumental and Roger Glover said to me, 'What are you calling this instrumental?' And I can't remember the title, it was some instrumental I called a German title. He said, 'Why is it in German?' And he was almost like a bit annoyed. And I went, 'It has to be in German just to annoy you, Roger. Every instrumental I do will be in German from now on.' It was, I felt, such a presumptuous, arrogant statement, I was really annoyed."

A live concert video, produced by Blackmore's own company, Minstrel Hall Music, was only made available at gigs, via his website or through fan clubs. Culled predominantly from the '97 Cologne show but also including extracts from the 1998 gigs, it reflected a less mysterious more relaxed Blackmore by including interviews and backstage footage.

Elsewhere Blackmore's hard rock was still being acknowledged. In its seemingly endless series of musical lists, UK's Channel Four TV broadcast a programme on the Top 10 Heavy Metal bands based on British sales, which saw Rainbow at number five and Deep Purple at number three. Interestingly Black Sabbath were at number two but only because the solo sales of Ozzy Osbourne were taken into account. Had the same rationale applied to Purple and their offshoots, they would probably have knocked Iron Maiden from the top honour.

Surprisingly Blackmore agreed to be interviewed and for those viewers unaware of his current musical incarnation there was one particular comment – "I just want to live in a musical little roundabout. I want to be at the bottom of my garden, living with the fairies, playing the music that is very dear to me" – that indicated the man had lost the plot. After years of constant pranks and wisecracks, it was amusing to find so many still taken in by Blackmore's straight faced humour.

Following Cozy Powell's tragic death the previous year, a tribute concert was arranged at the Buxton Opera House on May 1. An announcement had been posted on the official Powell website since January that stated, "Many well known artistes, including Ritchie Blackmore of Deep Purple, will appear in this one night gala concert." Blackmore's management was initially cagey on this issue, before finally forcing the ticket office to send out a statement to all potential ticket buyers that due to other commitments, he would definitely not be appearing.

Given the importance of Powell in Blackmore's career his decision not to attend seemed heartless but he has always shied away from star gatherings and as Mark Welch reported in *More Black Than Purple*, "he probably made the right decision. The resultant show, while high on content, was low on quality, and was certainly high on 'showbiz'. Performances of songs that originally featured Cozy were done by a band consisting of his replacement in Rainbow, Bobby Rondinelli and Neil Murray, Tony Martin (ex Black Sabbath), Geoff Nichols (ex Black Sabbath) and guitarist Mike Casswell who played on Cozy's final album. Brian May of Queen completed the night with a few tunes including 'Since You Been Gone' but it all got a bit silly at the end, and Ritchie would certainly have been very uncomfortable at such an event."

At the time of the Powell tribute, preparations for the next Blackmore's Night tour were in force. For the summer '99 concerts the equipment cutbacks continued with Blackmore taking the unusual step of dispensing with a bass player, instead employing a second keyboard player in singer/song-writer Marci Gellar. Mick Cervino didn't seem too surprised. "Before I joined Blackmore's Night the line up did not include a bass player, I believe Jessie was to play an acoustic bass here and there if it was really needed. When I was not available for one of the tours, Ritchie hired a second keyboard player, who along with the violinist would cover the bass parts. I suppose that since the bass lines in many of Blackmore's Night recordings were done with synthesisers they probably thought it wouldn't make much of an impact to do the same live, rather than having an actual bassist. Obviously it made a difference since they called me back."

The tour opened in Bulgaria, the first time Blackmore had played the former communist country and the second of the two shows in the capital Sofia was filmed by Bulgarian TV with an hour later broadcast. Whether it was another cost cutting exercise is unclear but the quantity of Blackmore's own equipment was scaled back with only one Stratocaster taken on the road.* Such is the delicate nature of Blackmore's playing that he very rarely broke strings on stage but just such a situation occurred at a gig in Solingen, Germany. With Blackmore in full flow during the solo in 'Writing On The Wall,' he was forced to switch guitars, and with only one electric the drama of the moment was severely affected when completed on an acoustic.

During the tour a football game was slotted in one afternoon on a pitch in Waldeck, Germany. After an hour the groundsman appeared, shouting and telling the teams to get off the pitch. Blackmore's response was to ignore him and instructed the players to carry on with the game. The jobsworth walked off but soon reappeared on his lawn mower and drove straight onto the pitch. When Blackmore came into possession of the ball he stopped the game. "Watch this," he told the author, and proceeded to kick the ball towards the machine around 60 yards away. The ball sailed through the air and landed with neat accuracy among the mower's blades, where it promptly lodged itself.

Geyers Schwarzer Haufen was the support act on the German tour and with an ever growing bond between them Blackmore agreed to record a session to add to their forthcoming live album. Interestingly despite his growing love for their blend of ancient music the Geyers wanted to steer their style more towards the rock Blackmore had shied away from. However

---

* Some who were close to the Blackmore entourage say there was even the possibility of going on the road with backing tapes, but fortunately to date this hasn't happened.

he gladly agreed to provide his trademark Stratocaster sound to 'Götliche Devise.'

As the year 2000 fast approached, despite his limited knowledge of computers, Blackmore predicted major catastrophes would occur as a result of the so-called 'millennium bug,' with air traffic control problems among other things. His pessimism was thankfully proved wrong in this instance. However, his other predictions such as one made in 1997 – "We will go through a bad time in the next few years. I think Nostradamus was correct. It's not looking too good with the Middle East countries. I just see nothing but doom. It's just a matter of time before someone blows up New York with atom bombs in a suitcase. Think of all these religious fanatics" – would prove to be uncannily accurate

The first commitment for the new millennium was a five-date Italian tour which included a cancelled gig at the Palauniverso in Silvi Marina on January 29. As the shows were aimed at audiences around the 1,500 mark, a small amount of seats had been arranged in the middle of a hall that held approximately 8,000. The crew reported the acoustics were awful with the freezing cold and a power cut in the area only adding to their woes. Unable to see eye to eye with the promoters, the fans standing outside in the cold were finally told the show had been cancelled around the time the doors were due to open.

The rest of the brief tour went without a hitch, after which Blackmore and Candice flew to Britain combining a holiday with business arrangements over a record label while choosing venues for the first Blackmore's Night UK tour. For the first time in a long career Blackmore made himself more accessible to the media. However the usual stubbornness and belligerence were still to the fore. Having spent a couple of nights at Stirrups Hotel in Maiden Green, Berkshire, close to his father's home in Camberley, not being an early riser, Blackmore didn't want to checkout until three pm but the hotel insisted that guests had to depart by the original time of one pm. Blackmore refused to accept this and stood his ground. As Stevens told the *Bracknell News* in a front page story, "It was a ridiculous situation. They threatened to physically move Ritchie. We offered to pay extra for the two hours but they said no. They said we had no rights."

Rob Fodder: "I booked the hotel and stipulated that we wanted a later checkout. We only wanted another hour or so extra in the room. I was supposed to pick Ritchie up at about one, but Carole called me and said they were having problems with the hotel, saying that we didn't request the late checkout. Anyway, the manager insisted that Ritchie left the hotel. Ritchie even offered to pay for another half day's stay but the manager refused. Ritchie refused to leave [on time] and wanted to get the local press down there … maybe to pressurise the manager in to letting him stay, or just to humiliate him. The press came out and did a quick interview and photo shoot and the manager had called the police. We spoke to the police who were great about it and negotiated with the manager that Ritchie could have his room for the extra time as long as he paid the maid an extra hour overtime, which was cheaper than the half day rate that we'd already offered!"

With the aid of officers from Ascot Constabulary Blackmore got his own way. The hotel said, "They had requested a late checkout when they booked but we were not able to offer it. They were being very rude and abusive. They were just trying to cause trouble. The situation was settled amicably but they won't be staying here again." Fodder recalls, "I think that Candy left a few choice words with the manager on our departure!"

After touring for three years, Blackmore's Night finally made their British debut in England in May 2000. Although some fans had felt Blackmore was ignoring his homeland, finding a promoter sympathetic to his desire of not wishing to play conventional rock venues had proved difficult. Eventually with a certain degree of compromise, five dates were arranged starting at York's Grand Opera House. A support band had not been arranged and Blackmore was still looking right up to the last minute when Angela Goldthorpe, flautist with up and coming seven-piece rock outfit Mostly Autumn, and at the time also working as assistant to Tim Hornsby of the local promoter Fibbers, saw an opportunity.

Heather Findlay, Mostly Autumn's lead vocalist and multi-instrumentalist recalls how it came about. "At the time we were doing a lot of folky stuff in the set that made sense to break down as a three-piece. First of all we did it very much instrumentally. Initially Angie had got word that they wanted a pipe and drum player and Angie stretched that to bodhran and flute and it was a two-piece kind of female outfit. We rehearsed and tried it and it wasn't working, we needed a guitarist in there and Carole's initial response was 'We already have a guitarist on the stage.' That's when I think she decided to audition us, so it ended up being a three-piece [adding Bryan Josh, Mostly Autumn's leader and principal songwriter] so we'd already twisted the rules a little bit to get the support at that particular show and we ended up with an audition on the afternoon of the gig. It may have even been the day before."

Mostly Autumn had heard of Blackmore's temperamental reputation and entered into the tour with a great deal of trepidation. At first they tried to be as inconspicuous as possible as Findlay remembers: "We used to tip toe around and take our bells off our ankles that we had strategically placed to make us look a bit more like a Renaissance outfit that we were professing to be at the time, but we would be all meek and mild. I remember the first time we met Ritchie was at the Cambridge Theatre in London and we heard Ritchie's bells coming down the corridor. Angie and I were just standing there and we all froze a little bit as this man all dressed in black came walking towards us and we were at the side of the stage a little bit trapped. The situation was different for Angie and me, but for Bryan he had grown up with Ritchie being his childhood hero. Bryan was on his way back from the bar and he had to get past Ritchie to give Angie and I our drinks, and he just stood there frozen; just speechless and stunned not daring to move or go past. So there was a lot of keeping quiet and keeping out of the way as we had heard he had a big reputation for sacking people he wasn't happy with."

A rapport soon developed and during the shows, Ritchie would invite the trio back on stage, normally to join in on 'Renaissance Faire'. Blackmore's typically warped humour ensured that Josh would have a hard time of it. "On occasions we used to join Blackmore's Night on stage and he showed me the chords just before the show, I joined them for the song and it sounded fucking awful, I then realised they were the right chords in a completely different key. One other occasion he ran through a whole host of chords again at the last minute; of which I had never even come across, at high speed with me trying to follow, getting rather flustered and worried, he then stopped and started laughing and told me they were nothing to do with the song at all, he was just winding me up."

Blackmore had been anxious about bringing Blackmore's Night to his homeland, expecting the British rock press to have a field day ridiculing him, but he needn't have worried. Since his departure from Deep Purple, the press were, by and large, ignoring him. Now that he had re-invented himself as an acoustic playing minstrel they were even less interested in giving him column inches. The UK shows were generally sold out and well received by fans. The press coverage that did appear was polite on the whole though most reviewers failed to fathom exactly what one of the world's greatest heavy rock guitarists was up to with this acoustic music.

CHAPTER 17

Beyond The Sunset: A New Millennium (2001–03)

The New Year kicked off with personal tragedy. When the news came through that Blackmore's father was severely ill and had been admitted to hospital in London, Ritchie took the first available flight from New York to be by his side, but regrettably Lewis failed to pull through. If it's possible for anything positive to have come out of his father's death, Blackmore was inspired to write 'Again Someday' with suitably melancholic lyrics from Candice.

Brighter developments came in the shape of a major new record deal with German company SPV who spared no expense in promoting the forthcoming *Fires At Midnight* album. Blackmore picked the venue of Lumley Castle in Chester Le Street, County Durham – a favoured locale he had stayed at many times over the years. SPV hired the lavish setting for a fortnight and arranged for journalists from around Europe to be flown in for four special performances featuring Mostly Autumn as part of the band.

Heather Findlay: "I think he was very much into the idea of helping us out, knowing there would be press there and some sort of exposure. There was quite a lot of parallels between us and Blackmore's Night at the time, we were into nature and spirituality. He would say things about us all that he couldn't possibly have known. He knew all sorts of things; he knew a lot of stuff about Angie's mother and herself, about myself and my dad, he knew about the relationship Bryan had with his dad, it was almost as if they had checked us out on some other level, he knew where I had spent my

childhood holidays, knew I had an affinity with the Jamaica Inn, it was really strange. He knew stuff that was impossible to know, stuff I have never spoken about. Another time when I was having a phone call with them, I was just looking out the window and there was a big ginger cat, which used to visit my house. As I was talking to [him] on the phone that cat was just wandering about in the garden, way across the other side of the big main road, and Ritchie just stopped the conversation and said, 'Is there a cat there?' I said, 'Er … yeah there is!" He said, 'A ginger one?' 'Yeah!' I mean like I'm in York, he's in Long Island, crazy! There's definitely a lot more to Ritchie. He's definitely in touch with that realm."

Bryan Josh: "I remember some really enjoyable late night discussions sat in old dimly lit castles on supernatural and spiritual subjects, sometimes he would just come out with information about my past, of which he couldn't possibly have know about, often about my late father. I have always had the feeling there is something otherworldly about Ritchie, in his playing and his character, I think you would feel he was in the room before you saw him."

When *Fires At Midnight* was released that summer it once again combined the familiar Renaissance themes along with more traditional Blackmore styles. Tracks such as 'The Storm' and the title track with its heavy, lengthy electric solo showed that the rocker was still there, and while fickle audiences in Britain and America still didn't take to Blackmore's Night, the album entered the national German charts at a very respectable number nine.

The German summer tour that followed included a show at the Serenadenhof in Nuremberg on July 26 witnessed by the author. Rainbow had played the same venue five years earlier, and on that occasion it was a lengthy show complete with a long encore. This time around things were somewhat different after the concert organisers had informed Blackmore's entourage that the venue had a ten o'clock curfew. Although the place was an open courtyard, it lay within the confines of the incomplete Congress building, erected by the Nazis during the war, which remains in the same unfinished state to this day. Being situated on the edge of the city, and with no residential area directly adjacent, the curfew appeared somewhat illogical. The simple thing would have been to go on stage earlier but Blackmore purposely delayed the start, not just of his own band but also the support act.

Heather Findlay: "I remember being shut in the toilets backstage with Carole, Candice, Angela and Bryan and being made to stay in there because the promoter was running round the venue trying to find the support band. So we'd been used as a bit of an instrument in breaking the curfew before anybody had even gone on stage. I can only presume that Ritchie had had a rough time with the promoters up to that point and wanted to piss these people off, so we'd been made to hide with Ritchie's manager and Candice and wind this guy up. I think there was a whole lot of awkwardness going on and Ritchie took a disliking to it and rightly so. He'd packed the venue and he really should have been given a lot more leeway with his say as to what went on."

Despite cutting songs from the set Blackmore threw in the surprise choice of Rainbow's 'Temple Of The King', to the bemusement of the rest of the band, as it had not been rehearsed. While a technical problem with the drums was being sorted, he and Candy entertained fans with an impromptu performance of Randy Newman's 'I Think It's Gonna Rain Today.' With the popular 'Spanish Nights' being one of several numbers omitted due to the time constraints, at 10:10 the show finished with 'Renaissance Faire.' Candy stated that would be all as they left the stage.

Although the audience continued to demand an encore for a further 10 minutes, Blackmore's assistant Richard Michaels returned to explain that the band would love to continue playing but were not allowed to. At the same time his hand signals were designed to get the crowd cheering for more. By now, half the audience had left, while those who remained continued cheering for an encore. Almost 20 minutes since the band left the stage they returned after the authorities had obviously relented, fearing the possibility of a mini-riot. The crowd moved forward onto the bank of shrubs that separated the stage from the audience, while the one security man who was employed to stop people walking up the steps at the side of the stage, looked on in dismay. With Blackmore having strapped on his Stratocaster, the band played a fine version of 'Writing On The Wall' followed by the other Rainbow-esque rocker, 'Gone With The Wind.'

After little more than a minute into the song the power was cut. Judging from this, the organisers had insisted that only one song could be performed. Blackmore did not seem perturbed in the slightest. He shrugged his shoulders and went along the front of the crowd, shaking hands, laughing his head off. When he saw the author, he said, 'We haven't finished yet.' Michaels stood on stage and told everyone to sit down and be quiet. As fans sat on the stage, Blackmore picked up his acoustic 12-string and with Candy he played 'Now And Then' totally unplugged. It could hardly be heard but once again, not wanting to be beaten by authority, Blackmore made sure he had the last laugh. The following night in Memmingen, all the stops were pulled out as the band produced an astonishing show of three hours duration.

Imagining the way that a tabloid press report would portray Blackmore's 'bad boy' image the author and the staff of *More Black Than Purple* concocted a spoof newspaper review of the Nuremberg show for the magazine, depicting events in the style of 'Blackmore causes a riot at concert.' The less than subtle approach of producing a mock up of a German newspaper, with the report written in English, complete with deliberate factual errors was too subtle for Carole Stevens. With irony often being lost on Americans the article's humour went right over her head. Stevens criticised the magazine for publishing a negative report, claiming that it would dissuade promoters from booking Blackmore's Night for future tours.

When representing an artist whose 30 year career of mayhem extended to the destruction of TV cameras and entire venues being smashed up because of his refusal to do an encore, while also taking into account the situation at the British hotel earlier in the year, such comments seemed astonishing. The value of publicity – bad or good – was lost on the inexperienced Stevens.

A second tour of the UK was booked for September but with the horrific events of September 11 it was touch and go whether or not Blackmore and Candy would fly over for the tour. Even though the first show (in Scotland on the 21st) was cancelled they arrived in time for the rest of the tour, starting off at Liverpool's Philharmonic Hall the following day. It was the first time Blackmore had played there since that night in 1970 when his beloved Strat was stolen from the stage, but this time around the mood was sombre. After the first couple of numbers Candy spoke about the events in New York and explained that they had decided the tour should go ahead to at least try and bring a bit of happiness into the lives of some people. It was a poignant moment, setting the scene for the rest of the somewhat subdued performance.

Things were more light-hearted for the rest of the tour. After running over the curfew in York with an encore of 'Black Night,' a high-spirited Blackmore briefly returned to the stage armed with a yard broom. A quick sweep of the stage and he ran off. He was clearly in a boisterous mood that night, much to Josh's detriment: "After chatting in the hotel lounge, as he was retiring to bed, he decided to throw a cushion from a distance at our table which was covered in bottles and glasses, it was an accurate shot and with a load of noise they went everywhere including all over me. He then ran upstairs very swiftly, the night porter came out and thought I was responsible and gave me a right bollocking. He refused to believe anyone else was involved."

Among the UK shows was the Stables Theatre in Milton Keynes, a laid back and relaxed venue that traditionally did not hire security. This held no sway with Blackmore who insisted security be in place on the night and furthermore, that all staff had to be at the premises far earlier than usual. From a staff viewpoint it was the biggest logistical nightmare the venue had ever encountered. The heavy handed security guarding the entrance to the backstage area initially wouldn't even let the building's staff through. However the gig's most surreal sight had nothing to do with Blackmore's dictatorial demands. When he had requested fans to dress in period costume, two devotees took this to extremes by attending the show in full suits of armour. Because of this less than flexible attire, they had difficulty sitting down and stood to each side of the stage for the entire concert like two guards on parade. Not only was it incredibly hot inside the theatre, but the sound must have resembled an echo chamber within their tin helmets. It only served to highlight the extraordinary lengths that some of Blackmore's followers were prepared to go.

In 2002, Blackmore visited Russia for the first time, where he had always had a strong fan base, playing in Moscow on his 57th birthday. Despite his desire to perform before smaller crowds the concert at the Luzhniki Sport Palace attracted around 8,000. In the middle of the show, some of the audience started singing 'Happy Birthday.' Blackmore waved at them and raised a glass of beer. During the show a fan clutched a huge bouquet of 57 red roses. After a few seconds of doubt Blackmore finally went to the front of the stage to accept the gift.

The tour concluded in Belgium at the 14th Labadoux Folk Festival in Ingelmunster. A summary of a report from promoter and organiser Jean-Pierre Deven follows: "I knew that by inviting Ritchie Blackmore there was a great chance that I'd encounter all kinds of difficulties…. When the Belgian premiere came closer, the amount of paper, faxes, e-mails and negotiations grew steadily. The never-ending changes of the band members and transport didn't happen by the day but by the hour. With the longest rider ever in my hand I began to understand the fear of the promoters. Rather special to say the least! They demanded it; well it was there when they entered the dressing rooms. So were the six bales of straw and the eight candlesticks that were requested at the last moment.

"According to their contract no channels [were to be] split with other bands on the sound mixing desk. That is very unusual for a music festival within a concert tent; the different bands preceding Ritchie were nearly all acoustic. The deal was that the material would be brought on stage during the daytime. But when we saw all the amplifiers and accessories displayed and compared it to the not so large stage, we realised this couldn't be done at the same time as the other bands.

"The road manager Ian said they wouldn't bring the material on stage until just before the concert. He had been at the site earlier with the band and those responsible for light and sound. A couple of hours later Ritchie, Candice, Carole, her husband, and bodyguard Richard arrived as well. As a promoter I've always seen it as my duty to shake hands with the artists as a welcome. I heard how Ritchie immediately said to his bodyguard that not many people should be allowed backstage. Right! There were no more problems with the soundcheck but the heaviest back line and soundcheck was to be for the band that played after Ritchie: Mory Kante, UN ambassadors of music.

"When we had asked all the concert attendees [about 1,000 people] to leave the tent to go into the cold and wet night they did a soundcheck on a stage set up that was not realistic for a festival. Two heavy PA systems crammed into a relatively small tent was very impressive but the extra work to change all the multi-cables is a real challenge for any respectable PA company. Meanwhile Ritchie and company had left for the hotel when I suddenly got another phone call. The hotel booked by our organisation didn't meet their demands. It had taken me much time to find a four-star hotel containing rooms without the numbers 13, 26, 39 … They had originally agreed with the rural hotel site when they visited it.

"After many enquiries by telephone I booked Ritchie and his people into a hotel in Kortrijk [Courtrai]. I was told they intended to move to this new hotel with the whole band. So now we had two mixing tables and two hotels and our own catering services that they objected to. Back at the site someone from our organisation was obliged to see that nobody would pass by while Ritchie was in his dressing room. The dressing rooms of Mory Kante and his band were in that area as well, so even the UN ambassador couldn't go to his own dressing room. As promoter I then had to use a lot of friendly words to help such an important person step on stage with the necessary enthusiasm.

"During the Blackmore's Night concert, no one in our own organisation was allowed backstage … but it didn't matter anymore to me. The metamorphosis that the festival underwent, the non-stop tension in the air, that wasn't the Labadoux festival. Because of the never-ending soundcheck the Blackmore's Night concert had to be halted after an hour and a half to allow the performances of the two remaining groups, Mory Kante and Apparatschik a fair chance. Mory Kante had allowed Blackmore & co. 30 minutes extra. They thanked them by saying the next band made them stop.* Despite the hour's delay and everything else we closed the night and the festival in a pleasant mood."

Overlooking Blackmore's outrageous demands Jean-Pierre's assistant, Rudi Bral described the show itself: "It was a great concert with songs like 'Shadow Of The Moon,' 'Written In The Stars,' 'Play Minstrel Play,' 'The Times They Are A-Changin' [for the Dylan fans at the folk festival, according to Candice], 'Fires At Midnight,' 'Wish You Were Here,' 'Under A Violet Moon,' etc. I was told Ritchie had cold hands and that was probably why I figured some solos that are normally done by him were now done by the violinist."

The Belgian show was one of four recorded for a live album, but on returning to Long Island Blackmore elected to use the previous night's show in Groningen, Holland. As an indication of his passion for the music he was now making, it was the first time in his career that he oversaw and personally selected the recordings to be used for a concert release. Not happy with the version of 'Sixteenth Century Greensleeves' as performed at the gig, the band went into a New York studio and laid down a spontaneous version that was neatly slotted into the album with very few people aware it was actually not recorded in front of an audience.†

The resultant double album *Past Times With Good Company* was released in October. A relatively unnoticed act of charity occurred when Blackmore donated a portion of the proceeds from the sales of the 'Home Again' single to the Red Cross in Germany to help victims of the devastating floods that occurred in Eastern Germany and the Czech Republic. Blackmore Productions released a second live video filmed during the 2000 German tour, suitably called *Under A Violet Moon Castle Tour 2000* that once again wasn't put on general release.

The summer leg of the 2002 tour included two nights at Wartburg Castle in Eisenach. The combination of playing at a superb venue in Johann Sebastian Bach's hometown should have been an inspirational moment but

---

* A fan that attended the show reported that Candice announced, "We have bad news, we have to stop, the promoter told us the next act [Mory Kante] is getting cold and wants to come on stage."
† A version of 'Street Of Dreams' was also taped at the same session but has yet to see the light of day.

once Blackmore discovered the promoter had switched the location from the smallest, most intimate hall within the castle complex he was incensed. When the author suggested to Blackmore that his fans probably didn't object to paying slightly more to see him perform in such a place, he disagreed and as a conciliatory gesture, paid for a pre-gig buffet for fans to counteract what he saw as exploitation. The contradictory nature of the man resulted in him putting on one of the most lacklustre performances of his entire career. Kicking off the show with 'No Second Chance,' a number the band had not rehearsed, immediately caused confusion and disbelief among his fellow musicians who struggled on valiantly. Candice tried to remain upbeat and performed in a professional manner, with the band doing their utmost to play well but their leader was totally disinterested and made no attempt to communicate with anyone in the band. Within a couple of songs the audience knew this was one show where there were not going to be any special moments and most seemed somewhat relieved when it was over.

A football match was arranged for the following afternoon and afterwards, the contrast in the man from the night before couldn't have been greater. As he and the author walked off the pitch together, the subject of old Sixties bands was raised. Blackmore said, "I remember in the Seventies when bands like the Hollies and the Searchers were still going I used to think 'What a bunch of wankers, why don't they pack it in?' Now all these bands are doing the nostalgia tours and I think it's great. If they weren't doing that they'd probably be working in factories. I know if I hadn't got lucky I'd be working in a factory now."

"But you had a lot of talent, surely that's why you made it?" the author queried. "There were a lot of guys around then, just as talented who never got the breaks – I just got lucky." It seemed that now, in his late fifties, Blackmore acknowledged his privileged position, being able to live comfortably and travel the world playing music the way *he* wanted. His humble stance helped forgive the poor performance the night before, revealing another side to a man that all too often came across as arrogant and self-centred. With the second night's show being filmed for a potential DVD release a more professional performance was delivered and 'Shadow Of The Moon' returned as the familiar opening number.

The October issue of Germany's *Eclipsed* magazine carried an exclusive interview with Blackmore. When asked if he had finished with Deep Purple and Rainbow, he responded, "Not with Rainbow, we'll even go on tour again next year. It'll be a very nostalgic affair. We do this really only because of the thousands of fans all over the world, who have asked and begged for it. With Deep Purple I only have to integrate some of the old songs in to the Blackmore's Night concept, however in acoustic form and interpreted by Candice, like 'Soldier Of Fortune' from the *Stormbringer* album. I'm still friends with Jon Lord but for the rest of Deep Purple it's a long past era, on which I'm proud, but with whom I've since been cut off for ages." He also dispelled any notion that a reunion would be done for financial reasons. "I don't need it thank God – because of my Purple and Rainbow royalties I can have a splendid life. I don't need to work in this life ever again and still have a good life. I really only do it for what brings me pleasure, respectively, in the case of Rainbow, the fans."

Because the interview had been translated into German, then back into English, allowed for certain inaccuracies and shortly after its publication Blackmore informed one fan that his words weren't reported correctly and that he would not be touring with Rainbow in the future. Throwing an additional spanner in the works, *Classic Rock* magazine reported news that Jon Lord was trying to arrange an event for the following year, bringing together all living members of Deep Purple past and present for a one-off concert, recording and filming it in the process. Surprisingly, Coverdale pitched in by saying he would do it providing Blackmore was involved, saying that without him it "wouldn't make sense." Reportedly Blackmore had said he would do a one-off performance with Purple providing Bruce Payne wasn't manager but would it actually happen?

CHAPTER 18

Castles And Dreams
(2003–06)

In 2003 the fourth Blackmore's Night studio album *Ghost Of A Rose* was followed by a compilation, *Beyond The Sunset* complete with a live DVD performance and a three-track Christmas single, the latter being surprising considering Blackmore and Candice have gone on record several times as being Pagans.

In 2004 Blackmore played a second session for Geyers on its first ever rock album, once again providing electric guitar to one track, 'God's Gospel.' That year, while Blackmore's Night were touring Germany, the author had a potentially serious health issue that was aggravated from playing football. After the game Dr. Blackmore was quick to give his diagnosis and suggestions for a remedy. Back at the castle in Abenberg he brought out a rather dog-eared medical book, explaining that its condition was due to the fact that he carried it with him wherever he travelled. By good fortune that evening Blackmore had dinner with a doctor which resulted in the author's visit to a surgery the following morning. The Jekyll and Hyde nature in Blackmore showed itself later that day. While chatting in the castle courtyard, even though the author had been given the all-clear, he showed genuine concern and interest. During their conversation a fan approached holding a Deep Purple photo book to be autographed, innocently trying to engage Blackmore in conversation by asking if he was familiar with the book. Obviously not wanting to look back at photos of his life, Blackmore snapped, "Just give me the fucking book," which he signed whereupon the chastised fan slunk off.

In January 2005, with Blackmore fast approaching his landmark 60th birthday a bizarre news story emerged which claimed he had suffered a heart attack. The *Southampton Evening Echo* reported that he had taken ill during a gig at Portsmouth Guildhall and was being treated in Southampton General Hospital. For anyone with a modicum of knowledge about Blackmore's career, the article was suspect. The journalist obviously hadn't done any research and the report claimed he was now known as "Sir Ritchie Blackmore, having recently been knighted in the New Year's honours list." Just as oddly it claimed that he had been living in Los Angeles, performing with his band under the name of the Black Knights and that he was accompanied on the tour by Roger Glover. Another news article stated "Police in Southampton, England, are on the lookout for a man impersonating Ritchie Blackmore. According to reports, the man has been making personal appearances, collecting money by selling his autograph and then disappearing. Police got a tip that he had checked into a hospital, but he was gone when they got there. A nurse said the impostor even wrote her a song."

To Blackmore it must have felt like déjà vu in recalling the incident in America, over 30 years earlier. His flippant response to being the victim of identity theft, second time around, was "Why didn't he pick on someone more famous?"

In 2005 a double DVD of live performances was released as *Castles And Dreams* while the fifth Blackmore's Night album *The Village Lantern* continues to divide fan opinion, in particular the re-workings of the Purple and Rainbow classics 'Child In Time' and 'Street Of Dreams.' However the greater use of electric playing throughout the album seems to have satisfied those who still refused to accept Blackmore as anything other than a rock guitarist. Indeed the album moved away from the Renaissance themes for the most part. Essentially an eclectic mix of styles, the title track owes more to Abba than to Tielman Susato and a similar type number could have been produced had Blackmore's desired collaboration with Agnetha Fältskog materialised back in the early Eighties. In fact the album slotted comfortably into the pop rock genre that he had always admired.

Whether or not this is a direction he will continue in is anybody's guess. Talk of Deep Purple reunions continues with alarming regularity, sometimes stoked by Blackmore himself. During his most recent UK tour in 2005, in an interview for BBC Radio Tyne he let slip, "I might think about doing one or two shows with Deep Purple but their management couldn't be involved. It wouldn't be for recording – just for the fans for nostalgia."

However, interviewed around the same time by the website *Metal Shrine* Ian Gillan had other ideas. "He's dreaming! Why on earth would we do something with that guy … that brought the band to the edge of ruination. It's just ludicrous! We spent the last 10 years rebuilding the reputation and the style and the quality of the music. There's no way on earth that will happen!"

If Gillan's comments appeared to be unequivocal in another recent on-line interview Glenn Hughes spoke about the intriguing possibility of a Deep Purple MK III reunion: "I would love to do it, Jon Lord would love to do it. David Coverdale has expressed an interest. Maybe some live shows, maybe a DVD or something special like that. I think it would be fantastic for people to see the MK III Deep Purple again. We'd like to do it just for the crack but everything has to be just right. Deep Purple split up with a lot of strong feelings and bitterness so it would be nice to heal that in a way. We all talk to each other. There's no hard feelings at all. It was all so long ago. MK III was unfinished business I think." As to whether or not Blackmore would entertain the idea, Hughes said, "Ritchie is in a very comfortable place right now, doing his own thing, making his own rules, so that in itself is very important. Everything is open. There's probably someone talking about this behind the scenes right now."

Whatever the merits or otherwise of a Deep Purple or Rainbow reunion, to date it has not eventuated.

As Hughes pointed out, Blackmore is in "a very comfortable place" and it's fair to say that at this stage in his life he probably has little desire to move. While over the years he has talked about doing an instrumental album or a blues album and while some fans have difficulty fathoming why he has taken such a leftfield career move, the hints he dropped over the preceding decades should have prepared them for it. In the same way that certain fans struggled to accept Rainbow's more commercial sound after Ronnie Dio's departure, so they refuse to accept Blackmore's Night. However Blackmore's new style of music has also attracted many new converts and for someone who for 30 years was seen solely as a hard rock guitarist, it is undoubtedly, personally fulfilling to have achieved success within a new genre, albeit on a smaller scale than with his previous bands.

Elsewhere his seemingly self-centred approach appears to continue. Since the tragic suicide of Screaming Lord Sutch in 1999, an annual memorial concert has been performed, largely organised by Sutch stalwart Carlo Little. Many whose careers had been started with the help of Sutch regularly attend but Blackmore has always kept away from events of this nature.

While in the preparation stages of this book the author attended the sixth Sutch memorial night at London's Ace Café in June 2005, primarily to meet many of the musicians who had worked with Blackmore over the years. Neil Christian, Tony Dangerfield, Rodger Mingaye, Nick Simper and many more were present. Even Carlo, who was suffering terribly with cancer, made the trip from his home in South Shields. Little made no attempt to disguise his contempt for Blackmore at failing to keep in contact with any of his old band mates. In fact his words to the author were, "He's up his own arse!" Sadly Little died a short while after. His wife Iris arranged an evening in honour of his memory at Twickenham on March 26, 2006. Although it's unclear if Blackmore was contacted there was no communication forthcoming (even the Rolling Stones made donations) and such a thoughtless attitude only acted as ammunition for his detractors.

However the public's perception of such insensitivity doesn't accurately portray the full picture and the generosity Blackmore can show to people he cares for. When a lifelong fan died in 2004, Blackmore arranged and paid for both the fan's partner and best friend to fly over to New York, stay at his home and sprinkle the ashes in his garden.

The uncompromising image he cultivated over the years enabled him to hide behind his shyness and insecurity. It has also helped keep many people at bay, though to some extent he has let his defences down in recent years and the Mr. Nasty image seems to have been replaced with one more akin to the "pussycat" that Ian Anderson observed. As far back as 1980, Blackmore noted: "It's incredible how I've got this name in this business for being a bastard, maybe it's just bad publicity. The people that know me know that I'm not an ogre. The people that don't like me are the people that I don't want to like. Even close friends say, 'Well yeah you can be a nice guy, but sometimes I don't understand you.' But that's because I don't understand myself. If someone asked me where I was at, I really couldn't say 'cause I don't know."

As for the "hard taskmaster" reputation that seems impossible to shake off, just how accurate is it? Raymond D'addario worked with Blackmore for over 20 years in various crew capacities and is as well placed as anyone to comment on Blackmore's reputation as a disciplinarian. "I never thought so but only because I had seen people like Ian Anderson. We'd done gigs with him and I'd seen people play their parts for him and he would berate them in front of people for not playing their stuff right. Ritchie never seemed that way, it was like you know what you're supposed to be doing and go ahead and do it. It was when you didn't do it then you heard from him. Other people are constantly yelling at you, constantly drumming things into you and treating you like children. He always gave you the freedom and the room to be yourself but do what is expected of you, do what's required, if you're the sound guy or the singer. He's a perfectionist. He didn't want anyone in the band that would not be playing good or anyone in the crew who would be drunk or dropping stuff and breaking stuff. As I said I'd seen other people a thousand times worse. There always seem to be a reason when Ritchie had a voice to complain or there's a problem. Whereas other people seem to just need to show off or show they are in charge and complain about stuff that is idiotic, whereas Ritchie would only complain when it seemed to be something important. I always thought he treated all the people as professional as anyone I ever saw."

It's not easy analysing anyone as complex as Blackmore but in many ways his black and white appearance is also a reflection of his basic approach to life. "I love to exercise, kick a ball around and play soccer. The average day would be waking up with my cats: I love animals. Tuning into Europe, trying to find any soccer games that are on. I have this ridiculous satellite set up that I can pick up games in Romania if I want to."

Of all his characteristics, the reputation for minimalist conversation and moodiness is perhaps best summed up by former Rainbow drummer Bobby Rondinelli: "I don't really believe he's that way. I believe he talks when he wants to talk to whom he wants to talk to and he's very talkative. When I was in the band we'd sometimes talk on the phone for hours and we'd hang out almost every night so it depends on your relationship with him I guess. You know Ritchie, if he's on and having a good time he could be the life of the party but when he's not just turn and walk away. But I always thought he was a good conversationalist and very funny. When he's in the mood Ritchie can be one of the funniest guys on the planet and if it's someone he doesn't want to deal with then he's not going to deal with them. You know there's like sort of friendly, very friendly, extremely friendly – Ritchie doesn't have all those different degrees of friendly. He's either 'Hello, Goodbye' or very friendly and there's not a lot in between, but I always found him to be very sociable and funny. Any of my friends who met him thought he was a really funny guy. And he's very intelligent but sometimes he's not very sociable and that's what people see and that's all they remember.

"He might be a guy that fires a lot of musicians but he got a lot of musicians started. He got me started. I took Cozy Powell's place; he put me on the map. He did a lot more good for people than bad. He had a good knack for picking good people. He's a great musician, very aware of what was going on, he's fucking Ritchie Blackmore! He's also a guy that helped create a style of music. He's one of the most recognisable guitar players on the planet. I always think it's so easy to pick bad things about anybody but you wouldn't be talking about bad things if there weren't so many good things. Nobody would give a fuck. Somebody asked me is Ritchie as diffi-cult as people say and I said, 'In every walk of life people can be difficult. You can work for a guy at a grocery store that can be difficult.' But Ritchie's a genius, he was the boss, he knew what he wanted and if you were in the band and you didn't know that was the case you shouldn't have been in the band. It was called Ritchie Blackmore's Rainbow. He knew what he wanted and that was the way it was."

Whatever conclusions one has of Blackmore as a person, the impact his playing has had on numerous other musicians should not be overlooked. With his onstage mannerisms, Janick Gers, who ironically joined Ian Gillan's band in the early Eighties, was Blackmore reincarnated. He has sub-sequently attained massive success with Iron Maiden. Phil Collen, guitarist with Def Leppard, happily admits: "I saw Ritchie Blackmore when I was 14 and went, 'OK, I want to do that for a living.' I pestered my mum and dad for two years to get me a guitar." Bryan Adams has been a big fan ever since he saw Deep Purple in Canada in the early Seventies: "I never heard a guitar player like Ritchie Blackmore. No matter how fast I tried to make my fingers go, it never made sense like Ritchie Blackmore. I'm still not worthy..."

Blackmore's use of classical structures influenced the breed of guitarists referred to as the "neo-classical" brigade of whom Yngwie Malmsteen is the ultimate exponent: "I first heard Ritchie on *Fireball*. My sister gave it to me for my eighth birthday. Wow! It truly was a revelation to me. It inspired me to play my guitar day in and day out, driving everyone around me crazy in the process." To this day Deep Purple and Rainbow songs adorn his soundchecks and Blackmore DVDs are watched daily on Malmsteen's tour bus.

Within the post-Blackmore Deep Purple line up, Joe Satriani who acted as temporary replacement in 1993, jumped at the opportunity to play Blackmore's riffs. Steve Morse, the man who ultimately got the long term job told the author: "When I was a kid the very first song I heard with Deep Purple was 'Hush' back in the Sixties. We played that, my brother and I in our little band because we just loved it. We loved Deep Purple especially in that *Machine Head* era when they really hit their stride." Italian guitarist Dario Mollo, who has worked alongside Glenn Hughes, as well as Ritchie's former Rainbow band mates Graham Bonnet and Don Airey says, "I consider Ritchie Blackmore one of the greatest artists, his contribution to the development of rock 'n' roll music has been awesome. During high school a friend of mine played me the 'Smoke On The Water' riff and it blew me away, I was so enthusiastic that I decided immediately to become a rock guitarist. The first rock gig I saw was Rainbow in Grenoble during the 'Down To Earth' tour."

As for his undoubted abilities as a guitarist in 1989 Jon Lord said: "Ritchie doesn't play the guitar the standard way; he has an odd way of looking at things. Different chord shapes that most guitarists may not be able to come up with, or maybe wouldn't even want to come up with. Because he's such an individual type of player, I have to be on my toes."

For his friend Stuart Smith, Blackmore is "the ultimate guitarist – he's got phenomenal technique, he's also very passionate in his playing – he can emote very well – he controls every note to the point that he can bring a lot of feeling out in every single note and when you are doing that at some of the speeds he's doing it is mind blowing. He knows how to play the guitar as well. It's not like someone like Yngwie [Malmsteen] who becomes an incredible technician and just tears up and down the neck without any thought whatsoever. Things that he has taught me over the years about putting yourself into the mindset of what the song is all about, like a character actor. If you're playing a blues song about having your heart broken then you go back in time in your mind to when that happens to you or when you've been angry or whatever the song calls for, which is basically how he manages to challenge that incredible emotion on each thing he plays.

"Ritchie will play for the song; he'll work out what the songs about, what the moods about. Sometimes even if the lyrics aren't written he'll get a vibe as to where the songs going and play with the melody and if he does put in a fast lick it's more as an embellishment, like the cherry on the cake as opposed to look how fast I am. I remember we sat once watching TV and I think there was something on about the old actors, Cary Grant and all this, which Ritchie really loves. He's got no time for the modern stuff. If he rents a video or something, it's like Cary Grant. But we were talking about how they basically become character actors and put themselves into the part and reach back inside themselves to when they had experienced that, whatever it is they are trying to act. I remember I was playing something and he said, 'You're not really playing for the song you've got this aggressive solo and the song is about someone who has lost someone. What you need to do is reach into yourself and go back to all the pain you felt. I know you've done it.' And Ritchie rescued me from the depth of despair sometimes when I've been through break-ups so he said, 'I know you've been there so go back in your mind to that point then play the solo.'

"That was a turning point because it taught me how to bring more emotion out in myself and that was one of the things I thought was just incredible. Take something like 'I Surrender,' just the tone on that, I remember asking Roger Glover once how did you just get that singing tone on the guitar what effect did you put on it, he said, 'I didn't put any effect on it that's Ritchie just playing,' which just blew me away because it feels like it's got some chorus on it or something."

Outside of the guitar world, Iron Maiden singer Bruce Dickinson has hosted radio shows devoted to Deep Purple while Metallica drummer Lars Ulrich regularly talks about the galvanising effect of first seeing Purple in 1972. Blackmore's popularity even extends outside the circle of rock musicians. World renowned spoon bender, Uri Gellar is a great admirer and has in the past invited Blackmore for dinner at his home (he didn't take up the offer). Tony Blair, Britain's Prime Minister since 1997 skipped college when he was studying at university to catch a local Deep Purple show in Edinburgh. Just before being elected to office he wrote to Blackmore, telling him how much he admired his playing.

Blackmore's musical influence continues to appear in some of the most unlikely instances: a hillbilly version of 'Smoke On The Water' by the bizarrely named Al Gringo & the Original Psychobilly Krautboys and an equally radical version by Australian entertainer Rolf Harris are just a couple of examples. In the Seventies the James Last Orchestra did astonishingly off the wall versions of several Purple classics including 'Fireball' that defies description. 'Smoke On The Water,' in particular, has been regularly used through the years in adverts, TV and films while a recent West End play on the life of Joe Meek included Ritchie Blackmore (played by David Hayler) among the characters.

While many have heavily criticised his sometimes enigmatic behaviour, those who have worked with or befriended Ritchie Blackmore would ultimately own up to admitting their lives had been touched by the experience.

"He is very insecure," says Ian Gillan, "he's got a personality blockage somewhere. He doesn't like to be amongst people, which involve conversation or any of the normal sorts of intercourse that people go through. He likes to be quiet and on his own and unquestioned. He also likes to be difficult for no apparent reason other than he gets fun out of it. If he had been a mere mortal someone would have smacked him in the face years ago or fired him or whatever but he is something special. That's why his behaviour has been tolerated over all the years: One, his dedication to Purple or whatever project he's in and two, his guitar playing. As far as that's concerned that's all you can ask. You can't ask people to change their character, and in all essence the final observation I made – without him, wouldn't life be boring?"

DISCOGRAPHY

*F*or someone who has been involved with recorded music for forty-five years it will come as no surprise to discover that Blackmore's discography is, to say the least, quite large! To include every variation and release would in itself require a full book and is outside the remit of this publication. This discography only lists UK releases except for a few unique exceptions that contain material that was not released in Blackmore's homeland.

The discography is divided into five sections. Part one covers Blackmore's groups and session work up to the formation of Deep Purple. Part two covers Deep Purple recordings between 1968–75 and 1984–93. Part three covers Rainbow between 1975–84 and 1994–97. Part four, the sessions since the start of Deep Purple, and finally part five covers his current work with Blackmore's Night.

PART ONE – GROUPS & SESSIONS 1961–67

With regards to the work done for RGM productions between 1962 and 1966, it has primarily been confined to original releases. Blackmore didn't necessarily play on both sides of single releases, and where it is generally considered he has no involvement these tracks are indicated in italics.

SINGLES

MIKE DEE & THE JAYWALKERS Stolen Hours / My Blue Heaven [Decca, 1961 **unreleased**]

JAMIE LEE AND THE ATLANTICS In The Night / *Little Girl In Blue* [Decca F11571, January 1963]

THE OUTLAWS The Return Of The Outlaws / Texan Spiritual [HMV POP 1124, February 1963]

MICHAEL COX Don't You Break My Heart / Hark Is That A Cannon I Hear [HMV POP 1137, March 1963]

CHAD CARSON They Were Wrong / Stop Picking On Me [HMV POP 1156, April 1963]

GLENDA COLLINS *I Lost My Heart At The Fairground* / I Feel So Good [HMV POP 1163, May 1963]

HEINZ Dreams Do Come True / Been Invited To A Party [Decca F11652, May 1963]

FREDDIE STARR & THE MIDNIGHTERS Who Told You? / *Peter Gunn Locomotion* [Decca F11663, May 1963]

HOUSTON WELLS & THE MARKSMEN Only The Heartaches / *Can't Stop Pretending* [Parlophone R5031, May 1963]

BURR BAILEY & THE SIX SHOOTERS *San Francisco Bay* / Like A Bird Without Feathers [Decca F11686, June 1963]

JENNY MOSS Hobbies / Big Boy [Columbia DB7061, June 1963]

HEINZ Just Like Eddie / Don't You Knock At My Door [Decca F11693, July 1963]

THE OUTLAWS That Set The Wild West Free / *Hobo* [HMV POP 1195, August 1963]

GEOFF GODDARD Sky Men / Walk With Me My Angel [HMV POP 1213, October 1963]

MICHAEL COX Gee What A Party / Say That Again [HMV POP 1220, October 1963]

PAMELA BLUE My Friend Bobby / Hey There Stranger [Decca F11761, October 1963]

HEINZ Country Boy / Long Tall Jack [Decca F11768, November 1963]

FREDDIE STARR & THE MIDNIGHTERS It's Shaking Time / Baby Blue [Decca F11786, November 1963]

GLENDA COLLINS If You Gotta Pick A Baby / In The First Place [HMV POP 1233, November 1963]

GUNILLA THORN Merry Go Round / Go On Then [HMV POP 1239, December 1963]

JOE MEEK ORCHESTRA The Kennedy March / The Theme of Freedom [Decca F11796, December 1963]

THE OUTLAWS Law And Order / Do-Da-Day [HMV POP 1241, December 1963]

THE SHARADES Dumb Head / Boy Trouble [Decca F11811, January 1964]

KIM ROBERTS I'll Prove It / For Loving Me This Way [Decca F11813, January 1964]

JIMMY LENNON & THE ATLANTICS I Learned To Yodel / Louisiana Mama [Decca F11825, January 1964]

HEINZ You Were There / No Matter What They Say [Decca F11831, February 1964]

BURR BAILEY *Chahawki* / You Made Me Cry [Decca F11846, February 1964]

ANDY CAVELL Tell The Truth / *Shut Up* [Pye 7N15610, February 1964]

DAVY KAYE A Fool Such As I / It's Nice Isn't It [Decca F11866, March 1964]

THE PUPPETS *Baby Don't Cry* / Shake With Me [Pye 7N 15634, April 1964]

THE OUTLAWS Keep A Knockin' / Shake With Me [HMV POP 1277, April 1964]

HOUSTON WELLS Galway Bay / Living Alone [Parlophone R5141, May 1964]

HEINZ Please Little Girl / For Lovin' Me This Way [Decca F11920, June 1964]

TANYA DAY *His Lips Get In The Way* / I Get So Lonely [Polydor NH 52331, 1964 *Non RGM production*]

GLENDA COLLINS Lollipop / Everybody's Got To Fall In Love [HMV POP 1323, July 1964]

THE RALLY ROUNDERS The Bike Beat Pt 1 / The Bike Beat Pt 2 [Lyntone LYN 573/4, 1964]

FREDDIE STARR Never Cry On Someone's Shoulder / Just Keep On Dreaming [Decca F12009, October 1964]

HEINZ Questions I Can't Answer / The Beating Of My Heart [Columbia DB7374, October 1964]

VALERIE MASTERS Christmas Calling / He Didn't Fool Me [Columbia DB 7426, November 1964]

HEINZ WITH THE WILD BOYS Digging My Potatoes / She Ain't Coming Back [Columbia DB 7482, February 1965]

ALAN DEAN AND HIS PROBLEMS Thunder and Rain / As Time Goes By [Pye 7N15749, February 1965]

DAVY KAYE In My Way / All The Stars In Heaven [Decca F12073, February 1965]

RITCHIE BLACKMORE Getaway / Little Brown Jug [Oriole CB 314, March 1965 *Derek Lawrence production*]

THE OUTLAWS *Don't Cry* / Only For You [Smash, S2025, 1965, *Derek Lawrence production American only release*]

THE LANCASTERS Satan's Holiday / Earthshaker [Titan FF 1730, 1965, *Derek Lawrence production American only release*]

THE SESSIONS Let Me In / Bouncing Bass [Fontana, catalogue number unknown 1965, *Derek Lawrence production American only release*]

MURMAIDS To Know Him Is To Love Him / *B-side unknown* [Chattahoochie, catalogue number unknown 1965, *Derek Lawrence production American only release*]

HEINZ WITH THE WILD BOYS Don't Think Twice It's All Right / Big Fat Spider [Columbia DB 7559, April 1965]

PETER COOK *Georgia On My Mind* / There and Bach Again [Pye 7N15847, April 1965]

TOM JONES Little Lonely One / That's What We'll Do [Columbia DB7566, 8th May 1965]

THE TORNADOS Early Bird / *Stompin' Through The Rye* [Columbia DB 7589, May 1965]

JESS CONRAD Hurt Me / It Can Happen To You [Pye 7N15849, May 1965]

SCREAMING LORD SUTCH The Train Kept A Rollin' / Honey Hush [CBS 201767, June 1965]

GLENDA COLLINS Johnny Loves Me / Paradise For Two [HMV POP 1439, July 1965]

GLENDA COLLINS Thou Shalt Not Steal / Been Invited To A Party [HMV POP 1475, September 1965]

TOM JONES Lonely Joe / I Was A Fool [Columbia DB 7733, October 1965]

PETER LONDON Bless You / Baby I Like The Look Of You [Pye 7N15957, October 1965]

HEINZ Movin' In / I'm Not A Bad Guy [Columbia DB 7942, June 1966]

RONNIE JONES My Only Souvenir / Satisfy My Soul [Smash S2047, 1966, *Derek Lawrence production American only release*]

SOUL BROTHERS Goodbye Babe, Goodbye / My Only Reason For Living [Mercury 72632, 1966, *Derek Lawrence production American only release*]

HEIDI BACHERT Super – Boy / Blumen Für Die [Polydor 52 738, 1966 **German release, Blackmore's involvement unconfirmed**]

NEIL CHRISTIAN & THE CRUSADERS My Baby Left Me / Yakkety Yak [Deutsche Vogue DV 14744, 1968, **German only release**]

EPs

HEINZ – HEINZ [Decca DFE 8545, UK October 1963]
I Get Up In The Morning / Talkin' Like A Man / That Lucky Old Sun / Lonely River /

HEINZ – LIVE IT UP [Decca DFE 8559, UK November 1963]
Live It Up / Don't You Understand / Dreams Do Come True / When Your Loving Goes Wrong /

HOUSTON WELLS & THE MARKSMEN – RAMONA [Parlophone GEP 8914, UK August 1964]
Ramona / Girl Down The Street / I Wonder Who's Kissing Her Now / Nobody's Child /

TOM JONES – TOM JONES [Columbia SEG 8464, UK December 1965]
Lonely Joe / I Was A Fool / Little Lonely One / That's What We'll Do /

ALBUMS

VARIOUS ARTISTS – THANK YOUR LUCKY STARS VOL 2 [Decca LK 4554, June 1963]
Includes Just Like Eddie (Heinz)

VARIOUS ARTISTS – READY STEADY GO [Decca LK 4577, July 1963]
Includes Just Like Eddie / Country Boy (Heinz)

HEINZ – TRIBUTE TO EDDIE [Decca LK 4599, September 1963]
Tribute To Eddie / Hush-A-Bye-Baby / I Ran All The Way Home / Summertime Blues / *Don't Keep Pickin' On Me* / *Cut Across Shorty* / *Three Steps To Heaven* / Come On And Dance / 20 Flight Rock / *Look For A Star* / *My Dreams* / I Remember / *Rumble In The Night* / Just Like Eddie /

VARIOUS ARTISTS – 16 BEAT GROUPS FROM THE HAMBURG SCENE [Polydor 237639, Germany 1964]
Includes the Tanya Day track.

ROY HARPER – THE SOPHISTICATED BEGGAR [Strike SYB 7, UK 1966]
Blackmore is rumoured to play on the track 'Committed.'

POSTHUMOUS RGM COMPILATION ALBUMS

All of the following include RGM recordings, with the exception of the Gene Vincent releases, which include the sessions done by The Outlaws for BBC's Saturday Club *broadcast. Since the advent of CD there has been an endless stream of posthumous compilations of Joe Meek productions but only a select few have been listed: Most notably those that contain a large percentage of tracks featuring Blackmore and those that include tracks that were not originally released during Joe Meek's lifetime. These recordings are referred to as the 'Tea Chest Tapes' due to the way they were stored and discovered after Meek's death. For a full comprehensive list of released RGM recordings featuring Blackmore, including overseas releases, check the More Black than Purple website.*

HEINZ – REMEMBERING … HEINZ [Decca REM 7, UK 1977]

VARIOUS ARTISTS – THE JOE MEEK STORY [2LPs Decca DPA 3035/6, UK April, 1977]

RITCHIE BLACKMORE – ROCK PROFILE VOL 1 [2LP / 1CD Connoisseur Collection RP VSOP LP 143 / VSOP CD 143, UK 15th October 1989]

GLENDA COLLINS – BEEN INVITED TO A PARTY! THE SINGLES 1963–1966 [1LP / 1CD Connoisseur Collection CSAPLP 108 / CSAPCD 108, August 1990]

THE OUTLAWS – RIDE AGAIN (THE SINGLES A's & B's) [LP / CD: See For Miles SEE 303 / SEE CD303, UK 1990]

VARIOUS ARTISTS – THE JOE MEEK STORY – THE PYE YEARS [2CD Sequel NEX CD 171, UK 1991]

RITCHIE BLACKMORE – ROCK PROFILE VOL 2 [2LPs / 1CD Connoisseur Collection RP VSOP LP 157 / RP VSOP CD 157, 15th April 1991]

RITCHIE BLACKMORE – TAKE IT! SESSIONS 63/68 [RPM, RPM 120, UK 1994]

VARIOUS ARTISTS – LET'S GO! JOE MEEK'S GIRLS [RPM, RPM 166, UK 1996]

GLENDA COLLINS – THIS LITTLE GIRLS GONE ROCKIN! [RPM, RPM 182, UK October 1997]

GENE VINCENT – REBEL HEART VOL 4 [Magnum Force CDMF 097, 1997]

GENE VINCENT – REBEL HEART VOL 5 [Magnum Force CDMF 099, 1998]

DAVE ADAMS – THE DAVE ADAMS STORY [Diamond Recordings GEMCD 013, 1998]

JOE MEEK – HIDDEN GEMS [Diamond Recordings GEMCD 022, 1998]

HEINZ – THE COMPLETE HEINZ [2CDs, Repertoire REP 4718-WR, *German only release* 1999]

GENE VINCENT – BLUE 'GENE' BOP [Rockstar RSRCD 025, 2005]

JOE MEEK – POTRAIT OF A GENIUS [4CD box set Castle CMXBX783, 19th September 2005]

RITCHIE BLACKMORE – GETAWAY 2CDs [Castle CMEDD1029, 26th September 2005]

THE TEA CHEST TAPES

Those that 'have been documented' that Blackmore recorded during his years working at 304 Holloway Road, which are still unreleased are listed below. Meek left hundreds of hours of recordings that have never seen the light of day and are now in the hands of one individual who despite regular pleas has refused to allow them to be released or accessed. It is fair to say there is an enormous amount of Blackmore's session work to be found amongst those said reels of tape.

DAVE COLT	Oh How We Danced	1963, still unreleased
DAVE COLT	Four Leafed Clover	1963, still unreleased
DAVE COLT	Hello Sir Echo	1963, still unreleased
GLENDA COLLINS	Walk On By	still unreleased
KIM ROBERTS	Everytime	still unreleased
FREDDIE STARR	I'm Not A Juvenile Delinquent	still unreleased
JOE MEEK &		
THE OUTLAWS	It's Me (demo)	still unreleased
THE OUTLAWS	Dance Music	heard in the background in the film 'Live It Up'
GENE VINCENT &		
THE OUTLAWS	Temptation Baby	unreleased, alternative version to song featured in 'Live It Up'
GLENDA COLLINS &		
THE OUTLAWS	Yeah Yeah Yeah	Radio London Jingle
HEINZ	Come On Let's Go	still unreleased
HEINZ	I Get Up In The Morning	alternative version, still unreleased
HEINZ	Big Johnny Rhythm	still unreleased

HEINZ & THE WILDBOYS	What Was It That The Wise Man Said	still unreleased
TOM JONES	Unknown title	still unreleased
TOM JONES	Chills & Fever	still unreleased
TOM JONES	Breathless	still unreleased
TOM JONES	Baby I'm In Love	still unreleased
GUNILLA THORN	He's Mine	February 1964, still unreleased
GUNILLA THORN	Blueberry Hill	February 1964, still unreleased

PART TWO – DEEP PURPLE 1968–75, 1984–93

This list is essentially confined to original UK releases and remastered CD versions that contain extra material. In general, compilations that simply duplicate the same material have been avoided, as there are enough to fill another book! The exceptions are those that contain material that is unavailable elsewhere. Regarding such releases, any tracks that include line-ups of Deep Purple not featuring Ritchie Blackmore are listed in italics.

SINGLES

HUSH / ONE MORE RAINY DAY [Parlophone R-5708, June 1968]

KENTUCKY WOMAN / WRING THAT NECK [Parlophone R-5745, December 1968]

EMMARETTA / WRING THAT NECK [Parlophone R-5763, February 1969]

HALLELLUJAH / APRIL (PART 1) [Harvest HAR 5006, July 1969]

BLACK NIGHT / SPEED KING [Harvest HAR 5020, May 1970]

STRANGE KIND OF WOMAN / I'M ALONE [Harvest HAR 5033, February 1971]

FIREBALL / DEMON'S EYE [Harvest HAR 5045, October 1971]

NEVER BEFORE / WHEN A BLIND MAN CRIES [Purple PUR 102, March 1972]

MIGHT JUST TAKE YOUR LIFE / CORONARIAS REDIG [Purple PUR 117 March 1974]

SMOKE ON THE WATER live / CHILD IN TIME live / WOMAN FROM TOKYO edit [Purple PUR 132 March 1977]

NEW, LIVE AND RARE –VOL 2: BURN live / CORONARIAS REDIG / MISTREATED live [Purple PUR 137, September 1978]

BLACK NIGHT / STRANGE KIND OF WOMAN [Harvest HAR 5178 [7″ single] / 12 HAR 5178 [12″ single], April 1979]

BLACK NIGHT live / SPEED KING live [Harvest HAR 5210, July 1980]

NEW, LIVE AND RARE –VOL 3: SMOKE ON THE WATER live / BIRD HAS FLOWN live / GRABSPLATTER live [Harvest SHEP 101, October 1980]

BLACK NIGHT / SPEED KING / INTO THE FIRE [Harvest 12 HAR 5233, February 1985, 12″ single]

STRANGE KIND OF WOMAN / I'M ALONE / HIGHWAY STAR [Harvest 12 HAR 5234, February 1985, 12″ single]

FIREBALL / DEMON'S EYE / ANYONE'S DAUGHTER [Harvest 12 HAR 5235, February 1985, 12″ single]

SMOKE ON THE WATER / CHILD IN TIME / WOMAN FROM TOKYO [Harvest 12 HAR 5236, February 1985, 12″ single]

SMOKE ON MY MEGA-MIX / MIXED ALIVE [EMI Records PSR-474, 1985]
If you collected the four twelve inch singles as listed above and mailed the stickers to EMI, this "stars on 45" type single based on 'Smoke On The Water' was supplied.

PERFECT STRANGERS / SON OF ALERIK [7″ single, Polydor POSPP 719, October 1984]

PERFECT STRANGERS / SON OF ALERIK [12″ single, Polydor POSPX 719, October 1984]

KNOCKING AT YOUR BACK DOOR / PERFECT STRANGERS [7″ single, Polydor POSP 749 October 1984]

KNOCKING AT YOUR BACK DOOR long / PERFECT STRANGERS / BBC INTERVIEWS [12″ single, Polydor POSPX 749 October 1984]

CALL OF THE WILD / STRANGEWAYS long version [7″ single, Polydor POSP-843, 1987]

CALL OF THE WILD / STRANGEWAYS long version [12″ single, Polydor POSPX-843, 1987]

HUSH '88 live / DEAD OR ALIVE live [7″ single Polydor POC 4, June 1988]

HUSH '88 live / DEAD OR ALIVE live / BAD ATTITUDE live [12″ single, Polydor PZ-4, June 1988]

KING OF DREAMS edit / FIRE IN THE BASEMENT [7″ single RCA/BMG Records PB-49247, October 1990]

KING OF DREAMS edit / FIRE IN THE BASEMENT / KING OF DREAMS album version [12″ single, RCA/BMG Records PT-49248, October 1990]

LOVE CONQUERS ALL edit / TRUTH HURTS [7″ single, RCA/BMG Records PB-49225, March 1991]

LOVE CONQUERS ALL edit / TRUTH HURTS / SLOW DOWN SISTER [12″ single, RCA/BMG Records PT 49212, March 1991]

BLACK NIGHT (remix) / BLACK NIGHT (original) / SPEED KING (matching mix) [CD, EMI 7243 8 82214 2 9, 1995]

ALBUMS

SHADES OF DEEP PURPLE [Parlophone, PMC / PCS 7058, September 1968 / CD, EMI 498 3362, February 2000]
And The Address / Hush / One More Rainy Day / Prelude: Happiness / I'm So Glad / Mandrake Root / Help / Love Help Me / Hey Joe /

CD Bonus tracks: Shadows [out-take] / Love Help Me [instrumental version] / Help [alt. take] / Hey Joe [BBC Top Gear session] / Hush [live US TV]

BOOK OF TALIESYN [Harvest SHVL 751, July 1969 / CD, EMI 521 6082, February 2000]
Listen, Learn, Read On / Wring That Neck (Hard Road) / Kentucky Woman / Exposition: We Can Work It Out / Shield / Anthem / River Deep, Mountain High /
CD Bonus tracks: Oh No No No (studio out take) / It's All Over (BBC Top Gear session) / Hey Bop A Re Bop (BBC Top Gear session) / Wring That Neck (BBC Top Gear session) / Playground /

DEEP PURPLE [Harvest SHVL 759, November 1969 / CDEMI 521 5972, February 2000]
Chasing Shadows / Blind / Lalena / Fault Line / The Painter / Why Didn't Rosemary / Bird Has Flown / April /
CD Bonus tracks: The Bird Has Flown (alternate b-side version.) / Emmaretta (studio a-side) / Emmaretta (BBC Top Gear session) / Lalena (BBC radio session) / The Painter (BBC radio session)

CONCERTO FOR GROUP & ORCHESTRA [Harvest SHVL 767, January 1970 / EMI 07243 541006 2 8, 2CD, October 2002]
First Movement: Moderate – Allegro / Second Movement: Andante / Third Movement: Vivace – Presto /
CD bonus tracks: Hush / Wring That Neck / Child In Time / Third Movement: Vivace – Presto (encore) /

DEEP PURPLE IN ROCK [Harvest SHVL 777, June 1970 / CD, EMI CDDEEPP 1, October 1995]
Speed King / Bloodsucker / Child In Time 2 Flight Of The Rat / Into The Fire / Living Wreck / Hard Lovin' Man
CD Bonus tracks: Speed King (piano version) / Cry Free / Jam Stew (inst) / Flight Of The Rat (remix) / Speed King (remix) / Black Night (remix) /

FIREBALL [Harvest SHVL 793, September 1971 / CD, EMI CDDEEPP 2, September 1996]
Fireball / No No No / Demon's Eye / Anyone's Daughter / The Mule / Fools / No One Came /
CD Bonus tracks: Strange Kind Of Woman / I'm Alone / Freedom / Slow Train / Demon's Eye (remix) / The Noise Abatement Society Tapes (out-take) / Fireball (instrumental out-take) / Backwards Piano (out-take) / No One Came (remix)

MACHINE HEAD [Purple TPSA 7504, May 1972 / CD, EMI CDDEEPP 3, September 1997]
Highway Star / Maybe I'm A Leo / Pictures Of Home / Never Before / Smoke On The Water / Lazy / Space Truckin'
CD Bonus tracks: (all remixed unless noted) When A Blind Man Cries (remastered) / Highway Star / Maybe I'm A Leo / Pictures Of Home / Never Before / Smoke On The Water / Lazy / Space Truckin' / When A Blind Man Cries / Maybe I'm A Leo (quad) / Lazy (quad) /

MADE IN JAPAN [Purple TPSP 351, December 1972 / 2CD, EMI 7243 8 57864 2 6, February 1998]
Highway Star / Child In Time / Smoke On The Water / The Mule / Strange Kind Of Woman / Lazy / Space Truckin' /
CD Bonus tracks: Black Night / Speed King / Lucille /

WHO DO WE THINK WE ARE [Purple TPSA 7508, March 1973 / CD, EMI 521 6072, October 2000]
Woman From Tokyo / Mary Long / Super Trouper / Smooth Dancer / Rat Bat Blue / Place In Line / Our Lady /
CD Bonus tracks (all remixed unless noted): Woman From Tokyo / Woman From Tokyo (bridge) / Painted Horse (out-take) / Our Lady / Rat Bat Blue (writing) / Rat Bat Blue / First Day Jam

BURN [Purple TPS 3505, February 1974 / CD, EMI 473 5922, September 2004]
Burn / Might Just Take Your Life / Lay Down Stay Down / Sail Away / You Fool No One / What's Going On Here / Mistreated / 'A' 200 /
CD Bonus tracks Coronarias Redig (b-side remix) / Burn [remix] / Mistreated [remix] / You Fool No One [remix] / Sail Away [remix]

STORMBRINGER [Purple TPS 3508, December 1974]
Stormbringer / Love Don't Mean A Thing / Holy Man / Hold On / Lady Double Dealer / You Can't Do It Right / Highball Shooter / The Gypsy / Soldier Of Fortune /

MADE IN EUROPE [Purple TPSA 7517, October 1976]
Burn / Mistreated / Lady Double Dealer / You Fool No One / Stormbringer /

POWERHOUSE [Purple TPS 3510, 9th November 1977]
Painted Horse / Hush / Wring That Neck / Child In Time / Black Night / Cry Free /

IN CONCERT 1970–72 [Harvest SHDW 412, December 1980 / 2CD, EMI CDEM 1434, 1992]
Speed King / Wring That Neck / Child In Time / Mandrake Root / Highway Star / Strange Kind Of Woman / Lazy / Never Before / Space Truckin / Lucille / CD1 Speed King / Child In Time / Wring That Neck / Mandrake Root / CD2 Highway Star / Strange Kind Of Woman / Maybe I'm A Leo / Never Before / Lazy / Space Truckin' / Smoke On The Water / Lucille /

LIVE IN LONDON [Harvest SHSP 4124, 23rd August 1982]
Burn / Might Just Take Your Life / Lay Down, Stay Down / Mistreated / Smoke On The Water / You Fool No One – The Mule /

PERFECT STRANGERS [Polydor, POLH16, 1984 / POLHP16, 1985, picture disc with extra track★ / CD, Polydor 546 045-2, June 1999]
Knocking At Your Back Door / Under The Gun / Nobody's Home / Mean Streak / Perfect Strangers / A Gypsy's Kiss / Wasted Sunsets / Hungry Daze / Not Responsible★ / CD bonus track: Son Of Alerik /

THE HOUSE OF BLUE LIGHT [Polydor, POLH32, / CD, 831 318-2, 12th January 1987]
Bad Attitude / The Unwritten Law / Call Of The Wild / Mad Dog / Black & White / Hard Lovin' Woman / Spanish Archer / Strangeways / Mitzi Dupree / Dead Or Alive / *Some tracks longer on CD. NB: 1999 remastered CD included shorter versions as per original vinyl release. Avoid like the plague!*

SCANDINAVIAN NIGHTS [Connoisseur Collection DPVSOPLP 125, 17th October 1988 / Purple Records PUR 338D, 4th April 2005]
Speed King / Into The Fire / Child In Time / Wring That Neck / Paint It Black / Mandrake Root / Black Night /
Re-issued under new title 'Live In Stockholm 1970' with slightly longer running time.

NOBODY'S PERFECT [Polydor, PODV 10, 1989 / 2CD Polydor 546 128-2, June 1999]
Highway Star / Strange Kind Of Woman / Perfect Strangers / Hard Lovin' Woman / Knocking At Your Back Door / Child In Time / Lazy / Space Truckin' / Black Night / Woman From Tokyo / Smoke On The Water / Hush / CD bonus track: Dead Or Alive /

RITCHIE BLACKMORE – ROCK PROFILE VOL 1 [2LP / 1CD Connoisseur Collection RP VSOP LP 143 / VSOP CD 143, UK 15th October 1989]
Although listed under part one of the discography this release also features previously unreleased versions of Highway Star, No No No (*edited on CD*), and previously unreleased studio outtakes; Playground, Guitar Job, & Show Me The Way To Go Home (*latter track omitted from CD*).

IN THE ABSENCE OF PINK KNEBWORTH '85 [2CD, Connoisseur Collection DP VSOP CD 163 July 1991]
Highway Star / Nobody's Home / Strange Kind Of Woman / Gypsy's Kiss / Perfect Strangers / Lazy / Knocking At Your Back Door / Difficult To Cure / Space Truckin' / Speed King / Black Night / Smoke On The Water /

SLAVES & MASTERS [CD, BMG RCA PD 90535, October 1990]
King Of Dreams / The Cut Runs Deep / Fire In The Basement / Truth Hurts / Breakfast In Bed / Love Conquers All / Fortuneteller / Too Much Is Not Enough / Wicked Ways /

FIRE, ICE & DYNAMITE [CD, Ariola 261 149CD, November 1990]
Various Artists, soundtrack album includes 'Fire, Ice & Dynamite', recorded for Slaves & Masters but unavailable elsewhere.

THE BATTLE RAGES ON [CD, BMG / RCA 74321 15420-2, 26th July 1993]
The Battle Rages On / Lick It Up / Anya / Talk About Love / Time To Kill / Ramshackle Man / A Twist In The Tale / Nasty Piece Of Work / Solitaire / One Man's Meat /

GEMINI SUITE LIVE [RPM 114, July 1993]
First Movement: Guitar, Voice / Second Movement: Organ, Bass / Third Movement: Drums, Finale /

LIVE IN JAPAN [3CD, 7243 8 27726 2 0, September 1993]
CD1 Highway Star / Child In Time / The Mule / Strange Kind Of Woman / Lazy / Space Truckin' / Black Night /
CD2 Highway Star / Smoke On The Water / Child In Time / The Mule / Strange Kind Of Woman / Lazy / Space Truckin' /
CD3 Highway Star / Smoke On The Water / Child In Time / The Mule / Strange Kind Of Woman / Lazy / Space Truckin' / Speed King /

COME HELL OR HIGH WATER [CD, BMG 74321 23416 2, November 1994 / ★BMG, BVCP766, 1994, Japan]
Highway Star / Black Night / Twist In The Tale / Perfect Strangers / Anyone's Daughter / Child In Time / Anya / (Lazy★ / Space Truckin★ / Woman From Tokyo★) Speed King / Smoke On The Water / (★ bonus tracks on Japanese edition)

CALIFORNIA JAMMING – LIVE 1974 [EMI Premier PRMUCD2, 1996]
Burn / Might Just Take Your Life / Mistreated / Smoke On The Water / You Fool No One – The Mule / Space Truckin' /
Re-issued as JUST MIGHT TAKE YOUR LIFE, 1974 [Sonic Zoom PUR 208, 2004] with extra track, Lay Down, Stay Down.

MKIII – THE FINAL CONCERTS [Connoisseur Collection DPVSOP CD 230, 2CD, 29th July 1996]
CD1 – Burn / Stormbringer / Gypsy / Lady Double Dealer / Mistreated / Smoke On The Water / You Fool No One /
CD2 – Space Truckin' / Going Down – Highway Star / Mistreated (alt version) / You Fool No One (alt version) /

THE BOOTLEG SERIES 1984–2000 [12CD Box set, Thames Thompson 6 97593 00074 8, 2000]
CD1 'Highway Stars': Highway Star / Nobody's Home / Strange Kind Of Woman / A Gypsy's Kiss / Perfect Strangers / Under The Gun / Knocking At Your Back Door / Lazy /
CD2 'Highway Stars': Child In Time / Beethoven's Ninth / Organ solo / Space Truckin' / Organ solo / Guitar solo / Space Truckin' cont. / Black Night / Speed King / Smoke On The Water /
CD3 'Third Night': Introduction / Highway Star / Nobody's Home / Strange Kind Of Woman / A Gypsy's Kiss / Perfect Strangers / Under The Gun / Lazy / Drum solo / Child In Time /
CD4 'Third Night': Knocking At Your Back Door / Beethoven's Ninth / Organ solo / Space Truckin' / Woman From Tokyo / Black Night / Smoke On The Water /
CD5 'Hungary Days': Intros / Highway Star / Strange Kind Of Woman / The Unwritten Law / Blues / Dead Or Alive / Perfect Strangers / Hard Lovin' Woman / Bad Attitude / Child In Time / Difficult To Cure / Organ solo /
CD6 'Hungary Days': Knocking At Your Back Door / Hungarian dance / Lazy / Space Truckin' / Black Night / Smoke On The Water / Speed King / Call Of The Wild / Woman From Tokyo / World tour outro
CD7 'In Your Trousers': Intro / Highway Star / Black Night / Talk About Love / A Twist In The Tale / Perfect Strangers / Difficult To Cure / Organ solo / Knocking At Your Back Door / Anyone's Daughter / Child In Time /
CD8 'In Your Trousers': Guitar solo / Anya / The Battle Rages On / Lazy / Drum solo / Space Truckin' / Woman From Tokyo / Paint It Black / Hush / Smoke On The Water / *Discs 9–12 without Blackmore*

SPACE VOL 1 & 2 [Sonic Zoom, PUR 202, July 2001]
Wring That Neck / Black Night / Paint It Black / Mandrake Root /
Re-issued as 'Live In Aachen 1970', Purple Records PUR 252, 13th March 2006

ON THE ROAD [4CD, Connoisseur Collection, DPBOX400, September 2001]
CD1: Hush / Child In Time / Into The Fire / Black Night / Highway Star /
Wring That Neck / No No No /
CD2: Speed King / Strange Kind Of Woman / Lazy / Fireball / Perfect
Strangers / Bad Attitude / Space Truckin' / Dead Or Alive / Anya /
CD3: Burn / Mistreated / Smoke On The Water / Going Down / You Fool No
One /
CD4: *Lady Luck / Love Child / Gettin' Tighter / You Keep On Moving / This Time
Around / Owed To 'G' / Wild Dogs / Stormbringer /*

LIVE IN DENMARK '72 [Sonic Zoom PUR 203D, December 2002]
Highway Star / Strange Kind Of Woman / Child In Time / The Mule / Lazy /
Space Truckin' / Fireball / Lucille / Black Night /

LIVE IN INGLEWOOD, 1968 [Sonic Zoom PUR 205, 2002]
Hush / Kentucky Woman / Mandrake Root / Help / Wring That Neck / River
Deep, Mountain High / Hey Joe /

LISTEN, LEARN, READ ON [EMI 540 9732, 28th October 2002]
Six CD box set including remastered and previously unreleased recordings with
120 page book.
Tracks: CD1: Keep A Knockin' (The Outlaws) / *You'll Never Stop Me Loving You /
Only Time Will Tell (M.I.5) / Send For That Girl (Johnny Kidd & The Pirates) /
Porcupine Juice (Santa Barbara Machine Head) / I Can See Through You / Mr Universe
(Episode Six) / Medusa (Trapeze) / Does Anybody Really Know What Time It Is (The
Government) / See My People Come Together (Zephyr) /* Hush / Help / Shield /
Listen, Learn, Read On/ Kentucky Woman/ Playground/ Emmaretta /The Bird
Has Flow (single version) /
CD2: Why Didn't Rosemary / Hallelujah / Ricochet (unreleased) / Bird Has
Flown (BBC session) / Hush (live, Royal Albert Hall) / Concerto 3rd Movement
encore (live, unreleased) / Wring That Neck (live, unreleased) Jam Stew (BBC
session) / Speed King (BBC session) / Cry Free / Hard Loving Man (BBC
session) / Bloodsucker (BBC session) / Living Wreck (BBC session) / Studio
Chat / Jam / Flight Of The Rat /
CD3: Mandrake Root (live, Stockholm) / Grabsplatter (BBC session) / Child In
Time (BBC session) / Jon Lord interview (BBC session) / Black Night (BBC
session) / Into The Fire (BBC session) / Fools (unreleased version) / Fireball /
No One Came / Demon's Eye /
CD4: No No No (live) / Highway Star (live) / Smoke On The Water (Quad
Mix) / Never Before (Quad Mix) / When A Blind Man Cries / Strange Kind Of
Woman (live, Paris Theatre) / Lazy (live, Tokyo '72) / Black Night (live,
unreleased, Osaka, '72) / Woman From Tokyo / Smooth Dancer / Mary Long
(unreleased remix) / Burn / Might Just Take Your Life /

CD5: Sail Away / Coronarias Redig / You Fool No One (live, Cal Jam) / Mistreated (live, San Diego) / Space Truckin' (live, unreleased, Kilburn) / CD6: Stormbringer (Quad Mix) / Soldier Of Fortune (Quad Mix) / Hold On (Quad Mix) / Highball Shooter (instrumental) / The Gypsy (live, Paris) / *Drifter (live rehearsal) / Dance To The Rock 'n' Roll (live jam) / This Time Around / Owed To 'G' / Love Child / Wild Dogs (live, Tokyo) / Lady Luck (live, Long Beach) / Gettin' Tighter (live, Long Beach) / You Keep On Moving /*

KNEEL & PRAY [2CD, Purple Records PUR207D, 2002]
Speed King / Kneel & Pray / Hush / Child In Time / Wring That Neck / Paint It Black / Mandrake Root / Kentucky Woman /

PERKS & TIT – LIVE IN SAN DIEGO 1974 [CD, Purple Records PUR206, January 2003]
Burn / Might Just Take Your Life / Lay Down, Stay Down / Mistreated / Smoke On The Water /

NEW, LIVE & RARE [Sonic Zoom PUR 209, 2003]
Wring That Neck / Child In Time / Black Night / Strange Kind Of Woman / Into The Fire / Demon's Eye / Wring That Neck (edit) / Mandrake Root (edit) /

THE EARLY YEARS [CD EMI, 596 6112, 1st March 2004]
And The Address / Hush / Mandrake Root / I'm So Glad / Hey Joe / Kentucky Woman / Listen, Learn, Read On / Shield / Wring That Neck / Anthem / Bird Has Flown / Blind / Why Didn't Rosemary / Lalena /
Although a compilation it contains two previously unreleased alternative takes.

LIVE IN PARIS 1975 [2CD, Purple Records PUR330D March 2004]
Burn / Stormbringer / Gypsy / Lady Double Dealer / Mistreated / Smoke On The Water / You Fool No One / Space Truckin' / Goin' Down / Highway Star /

LIVE IN EUROPE 1993 [BMG 82876 759042, January 2006]
Live At Birmingham NEC: Highway Star / Black Night / Talk About Love / A Twist In The Tale / Perfect Strangers / Beethoven's Ninth / Jon's Keyboard Solo / Knocking At Your Back Door / Anyone's Daughter / Child In Time / Anya / The Battle Rages On / Lazy / Drum Solo / Space Truckin' / Woman From Tokyo / Paint It Black / Hush / Smoke On The Water /
Live In Stuttgart: Highway Star / Black Night / Talk About Love / A Twist In The Tale / Perfect Strangers / The Mule / Beethoven's Ninth / Knocking At Your Back Door / Anyone's Daughter / Child In Time / Anya / The Battle Rages On / Lazy / In The Hall Of The Mountain King / Space Truckin' / Woman From Tokyo / Paint It Black / Speed King / Hush / Smoke On The Water /

PART THREE – RAINBOW 1975–83, 1994–97

SINGLES

MAN ON THE SILVER MOUNTAIN / SNAKE CHARMER [Oyster, OYR 103, October 1975]

KILL THE KING / MAN ON THE SILVER MOUNTAIN / MISTREATED [Polydor, 2066 845, August 1977]

LONG LIVE ROCK 'N' ROLL / SENSITIVE TO LIGHT [Polydor, 2066 913, March 1978]

L.A CONNECTION / LADY OF THE LAKE [Polydor 2066 968, September 1978]

SINCE YOU BEEN GONE / BAD GIRL [Polydor, POSP 70, August 1979]

ALL NIGHT LONG / WEISS HEIM [Polydor, POSP 104, February 1980]

I SURRENDER / VIELLEICHT DAS NÄCHSTE MAL [Polydor, POSP 221, January 1981]

CAN'T HAPPEN HERE / JEALOUS LOVER [Polydor, POSP 251, June 1981]

STONE COLD / ROCK FEVER [Polydor, POSP 421, April 1982]

STREET OF DREAMS / ANYBODY THERE [Polydor, POSP 631, August 1983]

CAN'T LET YOU GO / ALL NIGHT LONG (live) [Polydor, POSP 654, October 1983]

CAN'T LET YOU GO / ALL NIGHT LONG (live) / STRANDED (live) [Polydor, POSPX 654, 12" version, October 1983]

ARIEL (radio edit) / ARIEL (album version) / TEMPLE OF THE KING (live) [BMG, 74321-32982-2, November 1995]

ALBUMS

RITCHIE BLACKMORE'S RAINBOW [Oyster, OYA2001, August 1975]
Man On The Silver Mountain / Self Portrait / Black Sheep Of The Family / Catch The Rainbow / Snake Charmer / The Temple Of The King / If You Don't Like Rock 'N' Roll / Sixteenth Century Greensleeves / Still I'm Sad /

RISING [Polydor, 2490 137, May 1976]
Tarot Woman / Run With The Wolf / Starstruck / Do You Close Your Eyes / Stargazer / Light In The Black /

ON STAGE [Polydor, 2657 142, July 1977]
Kill The King / Man On The Silver Mountain / Blues / Starstruck / Catch The Rainbow / Mistreated / Sixteenth Century Greensleeves / Still I'm Sad /

LONG LIVE ROCK 'N' ROLL [Polydor, POLD 5002, 14th April 1978]
Long Live Rock 'N' Roll / Lady Of The Lake / L.A. Connection / Gates Of
Babylon / Kill The King / The Shed (Subtle) / Sensitive To Light / Rainbow
Eyes /

DOWN TO EARTH [Polydor, POLD 5023, August 1979]
All Night Long / Eyes Of The World / No Time To Lose / Makin' Love / Since
You Been Gone / Love's No Friend / Danger Zone / Lost In Hollywood /

MONSTERS OF ROCK [Polydor, 2488 810, October 1980]
Various artists compilation recorded live at Donington. Includes Stargazer & All
Night Long.

DIFFICULT TO CURE [Polydor, POLD 5036, February 1981]
I Surrender / Spotlight Kid / No Release / Magic / Vielleicht Das Nächster Zeit★ /
Can't Happen Here / Freedom Fighter / Midtown Tunnel Vision / Difficult To
Cure / *★This track was also titled in brackets with its English equivalent; 'Maybe Next
Time.' Because of Blackmore's grammatical error with the German title, it was corrected on
later releases of the album and consequently listed as 'Vielleicht Das Nächste Mal.'*

STRAIGHT BETWEEN THE EYES [Polydor, POLD 5056, June 1982]
Death Alley Driver / Stone Cold / Bring On The Night / Tite Squeeze / Tearin'
Out My Heart / Power / Miss Mistreated / Rock Fever / Eyes Of Fire /

BENT OUT OF SHAPE [Polydor, POLD 5116, September 1983]
Stranded / Can't Let You Go / Fool For The Night / Fire Dance / Anybody
There / Desperate Heart / Street Of Dreams / Drinking With The Devil /
Snowman / Make Your Move /

FINYL VINYL [Polydor, PODV 8, February 1986]
Spotlight Kid / I Surrender / Miss Mistreated / Street Of Dreams / Jealous
Lover / Can't Happen Here / Tearin' Out My Heart / Since You Been Gone /
Bad Girl / Difficult To Cure / Stone Cold / Power / Man On The Silver
Mountain / Long Live Rock 'n' Roll / Weiss Heim /
*All the albums were reissued on remastered CDs by Polydor in 1999 and with the
exception of Bent Out Of Shape that contained longer versions of two tracks, previously
only available on the original cassette version, and Finyl Vinyl that included a bonus track
also previously only available on the original cassette version, not a great deal of thought was
put in to them, with regards to bonus material or improved artwork.*

LIVE IN GERMANY 1976 [Connoisseur, DP VSOP LP 155, November 1990]
Kill The King / Mistreated / Sixteenth Century Greensleeves / Catch The
Rainbow / Man On The Silver Mountain / Stargazer / Still I'm Sad / Do You
Close Your Eyes /

Discography

RITCHIE BLACKMORE – ROCK PROFILE VOL 2 [2LPs / 1CD
Connoisseur Collection RP VSOP LP 157 / RP VSOP CD 157, 15th April
1991]
*Although listed under part one of the discography, this compilation also includes Sixteenth
Century Greensleeves & Man On The Silver Mountain from the same tapes used for the
Live In Germany 1976 double album but these are alternative versions.*

STRANGER IN US ALL [BMG, 74321-30337-2, September 1995]
Wolf To The Moon / Cold Hearted Woman / Hunting Humans (Insatiable) /
Stand And Fight / Ariel / Too Late For Tears / Black Masquerade / Silence / Hall
Of The Mountain King / Still I'm Sad /

DEUTSCHLAND TOURNEE 1976 [VAP, VPCK85354, 24th May 2006, 6 CD
box set, Japan only]
CD 1 Intro (Over The Rainbow) / Kill The King / Mistreated / Sixteenth
Century Greensleeves / Catch The Rainbow / Man On The Silver Mountain /
CD 2 Stargazer / Still I'm Sad / Do You Close Your Eyes /
CD 3 Intro (Over The Rainbow) / Kill The King / Mistreated / Sixteenth
Century Greensleeves / Catch The Rainbow / Man On The Silver Mountain /
CD 4 Stargazer / Still I'm Sad /
CD 5 Intro (Over The Rainbow) / Kill The King / Mistreated / Sixteenth
Century Greensleeves / Catch The Rainbow / Man On The Silver Mountain /
CD 6 Stargazer / Still I'm Sad / Do You Close Your Eyes /
*(Three complete concerts from German tour, parts of which were originally released on Live
In Germany 1976)*

LIVE IN GERMANY 1977 [2CD, Eagle Rock, EDGCD315, 12th June 2006]
Kill The King / Mistreated / Sixteenth Century Greensleeves / Catch The
Rainbow / Long Live Rock 'n' Roll / Man On The Silver Mountain / Blues /
Still I'm Sad / Do You Close Your Eyes /

LIVE COLOGNE SPORTHALLE [2CD, Purple Records T2CD0105, 10th July
2006]
Intro (Over The Rainbow) / Kill The King / Mistreated / Sixteenth Century
Greensleeves / Catch The Rainbow / Man On The Silver Mountain /
CD 2 Stargazer / Still I'm Sad / Do You Close Your Eyes /
(First two discs from Deutschland Tournee 1976 Japanese box set.)
There have also been numerous compilations duplicating material from the above albums.

PART FOUR – SESSIONS 1968–PRESENT DAY

SINGLES

BOZ I Shall Be Released / Down In The Flood [Columbia DB 8406, May 1968]

SUNDRAGON Five White Horses / *Look At The Sun* [MGM MGM 1458, 1968]

ANAN Madena / Standing Still [Pye 7N17642, November 1968]

RANDY PIE & FAMILY Hurry To The City / *Looking With Eyes Of Love* [Atlantic ATL10290, Germany 1973]

ROCK AID ARMENIA [Life Aid Armenia, ARMEN 001 / T001, 7″ / 12″, UK 1990]
Smoke On The Water / *Paranoid (Black Sabbath 1970)* /

SWEET LIVE EP [CD, Sweet Fan Club release, PR001, UK 1996]
Alright Now / *Hellraiser* / *Restless* /

ALBUMS

SUNDRAGON – GREEN TAMBOURINE MGM [MGM-C (S) 8090, UK, December 1968]
Blackmore on four tracks only: I Want To Be A Rock 'n' Roll Star / Peacock Dress / Five White Horses / Love Minus Zero /

GREEN BULLFROG [MCA, MCA 2021, March 1972 / Connoisseur Collection NSP CD 503, 1991]
My Baby Left Me / Makin' Time / Lawdy Miss Clawdy / Bullfrog / I Want You / I'm A Free Man / Walk A Mile In My Shoes / Lovin' You Is Good For Me Baby /
CD bonus tracks: Ain't Nobody Home / Louisiana Man / Who Do You Love /

LORD SUTCH & HEAVY FRIENDS – HANDS OF JACK THE RIPPER [Atlantic K40313, 1971]
Gotta Keep A-Rocking / Roll Over Beethoven / Country Club / Hands Of Jack The Ripper / Good Golly Miss Molly / Great Balls Of Fire / Bye Bye Johnny / Johnny B Goode / Tutti Fruiti Medley /

ADAM FAITH – I SURVIVE [Warner Bros K 56054, 1974]
Blackmore only appears on intro to 'I Survived'

JACK GREEN – HUMANESQUE [RCA RCALP 5004, March 1981]
Only appears on one track, 'I Call, No Answer'

LAURENT VOULZY – CACHÉ DERRIÈRE [CD, Ariola, 262970 BM650, France 1992]
Only appears on one track 'Guitarre Hieraut'

VARIOUS ARTISTS – TWANG A TRIBUE TO THE SHADOWS [CD, Pangea, 72438 33928 2 7, 1996]
Only appears on one track, 'Apache'

PAT BOONE – IN A METAL MOOD In A Metal Mood – No More Mr Nice Guy [CD, Hip-O, HIPD-40025, USA January 1997]
Only appears on one track, 'Smoke On The Water'

GEYERS SCHWARZER HAUFEN – LIVE '99 [CD Horse Records, CM 31.0545, Germany 2000]
Only appears on one track, 'Götliche Devise'

GEYERS – HISTOROCK LÄSTERZUNGEN [CD, Geyers Records, 012004, Germany 2004]
Only appears on one track, 'God's Gospel'

PART FIVE – BLACKMORE'S NIGHT 1997–PRESENT DAY

CD SINGLES

SHADOW OF THE MOON (radio edit) / SHADOW OF THE MOON (album version) / MOND TANZ [Edel 0099115WHE, Germany, May 1997]
THE TIMES THEY ARE A-CHANGIN' / SAKE OF SONG / THE TIMES THEY ARE A-CHANGIN' (video track) [SPV 085-72432 CDE, July 2001]
ALL BECAUSE OF YOU / HOME AGAIN [CD, SPV 055-72733 CDE, Germany, September 2001]
HOME AGAIN (edited version) / WAITING JUST FOR YOU (remixed version) /
ALL BECAUSE OF YOU (remixed version) / HOME AGAIN (album version) [SPV, 055-74423 CDS, Germany, 12th August 2002]
ALL BECAUSE OF YOU (Radio Romantic Mix) / ALL BECAUSE OF YOU (Regenwald Mix) / ALL BECAUSE OF YOU (album version) /
[SPV, SSSPV 055-69893, September 2004]
I'LL BE THERE (JUST CALL MY NAME) / OLD MILL INN [SPV, 055-99693, 5th September 2005]
STREETS OF LONDON / OLD MILL INN [SPV, 99403 CDS, April 2006]

CD ALBUMS

SHADOW OF THE MOON [Edel, 0099022WHE, July 1997 / HTD Records, HTDCD84, 1998 reissue with extra track★]
Shadow Of The Moon / The Clock Ticks On / Be Mine Tonight / Play Minstrel Play / Ocean Gypsy / Minstrel Hall / Magical World / Writing On The Wall / Renaissance Faire / Memmingen / No Second Chance / Mond Tanz / Spirit Of The Sea / Greensleeves / Wish You Were Here / Possum's Last Dance★ /

UNDER A VIOLET MOON [Candlelight PCCY 01377, 21st June 1999]
Under A Violet Moon / Castles And Dreams / Past Time With Good Company /
Morning Star / Avalon / Possum Goes To Prague / Wind In The Willows / Gone
With The Wind / Beyond The Sunset / March The Heroes Home / Spanish
Nights (I Remember It Well) / Catherine Howard's Fate / Fool's Gold / Durch
Den Wald Zum Bach Haus / Now And Then / Self Portrait /

FIRES AT MIDNIGHT [SPV, SPV085-72432 / Limited Edition version,
SPV08872430, August 2001]
Written In The Stars / The Times They Are A Changin' / I Still Remember /
Home Again / Crowning Of The King / Fayre Thee Well / Fires At Midnight /
Hanging Tree / The Storm / Midwinter's Night / All Because Of You / Waiting
Just For You / Praetorius (Courante) / Benzai-Ten / Village On The Sand / Again
Someday /
Limited edition includes: Velvet box with photo cards, poster, bonus track
(Possum's Last Dance) and video track (The Times They Are A Changin')

PAST TIMES WITH GOOD COMPANY [SPV, SPV 092-74492 DCD /
Limited Edition version in special digi pack, SPV 095-74490, 28th October 2002]
Shadow Of The Moon / Play Minstrel Play / Minstrel Hall / Past Time With
Good Company / Fires At Midnight / Under A Violet Moon / Soldier Of
Fortune / Sixteenth Century Greensleeves / Beyond The Sunset / Morning Star
/ Home Again / Renaissance Faire / I Still Remember / Durch Den Wald Zum
Bachhaus / Writing On The Wall / Limited edition bonus tracks: Fires At
Midnight (Acoustic) / Home Again (Greek) /

GHOST OF A ROSE [SPV, SPV 085-74992 CD / Limited Edition version, SPV
089-74990, 30th June 2003]
Way To Mandalay / Three Black Crows / Diamonds And Rust / Cartouche /
Queen For A Day (part 1) / Queen For A Day (part 2) / Ivory Tower / Nur Eine
Minute / Ghost Of A Rose / Mr. Peagram's Morris And Sword / Loreley /
Where Are We Going From Here / Rainbow Blues / All For One / Dandelion
Wine / Limited edition bonus tracks: Mid Winter's Night (live acoustic version /
Way To Mandalay (radio edit) /

BEYOND THE SUNSET – THE ROMANTIC COLLECTION [SPV, SPV
087969900, 13th September 2004]
CD Tracks: Once In A Million Years / Be Mine Tonight / Wish You Were Here /
Waiting Just For You / Durch Den Wald Zum Bach Haus / Ghost Of A Rose /
Spirit Of The Sea / I Still Remember / Castles And Dreams / Beyond The
Sunset / Again Someday / Diamonds And Rust / Now And Then / All Because
Of You. DVD tracks; Written In The Stars / Morning Star / Play Minstrel Play /
Minstrel Hall / Under A Violet Moon /
Special limited edition compilation CD & DVD plus 3 track Christmas single;
Christmas Eve / Emanuel / We Three Kings /

THE VILLAGE LANTERNE [SPV, SPV 99702 / Limited Edition 2 disc version,
SPV 99700, 27th March 2006]
25 Years / Village Lanterne / I Guess It Doesn't Matter Anymore / The
Messenger / World Of Stone / Faerie Queen / St. Teresa / Village Dance / Mond
Tanz / Child In Time / Streets Of London / Just Call My Name (I'll Be There) /
Olde Mill Inn / Windmills / Street Of Dreams /
Limited edition bonus disc: Call It Love / Street Of Dreams (feat. Joe Lynn
Turner) / DVD interview /

FILMOGRAPHY

Only concert, TV and film recordings that have been commercially released have been included.

LIVE IT UP! [VHS, DD video, DD.06050, 2003]
1963 film featuring The Outlaws.

CONCERTO FOR GROUP & ORCHESTRA [VHS, BBC, BBCV 3027, 1986 / DVD, EMI, 492 9419 30th September 2002]

DEEP PURPLE EP BEAT CLUB [DVD, Classic Pictures DVD7013X, 23rd September 2002]
Hallelujah / Highway Star / No No No / [also issued on Masters From The Vaults, Classic Rock Legends, CRL1507, 17th November 2003]

DOING THEIR THING [Castle Music Pictures, CMP 3001, October 1990]
Speed King / Child In Time / Wring That Neck / Mandrake Root /
Granada TV broadcast from 1970 re-issued on Masters From The Vaults, Classic Rock Legends, CRL1507, 17th November 2003)

ROCK REVIEW 1969–1972 [DVD Ragnarock, DVDL021D, 30th August 2004]
Includes Wring That Neck & Mandrake Root from French TV broadcast 1970)

SCANDINAVIAN NIGHTS [VHS, Connoisseur CCV 1000, 1990]
Highway Star / Strange Kind Of Woman / Child In Time / The Mule / Lazy / Space Truckin' / Fireball / Lucille / Black Night /
Recorded live in Copenhagen, March 1972 (monochrome footage)

LIVE IN CONCERT 72/73 [DVD, EMI 331 7729, 25th July 2005]
Copenhagen, March 1972 (monochrome footage): Highway Star / Strange Kind Of Woman / Child In Time / The Mule / Lazy / Space Truckin' / Fireball / Lucille / Black Night / New York, May 1973, (colour footage): Strange Kind Of Woman / Smoke On The Water / Space Truckin' / Burn (bonus live track from Live At California Jam, 1974)

ROCK FLASHBACK (CALIFORNIA JAM) [VHS, BBC, BBCV 3000, September 1981 / DVD, EMI 094634467797, 21st November 2005]

Burn / Might Just Take Your Time / Lay Down Stay Down★ / Mistreated /
Smoke On The Water / You Fool No One / Space Truckin' /
★ *DVD version contains extra track and re-titled Live At The California Jam 1974*

THE VIDEO SINGLES [Channel 5, CFV 04182, 1987]
Bad Attitude / Call Of The Wild / Perfect Strangers / Knocking At Your Back
Door / Nobody's Home /

HEAVY METAL PIONEERS [VHS, Warner Music Vision, 8536 50265-3, 1991]

COME HELL OR HIGH WATER [VHS, 74321 22443 3, November 1994]
Highway Star / Black Night / Talk About Love / A Twist In The Tale / Perfect
Strangers / Beethoven's Ninth / Knocking At Your Back Door / Anyone's
Daughter / Child In Time / Anya / The Battle Rages On / Lazy / Drum Solo /
Space Truckin' / Woman From Tokyo / Paint It Black / Smoke On The Water /

NEW, LIVE & RARE THE VIDEO COLLECTION 1984–2000 [DVD, Thames
Thompson, this release has no catalogue number, 2000]
Includes promo videos and live concert footage

MACHINE HEAD [DVD, Eagle Vision, EREDV259, 27th November 2002]

RAINBOW

LIVE IN MUNICH 1977 [DVD, Eagle Vision, EREDV573, 21st August 2006]
Kill The King / Mistreated / Sixteenth Century Greensleeves / Catch The
Rainbow / Long Live Rock n' Roll / Man On The Silver Mountain / Blues /
Still I'm Sad / Do You Close Your Eyes / Long Live Rock n' Roll promo / Gates
Of Babylon promo / LA Connection promo / Bob Daisley interview / Colin
Hart interview /

LIVE BETWEEN THE EYES [VHS, Polygram / Spectrum, 790587-2, 1982]
Over The Rainbow / Spotlight Kid / Miss Mistreated / Can't Happen Here /
Tearin' Out My Heart / All Night Long / Stone Cold / Power / Blues / Difficult
To Cure / Long Live Rock 'n' Roll / Kill The King / Maybe Next Time /
Smoke On The Water /

LIVE IN JAPAN '84 [VHS, Toei, TEM 585, 1984, Japan only]
Spotlight Kid / Miss Mistreated / Can't Happen Here / I Surrender / Catch The
Rainbow / Power / Street Of Dreams / Fool For The Night / Difficult To
Cure / Blues / Stranded / Death Alley Driver / Firedance / Maybe Next Time /
All Night Long / Since You Been Gone / Smoke On The Water / Interviews /

FINAL CUT [VHS, Polygram/ Spectrum, 041 385.2, 1985]
Spotlight Kid / Death Alley Driver / I Surrender / All Night Long / Can't
Happen Here / Difficult To Cure / Can't Let You Go / Power / Since You Been
Gone / Stone Cold / Street Of Dreams /

BLACKMORE'S NIGHT

SHADOW OF THE MOON (BEHIND THE MUSIC) [VHS, BMG BVVP-149, Japan, 23rd April 1997]
Shadow Of The Moon / No Second Chance / Renaissance Faire / plus interview & Ritchie's guitar collection / (also issued by Minstrel Hall Music)

LIVE IN GERMANY 97–98 [VHS, Minstrel Hall Music, 1999]
Shadow Of The Moon / The Clock Ticks On / Play Minstrel Play / Minstrel Hall / St Theresa / Under A Violet Moon / Magical World / Sixteenth Century Greensleeves / Renaissance Faire / No Second Chance / Writing On The Wall / Mond Tanz / Be Mine Tonight / Memmingen / Maybe Next Time /

UNDER A VIOLET MOON CASTLE TOUR 2000 [VHS, Minstrel Hall Music 2002]
Written In the Stars / Morning Star / Renaissance Faire / Possum Goes To Prague / Under A Violet Moon / Spanish Nights / Past Time With Good Company / March The Heroes Home / Gone With The Wind / Fires At Midnight / Now & Then / Durch dem wald zum Bachhaus /

CASTLES & DREAMS [2 DVDs, SPV, SPV56399157, 6th June 2005]
DVD 1: Concert Burg Veldenstein 2004: Cartouche / Queen For A Day I & II / Under A Violet Moon / Minstrel Hall / Past Time With Good Company / Soldier Of Fortune / Durch den wald zum Bachhaus / Violin – Improvisation Of Tudor Rose / Once In A Million Years / Mr. Peagram's Morris And Sword / Home Again / Ghost Of A Rose / Child In Time / Mond Tanz / Wind In The Willows / Village On The Sand / Renaissance Faire / The Clock Ticks On / Loreley, All For One / Black Night / Dandelion Wine / Bonus material – Behind the Scenes / Ritchie Blackmore's Guitar Special /
DVD 2: 1. Acoustics – I Think It's Going To Rain Today / Christmas Eve. Burg Abendberg '04 – Shadow Of The Moon / Queen For A Day / Under A Violet Moon 2. Videos – Hanging Trees (real) & (animated) / Once In A Million Years / The Times They Are Changing / Way To Mandalay / Christmas Eve. 3. Documentations – Blackmore's Night – The Story / 1. Blackmore's Night – The Story / Once upon a Time – The Candice and Ritchie Story / Tourstart St. Goar 2004 / Hanging Tree – making music with our friends / "Schlossgeister" – German TV Special / "Goldene Henne" – German TV Appearance / "ZDF - Fernsehgarten" – German TV Appearance feat. All Because Of You. 4. Proclamation – Discography – Blackmore's Night / Biography – Candice Night / Biography – Ritchie Blackmore / Interview – Band & Members 5. Special Bonus – Slideshow / Candice's Private Cam /

BIBLIOGRAPHY

Books:

Brans, Marc. *Purplistory* (Belgian DPFC – CD-Rom Format Only)
Buell, Bebe With Bockris, Victor. *Rebel Heart* (St Martin's/Griffin)
Charlesworth, Chris. *The Illustrated Deep Purple Biography* (Omnibus Press)
Davies, Roy. *Rainbow Rising* (Helter Skelter)
Gillan, Ian & Cohen, David. *Child In Time* (Smith & Gryphon)
Heatley, Michael. *The Complete Deep Purple* (Reynolds & Hearn)
Henderson, Derek. *Gene Vincent: A Discography* (Spent Brothers)
Logan, Nick/Woffinden Bob. *The Illustrated Encyclopedia Of Rock* (Salamander Books)
Popoff, Martin. *Rainbow: English Castle Magic* (Metal Blade)
Popoff, Martin. *The Top 500 Heavy Metal Albums Of All Time* (ECW Press)
Repsch, John. *The Legendary Joe Meek* (Cherry Red Books)
Rice, Tim & Jo/Gambacinni, Paul/Reid, Mike. *The Guinness Book Of British Hit Singles* (Guinness Publishing)
Rice, Tim & Jo/Gambacinni, Paul/Reid, Mike. *The Guinness Book Of British Hit Albums* (Guinness Publishing)
Sharpe, Graham. *The Man Who Was Screaming Lord Sutch* (Aurum Press)
Thompson, Dave. *Smoke On The Water* (ECW Press)
Wallis, Ian. *American Rock 'N' Roll: The UK Tours 1956–72* (Music Mentor Books)
Zappa Frank/Occhiogrosso Peter: The Real Frank Zappa Book (Picador/Pan Books)

Music Magazines:

Acoustic Musician, Bravo, Circus, Darker Than Blue, Guitar Player, Guitar World Guitarist (December 1990), *Kerrang!, Mojo* ('On The Roundabout With Deep Purple' by Kieron Tyler), *Muziekkrant Oor, The Official Rainbow Fan Club* magazine 1980–81, *Raw, Record Collector, Rock Hard, Stargazer, Thunderbolt* (Joe Meek Appreciation Society magazine), *Vintage Guitar* 1997, *Zig Zag* (article by Steve Peacock, August 2–6, 1970)

Also the archives of *More Black Than Purple – The Ritchie Blackmore Magazine* (established 1996). For subscription details enclose a stamped self-addressed envelope (or an International Reply Coupon if outside the UK) to MBTP, PO Box 155, Bedford, MK40 2YX, England or call +44 (0) 1234 326691 or check the website www.moreblackthanpurple.co.uk

Music Papers:

New Record Mirror 1961–1963, *Record Mirror* 1963–1991, *Rolling Stone, Melody Maker, New Musical Express, Sounds*

Provincial Newpapers:

Weston Mercury & Somersetshire Herald April 1945, *Bedford Record* 1961–63, *Shrewsbury Chronicle* 1963, *The Salisbury Times* 1964, Wolverhampton; *The Chronicle* 1963, Dublin *Evening Press* January 1964, Doncaster *Free Press and Courier of Coming Events* Nov/Dec 1964, Doncaster *Gazette & Chronicle* Nov/Dec 1964, *The Eastern Evening News* Dec 1964/Jan 1965, *Eastern Daily Press* Dec 1964/Jan 1965, *Acton Gazette* 1969, *Dunstable Gazette* 1970, *The Florida Times-Union* 1976

National Newspapers:

News Of The World 1963 & 1993, *Daily Mirror, Sunday Mirror* 1963, *The Sun* 1980

Other published articles:

Reflections (David Coverdale, Whitesnake.com)

ACKNOWLEDGEMENTS

Any book of this magnitude would not have been possible without the help and co-operation of many people. Firstly I would like to thank those who have either been personal friends or acquaintances, or worked with Ritchie in some capacity throughout the years and were gracious enough to chat to me for this book, or who have chatted to *More Black Than Purple* over the years.

They are (in alphabetical order): Don Airey, Alex Alexander, Frank Allen, Arvid Andersen, Graham Bonnet, Tony Carey, Mick Cervino, Neil Christian, Mark Clarke, Raymond d'Addario, Bob Daisley, Tony Dangerfield, Mike DiMeo, Heather Findlay, Rob Fodder, Ian Hansford, Pauline Hardy (neé Walton), Jessie Haynes, Valerie Horwood (neé Morris), Glenn Hughes, Derek Lawrence, Albert Lee, Freddie 'Fingers' Lee, Barry Lovegrove, Ken Lundgren, John McCoy, Hugh McDowell, George McManus, Rodger Mingaye, David Moore, Ricky Munro, Neil Newsome, Gerry Oxford, Patrick Pink (NKA Robbie Duke), the late Cozy Powell, Don Preston, Bobby Rondinelli, Andy Scott, Bob Simon, Nick Simper, Stuart Smith, Jim Sullivan, Joe Lynn Turner, Mick Underwood, Houston Wells, Dave Watts, Dave Wendels, Mike Wheeler, Dougie White, Brian Woods.

Many others were instrumental in various capacities, such as coordinating interviews, translations, research, technical data, supplying anecdotes and above all correcting or supplying vital facts and figures: Kingsley Abbott, John Acock, Pete Aylmore, Alan Barratt, John Braley, Elisa Bonora, Marc Brans, Tom Casey, Neil Davies, Julian Dawson, Didier Delcourt, Roger Dopson, Roger Drew, Melvin Edwards, Bob Erskine, Matteo Fillippini, Matthew Fisher, Trevor Fontaine, Mike Fred, Helmut Gerlach, Andrew Good, Angela Gordon (neé Goldthorpe), Ron Harper, Colin Hart, Paul Hartshorn, Derek Henderson, Mike Hill, Artie Hoar, Graham Hough, Rob

Huxley, Billy James, Bryan Josh, Dr Jim Marshall OBE, Ketil Michelsen, Dennis Munday, Mark Newson, Pauline O'Pray, Jerry Packer, Ainhoa Prieto, Graham Sharpe, Tonny Steenhagen, Lisa Walker, Jim Watt, Steve Woodward, Joe Wright.

Special thanks to Mike Eriksson, Neil Jeffries, and Alan Whitman who supplied or gave permission to use interviews they had conducted with either the 'Man In Black' himself or with others relevant to the story.

Finally a big thank you to all those who gave words of advice, encouragement and general support:

Firstly my father and mother, without whom I wouldn't be here in the first place, and despite constantly telling me to "Turn that racket down" during my youth have always helped and supported my chosen path throughout the years; Major Mark Adkin, Michael Heatley, John Repsch, Mark Welch, the readers of *More Black Than Purple* and of course Chris Charlesworth for having faith in the project; his editorial assistant, Andy Neill; and last but not least Rene Nethitt, who made the research so much easier and without whom the project would have taken twice as long.

The author would love to hear from anyone else not listed above who has worked with or had associations with Ritchie Blackmore in some capacity over the years who would like to contribute stories for future revised and expanded editions of this biography. Please contact the author via the magazine, *More Black Than Purple,* PO Box 155, Bedford, MK40 2YX, England.